JOHN MASTERS

JOHN MASTERS

A REGIMENTED LIFE

John Clay

LONDON
Michael Joseph

MICHAEL JOSEPH LTD
Published by the Penguin Group
27 Wrights Lane, London W8 5TZ
Viking Penguin Inc., 375 Hudson Street, New York, New York 10014, USA
Penguin Books Australia Ltd, Ringwood, Victoria, Australia
Penguin Books Canada Ltd, 10 Alcorn Avenue, Toronto, Ontario, Canada M4V 3B2
Penguin Books (NZ) Ltd, 182–190 Wairau Road, Auckland 10, New Zealand

Penguin Books Ltd, Registered Offices: Harmondsworth, Middlesex, England

First published in Great Britain May 1992

Typeset in 11/12 pt Times
Printed in England by Clays Ltd, St Ives plc

A CIP catalogue record for this book is available from the British Library.

ISBN 0 7181 2945 8

For Y, F and A
– where the twain shall meet

'I always want to win, but I discovered long ago, at Wellington, that it's not good winning on false pretences.'

Rodney Savage in *Bhowani Junction*

'Each man's real life is led in his head and is known to none but himself.'

Mark Twain

CONTENTS

Acknowledgements   viii

1   Family Origins   1

2   India 1914–1919   14

3   England 1920–1927   18

4   Wellington 1928–1932   23

5   Sandhurst 1933–1934   33

6   India 1934–1938   42

7   USA 1938–1939   75

8   India and Quetta 1940–1942   81

9   Chindits and Burma 1943–1945   103

10   Delhi 1945–1946   142

11   England 1946–1948   150

12   USA 1948–1952   160

13   *Bhowani Junction* 1953–1954   211

14   USA 1955–1957   228

15   *Fandango Rock* 1958–1959   238

16   At Home and Abroad 1960–1969   243

17   Santa Fe 1970–1973   282

18   Chili and Marching Society 1974–1975   296

19   *Loss of Eden* 1976–1982   312

20   Final Months 1983   336

Appendix   343

Notes   346

Bibliography   365

Index   367

ACKNOWLEDGEMENTS

My greatest debt by far is to Barbara Masters for her open-handed generosity in talking to me at length about her husband and in putting his papers at my disposal and, as his literary executor, for permission to quote from his published and unpublished letters and other texts.

My thanks extend to other members of the Masters family – to Alex Masters for sharing his perspective on his brother and letting me use family correspondence and photographs in his possession, to Susan Masters Kyger and Martin Masters for their talks with me, and to Barbara's two children by her first marriage, Liz and Mike Rose, for their help. A special word of thanks goes to Mike and Angela Rose's son, Edward, whose mini-biography of his step-grandfather, written as a school project, is a worthy precursor to this work. I would also like to thank John Masters's first cousins, Maj-Gen Cyril Edge, Diana Gray and Joan Masters, for providing valuable background and family material.

Among John Masters's literary associates particular thanks go to the staff at Michael Joseph in London and at Viking in New York for their co-operation in putting archive material relating to John Masters at my disposal. Gerald Pollinger of Laurence Pollinger Ltd generously opened his firm's files on John Masters and gave me detailed information about the UK sales of his books, which appears in the Appendix. I am most grateful to Maj Maurice Biggs, Hon Secretary of the 4th Prince of Wales's Own Gurkha Rifles Association, for information about the 4th Gurkhas and for supplying me with relevant back numbers of the 4th Gurkhas Newsletter.

Among the numerous people with whom I spent many enjoyable and informative hours discussing John Masters or with whom I corresponded, I should like to thank:

In England: Fernand Auberjonois, Marjorie Barrie (formerly Caton-Jones), M. Bass, Brig Shelford Bidwell, Lt-Col Tim Brennan, Alan Brooke, Maj-Gen R. Burges, Brig Michael Calvert, Rev Peter Cane, Dr Lionel Carter of the Centre for South Asian Studies, Cambridge, Norah Collins, Hazel Craig, Col David Davidson, Maj David Day, George and Jean Depree, Lt-Col E. Edlmann, Lt-Col F. Edmeades, Edmund Fisher, Patrick Flatt, Diana Foord-Kelsey, Dennis Foxall, Maj Martin Fuller, John Hadfield, Mark Hamilton, Lt-Col Alec Harper, Theo Hetherington, Maj Robin Hodson, F. G. Holliday, Phoebe Jervis, Mollie Kaye, Lt-Col Lionel Leach, Valentine Lebern (formerly

Roberts), Lt-Col J. W. A. Lowis, Sir Robert and Lady Lusty, Kamala Markandaya, Lt-Col Donald McCutcheon, Dr C. W. F. McKean, Peg Man, Philip Mason, Lt-Col Paddy Massey, Brig Peter Mead, Ismail Merchant, Maj Ainslie Miller, Geoffrey Moorhouse, Victor Morrison, Col Iain Murray, Dr M. O'Flynn, Richard Peel, Brig H. C. Pulley, Lena Rainbird, Richard Rhodes-James, Wilfrid and Sheila Russell, Victoria Schofield, Hilary Spurling, J. R. Strachan, Lt-Col John Strickland, Bill Travers, Raleigh Trevelyan, Maj Frank Turner, Lt-Col P. C. Turner, Edwin Waight, Lt-Col D. Wakely, Mrs Eileen Whitcomb, Dr Desmond Whyte, J. Wilkinson, Lt-Col R. N. D. Williams, Air Marshal Sir Peter and Lady Wykeham. I should also like to thank Nigel Grandfield for timely patronage, Drue Heinz and the staff at Hawthornden International Retreat for Writers for my stay there, the staffs at the Imperial War Museum, India Office, London Libraries and the Trustees of the National Library of Scotland, Edinburgh. Many of those listed above have been kind enough to let me see and use copies of their letters from John Masters.

In the USA: Alan and Nancy Anderson, Mickey Bogert, Sue Bontecue, Carl and Clare Brandt, Bob and Priscilla Bunker, Joan Buresch, Phil and Ann Casady, Bill Chudd, Katya Clark, F. A. de Caro, Col Bill Dodds, Betsy Fuller, Armon and Lucie Glenn, Howard Gottlieb and staff at Mugar Memorial Library, Boston University, Tom Hamill, Vald Heiberg, Phyllis Jenkins, Keith and Emily Jennison, Chester Johnson, Rosan Jordan, Allen Kaufman, Paul Kinslow, David Kyger, Rex Lardner, Bruce Lee, Alice Mathews, Stan and Nancy Noyes, Carl Overhage, Polly Robertson, Tina Rousselot, Capt Reginald Sawhny, Romona Scholder, Phil and Jo Shultz, Richard and Dot Stern, John Talley.

In India: Brig Raj Bir Chopra, David Gilani, Manohar Malgonkar, Dr Sujit Mukerjee, Maj-Gen G. S. Nagra, Maj-Gen M. K. Palit, Lt-Gen Moti Sagar, Col Arvind and Mrs Sharma at Bakloh, Khushwant Singh, Mark Tully.

In Pakistan: Maj-Gen S. Shahid Hamid and his family, Masud Salahuddin and the Commandant at Staff College, Quetta.

In Spain: Antonio and Alegria Lacoma, Julio and Eva Nogues.

Finally, a special word of thanks to my daughter, Farida, for typing skills performed beyond the call of filial duty, to Clare Wildey for tape transcriptions, and to my editor, Louise Haines, and her assistant editor, Arianne Burnette, for their invaluable editorial help.

1

FAMILY ORIGINS

Men who write exciting novels seldom lead exciting lives. John Masters was an exception. He lived his life to the full in two continents, first in India, then in America. England played a relatively small part in his life: he went to school and Sandhurst there and he visited often enough to stay with members of his family, but he preferred to make his own home elsewhere. 'Home' was an emotive word to him, as it was to many of the British in India.

He was born in Calcutta in 1914, the fifth generation of his family to live in India. India was in his blood, literally so, and an earlier cause of dissension to his family and a perennial source of ambivalence in himself. Most people assumed he was at least partly Anglo-Indian, an allegation that stuck and to which he reacted characteristically by making himself more noticeable, more successful than many of his contemporaries. His best-known book, *Bhowani Junction*, deals with the Anglo-Indian issue, and the assumption was that he was writing from personal experience. He was, but not in the way most readers thought.

To be Anglo-Indian, or even to be thought of as Anglo-Indian, during the height of the British Empire in India was a dreadful stigma. People so 'tainted' went to enormous lengths to conceal the fact. It led to social ostracism and exclusion from the officer class of the best regiments and the best clubs. Yet many families whose stay and service in India were as long as the Masterses' had intermarried. The curious, and less explicable, point is that only some families seemed to have been singled out and suffered from this attribution. The Masters family was one of those.

John Masters did not look particularly Anglo-Indian, with tall, rather craggy features when he was young, and a skin colour certainly no different from that of many a growing child or young man who had spent his first years in the tropics. His father, though, did have a much darker complexion, and this would have been noticed in the race- and class-conscious climate of the 1920s. For anyone brought up in that era and that milieu, having a 'touch of the tarbrush' was viewed as shameful and ignominious, and meant the person was usually relegated to an in-between status, neither belonging nor outcast. Masters had to contend with this from early on. At school and at Sandhurst rumours circulated about his origins. Yet he turned this half-hidden family secret, which could never be openly acknowledged, into a positive driving force in his life. Only much later on, in his forties, did he learn the true facts of his inheritance. By then, like many family secrets, it had been forgotten and buried by the family members, so keen were they to escape its shadow. Masters's impetus to succeed led to what many people felt was a certain 'chippiness' that often put people's backs up. He could be abrasive, but he could also be charming and the best company in the world.

The Masters family's connection with India began in 1804. The first to go there was William Masters, a soldier-adventurer from a Wiltshire family of weavers. He arrived in Calcutta, aged thirty, with his regiment, The King's Royal Irish Light Dragoons, accompanied by his Irish wife, Charity Hardy from Tipperary, and their two young children, William and Martha. They lived in Fort William, but his regiment soon left to fight against the Princely States for the East India Company. The unhealthy, typhoid-ridden climate of Calcutta took its toll on Charity and she died not long afterwards, leaving the two children effectively orphaned. Family friends in the Chowringhee district looked after them. They were intelligent children and went to privately-run schools nearby: Martha to Mrs Durell's School on Clive Street and William to Mr Farrell's Classical and Commercial Academy. Their father eventually became quartermaster of his regiment, but could rarely get back to Calcutta, and he relied on their monthly letters for news of their progress, gratified to learn that William, for instance, had obtained gold medals for proficiency, and was top of his class.

Then William senior died of illness at Meerut on 27 May 1819, aged forty-five. Martha, who was eighteen years old, was fortunate enough to marry Cornelius Cardew, of the well-known West Country family, a young civil servant in the East India Company in Calcutta and a good match. William, two years younger and unsure of his future, went back to England and stayed with his grandparents, but the call of India was too strong and he returned in 1823, aged twenty. His friends and contacts were in educational circles, and Chowringhee was also where many of the Eurasian (as Anglo-Indians were then called) community resided. The community was in a state of turmoil, suffering from the effects of extensive and, in their eyes, quite unjustified discrimination by the East India Company.

The reason for this highlights one of the less savoury episodes in

British rule in India, and dates back to an earlier time. It needs to be seen as part of changing attitudes towards racial integration in the Empire as a whole.

From the post-Reformation onwards, with the collapse of the idea of Christian unity on earth, new formulations began to be made about the separate racial and ethnic identities of mankind and their unequal development. The spread of Empire used these formulations to justify slavery and protective servitude, and to divert attention away from more commercial motives. Later, with this growth of 'scientific' thinking, the urge for classification increased. A hierarchical, evolutionary scale was introduced – a version of the Great Chain of Being – in which those of black skin were placed at the bottom. 'Scientific measurement' included both body and mind – the tall, white blond races came out as superior, with the dark, short, 'squarer-visaged' people inferior. The neoclassical revival at the end of the eighteenth century brought with it a cult of Greco-Roman art, with its manifestly superior white marble statuary. By the mid-nineteenth century nearly every British school boasted a wall-chart with the main stocks of races – Caucasian, Negroid, Asiatic – delineated on it in a descending evolutionary scale, while the map alongside it blushed pink with the achievements of the British Empire. When the great apes of Africa were discovered, the European mind, already fevered by evolutionary imaginings, saw these animals as proximate ancestors of what were deemed the lower orders of the human race.

In India, attitudes towards racial mixing began to harden only in the last part of the eighteenth century. The early days of the East India Company, certainly from 1650 onwards, were free-wheeling, as its officials sought to work closely with the local community. The East India Company was first and foremost a trading company interested in making money. It employed locals and readily encouraged intermarriage, which was important for strengthening the commercial links with the community, as well as for keeping its officials away from the dangers of drink and prostitution. The army that protected the interests of the East India Company also intermarried or came to equivalent arrangements. The following generation continued to work for the East India Company, and had access to its better (i.e. covenanted) posts and similar ones in the army. By the end of the eighteenth century as large a number of Eurasians were employed by the East India Company and in the army as of British.

Then attitudes started to change. The impact of the French Revolution in 1789 brought a universal and widespread fear of natives rebelling, as had happened with the mulattos in Haiti. Eurasians were quickly seen as a threat, a possible danger if they rose above their station. The Cornwallis Acts of the 1790s were passed to restrict their progress as Company servants, with the result that they were soon denied access to senior and profitable posts in the Company; they were also prevented from holding commissions in the army. With a deft sleight of hand, the Company managed to transfer its own sense of shame at rejecting these loyal, long-standing servitors on to the subjects, the Eurasians themselves. The Eurasians soon became an unwanted and despised community, inhabiting a no-man's-land in British India, welcomed neither by the land of their fathers, Britain, nor by that of their mothers, the Hindu community, with its restrictive caste system. Half-breeds throughout history have usually had a rough time of it. De Tocqueville referred to them as 'the natural link between civilization and barbarism'. They aroused fears of degeneracy, as if only the worst attributes of each component race would come out in succeeding generations.

By the 1820s, intent on fighting back against East India Company discrimination, the Eurasian community in Calcutta had decided to open its own schools, inspired by the efforts of its leader, John (J.W.) Ricketts. Eurasians had already been barred from attending the official East India College in England, which had opened in 1806 and later became Haileybury. Education there was now a prerequisite for serving with the Company. William Masters offered his services to the community. With his educational record, he was quickly appointed the first headmaster of the Parental Academy when it opened its doors in 1823. His youthful enthusiasm and his gifts as an educator were soon apparent. A commentator wrote: 'The education imparted in the Parental Academy was more progressive than in any government, church or private school in India at that time. The course of instruction included Scripture, English Literature and Grammar, an Indian vernacular, Geography, Roman, Greek and Indian History, Astronomy, Natural Philosophy, Latin, Maths and Political Economy, a truly liberal education with a curriculum that could serve as a model for any progressive school of today's standards.' His school relied financially on subscriptions and donations from within the Eurasian community; the East India Company remained typically stand-offish, though it was prepared to open schools for Hindus and Mohammedans. No mention of Eurasian schools was made later in Macaulay's famous Minute of 1835, nor in the more liberal Wood Despatch of 1854.

By 1828 William had moved to another, newly-founded school, Verulam's Academy, again as its head, using similar progressive teaching methods, that is, no lesson was repeated by rote and classes changed tutors and subjects every hour and a half. Then in 1836 an important new school in Park Street was proposed. William seemed the obvious choice as its first headmaster. This was La Martiniere, the foundation of which came about in a curious way. A French military adventurer, Major-General Claude Martin, had died in Lucknow in 1800, leaving a sizeable fortune with his bizarre palace-type edifice, called Constantia, which still stands. Under the terms of his will, he decreed that the bulk of his fortune should go to found three schools, each bearing his name: one at Lyons in France, one at Lucknow (where Kipling's Kim was sent) and one at Calcutta. Martin had started life as a Catholic, become disillusioned with it and looked into other religions but, finding no substitute, reverted to Catholicism, hence the schools had to be Christian-run.

William was now thirty-three years old and, in keeping with the prestige of his new post, he decided to marry. His bride was Caroline Crow, then a mere fourteen years old, though in those days early marriage was common enough. William Masters, well-placed as he was to interpret the changes in the Eurasian community, must have felt that taking a Eurasian wife – for her dark and striking looks placed her unmistakably in this category – conferred no disadvantages.

The prospects for the Eurasian community were then improving. William Masters would have been aware of two recent events. First, J. W. Ricketts took his East Indian Petition to both Houses of Parliament in London demanding better rights for Eurasians. Secondly, reform was in the air: the Great Reform Bill of 1832 had just been passed and the new Charter of the East India Company in 1833 stipulated that henceforth posts in the Company's service should be open to all, and religion, birthplace, descent or colour should not be a bar to official employment. As he stood at the altar of St John's Cathedral, Calcutta, on 1 February 1836, he could have had little reason to think that his marriage would be anything but an adornment. Certainly he could have had no idea that it was to cast such a shadow over his family for the next hundred years or so.

Caroline Crow was the daughter of Cecilia Crow, the widow of a failed European trader, Richard Crow, who had ended his days in Calcutta, more or less bankrupt and working for Armenian merchants. Her mother was one of two children of a longstanding liaison between William Steuart, whose family originated from Edinburgh, and Singhi Kaum, a Muslim lady from Delhi, hence the origin of the Indian ancestry in the Masters family.

*

William Steuart had gone out to India in 1780 at the age of eighteen to join the army in the Bengal Establishment. He was sponsored by his uncle, Charles Steuart, a man of some importance as he had been the last British Receiver-General of Customs in North America in the 1770s. Fighting in the Second Mahratta War and with Scindia's army at the capture of Delhi in 1785, William rose through the ranks. He kept up a regular correspondence with his uncle, though ship-borne letters at the time could take six months to go back and forth. His letters are of interest in that they show contemporary attitudes to intermarriage and the differences between British and Indian viewpoints.

It was while he was fighting in Delhi in 1785 that William's Indian mistress had come into his life. Yet it took him five years before he could summon up enough courage to tell his uncle in England about it. In his letter he was at pains to justify his decision to take up an Indian mistress. It was, he wrote, in keeping with 'the generally approved custom in the East for officers to keep women, notwithstanding the disadvantage of getting black children, in preference to the certain destruction proceeding from a promiscuous dealing with the prostitutes of the country.' He quotes the example of some of his fellow officers who had already acted similarly: 'James Anderson was favoured with a daughter, Lt Kinloch with a son and Dr Cochrane, the remaining member of our party, with a daughter.' But he sounded a warning note about another officer, one Macgregor, whose countenance was now 'pale as snow' and whose 'constitution has been ruined by debauchery'. Macgregor was clearly one of those officers who had become 'maimed and rendered unfit for service at an early age by the sad effects of their unlimited passions.'

William says he had spoken at length to a Mrs Murray, wife of a fellow officer, who advised him in May 1785 to 'hire a young woman of good family.' So Singhi Kaum became his mistress, his 'bibi', and followed him on his travels. His career prospered. He was soon promoted to command a company of grenadiers in Scindia's army, and in 1790 was sent by Lord Cornwallis as secretary to the embassy of the Nizam of Hyderabad, then at war against the notorious Tippoo Sultan. It was only at this point that he felt confident enough, and rich enough, to tell his uncle about his mistress.

He tried to make his peace with his uncle, writing, 'I abhor the very idea of deceit and am induced to trouble you with an information which may hurl me from the summit of your fond affection to the deepest pit of your detestation ... I freely avow to you that I have a son three years old, who dares not pronounce the name of Charles which I wish to give him. The boy is as fair as I am, and having white hair, I shall not be ashamed of giving him an English education.' He was tempted, he says, to keep this 'profound secret closed up for ever in the womb of time', but the pressure of shame proved too strong. It was not so much the fact that his child was born 'out of wedlock', but his mixed racial origin, that caused William to beg his uncle's forgiveness. His uncle was a relatively liberal and broad-minded man; besides, there was a family legend that he had fathered an illegitimate son in America. William was less sure about imparting the news to the rest of his family. 'I see no purpose to be answered by spreading the news to the Northside of the Tweed [his family lived in Cleveland Gardens, Edinburgh] except that of depriving me of part of the affections of my revered parents and sisters whose ideas must be to my certain knowledge too strict to admit of my pardon.' His hope was that his uncle was free enough of 'confirmed prejudices' to prevent the 'awful dissolution of the ties of friendship you have hitherto retained for me.' To lose these would make him 'miserable beyond remedy'. He begs his uncle to bring about a 'speedy termination to the torture of suspense under which I labour, worse than having to face the cannon's mouth.'

His uncle did reply, accepting his explanations. In 1794 William became Assistant Resident at Hyderabad and had the 'possibility of being ADC' and 'if I do well, a fair prospect of being an Ambassador at an Indian Court', as he wrote later to his uncle. Then, suddenly, he was struck down by a fever and he died in Hyderabad in September 1795, aged thirty-two, leaving behind his mistress and his two children by her, Charles and Cecilia. Cecilia married first a Mr Hollingberry and had two children by him, but then he died and she married Richard Crow. They had three children; the youngest, Caroline Louisa, married William Masters.

La Martiniere got off to a good start, and its roll of pupils steadily increased. It soon earned the reputation of being one of the foremost schools in India, which it retains to this day. William and Caroline had a large family: six children were born in quick succession at La Martiniere. The youngest, John, the grandfather of the author John Masters, was born in 1844.

1844 was the year William's fortunes took a turn for the worse. In November he was relieved of his post. There is a family history dated 1903, written by William's son Alexander, that provides details but is evasive about the origins of this dispute. The history speaks about William being 'supplanted in this appointment by a University Graduate from Home.' The undercurrent of strong feeling in this brief statement implies an unjust replacement. William Masters was clearly a man of merit with much educational success to his credit. To be replaced by a younger and less experienced 'University Graduate' must have been humiliating. The unfair advantage of a degree – a sore point for the discriminated-against Eurasians – was making itself felt. William was beginning to suffer from his Eurasian association.

The 'University Graduate' was one A. M. W. Christopher, a graduate of Jesus College, Cambridge, who stayed in his post for four years before leaving in 1848 to take up Holy Orders. The possession of a university degree was only one consideration in what had now turned into a scramble for India. More and more posts were being filled by candidates from England, usually nominated by the Directors of the East India Company. Many British-based families had seen nabobs returning from India laden with personal fortunes earned in the Company's service, and had gazed longingly at them while making preparations for their younger sons to go there. They quickly filled all available posts. The so-called 'liberalising' East India Company Charter of 1833 had made little difference to the Eurasians. In fact, the number of Britons in India trebled to 126,000 between the 1830s and 1860s. Eurasians remained excluded; indeed their plight worsened once the memsahibs arrived.

Improved conditions of travel and the general amenities within India had encouraged more Englishwomen to come out. They brought with them the mores of the Victorian era then at its height. Prudishness and an emphasis on correct appearance became the order of the day. Memsahibs needed to maintain a sense of superiority, and Indians, the subject race, soon came to be thought of as inferior – or worse. Any Indian mistress was quickly dismissed. The memsahib tolerated no future rivals for her husband's affection.

The men, guilt-driven and newly influenced by their white consorts, changed their attitudes and consented to the dismissals, seized by the apprehension that their white women might become defiled or polluted by contact with Indians – Eurasians fitted into this category as well. Eurasian doctors were no longer allowed to examine white women. The embargo went further; Indians were now seen as lascivious by nature, with the evidence of child marriage and polygamy ready to hand. School books were soon scoured for texts that might prove inflammatory to the more 'primitive' Hindu or Muslim mind.

It was not prurience, but a massive effort to ensure that white women might not be put at risk. Behind it was the fear, always lurking just below the surface with a dominant elite, that sexual relations might take place between their women and men of subordinate groups.

Shakespeare had voiced a similar fear in *Henry VIII*: 'Or have we some strange Indian with the great tool come to court, the women so besiege us?' It touches upon the whole question of sexual energy as a factor in imperial expansion, and whether people went out to the Empire to pursue sexual tastes and appetites that simply were not available to them at home. It almost certainly led to the increase of guilt felt by British men in India once the memsahibs had arrived, and to their apparent volte-face and full-scale espousal of propriety.

After the 1857 Mutiny, which to many English eyes had shown the dangers of 'native freedom', India became a sort of testing-ground for moral uprightness. This newly-acquired 'proper' manner meant keeping aloof from the natives. The more distance put between them, the less chance corruption or disease had to spread. Cantonments for Europeans were built far from the native town and bazaar. A hierarchy of races developed and the 'babu' mentality was used as a justification for incipient racism. Eurasians got the worst of both worlds and were shunned by both communities. They were regarded with uneasy disfavour, as threatening to bridge the social distance between the ruling race and the people. Individuals associated with Eurasians, such as William Masters, were inevitably caught up in the hostilities.

The family history points out how on 'severing his connection with La Martiniere he was presented with a silver vase by the students, past and present, as a token of esteem and gratitude.' Clearly there was no disfavour from that quarter. He next went to Patna College as headmaster, a step down from La Martiniere. No doubt disillusioned by recent events, in 1846 he sent his three eldest children to his sister, Martha Cardew, in Plymouth to seek better opportunities there. William then gravitated back to Calcutta and tried unsuccessfully to set up a school of his own. He went to England in 1852 in the 'hopes of securing a good appointment through the Authorities at Home, as the best posts in India were being conferred on candidates sent out from the Universities, but in this he was disappointed.' A year later, in 1853, he was back in India, where he settled at 1 Lower Circular Road, Calcutta, and began working at the Hindu Metropolitan College. His luck turned in 1860 when he became headmaster of Kishnagur College. His time there was a 'happy period of his life' and he later became Professor of Mathematics before he died, aged sixty-five, in 1868. A white marble plaque was put up in the hall at Kishnagur College by his 'loving and grateful pupils in recognition of his zealous efforts to promote their intellectual and moral welfare.'

William had passed his declining years in reasonable contentment, but was determined his children should avoid the buffeting he had been

through. The family history states, 'He was strongly impressed by the
gross injustice of his repeated supersessions by youthful graduates from
Home, which crushed his legitimate expectations of advancement, that
he was determined to send his younger sons Home to enable them to
qualify there for the more desirable appointments. This was a bold and
adventurous decision, considering the limited pecuniary resources, but
his own cruel treatment in the uncovenanted service determined him to
make every effort to give his younger sons at least a fair start in life.' In
fact, his sons, after a spell in England, all came back to India: William
went into the Opium Department and Cornelius into law (not before
being 'unjustly superseded' in the Opium Department). Two other
brothers, Alexander, the writer of the family history, and Edward, went
into the Indian Army, and John went into the police force. Theirs was
a family that had bound itself together to combat disadvantage. In true
Victorian fashion, they shared a dark family secret, and, just as typically, they sought by their drive and determination to overcome it.

The sixth son, John, was not sent to England for his education,
being 'not very studious in his early days', and was educated instead in
India by his father. His 'venturesome spirit' came out later when, at the
age of seventeen, he joined the police at Oudh. Soon he transferred to
the Bengal Police and became an assistant superintendent. From there
he was subsequently posted to Assam, where he met his future wife,
Annie Lewis, aged twenty. She was the daughter of a Rangoon river
pilot, Stephen Lewis of Welsh origin, working for the British India
Steam Navigation Company. She had come up to the north of Burma
with her mother to visit an uncle, a merchant in that area.

John and Annie were married at St Joseph's Roman Catholic Church
in Bankipore on 23 November 1880. Photographs show him as a rather
lugubrious thirty-five-year-old with mutton chop whiskers, while his
younger wife stands tall and striking, with dark hair and an imperious
look. He served as District Superintendent in Bengal, followed by
postings to Bhagulpore and Calcutta. In 1886 the Masterses took home
leave together with the express purpose of securing good schools for
their children – they were to have seven in all, four boys and three girls.
The eldest, another John and father of the author, was born in
Midnapore on 5 November 1883. They picked Bedford School, which
had many Indian and colonial connections, and bought a house in the
town, 16 Rathsay Road, where Annie planned to live when the children
were of school age. The house was named Ruswarp, after the suburb of
Whitby where part of her family had originally come from.

This concern to educate their children in the best possible manner
began to become almost an obsession with them. For John it was an

integral part of the family's efforts to rehabilitate itself. Education was a key route to doing this. When he got back to India he set aside most of his earnings for this purpose, stinting himself of extra amenities and reducing his personal expenditure to a minimum. In 1895 Annie returned to England to supervise the children's education. The sons went as day boys to Bedford, while the girls went first to a local day school and then to Blumenthal convent in Belgium. Annie was hardly ever to see her husband again, as he stayed in India. His health suffered as a result. He tried visiting German spas to improve matters but dared not stay away too long, for fear of losing his lucrative post and the pension that went with it, which were needed to pay for his children's education. In the end, he delayed proper treatment in order to complete his forty years of service; he got his full pension, though it proved to be a fatal delay. He died in the hospital at Fort William, Calcutta, in 1901, probably from a form of cancer; the family history describes it as a 'general breakdown of his internal organs'. However, before his death he had been promoted to the rank of Inspector-General of Bengal Police – a great distinction. The family history proudly states that this was 'the first instance of that post being given to an uncovenanted officer.'

Annie, ambitious in her own right, ruled her household with a firm and idiosyncratic hand. With seven children to educate, money was tight. She took in boarders from a nearby crammers, and in return her children were given extra free tuition. Her grandchildren remember her house, with its unmistakable echoes of India. On the walls were bison heads and buffalo, and tiger rugs lay on the floor, while in the dining room a text was hung on the wall behind the head of the table that read that someone was always keeping an eye on you. Most young children found it daunting and were in awe of her. She swung, in an echo of her colonial past, between extreme respectability and an earthiness that seemed initially mystifying.

She was determined to get all her sons into the Indian Army, because the pay was much better than the British Army. A family legend describes her sitting on the steps of the War Office to make sure they got in: they did. John was the first to leave Bedford and went on to Sandhurst in 1901. When all four sons were in the Indian Army (John in the 16th Rajputs, Oswald and Edwin in the Native Infantry, Alexander in the 34th Sikh Pioneers), she apparently insisted that they sent home part of their pay as subalterns. If they did not do it regularly, she wrote a sharp letter to the colonel, or to the medical officer asking for confirmation of their illness. For all her airs and graces, she was a plucky and courageous woman, admired and feared by her family, who called her the Mater.

John left Sandhurst and went out to India in 1904 to join the 16th Rajputs. By 1911 he was made a captain. In 1913 he and all three brothers in India managed to come home on leave together. John liked practical jokes and got them all to hold on to an electric wire – electricity had only just been installed – before switching the current on. Luckily, it was low voltage.

A family legend has it that he thought he might have put the maid in the family way and so he and one of his brothers skipped off to Scarborough, then a fashionable summer resort. There he met Ada Coulthard, aged thirty, still waiting for Mr Right to come along. She was one of four sisters of a local Yorkshire family that had come up in the world. Her father had started life as a coal-miner, but he injured his back in a pitfall of rock and became a successful shopkeeper. Ada, the second eldest, was of medium height, nice looking and warm hearted, with a good singing voice and a fondness for amateur theatricals. She had set her sights on getting more from life than her local town had to offer. John, always a bit of a talker and leg-puller, told her tales of his life in India, and she listened avidly. Their friendship grew, he proposed to her and she agreed to marry him. There was not much time to waste, as he was due to go back to India. Their marriage took place on 13 December 1913, and they set off for India shortly afterwards. Their first son, John Masters, was born ten months later, on 26 October 1914 at Fort William, Calcutta. By now the Great War had started in Europe and was casting its shadow even as far away as India.

Jackie, as he was called when young to distinguish him from his father, was born into a family whose dark secret of Indian blood had by now been well and truly buried. He was only to learn of it in his late forties, when a female cousin of his was carrying out research in the Steuart family archives in the National Library of Scotland in Edinburgh, and unearthed the letters mentioned above.

Masters gave his reaction in a letter he wrote to his brother Alex in August 1962:

> I didn't comment on the news of Singhi Kaum because there didn't seem much to say. It was always obvious that we were a 'country' family – vide great grandfather's wretched struggles with the genuine counterjumper straight from Home; and there was always the chance that someone had Blundered. I am quite glad I did not know for sure until my attitudes on a great many matters have hardened, as my feelings against race prejudice might have seemed to others and perhaps to me as a mere defence mechanism. Also I think we would

have been much more vulnerable when in India, either obsequious or takorari. So on the whole I think the older generation probably did the right thing in burying the poor girl without trace, since they were determined to follow a certain course and become pukka sahibs again. If they had decided to become like Jim Corbett, or the Skinners, and settle in India, it would have been different and so would we. As of now, I think it is high time and a good thing the great discovery was made, though I sympathise with Dad being outraged – he was in much closer touch with generations to whom it was desperately important not to be chee-chee, and he is of course 1/16th Indian, as compared to your and mine 1/32nd, that is, presuming no one else made a Blunder they never talked about . . .

The phrase 'I am glad I did not know for sure' is revealing. It showed a half-knowledge, and such a partial understanding informed much of his upbringing and early adulthood. Whenever its shadowy imprint emerged, he countered it by becoming more self-assertive, as if brashness was the surest way to dispel shame.

2
INDIA
1914–1919

Fort William, where Masters was born, was the most famous of the British forts in India. An imposing, impregnable mass, it was surrounded by bare, scorched grassland, and was the first thing every traveller saw when they sailed up the Hooghly river towards Calcutta. A large Union Jack flew from its top, and over the ramparts the roofs of grey barracks and the steeple of a church could be made out, while in front stood the squat black forms of cannon. Almost a third of a mile in diameter, it could house a garrison of ten thousand men, and serve, if need be, as a refuge for the European population of Calcutta. It was a world of its own. Inside the gaunt and spartan barrack-type buildings that were the married quarters, Masters spent his first few months. He was baptised by the garrison chaplain, Ormonde Birch, on 7 January 1915, and was given the same Christian name as both his father and grandfather.

His father's regiment, the 16th Rajputs, had been stationed at Jubbulpore, but when war was declared in Europe in August 1914, they were put on a war footing and came down to Fort William. They were to remain in India for the duration of the war, unlike many of their brother regiments that were sent to the Western Front. John's uncle, Alexander, lost his life at Festubert early in 1915 with the 34th Sikh Pioneers. John senior's duties with the regiment took him away from home for much of the time, and Masters saw little of him during the war.

Masters recounts little of his childhood in the volume of his autobiography that deals with that period of his life, *Bugles and a Tiger*. He summarises it thus:

> I travelled about India quite a bit with my mother while Daddy was off at the war. I don't remember anything till 1919, when the war was over and we were in Karachi. I had my fifth birthday there, and we went out in a boat to Sandspit, and there were thousands of crabs running sideways and diving down their holes, the sea washing over them. Ashraf, our bearer-cook, made a three-tiered cake with ladders of icing from one level up to the next. A wheel came off a horsed

carriage full of British soldiers, Tommies, Mummy called them, and they all spilled into the street. My father was not there.

It is strange that he did not want to dwell on his childhood, for we can be sure that his childhood was full of vivid experiences and was the bedrock of his lifelong attachment to India. Perhaps it was a protective device, guarding a treasured memory.

His father's absence is certainly remarked on. He was based in Ranikhet in 1916 and then was temporarily seconded to the Assam Military Police over an incident near Manipur when a district officer was killed and there was much unrest in the district. He left Masters in the care of his mother, with whom a close relationship developed, a closeness that was to remain all his life. With his father away at war, and before the birth of his brother in 1917, Masters may have filled the role of father substitute, which could have propelled him into a precocious or premature adult-like behaviour that belied his years. His mother was not especially keen on social life, on going out or entertaining in the usual cantonment way. She enjoyed the company of her son; her natural warmth and affectionate nature emerged in such a situation.

An Indian upbringing had much to do with the native ayah, or nurse, with whom a growing child spent a great deal of time. There are photographs of Masters's ayah, almost coal-black, dressed in sari and blouse, with a ring inserted in her nose. Like most ayahs, her temperament was gentle and sweet-natured. Young English babes-in-arms, such as Masters, were fortunate creatures in India and were treated as special beings. A boy, in particular, was lavishly attended to and called the chota sahib (little master). As he waited for his ayah, her arrival would be announced by the clanging of her bangles on wrist and ankle. Squatting down on her haunches, she would croon and sing to him, changing nursery rhymes into a curious kind of patois:

> Pussy cat, pussy cat, where have you been?
> I've come out from under the rani's chair

and then she would lull him to sleep with soft, beguiling words whispered in his ear: 'Roti, makan, chini, chota baba mini.' (Bread, butter, sugar, little baby asleep.)

Discipline was left to the parents, so ayahs were entitled to spoil their charges. Childhood thus became an idyllic state, with little boredom and always someone to talk to or play with, whether it was other children in the compound alongside the bungalow, or a manservant to make sandpies with, or the gardener to build a treehouse with, or the dewan down by the gate to talk to. Indian servants had the endearing capacity of becoming almost child-like themselves when playing with children. Hindi was used as the language between them, as parents feared their children might otherwise pick up a sing-song English, or the dreaded chee-chee (supposedly derived from the first Welsh missionaries in India) that characterised the lower classes and Anglo-Indians.

A highlight of the day would be a trip with the ayah to the native bazaar, full of exciting, colourful stalls covered with sticky sweets and silver paper and piles of fruit and tiny little flares that could be lit. The smell of spicy incense mingled with the constant heat and press of people, with lepers and beggars; kites flying overhead and temples with rows of brass bells in front of them were a treat for the imagination. At monsoon time, children were allowed to rush out into the garden to stand in the pelting rain, getting soaked to the skin, and at Christmas, the high point of the year, preceded by catalogues from the big Calcutta emporia or from the Army and Navy Stores in London, the celebrations belonged to the children as much as to the adults.

Such an upbringing was much less formal than the equivalent in English homes, where a tyrannical governess might still insist on children being seen but not heard. Here children were free 'to roam at will through every part of the house, prattling with all the artlessness of fearless childhood, and effectually twining themselves round the affections of every member of the family and visitors to the house.'

Indeed, the first five years of any child's life were lived with few shadows and provided indelible memories. It was a time of continuous sensual delight of colour and activity. 'I grew up in bright sunshine. I grew up with tremendous space. I grew up with animals. I grew up with excitement', was how a contemporary described it. We can be sure that this was the case for Masters too. 'My Hindustani went within six months of reaching England, but I remembered the taste and look of the bazaar candles for ever, the yellow balls made of coarse sugar and corn meal.' After that age, the prospect of England and school loomed. Mothers looked wistfully at their children, soon to be gone, which may explain why children in India were 'peculiarly objects of passionate love' and perhaps why parents allowed such rich stores of memories of a happy childhood to be built up. Of course, there was always the risk of illness and premature death. Cemeteries throughout India testified to the high incidence of typhoid and dysentery among the young. A familiar sight of children going to a tea party was of each carrying his own hygienically-boiled bottle of milk, wrapped in tissue paper.

The age of seven was considered the last possible moment to remove children from India, a legacy from the Victorian view that otherwise the 'mores of India would inescapably handicap them in the race of life.' Middle-class mothers would now be faced with the invidious choice of staying on with their husband in India and the prospect of a silent home, or going back to England with their children. Usually they stayed, and had more children to replace the departed ones. It is easy to see why children brought up in this way never thought of England as home; India was their home. England was a distant land where parcels came from, with toy soldiers and tins of chocolate biscuits.

The Masters family moved to Karachi, where John's brother Alex was born, and then John senior had been transferred to the 10th Rajputs as a temporary lieutenant-colonel to take part in the 1919 campaign in Waziristan, on the North-West Frontier. The Third Afghan War had broken out in May of that year; Masud and Wazir tribes had joined in, many of them defectors from Indian Army battalions raised during the Great War and therefore still armed with rifles which they had pilfered from their time in Mesopotamia. It was a hard-fought campaign, as always on the Frontier. John had a bullet shot through his cheek, but he clearly distinguished himself and was awarded a DSO for his efforts.

By the time the campaign was over in 1920, it was time for home leave, to take young Masters to England to make arrangements for him to start his schooling there, now that he was nearing the age of seven.

3

ENGLAND
1920–1927

Thus it was in the early summer of 1920 that Masters first set foot in England. How strange and unfamiliar the sight and sounds of England must have seemed after the bustle and activity of India, the cold, grey skies contrasting with the brilliance he had known. His parents went to Eastbourne, a fashionable South Coast resort with strong colonial connections. There was something about these seaside resorts, like Hastings and Bexhill, with their villas, bandstand, promenade and seafront, that appealed to old India hands. In Ada's photo album, which she took everywhere with her, the photographs of Eastbourne are numerous and much thumbed-through – their stay there must have signified something special for her. In keeping with their station in life, they acquired a nanny for the boys, Nurse Hilda Giddings from Woodborough, near Pewsey in Wiltshire.

We can only imagine Masters restlessly seeking out some of the variety and colour he missed from India. He spent much of his time on the seafront and beach, away from the dignified Palm Court atmosphere of hotels and boarding houses. He and his brother Alex, wearing only khaki shorts and shirt and no shoes, ran in and out of the sea, and earned pocket money helping old ladies up the planks on to boats that went round Beachy Head lighthouse, or searched for pennies among the pebbles where people had been sitting. He struck up a friendship with a boatman, who called him Bombay and pronounced it Bombye. It was a carefree, summer existence, even though Masters once fell off a breakwater into deep water, causing momentary alarm.

Cheltenham Junior School had already been selected for Masters. It had two advantages: first, its strong Indian Army connections (it had been set up principally for the sons of Indian Army officers); and secondly, because his aunt, John's sister Mary Edge, lived in the town with her husband, who had recently retired from India where he had been an engineer in the Public Works Department, Masters could lodge with them and join two of the Edge children as a day boy at Cheltenham Junior School.

His father's leave soon ended and he returned to India. Ada took the children across to Cheltenham to stay with the Edges before Masters's term started in September 1921. Just before she left to go back to India with Alex, Masters gave her something to read on the ship to remind her of him: it was a small notebook in which he had written three 'short stories' covering six pages in large handwriting, ten words to the page.

Masters was two years younger than Cyril, the youngest of the Edge children. Looking back, Cyril reckons they were not particularly nice to Masters. 'It was hard to have someone foisted on you. No small child likes being anywhere but home. We thought him a bit pompous for a child, a bit of a know-all, a king of the castle. He was a very brainy child from the word go, but on the defensive. He must have missed his parents a lot and felt a bit foreign coming to our house at the age of seven with his parents in India.'

There is a photograph of Masters not long after his arrival at Cheltenham in his school rugger shirt, dark haired, taller than average, a bemused, slightly wry and pained look on his face, and another of him sitting in a garden deckchair looking away from the camera. The cold grey corridors and stone-flagged floors of Cheltenham Junior School contrasted with his colourful and cosseted upbringing in India. There, all was touch and sensation; here, it was austere and impersonal. Yet his resilience was sufficient for him to merge into the environment of the school, even though it meant having to suppress some of his inner feelings. This later became a lifelong habit. Others like him had parents in distant lands, and must have felt similar sadness and nostalgia. 'All through the time I was at school and growing up, India was a land of promise, something I would go back to. One was sustained throughout all those years by the thought one would go back', a contemporary recalled. It must have marked such children for life and made them develop an unusually precocious maturity. In Masters it certainly bred an early self-reliance. Kipling had been through similar experiences and it was no accident that he prefaced his autobiography *Something of Myself* with the Jesuit quote, 'Give me the first six years of a child's life and you can have the rest.'

Separation was a theme that dominated such childhoods, a pattern perpetrated by boarding schools in England. Another contemporary reiterated this point: 'Separation made us immensely independent and to some extent independent of love. I think it probably hardened us. My brother, I remember, would pack his school trunk alone from about the age of eight. We got used very early on to making our own arrangements for travelling or doing whatever it was, learning at a very vital age to manage on our own, to cope with life.'

Masters's first Christmas was spent with his mother's relations in the north. The Headmaster, Mr Thornton, put him on the train and insisted on tying a label to his waistcoat saying who he was and where he was going. As soon as Masters had boarded the train, in the care of the guard in whose van he travelled, he tore it off and threw it out of the window.

Cheltenham Junior School is described only fleetingly in his autobiography: 'prep school was long corridors and Eton collars and mortar boards and secret societies, and struggles and pushes and yelling in the corridors over Oxford and Cambridge.' Academic performance was important, but the records show no outstanding achievement on his part, either academically or in the sporting field.

Holidays were spent first of all with the Edges, but when his brother Alex joined Masters at Cheltenham Junior School in 1925, they spent their holidays mostly with their Eastbourne nanny, Hilda Giddings, at her family house, Rose Cottage, Bottlesford, near Woodborough. Hilda was a warm-hearted, motherly sort – just what emotionally-starved schoolboys needed. Her cottage became a second home for them in England. It backed on to the main Great Western Railway line from London to Penzance, and a favourite pastime for Masters was to take a chair, a pile of bread and marmalade sandwiches, and sit at the end of the garden, watching the trains go by, a notebook on his knee to jot down the engine names and numbers. He could soon tell what class of engine was coming by the sound of its exhaust beat 2 miles away, whether it was a Castle coming down the bank from Pewsey or a King with the Torbay Limited labouring up from Woodborough. It was the start of his lifelong passion for railways, which he later described as 'closed compartments, the rest of the world shut out', which nevertheless held out the promise of going somewhere, of escape.

Masters grew to love the English countryside, and went for long walks. During the spring holidays, he went bird-nesting, climbing elm trees for rooks' eggs or wading up the River Avon in search of moorhens' nests. Woodborough was a small rural community and he made friends with the local boys. The Waight family had a farm nearby, and had lived there for over four hundred years. Young Eddie Waight was much the same age as Masters, and they became special friends. Masters would visit most days; Eddie remembers him singing cheerfully as he came down the lane. With other children of their age they made up a small group that would often go walking to the springy turf of the Wiltshire downs, or camp by the White Horse of Wilcot, taking a light tent, sleeping in their clothes and eating emergency rations of bread and hard-boiled eggs.

Masters was very much the dominant figure of this group. He liked being its leader, and the part suited him. If he could not have life the way he wanted (with parents away in India this was clearly impossible), then he would make damned sure he was in charge of what was happening here and now. Once they went camping on Manningford Hill for the night, and got very wet when a big storm blew up. Masters kept them going, telling them bloodcurdling stories through the night. At another time, Eddie Waight remembers him building an elaborately constructed fort in an old stable at the Waights' farm, which he would then throw missiles at – an early taste for war games. Eddie mostly remembers him for his organising and planning ability, but towards his younger brother, Alex, another caring and protective side came out. Alex was more easy-going and affable, and had been given the pet name Buddha because of his chubby frame. Masters used to read him a bedtime story every night at Rose Cottage, very much playing the part of the supportive elder brother.

A little further away was the Odlum farm, where young Stanley Odlum lived. He was an American boy who had been sent over to stay with his uncle on his 800-acre farm and to go to prep school in England. His father was a multi-millionaire, who made his fortune from developing land by the side of the railway tracks he owned in the United States. The farm, with its American influence, had all the latest gadgetry: the first electric milking machine in England, the first imported herd of Friesian cattle. Masters was impressed; it was a new world to him. When Stanley's father came over, he was invited to stay with them at the Savoy Hotel in London for a week. Stanley's father made the then record transatlantic telephone call costing over $700. After this whirlwind visit, life in rural Wiltshire seemed tame in comparison. Masters now spent more time with the Odlums and Eddie Waight felt a bit left out. This early eye for the main chance was a way of counteracting the resentment he felt at being left out, with parents so far away in India.

His parents came over for summer leave in 1926 and the boys spent their holidays with them at Minehead in Somerset. His paternal grand-mother, the Mater, asked them to stay with her at Ruswarp in Bedford during the Christmas holidays. Her powerful and dominating personal-ity was much in evidence. She refused to give them sheets, only blankets, part of what she saw as a toughening-up process. Hardship was to be endured; it was character-forming. She took them with her to London, to visit the Natural History Museum. Catching a bus from the station, the two boys naturally enough moved to the front seats to get a better view. They chatted merrily away to their neighbour, another boy sitting next to them. Suddenly a loud voice came booming out from the back, 'Jackie and Alex, get away from that horrid, common boy in front.' It was a humiliating moment that Masters never forgot. A few days later he tried to run away from Ruswarp and vowed privately never to stay there again.

The Mater, with all her snobbery, represented for him a side of English life that he felt no part of. He hated being shown up in public like that; it was embarrassing and only reminded him of the pretentiousness of that side of his family. He was seeking a separate kind of independence, away from those social aspirations. If he was looking elsewhere at all for a direction, then it was more to what he saw as the glamorous and new-fangled world of the Odlums.

4

WELLINGTON
1928–1932

M asters left Cheltenham Junior School in December 1927 after passing his entrance examination to Wellington. He and Alex spent Christmas at Rose Cottage. An exceptionally heavy snowfall on Christmas Eve left a thick mantle of snow on the countryside for the next week, and the road in front of Rose Cottage had to be dug out. Preparations were in hand for his first term at Wellington in January 1928. He needed a blue suit, the daily uniform, and Mrs Giddings made one for him out of serge, which turned out to have an embarrassingly homespun look to it. Most pupils got their regulation outfit from the Army and Navy Stores.

Wellington was, and still is, primarily a military school. Founded in 1859 to commemorate the death of the Iron Duke in 1852, and set up originally to provide 'free education to the orphans of army officers', it was full of military associations. Dormitories, as the houses were called, were named after the Duke's fellow officers (Anglesey, Beresford, Orange and so on) and their busts lined the walls of the covered ways by the inner quadrangle. The school had a curious grandeur of its own, and was set in large and pleasant grounds surrounded by pine scrub. The big gate under the school clock opened on the first of two square, stone-paved red-brick courts, where the central building was a fine example of Victorian Renaissance. Classrooms were on the ground floor, schoolmasters' rooms above them, and on the top floor were the dormitories in which each boy had his separate cubicle.

It was a tough regime, deliberately so, and designed to convert boys into men, callow youths into future army officers. A large number of pupils would move on to the nearby Royal Military College at Sandhurst, from where they would look back on Wellington and refer to it, in semi-affectionate terms, as 'that little hell over the hill'. A contemporary of Masters remembers it as strenuous and physically hard: 'The day started with a cold bath every morning before we went to pre-breakfast lessons, Early School as it was known. Then we were given a full timetable, the aim being to keep pupils fully occupied for most of the day.'

In fact, the rigidity of this timetable was under scrutiny at the time. Lord Derby, the vice-president of the school, had received complaints from parents that the school was 'not popular with the boys. They never seem to have a moment to themselves the whole day long.' F. B. Malim, the Headmaster, who described himself as an 'impenitent Victorian', took note of this and blamed the complexity of the modern curriculum, but his aim was to keep the boys busy and out of mischief. Mischief might mean many things: it could mean laziness, or inefficiency, but, in the hothouse atmosphere of a public school, it often meant sex. T. C. Worsley, then teaching there, commented that Wellington was 'in every possible way thirty, forty, fifty years behind the times.' Inevitably repression led to overreaction. When the occasional cases of homosexuality were discovered, the guilty parties were banished from the school. As Worsley states, 'Squalid discoveries of sexual misdemeanours were constantly coming to light; and the inhuman ritual of banishment to the sanatorium, roped playboxes, and the summoning of weeping parents was all too common an occurrence.'

Wellington was tough, too, in being a 'beating' school. Boys could be seen lined up outside a tutor's room waiting for the red light to go on to be given their corporal punishment. Prefects could also administer the cane, or 'tan' as it was known, and were even permitted to take a run at the unfortunate recipient bent over a chair. No beating, however, was allowed on a Sunday, the Lord's Day.

This was the milieu Masters entered. His first glimpse of the place was inauspicious. 'I arrived on a winter evening, carrying a suitcase all the way up from the station through the misty lamp-lit dusk towards the loom of the great buildings. I stopped at the narrow gate, iron-barred but open, and saw what was written above: the path of DUTY is the way to GLORY.'

It must have been unusual for a new boy to arrive on his own and his first days were probably something of an ordeal. New boys at Wellington were each assigned to a dormitory, which became the focal point of their life there; they were discouraged from speaking to boys in other dormitories. So rigid was the hierarchical system that new boys really only got to know well those who arrived in the same term as they did. To be a year older was to belong to another world, and these age gaps often persisted into later life. It bred an insularity and repetitiveness in their lives that many pupils found burdensome. Esmond Romilly, whose book on Wellington, *Out of Bounds*, caused an outcry when it was published in 1935, arrived there not long after Masters in 1931 and remarked:

The boy who came a term before you, was (for the first year or so at least) an infinitely superior being. Similarly you would never dream of demeaning youself as to make friends with a boy who came after you. I used to hate the meals at Wellington; one saw the same faces opposite one every day, breakfast, lunch or tea, term after term, year after year, always the same monotonous conversation. As a boy became older, he moved up the table and was able to swear and curse at the people below him; the number of terms one had been at school counted for everything.

Masters's dormitory was the Beresford. His three fellow newcomers ('pipsqueaks' or 'frostbitten cabbage' in the vernacular) were McKean, Cook and Venn. He struck up a particular friendship with William McKean, who remembers, 'Jack and I paired off and became good friends. We went for many a walk together, in the country and to the village shop.' McKean's first impression of Masters was that he was hard-up. Interestingly, Masters would talk readily of his father in the Indian Army but made no mention of his mother, so that McKean was left with the impression he had no mother. Either he was protective of her memory, not wanting to share her with anyone, idealising her as children often do of absent parents, or he might have felt ashamed of her, in the knowledge that she still had a Yorkshire accent and was not top drawer. A tendency to exaggerate and inflate his achievements became part of Masters's weaponry to counter what he must have felt to be his inferior status. Most public schoolboys are deeply competitive – the system, for all its emphasis on fair play, encourages it – and tend to brag endlessly about their fathers' pursuits or status or the places they visited in the holidays. Masters was no exception, and used to regale McKean with exciting tales of adventure during his holidays in Savernake Forest.

It was all part of his myth-making, since he rarely went to Savernake Forest. Generally, boys far from home are naturally adept at reinventing themselves, laying down fresh routes to memory and improving the plot so that sooner or later they come to believe their own fictions. The future storyteller, strong on narrative, was already at work. It was a thin disguise, and McKean, sensing Masters's loneliness at having parents away in India, wanted to ask him to stay at his home in Ledbury, a small Herefordshire market town where his father was a doctor, but he was put off, feeling that his parents were town people who had little to offer Masters after his tales of exciting country life in Wiltshire and Savernake. He recalls, 'Many times it was on the tip of my tongue to ask him to visit my home. I have regretted not opening

my mouth, thinking my holiday life would be too dull.' Yet the chances
are Masters would have been only too pleased, though pride and his
need to keep up a strong front were likely to have concealed it. Bravura
came out in other ways. Whenever they went to the school shop,
Grubbies, to buy sweets together, Masters would invariably say to
McKean, 'Here, have one of mine. Take a lot – take two'; the excess of
generosity being a deliberate display of largesse. He was learning to put
on a carapace of indifference in his determination not to show he
minded; sweets and parents were easily dispensed with. In later life he
would make sure he was not caught out again and would always seek
to be in charge of events. McKean recalls spotting this. 'He was
obviously proud and always showed a brave and cheerful face.'

New boys were kept constantly on the run and had a terror of being
late for things. A shout of 'Someone' from a prefect brought fags
running and the last fag to arrive would be sent on some trivial
mission. School prefects could waylay any unfortunate fag, whether a
room fag, a uniform fag, a boot fag or a running fag, and dispatch him
to do their bidding. New boys had little sense of their time being their
own (everything at Wellington was measured in units of a quarter of an
hour) and woe betide anyone who did not snatch his hands out of a
pocket when a prefect was coming.
    Hard work – a sort of grim, methodical discipline – shaped the day,
and was based on a form system, so that the form master taught as
many subjects as possible. This routine and the underlying spirit of
competition may have suited Masters. He had already adjusted his
temperament and disposition to it at Cheltenham. Not having a
parental home in England and with fewer roots there than most of his
contemporaries, he saw little reason not to compete and compete
furiously. He needed to run faster, to bowl faster than any of them.
Competition became a welcome substitute for the gnawing anxiety of
being rootless. He could outsmart the others. McKean recalls early on
a trick Masters developed of wiping his pen undetected on the lining of
his cap, a quick device that kept him a pace ahead. Others remember
how he would play jazz very loud on the dormitory gramophone,
proud of having acquired the latest hits on 78 rpm. 'We were always a
bit in awe of him as he was slightly ahead of his time,' recalled another
contemporary.
    Masters worked hard academically, keeping up with the exacting
standard. Each week the students had to write an English essay.
Masters remembered this: 'There were some very good English masters
– I mean that they had a very good idea of what the English language

ought to be about and how it should be handled. I usually did well in the essays, but the most valuable thing for later was learning to put your thoughts on paper, and not wasting space. You wanted to say something; so over the years you learned to say it, then stop.'

The head of the English department was R. St. C. Talboys. He was an outstanding teacher, something of an eccentric aesthete, but with excellent taste and a deep appreciation of English literature, and an in-built flair for getting the best out of the boys in his class. It was a measure of the esteem Masters held him in that he kept a copy of the jacket of his book, *A Victorian School*, in his personal scrapbook at home. Masters chose to retain in the same scrapbook an essay he had written on the foundations of Christianity for divinity, a subject taken by Malim, whose marginal notes attest 'Very Good'. We can assume Masters got on well with Malim. Others found him distant and autocratic, but for Masters he was the head, a necessary stepping-stone for future advancement.

Sport, a central feature of Wellington life, played an important role for him. He was a fast wing three-quarter at rugby and played for his dormitory team. McKean has kept a Beresford Michaelmas 1930 First XV dinner menu with signatures of all team members – the final 's' of Masters's surname rising up in a great swirl and swagger. At cricket he bowled fast, taking a long run up and then came 'thundering up to bowl, rather flat-footed, with a long whooshing sound', enough to frighten the batsman if not to demolish the stumps.

During his years at Wellington the army side had become a 'diminished and disparaged element in the School', a reaction against the militaristic fervour of the First World War. The early 1930s saw a swing towards other concerns, often political, with communism, pacifism and fascism vying for attention. The famous Oxford Union debate of 1933 on 'King and Country' epitomised this questioning of patriotic fervour. Wellington picked up some of the backwash; the Officer Training Corps declined in numbers and somewhat in efficiency during these years, even though they kept their Wednesday and Friday afternoon corps parades which Masters enjoyed and participated in, and by the time he left he had reached the rank of sergeant.

There is little sign that Masters was involved in any of these burgeoning political movements. The impression given is that he kept himself apart from such goings-on, keener on his own self-advancement. He was made a dormitory prefect in 1932, and ended up as the prestigious head of dormitory for his last term in Michaelmas 1932 and became one of the ten school prefects. For Masters to have achieved this much indicated considerable force of character and ability, but he was not always popular. A contemporary recalls him as a brilliantly clever but rather selfish boy, with few, if any, real friends, to whom conventional behaviour or popularity were of little account. Another writes: 'I only remember him there as a "character" with a very good academic brain who, while not generally popular, was considered to be "amusing" if a bit of a menace.'

Masters went in for his fair share of boasting. A fellow student in his German class recalls how uninhibited he was in talking about sex, even bragging about the fags he had 'had', pointing them out as they passed by. When he was higher up in the school, he advised a more senior contemporary that 'vicar's daughters were best', a reference to his own outside experience. His sexual initiation with a girl took place at the age of sixteen after a party during his holidays in Dorset.

His parents had moved to Dorset after his father had retired from the Indian Army in 1928. John and Ada had stayed for a while at Bottlesford. From there they moved to a 300-year-old house, Yew Cottage in Beach Street, Deal, Kent, close to the sea. They lived on his Indian Army pension of £600 per annum and the dividends from shares in Rover Cars Ltd. John Masters was not well off; he could just about afford the school fees at Wellington, not then one of the more expensive public schools. Sons of serving or living officers (about sixty-five per cent of the intake) paid reduced fees of £125 per annum (the maximum fees were £175 per annum). Paying for his sons' education (Alex went to Wellington in 1931) nevertheless took a sizeable chunk out of his pension, but education, the best available, had always been a family priority ever since the dark days of the nineteenth century.

However, the effects of the 1929 Wall Street crash began to be felt and the slump of 1931 followed. John Masters's financial position worsened considerably. He was forced to commute half his pension to help pay the school fees. His Rover shares lost their value, falling from 16s to 1s 6d, and he had £4,000 invested in them. He went to see his bank manager and negotiated an overdraft. Back home he opened a celebratory bottle of champagne, but it was only a temporary respite. It meant he had to seek employment, which was not easy for someone of his age and background. Eventually, he found a job on a farm at Stourton Caundle, near Stalbridge in Dorset, working as a glorified farm-hand, looking after the pigs, for the farm owner, an ex-military man though junior in rank. John Masters took to the work in his own inimitable style and could be heard towards evening calling the pigs in with a sort of Wild West whoop. He assured everyone this was the correct way to do it. He was adopting his own joking, self-disparaging manner to cope with adversity.

The Masterses lived in a Nissen hut, and this became the family home for the time being, an awkward and potentially embarrassing contrast to Masters's high life at Wellington. The advantage for him was that it was not far from Bottlesford, where his current girlfriend resided. She was Lois Jervis, the daughter of the vicar of nearby Woodborough, and had been part of the group he had grown up with. She was the same age as he was, brown-haired, vivacious, outgoing and keen to go places.

His last term at Wellington approached. Becoming head of dormitory and school prefect was undoubtedly the high point of his stay there. A photograph of the school prefects for that term, with the Headmaster, F. B. Malim, sitting in the front row with Masters behind to the left, shows an assured, almost arrogant Masters, as he stands four-square to the ground, self-confident and relaxed, looking straight at the camera – the only prefect to have his hands in his pockets. The others seem more deferential by comparison. He seems to be saying, 'I feel confident enough not to need others, I'm ready to take on the world.'

No doubt he enjoyed the inner world of power and privilege that school prefects inhabited; they were treated by the other boys with the greatest respect, and the behaviour and discipline of all boys outside the classroom really depended entirely on them. It was designed as a foretaste of the loyalties of regiment and Empire, and this much stayed with him, a punctiliousness that he never forgot. The prefects' privileged status allowed them to assume a loftiness that put them a cut above the rest.

Future Sandhurst entrants were in the Army Sixth. In his book, Talboys describes watching the Army Class setting out for London 'in the costume which they all seemed to affect – round pork pie hats and immensely long woollen scarves, mostly yellow and black fringes', and he clearly envied them their lifestyle.

Had I to spend a week in London with any one section of the School, unhesitatingly I should choose it to be with the Army Class; for then I should really see Life. And what an experience that would be! I should hop in and out of taxis, and skim confidently, though perhaps rather clumsily, over ice rinks. I should buy tobacco pouches in Burlington Arcade, and chat easily with dog fanciers and pugilists: I should dine generously in Soho and join in the noisier choruses at a Variety Show, and, if I were lucky, I should be thrown out of the Plaza, perhaps to exchange badinage with pert adventuresses sipping creme de menthe on red velvet sofas; and before going to bed I should

swing on the chandeliers at Brown's Hotel, like the young women in
Evelyn Waugh's books, just to see if they came down. Of course I
should be terribly tired by the end of the week; but when the train
steamed slowly out of Paddington, I should sit back and think it had
all been worth while.

Masters's report for Michaelmas 1932 shows him commended for
being alert and industrious in both chemistry and German, at French
he is described as 'not brilliant', physics, 'rather slapdash', drawing,
'fair, though not reliable'. His best subjects were English, 'much better',
and divinity, taken by F. B. Malim, 'interesting and thoughtful', but
the highest praise is reserved for his efforts outside the classroom. His
tutor at Beresford, A. L. Payne, writes: 'He has been a very good head
of dormitory, and a great asset. I am sorry he is going'; an even
stronger testimonial comes from the Headmaster: 'I am genuinely sorry
to lose this very friendly and conscientious prefect.' He had got the
plaudits where they counted. As in the case of F. B. Malim, Masters
had already sensed the importance of catching the commanding
officer's eye.

    As with his early years in India, little appears about his schooldays
in his autobiographies, no more than a couple of paragraphs in all.
Why was this? They were clearly crucial and formative years; his
achievements were by no means negligible and his final report from the
Master and tutor fully complimentary. Perhaps, beneath it, he was
unhappier than he cared to remember and was reluctant to reopen old
wounds. After leaving he never sought to keep up with Wellington nor
to have Old Wellingtonians among his friends. He did return there
once for a Speech Day, in 1961, taking with him some American
friends whom he was showing round Europe. He was apprehensive
about it, but was reassured when he was greeted as a famous author.
Perhaps the clue lies in the paragraph he devoted to Wellington in his
autobiography *Pilgrim Son*. 'It was always autumn at Wellington, the
woods brown and the chestnut leaves thick on the damp earth and
orange and black scarves going down to Bigside [the playing field],
cocoa brewing at the end of dormitory.' He seems to have chosen only
autumnal memories, the season of melancholy as Keats reminds us; the
eternal summer of his Indian childhood was over. Beneath all the
success, unease remained, though he does record the brief, proud
moments of glory, the sudden sense of belonging when he got his house
colours, 'and oh to wear a cap with a tassel swinging at the back of
my neck'.

    The overall impression is of someone keen to leave it all behind. He

WELLINGTON COLLEGE.

Army VI. and Upper School.   Michaelmas Term, 1932.

Dormitory or House *Beresford*   Term Report.

No. **303**   Name **Masters J**   Form **Army VI**

	Age on Dec. 31.	Term in Form.	Place at beginning of Term.	Present Place
	18.2	3	6	16

	SET.	NO. IN SET.	PLACE	
MATHEMATICS.	A2	17	[1]	Good. a?
EXTRA MATHEMATICS				
PHYSICS.	A2	17	11	rather "slap dash" HGV.C.
CHEMISTRY.	A1	17	14	Alert & interested T.dm
BIOLOGY.				
LATIN.				
GREEK.				
FRENCH.	A2	18	16	Not brilliant. A.N.
GERMAN.	1	15	3	Alert and industrious. x/gw
DIVINITY.	Interesting & thoughtful. F.B.M.			
ENGLISH.	Much better. GG			
HISTORY.				
GEOGRAPHY.				
DRAWING.	Fair, though not reliable. We			
PRIVATE TUITION.			MUSIC.	

TUTOR'S REPORT.   He has been a very good head of dormitory, and a great asset. I am sorry he is going. a.i.?

I am genuinely sorry to lose this very pleasant and conscientious Prefect. F.B.M.   MASTER.

FORMS IN THE UPPER SCHOOL.

	Av. Age on Dec. 31.	No. of Boys.	TAKEN BY		Av. Age on Dec. 31.	No. of Boys.	TAKEN BY
VI. CLASSICAL GROUP	17·6	13	THE MASTER.	REMOVE A.	16·9	33	MR. DENBY.
MODERN GROUP	17·7	12	MR. NOBLET.	REMOVE B.	16·9	31	MR. POTTER.
MATHEMATICAL GROUP	17·5	17	MR. BUCKLEY.	FIRST A.	15·11	29	MR. BROWNE.
ARMY GROUP	17·10	24	MR. MACDERMOTT.	FIRST B.	16·9	29	MR. GRIFFITH.
LOWER VI. ARMY	17·6	31	MR. LARMOUR.	FIRST C.	16·1	30	MR. FENN.
CLASSICAL	16·6	10	MR. WRIGHT.	FIRST D.	15·6	30	MR. CRAWLEY.
MODERN	17·4	29	MR. TALBOYS.				
SCIENCE	17·0	31	MR. WORSLEY.				

But all Subjects except English Subjects are taught in Sets.

Next Term begins on Friday, January 20th, 1933.

already knew that he was on a slightly different course to his contemporaries. He did not see himself as either belonging to, or keen to fit in to, the ideology of the ruling class. He wanted to get there on his own, on merit. He was impatient to cross the threshold of adolescence and move on to adulthood, to greater autonomy in the running of his life. His father was no sort of model for him in this respect, as he was too easy-going by far. Masters would have to make his own way, even if the price of such premature competence was to cause stirrings of dislike in others, tinged with envy at his grown-up manner. His occasional showing-off and his know-all appearance may have been a search for admiration or confirmation from others of his superior status. Beneath lay the inner unhappiness that from an early age he had sought to conceal once he knew his parents had gone back to India without him. Kipling in his memorable short story, 'Baa Baa Black Sheep', uses a haunting image of this in his description of two children, left by their parents in a boarding house at Southsea, running down to the sea when the news reaches them that their parents have indeed sailed back to India without them. They get to the beach and stand gazing out to sea hoping to catch sight of the ship. It is a poignant moment and, for Masters, such childhood memories had to be locked in an inner room of his mind. In their place he had put self-assurance and this new-found wish for admiration.

As he left Wellington at the age of eighteen, he was going to make the most of the moment, and there was fun and pleasure to be had out of life. He had a steady girlfriend, Lois, and others too were drawn to his conviviality, as the photo albums show, girls with names like Betty, Joanna and Barbara, crowded into the back seat of a sports car or, in summertime, in groups on the beach, or with Masters alone. One photograph of him and Joanna in bathing costumes, his arm around her shoulders, has the subtitle 'The Optimist', as his erection is clearly visible. Alex recalls that his brother preferred his girlfriends to be slightly older – 'not someone you had to argue about, nor did he want to be bothered sitting around all day with bunches of flowers.'

5
SANDHURST
1933–1934

Masters sat his entry examination for the Royal Military College, Sandhurst, in the final term at Wellington and passed fifth in order of merit. This meant he was awarded a Prize Cadetship of £37.10 per annum, a welcome addition to his father's strained finances. His father drove him to Sandhurst in his old Rover car in February 1933 for the start of the first term. Masters recalls that moment in *Bugles and a Tiger*: 'After we had taken my bags out of the car my father shook me by the hand and said, "Well good luck, Jackie." We did not embrace, because we never do, and anyway a sergeant with a red sash was talking to a group of young men beside us, and we would have been observed. I said, "Goodbye Daddy."'

It was more than just a traditional father-son parting. For Masters this marked a turning point and as he watched his father drive away, 'a small figure hunched over the steering wheel of his battered Rover in a greatcoat', he knew their paths were diverging, that his own fortunes were on the up while those of his father seemed to be heading downward. By the time *Bugles and a Tiger* was written, some twenty years later, in 1955, Masters was able to take a much more objective, even critical, look at his father. His portrait of him is affectionate, but also impatient and irritated. We can already catch some of this ambivalence when he deliberately mentions not embracing, as if part of him wanted to show affection to his father, but was held back from doing so, perhaps by the awareness of others being present. He was clearly embarrassed by the greatcoat his father was wearing, which had been given to him by an elderly woman friend who had converted it years ago from a carriage rug, and by the brand new pearl-grey Homburg hat on his head; neither was quite the right apparel. He had the look of a 'mysteriously sunburned refugee from Central Europe' – a not-so-concealed reference to his more noticeably darker, Anglo-Indian, complexion, now being exposed to public gaze. On Masters's first day at Sandhurst, such details would have been commented on, to his detriment.

There was a sense of relief, therefore, at watching his father drive away past the 'sacred gravel' of the square with its brass rows of

Waterloo cannon. Yet a flash must have passed through his mind, a fear that he too might end up with as little to show for it as his father, a retired lieutenant-colonel of the Indian Army with no money and few prospects. His father had taken early retirement after serving only twenty-six years in the Indian Army – fewer than most. He might have stayed on another ten, but perhaps he was wary of getting stuck in India as his father had done and of dying there prematurely. His reputation in the Indian Army was mixed; he was brave certainly, as his DSO would indicate, but otherwise he was seen as too easy-going and fond of an 'open-air type of soldiering'. He was fonder still of the ladies (he was a renowned bottom-pincher) and of drink – 'smell-of-a-cork Masters' was a less than charitable epithet used about him. He had never done a Staff College training course and so was never in line for the higher ranks of the Indian Army.

The truth was that Masters's father had not gone as far as he might. Now, looking at him, 'broke, with nothing to show for his service but a few fading photographs of himself among brown-skinned and turbaned soldiers, or in the jungle with his dog, or in the mountains in the dawn or by the banks of a great river, rod in hand,' Masters knew he would have to drive himself hard to avoid repeating the pattern. Sandhurst presented a particular challenge in this respect: it was grander than Wellington and any misgivings he felt about himself and of his possible inferior social status would soon be tested.

He had contemplated evading the family destiny through other careers. For a while he had thought of going into the navy, or becoming a barrister, but both needed a private income. His mood, therefore, on that first day at Sandhurst was one of 'sulky annoyance', yet he consoled himself with the knowledge that he had passed in fifth and was sufficiently brainy and good enough at athletic sports not to be labelled a 'swot'.

By now he was 6 feet tall and weighed nearly 11 stone. He had a thin, angular frame and a slightly sunken-cheeked look to his face, with bright, questioning eyes. As one of the thirty-five new Gentlemen Cadets in 5 Company, 'Lovely Five' as its Old Building was known, he was shown to his new quarters by his room servant, Bert King, late of the Rifle Brigade. The first nine weeks of term were taken up with drill practice, mostly the classic square-bashing conducted by NCOs. Cadets struggled to learn these new techniques. Oaths were heaped remorselessly on any falterer's head, but since they were Gentlemen Cadets, each piece of invective was preceded by 'Mr' and terminated with 'Sir'. Being yelled at from morning till dusk became a familiar routine. The slightest misdemeanour was seized upon and brought to notice. A speck of sand in the rifle sight or an ill-adjusted uniform merited the worst condemnation of all – 'Idle'. A sergeant-major would put his face inches away from that of the miscreant and bawl at the top of his voice, 'Idle, Mr Masters, Sir.'

Masters soon learnt there was no point trying to ingratiate himself with senior staff. A cordially boyish smile only got the retort: 'It's no laughing matter, Mr Masters.' But he managed to avoid the worst ignominy of all, being frog-marched to the guardroom with the cry, 'Gottim, sir', by two sergeants as they lifted the offender almost bodily off the parade ground, each of them bellowing incessantly in his ear, 'lef'righ', lef'righ'.' The road to success, he quickly surmised, lay in conspicuous keenness: 'in no time my rifle rattled louder than anyone's.'

If drill was designed to produce unquestioning discipline, the next stage was to generate confidence, and a mistake would now be met with a brusque word instead of a spine-curdling shriek. Pride was being inculcated as the basis for the future officer's code of self-esteem and proper conduct. Masters must have excelled at this phase, as he got his coveted stripes off the square and was awarded his chevron by the end of his junior term. He was promoted to the rank of lance-corporal in June 1933. This was quick progress.

Favour with the officers and instructing staff did not necessarily lead to popularity with his fellow cadets, however. Many did not like or really trust him. Sandhurst operated on a system of in-built assumptions about gentlemanly behaviour, unwritten codes of conduct close to the *pas trop de zèle* attitude of the upper class. Anyone deviating from this was bound to attract unfavourable attention. Masters seemed too full of himself, too cocky for most people's liking. At first it brought admiration, but that was only short-lived, and people soon moved away from him, in his words, 'as if instructed by a secret signal'. Masters had overdone the air of self-assurance and it had come out as superiority; others saw it as disdain. He had to admit later that this was true. 'In 1933 I disliked or despised more things and people than I loved or admired.' His superciliousness was as much a cover-up for his own insecurity at not being sure of the ground rules in this grander company and a hidden sense of shame – but that was the last thing he wanted people to see.

His cousin Diana Gray visited him that summer for the Passing-Out Parade and he told her of his dilemmas: how people had started liking him and then seemed to go off him. He related an unfortunate and humiliating incident that happened to him. He had returned to his room one evening to find that it had been wrecked and his clothes thrown out of the window. He had suffered a traditional Sandhurst punishment for someone acting above his station. Admittedly it was not the worst punishment, which was being 'laked', i.e. thrown fully-clothed into the lake, but this was bad enough and intensely humiliating. Tidying up the mess afterwards left no one in any doubt why his coats and shirts were being plucked out of the mud outside or why he was sweeping his floor clear of water and cigarette ash and torn paper.

The purpose of this clandestine form of revenge had been to 'teach him a lesson'. A contemporary, Peter Cane, remembers Masters as being impelled at that stage by three drives: person, promotion and pride. Each was an adjunct to his ambition. The punishment meted out to him showed both how little he seemed to care about people and how impervious he was to their reactions. Others in his year were more circumspect and tried to assess what was permissible. They knew when to brag, when to shut up and when to get on with it. Pranks and outrageous behaviour were far from frowned upon at Sandhurst. Memories of near-contemporaries, such as David Niven, show this. Yet Niven knew the rules and avoided putting people's backs up in the same abrasive way that Masters did. Part of the problem was the familiar one of moving from being kingpin at school to being a lowly cadet at the next place. It was all a question of where to draw the line.

Masters's solution was characteristic. 'I gritted my teeth and decided that this was something I was going to have to put up with for the rest of my life and it was no use getting worked up about it.' It was his own variant of the stiff upper lip; he was determined to do things his own way and be tough about it. His father's method of coping with adversity had been to joke and clown, in a form of self-defence. Masters was made of sterner stuff. Yet he was much valued for the good company he could be at other times; he was fun-loving and convivial, and had the rumbustious humour so beloved of his age group. Many of his Sandhurst colleagues recall him as a very companionable type, as eager as the rest of them to have a good time, or to drive up to London for a night on the town. But this did not distract him from his main purpose, which was to make himself his own man. 'I had already survived a prep school and Wellington, and had therefore twice been through this business of learning to live with a different set of people. This was the third time and it confirmed the pattern.' The solution, it was becoming clearer to him, was to follow his own star.

The correct civilian attire at Sandhurst was a tweed coat with two slits at back, grey flannel trousers and a tweed gorblimey cap, worn well forward on the head, with the peak sewn down to the rim of the brim. The high point of the social year was the June Ball. For his first year, in 1933, he joined a party got up by Iain Murray, a fellow cadet in 5 Company, who, Masters claims, taking rather a self-deprecating tone about himself, 'had been kind enough to take pity on my loneliness and invite me to join his party.' Perhaps he really did feel under-equipped socially. After all, Iain Murray was an Old Etonian, and life at Bottlesford and the pig farm had not exactly groomed him for this. He invited his cousin, Diana Gray, to come along, and she brought a schoolfriend, Eileen Burmingham, to make up numbers. To the recollection of these two, he behaved impeccably, but in *Bugles and a Tiger* he describes a different perspective. He relates how, to steady his nerves, he shared a bottle of whisky with another cadet beforehand. Champagne followed at dinner and he was soon sufficiently inebriated to be sophistication itself. By early morning, presumably after the girls had left, he was meandering round the dance floor, in a golden haze of bonhomie. He stayed up all night, or rather until 6 a.m., but had 'forgotten' he was on duty as orderly corporal and due to be on parade the next morning. He tried to attend this parade, but was forced to retire, 'the wine of life', in his memorable phrase, 'heaving like sour porridge in my stomach.' 5 Company Commander, Major Val Wilson, hauled him up and severely reprimanded him, reminding him of the essential principle that however much you drank the night before, you were always properly on parade the next morning. It was a lesson he took to heart, and he never repeated the error.

Education was an area he succeeded in at Sandhurst. It had gained in importance there after the war, following the same shift in emphasis as at Wellington. There was even talk of trying to turn Sandhurst into the English equivalent of West Point, to make it more like a military university. Education comprised forty per cent of eventual passing-out marks. Masters did so well academically that in February 1934 he was awarded one of the twelve annual Cadet Scholarships from the War Office worth £60 per year. It bolstered his father's finances, which were in a very rocky state. Prior to this, the War Office had sent his father a form to complete asking for details of his finances and of his occupation so that the award could be processed. With typical braggadocio, his father entered 'Swineherd' in answer to the question relating to occupation.

A further five scholarships worth £50 each and tenable for five years were available for candidates with the highest passing-out marks. Masters, now doing very well, seemed to be a candidate for one of these. He had been promoted to corporal in his intermediate term and studied hard, but then disaster struck and with it further chances of promotion and the hoped-for higher marks at the end of his final term. It was a bizarre incident involving a weekend pass.

Cadets who went on weekend leave had to produce written permission in advance from their family or whomever it was they were staying with. Masters wanted to go to Bottlesford, to the Giddings family, and, incidentally, to see his girlfriend, Lois Jervis. Like many a fellow cadet, he had left his weekend leave application much too late and therefore followed the well-established practice of writing out a letter of invitation purporting to come from the Giddings family. He handed it in. By some curious misfortune Giddings happened to be the surname of a well-known sergeant-major at the Royal Military College. It was immediately assumed, Masters's reputation being what it was, that he was deliberately making a fool of this sergeant-major by inventing a Giddings family. Foolishly, Masters had also made the lamentable mistake of failing to fold his letter in two, thus making his forgery only too apparent. Hauled up before Major Wilson again, he protested the truth of his intentions, namely that the Giddings family did really exist in Bottlesford and he often stayed with them. A telegram was dispatched to verify this. The answer came back in the affirmative, and he was cleared of deception, but the charge of forgery remained. As punishment he was demoted from the rank of sergeant, to which he had just been raised at the beginning of February, down to Gentleman Cadet again. It was a bitter blow, and very bad luck, not least because it ruined his chances of becoming a junior under-officer in his senior term and thus getting the expected higher marks in the final passing-out places.

Left with little option, Masters threw all his energies into his studies. At least he could aim to get top marks there. So knowledgeable was he that many other cadets turned to him for assistance with their own sluggish studies. The exams came and he skipped through, often leaving the room before the end of the exam much to the envy, and perhaps the irritated stares, of his fellow students. He achieved high marks in nearly all his papers, coming first in military history, economics and German and second in military law. For this he was awarded four monetary prizes, which he spent on a gold watch and on books, choosing, among them, H. L. Mencken's *Selected Prejudices* and books by the currently popular author, Aldous Huxley. By winning the first prize in military history, he was entitled to a sword specially engraved for him by the Wilkinson Sword Co.

In spite of all the setbacks, he still finished second overall in the final passing-out places out of the 134 cadets in his year. It was a prodigious effort considering his setback to promotion.

The first place went to Douglas Darling, also of 5 Company, then the senior under-officer and a squash blue. (He was later to make his name in the Western Desert and end up as a major-general). Masters won the highly-prized Norman Medal for obtaining the highest marks for an Indian Army candidate, and the five-year graduation scholarship he was seeking. By any standards he had done exceptionally well – testimony to his hard work and determination – and had every reason to feel pleased with himself. The staff, mindful of his earlier misdemeanours, now showered him with congratulations. 'Officers wobbled off their bicycles to clap me on the back.' The triumph was his, even though it had been something of a Pyrrhic victory.

By the time he left Sandhurst, his 'home' had moved again. His father had had a row with his employer at the pig farm; it had never been an easy relationship with an army officer junior in rank to himself. His parents had moved to Uplyme, just above Lyme Regis near the coast. They had bought a single-storey house, Bailey Gate, built in the 1920s but in appearance not unlike a bungalow in India, with its entrance porch and loggia by the back verandah. This was to be the family home where Masters would spend his leave and return for family reunions.

He had every reason to feel good about his final efforts at Sandhurst. He had ended up with what he had set out to achieve, though the memory of his demotion rankled. As he waited on the platform of the station nearest to Sandhurst to catch a train to Uplyme, he noticed a glamorous debutante waiting for the same train. She had been at the Passing-Out Ball a few nights before. Should he approach her? Would she remember him? He was caught undecided, aware now of the social gulf between them. The worlds of Uplyme and of Sandhurst seemed far apart. The train came, and the question was unresolved. He got into his compartment, noting that the engine was King Arthur, class 4–6–0 – at least that was something he was sure about.

Masters knew his posting to India would come through that summer, and he set out to enjoy himself as much as he could in the interval. Lyme Regis was a popular summer resort, with its famous Cobb, and nearby the beaches of Dorset beckoned. He made the most of it, taking Lois out in Salisbury, where her father was now canon at the cathedral and she was working in a tea shop. Life seemed full of promise to him. In August his official letter from the War Office came through appointing him to the Unattached List for the Indian Army and telling him to report to the Ist Battalion, the Duke of Cornwall's Light Infantry (DCLI), a British regiment stationed at Bareilly in India, by next October as a second lieutenant. He was more than pleased; it was the step into adulthood he had been waiting for.

Tel. No.—Victoria 9400.

Any further communication on this
subject should be addressed to:—
The Under-Secretary of State,
The War Office,
London, S.W. 1,
and the following number quoted.

THE WAR OFFICE,
LONDON, S.W. 1.

23 AUG 1934   A/6

100/India/2704. A.G.2.(0).

Sir,

    I am directed to inform you that action is being taken
to appoint you to the Unattached List for the Indian Army on
first appointment, and that you will be attached to the

1st Bn, The Duke of Cornwall's Light Infantry

which is stationed at Bareilly (for Razmak).

You will, therefore, join this battalion on arrival in India.

    I am to request that you will communicate in writing
forthwith with the Under-Secretary of State, (Military Department),
India Office, Whitehall, S.W.1., who will issue all further
orders and instructions.

    I am,
      Sir,
        Your obedient Servant,

          Director of Recruiting and Organization.

Gentleman Cadet
John Masters,
Bailey Gate, Uplyme, Lyme Regis, Dorset.
Copy to:- The Military Department,
        India Office.   R.2017.

Tel. No.—Whitehall 9400.

Any further communication on this
subject should be addressed to:—
The Under-Secretary of State,
The War Office,
London, S.W. 1,
and the following number quoted.

THE WAR OFFICE,
LONDON, S.W. 1.

4ᵗʰ September, 1934.

43/R.M.C./714 (S.D.3.a.)

Sir,

     I am directed to forward herewith the "Norman"
Medal which has been awarded to you on the recommendation
of the Commandant, Royal Military College, Sandhurst,
as the senior cadet appointed to the Unattached List for
Indian Army, for the recent term.

     Please acknowledge receipt.

         I am,
           Sir,
            Your obedient Servant,

Lt. Colonel.

Director of Staff Duties.

Second-Lieutenant J. Masters,
    Unattached List for Indian Army,
       Bailey Gate,
         UPLYME,
           Lyme Regis,
            Dorset.

6
INDIA
1934–1938

Masters travelled out to India on the troopship *Nevasa*, 'slow and dirty and full of soldiers vomiting in the troop deck.' On board with him were three Sandhurst colleagues, Robin Hodson, Bill Williams and Chris Pulley, all on the Unattached List with him and all joining the Duke of Cornwall's Light Infantry for a year before transferring to their chosen regiment in the Indian Army. This was an accepted tradition for all future Indian Army officers and gave them time to learn the native language they would need. The boat stopped in Port Said, where they got off to drink gin at a bar overlooking the harbour and to sample the tawdry night life. They docked in Karachi in October 1934, and Masters was immediately struck by the familiar chaos and confusion of India. It was fourteen years since he had been there last, and a glance at the noisy quayside with its clamouring porters brought memories of the India he knew flooding back.

From Karachi the four of them boarded a train for Bareilly, the DCLI's headquarters, east of Delhi, thirty-six hours away. Sitting on cane chairs, they drank soda water by the gallon as they passed through the arid wastes of the Sind desert, dust and sand blowing in through the slatted windows of their compartment. Further north the landscape changed to pale golden fields with bullock carts. At night the train often halted for long intervals at wayside stations. Through his window he could see crowds of white-robed people milling about, or squatting on the platform. The station area was alive with purposeful activity even at this late hour, the cries of the sellers of soda water or lassi ringing out. Trains had always exerted a strong fascination for Masters since his Bottlesford days and the Indian railways had a character all of their own.

They arrived at Bareilly at 2 a.m. and were met by John Strickland, about to join the 4th Gurkhas after completing his year in the DCLI. Horse-drawn tongas took them through the sleeping town to the officers' mess, a huge dark house, where four beds draped with mosquito nets had been placed in the central hall. Next day in the 'awe-inspiring and gloomy' splendour of the mess, Masters felt very much the new boy. When they sat down for tea, a large fruit cake sat in the middle of the polished table. Eyeing it with eager anticipation, he finally asked the captain next to him whether he might be allowed some. The captain turned to him and, with withering scorn, said, 'That's a mess cake. You're not at your prep school now.'

This incident is recorded in *Bugles and a Tiger*. Similar anecdotes abound, of an equal and surprising candour. Why should he choose to do this? Autobiography, usually an excuse to embellish the past and hide unfavourable moments, or for Augustinian self-purgation, became for Masters more a wish to set the record straight, telling it how it happened. He wrote the book in 1955, away from post-war Britain, living in the USA, not tied to any old boy network, nor with any particular axe to grind. *Bugles and a Tiger* comes across as an authentic and effective account of the pre-war era in India in the last phase of the Indian Empire. It is still used on officer training courses in both Pakistan and India, both for its historical value and for the vivid manner in which it describes the excitement and anxieties felt by a new recruit joining a regiment.

After a week's stay in Bareilly, the recruits left for Razmak on the North-West Frontier, where the first battalion of the regiment was stationed. The DCLI had been at the siege of Lucknow in 1857 and had a long association with India, but it was always part of the British Army. In India in those years there were two distinct military formations: the British Army, consisting of forty-eight battalions of infantry, four regiments of cavalry, and artillery; and the Indian Army, about three times the size, staffed mainly by British officers (ten Indian officer cadets attended Sandhurst each year). Inevitably there was rivalry between the two armies, each considering itself superior; the British Army thought they had the edge socially, while the Indian Army claimed military supremacy.

Razmak was in Waziristan, which he had heard his father speak of often, as he had fought there in 1919 and won his DSO. Masters looked forward to being in the North-West Frontier; it offered the chance of real soldiering, of shots being fired in anger, away from the so-called 'sloth stations' in mainland India. A standing army needs such first-hand practice, and perhaps the fighting was kept up partly for that purpose.

The North-West Frontier bred special qualities in officers stationed there. The harsh bitterness of the scenery seemed to give them a sixth sense, an eye for country that made them notice the slightest distortion. Masters cites the example of a major who spotted a funeral procession crossing the plain close to his camp. He suddenly ordered his men to fire on it. They hesitated, but he was right; the mourners were in reality armed tribesmen preparing to attack. Masters commented, 'No one ever found out how the major knew these things. He just did, in the same way that, tactically, he could see through a hill and know what the other side was like.' It was a knack Masters picked up as well, and in later years he would pride himself on his eye for country and put it to good use in the jungles of Burma and later on mountain expeditions.

They entrained again, travelling west as far as Bannu, from where they covered the last 70 miles to Razmak on foot. Masters was a second lieutenant in charge of a platoon of twenty-five men. This was what the first year in India was designed to test, the ability to command at that level.

Razmak was the largest garrison on the North-West Frontier, set in the heart of what was known as the Tribal Territory, a belt of land varying in width from 10 to 100 miles that straddled the Indian-Afghan border, itself defined politically, if not tribally, by the Durand Line drawn up in 1893. It was a mountainous region, stretching north to south from above Peshawar and the Khyber Pass to Quetta in Baluchistan. It was peopled by the Pathans, whose principal tribes were the Afridis, Mahsuds and Wazirs. War was almost a way of life for them, if not with the British, then as likely among themselves.

Razmak had been built by the British in 1923 as a central defensive fortress. It looked almost prison-like, with its low barracks in straight lines behind a stone perimeter wall 3 or 4 miles long, preceded by three double aprons of barbed wire. Electric lights on tall posts showed up hidden corners. It was a strange sight in the middle of the plain – almost like Aldershot transplanted from England – perched on this plateau 7,000 feet high, with mountains 10,000 feet surrounding it. It could contain a population of up to ten thousand men and house six battalions (usually one British and five Indian) in its upper and lower camp. It was an active station and therefore no women were permitted: only military personnel, the political agent – a key figure who liaised with the local Pathan tribes – and dentists, doctors and so on lived there. Across the plateau tribesmen could be seen striding slowly past with their characteristic full, free lilt, leading their camels behind them.

Tribal wars on the North-West Frontier were a constant feature of British rule in India. Since the mid-nineteenth century, the British had struggled to impose rule on the tribes, sometimes by a forward policy, at other times by a close border policy; neither had been successful. The forward policy supported the principle that the British should administer right up to the Durand Line, while the close border policy preferred British interference to be confined to the administration of the settled districts of the North-West Frontier Province up to the border with the Tribal Territory. Beyond that administrative line only the most elementary order should be kept, in accordance with Pathan standards of conduct. Over the years it was the close border policy that prevailed, as the tribes simply did not want to come under British protection. The Pathans then were as determined to keep their hills to themselves and their way of life uncontaminated by outsiders as they are today.

The Pathans' land barely supported human life at the simplest level, as little cultivation was possible on the mountainous slopes, so they were forced to rely on pillage for survival. Raiding the neighbouring administered areas seemed the most attractive solution. Never having called any man master, and 'as craggy as the country, unswerving in the most fundamental forms of Islam', the Pathans presented an almost insuperable problem of rule for the British, whose aim was to preserve the tranquillity of the administered areas in the belief that a person's right to go about his business without assault was the justification of their rule. The Pathans were a constant challenge to this notion.

At the back of their minds, the British always feared a Russian advance into India through Afghanistan, the 'Great Game' as it was then called. Masters was later to make this the subject of one of his novels, *The Lotus and the Wind*. British policy alternated between the view that it was better to let the Russians advance up to the mountains and have to fight their way through the hostile Pathans than to make a stand against them on the Afghan border itself and vice versa. Policy was confused but, since the Russian threat never fully materialised, the choice was never fully tested.

Nothing about the North-West Frontier was straightforward. It existed on a continuum of upheaval. No wonder Curzon had written, 'No man who has read a page of Indian history will ever prophesy about the Frontier.' The Pathans were belligerent by nature, and their raids into neighbouring areas led to an almost constant state of friction that regularly erupted into war. The British built a series of forts with garrisons at strategic intervals throughout the area as defensive measures, from which they would sally forth to retaliate against the Pathans. These forts, interconnected by newly-built roads, had a dual function: as lines of communication, and to give employment to the tribesmen in the hope of pacifying them and inducing a more settled way of life.

By the time Masters arrived at the North-West Frontier in October 1934, it was a relatively peaceful period. Razmak quickly taught him and other recruits the basic techniques of frontier life. For Masters it was a new type of soldiering. 'I unlearned my Sandhurst drill and learned a new type, light-infantry drill, where all movements were executed with extreme speed and a minimum of orders.' Training columns were its main feature, and were sent out to guard the transport convoys bringing supplies and arms from bases such as Bannu. The column might be made up of four hundred or so men and as many mules, a double string of men and animals in a defile up to 3 miles long. They would be watched constantly by the Pathans in the hills above, waiting to pounce if they perceived any mistake. Hence the need for piquets, small detachments that were sent in advance to occupy vantage points before the column arrived and which remained in position overlooking the valley until the column had gone by. Piqueting was exciting for the men, who shuffled up the hill at the double, pushing ahead as rapidly as possible, covered by machine and mountain guns, but it was often a slow business. Many of the hills were 1,000 feet above the road and the going was difficult and precipitous. It could take forty minutes for the piquet to reach the top. The column below could not move forward until the piquet was in position and once they had passed, the piquet had to leave the ridge as quickly as possible and scamper down at once. Tribesmen watched all this and had probably crept silently towards the ridges, ready to move in to the same spot, and attack the unwary piquet as it left. Early on, Masters encountered one such incident: a 'sudden storm of bullets, a rush of knifemen, a bloody hand-to-hand struggle', and then the piquet tumbled down the hill at full speed to rejoin its column.

At night on column they built a sangar, a low protective stone wall sufficiently high to be invulnerable to bullets. Mules would be put in the centre. Then, 'with the day's march done and the stone wall built, we sat, sweat-stained, around the cookers and smoked and drank strong tea, and then made our rounds of duty, the stars gleaming on the bayonets of the silent sentries along the wall.' They would sleep inside these sangars with their rifles chained to their wrists, in case Pathans crept in and stole them as they slept.

The officers generally liked being on frontier stations. 'There was always excitement, you would go out at night on training columns, with bullets hailing over you. There was a terrific camaraderie. It was very high-spirited coming back from a two or three week column to find the whole place bursting at seams,' David Davidson recalled. It epitomised much of what the Indian Army offered in terms of adventure and comradeship. Evenings were spent at the club, with frequent dinners with other regiments stationed there. People might drink a bit too much during the evening, though not during the day, but discipline was always very strong. Sport was regularly organised: football and hockey with the men, squash among the officers. Masters shared a room with Chris Pulley in the hutted accommodation in the camp. Pulley remembers him at the time as 'an ambitious person and intensely interested in a wide range of subjects, keen on the history of dress and tradition in army, knowledgeable on music and, above all, on the timings and workings of the Indian railway system.' Pulley noted his inquisitive mind but felt that his 'compunction about airing his views and arguing a case with more senior officers' did not always go down so well. Masters tended to get carried away and boast of his achievements, not least of his ability to charm the opposite sex. 'My chief memory is of a highly charged and dynamic personality, with a touch of romanticism about him', Pulley concluded. It is probably an accurate assessment of Masters at the time.

The need to boast left him feeling something of an outsider at times. During his first Christmas at Razmak he was orderly officer and accompanied his senior officers round the mess-halls of the battalion to drink a Christmas toast in each. Eventually they returned to their own mess for Christmas dinner. A regimental tradition at Christmas was that rank and discipline were forgotten for the day; junior officers could insult senior officers; food could be thrown about the table. Potatoes, legs of turkey were soon sent flying. Suddenly he realised, to his dismay, that, far from being included, he was being left out; no one was throwing anything at him. But then, after a while, he was included in the proceedings. 'Oh ecstasy! – hard fingers were rubbing brandy butter into my hair and stuffing Christmas pudding into my ears. I was forgiven, accepted! I flung myself with abandon into the riot, and the steaming rum punch flew faster round the table, and the snow fell thicker outside the windows.'

There is a wry irony in this account as he resurrects the memory of the occasion, which focuses on the central theme of his growing up, the sense of not belonging and what he did to counteract it. On occasions like this, which were more like tribal customs, the British Army reverted to its own. Bumptious newcomers like Masters were excluded for not being 'one of us', and any hint of his Anglo-Indian origins will have been taken into account. The price of acceptance was to be humiliated by having brandy butter rubbed into his hair. He speaks of it as if with exultation, but probably he was hurt by this singling out. Deep down his time with the British regiment may have been more trying than he lets on. British officers looked down upon those who did not quite belong, and Masters made himself an ideal foil for their taunts by striving so hard to be better and by trying at other times to please. His impatience with those less quick-witted than he would not have helped either.

It was never easy to enter a smoothly-running regiment as a newcomer. Masters, with his ambition to succeed, was particularly aware of this. Even after four months in the DCLI, he still saw himself as 'floundering about, like a blind puppy.' As a newly-appointed officer, he was particularly conscious of his first day of command. He stood tongue-tied when required to shout out the orders. It was a combination of nerves and over-eagerness to succeed. His fellow juniors, such as Hodson and Pulley, who had arrived at the same time as he, took things more slowly, just as eager to please and to succeed in the long run, but without Masters's impetuosity.

Masters made mistakes too. Once he told his platoon to proceed without waiting for his senior officer to arrive. A more experienced junior officer would have waited in spite of the risk of putting his men behind schedule. Revealingly, Masters concedes he did not admit to his senior officer it was his fault and allowed his sergeant to get the blame. How fragile his self-esteem must have been underneath; how strong his need to feel competent. Yet, and perhaps this is why he chose to describe those incidents, he was learning from these experiences, assimilating them for future use. Like many an ambitious person, the thought of not being able to live with himself was almost unbearable. Duty, loyalty and obedience were external attributes easily acquired. It was what he felt like inside that had to be protected. The mask of shame, the legacy of his family and their dark past, may still have troubled him, more so now that he was back in India. His return had heightened this awareness.

Another incident taught him a valuable lesson. He had complained to the Adjutant, Richard Bunbury, about another officer's act of unfairness and stupidity in dealing with his men. The Adjutant noted his comments and privately agreed this might well have been the case, but he pointed out that loyalty to fellow officers superseded such considerations. Without loyalty the army would be unmanageable. Masters learnt to tailor his sense of injustice to the requirements of the army – not an easy thing for him to do, since the idealist in him longed for the surrounding world to be perfect and his ambitious side wanted to clear opposition out of the way. 'My code has never been quite the same as anyone else's,' as he later wrote.

An even more typical example of his state of mind at this stage came in April 1935 when his regiment went to play in a cricket match at Tank against a team put together by the Political Agent of South Waziristan, Major Barnes, a respected political officer. After the match, they had the usual drinks at the Political Agent's bungalow. Masters's exuberance got the better of him and he became very high-spirited, 'lit up' in the phraseology of the day. He made some rather chancy remarks to Mrs Barnes, an older woman, who took exception to them. Dubious jokes and risqué language were no part of her social milieu. The others present noticed this and, once they got back to Razmak, the Senior Subaltern, Tom Cooper, felt he had to take action. Robin Hodson met Masters outside the mess later that week as he was about to be called in to be questioned. He was facing a subalterns' court martial, a rare and serious event. In the end he got a real dressing-down. Cooper told him his behaviour was unbecoming of a gentleman and of a member of the DCLI. One can sense how affronted Cooper, a senior subaltern of some seventeen years' service, must have felt at this newcomer's boisterousness, which, in this instance, was arguably almost a carbon copy of his father's behaviour on such occasions.

As summer approached, the four junior officers began to arrange their transfers to the Indian Army. Masters, ambitious as ever, had been keen to join a Gurkha regiment. He had an uncle, Hal Gordon, married to his mother's sister, who was in the 8th Gurkhas, and at Razmak he had watched the two Gurkha Rifle battalions stationed there and had liked what he had seen. He put in his request, and in July 1935 he was sent from Razmak to Bakloh in the Punjab where the 4th Prince of Wales's Own Gurkha Rifles were based. It was a much competed-for regiment, usually with four or more candidates after the same post. Vacancies only occurred when an officer retired or was seconded to staff. His visit was a way of being vetted or 'approved by ordeal'. It entailed a ten-day stay with the regiment, joining in their daily life to see if he was a good fit, as a potential member of the 'family'. When each candidate had visited in turn, the colonel called a mess meeting to select the most suitable applicant. Particular attention would be paid to the opinion of subalterns who lived with the applicant and were thus well placed to judge his suitability.

Masters was delegated James Fairweather, the junior subaltern, as his guide and mentor, but Fairweather failed to meet him at Tuni Hatti, the local bus stop, which he had reached after an uncomfortable two-hour, bouncing bus ride up from Pathankot, the nearest railhead. 'My watch must have stopped,' Fairweather assured him when they did meet. Masters was relieved that such foibles were tolerated. Also, Fairweather's absence gave him an opportunity to walk up the hill to Bakloh, past the native bazaar and the soldiers' quarters, across the parade ground hewn out of the hill and the officers' bungalows in the pine trees, the squash and tennis courts and small English-type Gothic church before reaching the officers' mess, which looked so English in parts, almost like a Virginia Water set in the foothills of the Himalayas. He liked it immediately, marvelling at its resplendent situation, especially the view from the glassed-in verandah at the front of the mess, which looked down a sheer drop to the Punjab plain, 4,500 feet below. Officers began to filter in, among them, somewhat sheepishly, James Fairweather. They greeted him warmly and he could sense the family atmosphere straightaway. It put him at ease – here he might be accepted without having to draw attention to himself. He was aware of being watched most of the time – after all it was the point of the exercise – however surreptitiously it was done. He tried to show himself keen and attentive, and inevitably appeared a bit thrusting. Then, a few days later, luck played him a good card.

Trouble and rioting had broken out in Lahore, the capital of Punjab, in the valley below. Tensions between the Sikh and Muslim communities had always been high. Now a flare-up had started over the Shadigamni Mosque which the Sikhs had destroyed. The battalion was ordered down to try and keep the peace, and Masters was allowed to join them. It was a tense, uneasy situation. Gurkhas had a long tradition of dealing with civil unrest and knew what to do to try to keep the two communities apart. Masters, on his mettle to show he could fit in, did his best without being too obtrusive. Bottle-throwing and unprovoked attacks were a constant hazard amid the commotion in the city. The situation calmed down eventually and the detachment returned to Bakloh. His conduct received favourable comment. The call to Lahore came just in time, because by then, by his own admission, he might have let his enthusiasm get out of hand. At Bakloh, he was already getting 'teed up' to display that 'erratic brilliance my years were incapable of controlling'.

He returned to Razmak and, a few weeks later, learnt to his great joy that he had been accepted by the 4th Gurkhas. By now he had mastered his chosen Indian language and was nearly fluent at Urdu, receiving seventy-six per cent in his Higher Standard Urdu exam in July 1935. Languages came easily to him and he later became a fluent Gurkhali speaker, with a more than passable command of Hindi.

The year with the DCLI was up, and they were off to new postings: Robin Hodson to the Guides, Chris Pulley to the 3rd Gurkhas and Bill Williams to the 14th Punjab Regiment. Masters could look back favourably on his year with the regiment. He said goodbye to Robin Hodson, who, looking back, remembers him as a 'bit of a know-all, justifiably so, as he knew a lot. He was always trying to find out about things. He was rather boisterous and wanted to get places and wouldn't

2/Lieut. J. Masters, M.H.A ald 1st Bn., S.C.L.I.

LANGUAGE EXAMINATION RESULT.

HIGHER STANDARD EXAMINATION IN URDU.

CANDIDATE'S INDEX NUMBER ONLY...13......

A/8

Place..Razmak.   Date.1. July .35.

Tests.	Full Marks.	Marks obtained.	Minimum pass marks required.	REMARKS.
PART I.—ORAL.				NOTE.
1. Translation from English	60	52	150 out of 250 in Part I, and 60 out of 100 in Part II.	1. A candidate who fails to obtain 60 per cent. of the total marks in Part I will be informed of the fact and his examination will not be proceeded with.
2. Translation from Urdu	60	47		
3. Reading and translating manuscript	30	80		2. If the candidate is for Part II only, the authority (District Orders, etc.) should be stated.
4. Conversation	100	20		
TOTAL	250	199		
PART II.—WRITTEN.				
1. Translation from English	60	33		
2. Translation from Urdu	40	35		
TOTAL	100	68		

Forwarded, together with the answer papers in Part II, to the Secretary, Board of Examiners, A.H.Q.

Supervising Officer,   Local Examiner.
for Part II (when appointed).

The Board of Examiners, having awarded marks in Part II and taken into consideration the marks awarded in Part I, declare that the candidate has passed/not passed.

Secretary, Board of Examiners A.H.Q.

Place... Simla...
Date......13/7/35...

Headquarters......Waziristan......District.

Forwarded to the candidate for information.

Place..Razmak.....
Date...31.7.35........

H. D. Hickman
Colonel
......District.

MGIPC—S5—1983 (O¹ I-B) MFP—(B-133)—1-2-35—500.

let things stand in his way.' The formality and hierarchical nature of the mess of a British regiment was different in this respect from an Indian Army one. With the DCLI, you were not expected to air your views unless the senior officers had aired theirs first. In Hodson's memory, people got rather cross with Masters about this. It was a failing he was having to come to terms with. A junior officer was expected to walk a narrow tightrope between being offensively bumptious and insignificantly dull. Conversationally he was expected to get his effects by offhand understatement, timed to catch the listener's attention at the right moment. This was not Masters's style. He was one of those discomfiting people who went to the truth straightaway and made other people feel inadequate in some way. The fact that he was supremely confident of his judgement and was not prepared to tolerate fools did not help either.

All that was behind him now. As he climbed into his train – the proverbial Heatstroke Express that crossed the burning desert to Mari Indus at little more than 10 miles per hour – he had time to reflect on his year with the DCLI. 'In the one year, I grew up ten', he later wrote. It had made a man of him. He was stronger, more self-reliant, resilient even, though he needed to curb his over-confident side. He was learning all the time, and he knew it. He sat in the restaurant room at Pathankot eating lunch before the bus ride up to Bakloh, aware of the change about to take place. He was entering India proper. As the red roofs of Bakloh appeared, crouched on its narrow, forested ridge in the foothills of the Himalayas, he felt a sudden elation.

Among his fellow junior officers in the 2nd Battalion were James Fairweather, John Strickland, 'Beetle' Lowis, 'Midge' Madge, 'Moke' Murray and 'The Boy' Stevenson-Hamilton. The nicknames indicate the familiarity of the atmosphere. The centre of activities was the officers' mess. Here were the accumulated mementoes of the regiment and of former officers, their names inscribed on the table silverware. It gave him a sense of belonging, of connecting with other generations that had preceded him. He thought to himself: 'One day my name will be on one of these.' As he sat back and watched his fellow officers, he let himself absorb the atmosphere; 'the sun shone level through the glass, the talk hummed lazily, china clinked'. It was 'like a dream before me.' The dream was fast becoming a reality. He had arrived. For the first time in years, he felt truly happy. He was being accepted for what he was, without the need to seek attention.

His bachelor quarters were in a bungalow known as the Rabbit Warren. Though spartan and primitive, they were adequate. His room had a narrow bed, a chest of drawers, a wardrobe, an easy chair, table and bookshelf, while next door was that notable Indian institution, the ghuslkhana or bathroom. In the middle of the room stood an oval zinc bathtub, with a table nearby with an enamel basin and jug, and in the corner was the thunderbox, or toilet. This was the domain of the sweeper or watercarrier, the 'bhisti'. The sweeper was summoned to heat water in four-gallon oil drums to be poured into the bath. Afterwards the bath water was tipped out through a hole in the outer wall that let the water out and, more often, snakes in. The sweeper also emptied the 'top hat' as the receptacle of the thunderbox was called. Altogether the ghuslkhana was, in Masters's words, 'a fine miniature of the Indian scene – barren, ramshackle, by turn too hot or too cold, yet full of interesting corners, strange expectations, and a mixed smell of woodsmoke and human excrement.' Many a traveller to India will recognise the accuracy of this description.

His bearer was a Gurkha called Biniram Thapa, old, grizzled and bent. Masters took to him immediately. 'He had no finesse and no professional charm but I liked him and everything about him.' Thapa helped him unpack and settle in. His rugged individualism, and stubbornness, was a characteristic of the Gurkhas, whose appearance was more Mongolian than Indian. They came from the hills of Nepal and were slant-eyed and hard-skulled; they shaved their head sometimes so that only a tuft at the crown remained, and their short, sturdy bodies were powered by a strong heart. Gurkhas, he soon realised, took immense pride in their turnout and in the smartness of their drill. They were straight as ramrods, and their discipline was firm and relentless. They ran awkwardly on the level, but fast uphill, and on a steep downhill no one could catch them. Aroused from slumber, they would go straight into battle.

Aside from their pride and straightforward loyalty, they liked practical jokes and had a rare gift for mimicry. They would look at you straight in the eye, but would not be very interested in you unless they knew you well. They liked gambling, rum and women. All in all they had an indefinable quality that even Masters, when he came to write about them later, found hard to pin down. 'Straightness, honesty, naturalness, loyalty, courage – all these are near it, but none is quite right, for the quality embraces all these.'

Gurkhas occupied a special position in British India ever since they first encountered the British in the Anglo-Nepalese war of 1814. Nepal was a separate kingdom that had come into existence in the eighteenth century when Rajput nobles had fled there from the Mogul domination in the plains of India and had taken over the area around the villages of Pokhara and Gorkha and introduced their Hindu religion and caste system. They recruited the local tribes into their armies which were the ones that strongly resisted the British, seeking to expand into Nepal. The Nepalese put up such a tough fight that after the war the British, in typical fashion, invited them to join their own side, a habit they had previously adopted in India by getting Madrassis to conquer Bengal, and men from Bihar and Oudh to conquer the Sikhs. The Nepalese were granted independence and thus were never part of the British Empire. In return, Nepal offered Gurkha recruits for three new regiments of the East India Company; the first Gurkha regiment was founded then.

The Gurkhas distinguished themselves on several occasions. During the 1857 Mutiny or Rising, they sided with the British and fought on the latter's behalf, which gave the Gurkhas their reputation for quelling civil disorders. New regiments were subsequently raised, including the 4th Gurkhas in 1857. The Gurkhas' code, 'I will keep faith', enshrines their sense of loyalty and they are reckoned by some to be the best foot soldiers in modern history. Gurkhas are noted for their kukris, a curved blade that in war can slice a man's head off in a single blow and in peacetime is used ceremonially at the festival of Dussehra when buffalo are sacrificed. Gurkhas are cunning and have proved themselves adept at psychological warfare too. During the Second World War legend has it that a Gurkha crept into a German tent at night near Cassino in Italy and neatly beheaded one of the two Germans sleeping there, replacing his head exactly and leaving it for his colleague to discover on waking the next morning.

Masters admired the Gurkhas from the start, and identified himself with their strong ties of loyalty. In the DCLI, a British regiment, he had at times come up against the underside of the British presence in India – the racial intolerance. He hated hearing the abuse directed at Indians, hearing them spoken of as 'niggers', 'wogs' or 'black-bellied bastards' – so often the standard terms of abuse of the British soldier and even, at times, of the British service officer. Masters could no more take part in the abuse than he could align himself with the haughty approach to India as a country which England owned and governed from a distance with distaste. He disliked the way Indians were treated like wayward children. Racial issues were never far from Masters's thoughts in these early days back in India.

In 1935, each Gurkha regiment consisted of two battalions each of about eight hundred men and thirty officers, commanded by the 'Colonel'. Each battalion went about its military business independently of the other. The colonel of the regiment as a whole was the only visible link between them; he was responsible for the selection of officers, and acted as arbiter for quarrels, as well as being the last authority in all matters of dress, tradition, custom, modes and manners. Bakloh, as a base or depot, had been founded in 1864, giving the Gurkha men a home in India as well as in Nepal. Most Gurkhas enlisted between the ages of sixteen and nineteen for an initial four-year period. The 4th Gurkhas drew their recruits from western Nepal, among the Magar and Gurung tribes. The key figure in each battalion was the subadar-major, the senior Gurkha officer, likely to have been with the regiment for fifteen years or more, and having a close and trusting relationship with the colonel. Other lesser ranks were: subadar, the equivalent of lieutenant; jemadar, second lieutenant; havildar, sergeant; naik, corporal; lance-naik, lance-corporal; and rifleman, private. Gurkha officers were undoubtedly the 'backbone of the Regiment'.

The 4th Gurkhas had added Prince of Wales's Own to their title after the First World War, when George V appointed his son, the Prince of Wales, as their Colonel-in-Chief. Their title and crest were then altered to include the Prince of Wales feathers and scroll, with his motto 'Ich Dien' on the crest and beneath that the traditional crossed kukris, both blades down, handles to the right, and a Roman IV in the lower fork of the kukris.

As his second year in India started, Masters realised he had found what he had secretly been looking for – a home in India a second time round. Donning his green 4th Gurkha uniform, with its black buttons, he felt a sense of pride and belonging. 'I had come to my home,' as he later described it.

One of his first initiation ceremonies was Guest Night, an age-old ritual of being 'dined into' the regiment under the watchful eyes of the assembled company. It was presided over by his Commanding Officer, Major, and Brevet Lieutenant-Colonel, David Murray-Lyon, DSO, MC. He put on black tie as required but, in his haste, had left his flies undone, to be met by Murray-Lyon with the cry of 'Stars in the east, I see, Masters.'

Drinks came first, a gimlet for him, whisky and sodas for the others. He needed to be careful this evening, as he would be judged on how well he held his liquor. Outside on the green lawn the band played 'The Roast Beef of Old England'. When dinner was called, Masters sat midway down the table, with the president and vice president at either end. Nervous as he was about this guest night, he soon noticed the imperturbability of his fellow diners, and this reassured him. Not only had they all been through it many times before, but they also were not out of discomfit him. He seemed to have crossed the invisible line between trial and acceptance. As the meal progressed, he relaxed, feeling 'the comradeship of those who had come before me to this table and been received in to this home'. Conversation rippled in comfortable waves around him and his glass was constantly filled; mindful of the June Ball a couple of years back, he limited his intake. At the end of the meal toasts were drunk to the King Emperor, the water glasses having first been removed (a reference to the Jacobite habit of drinking to the 'King over the Water'). The bandmaster came in, the pipers played. It was a warm and convivial occasion. Perhaps the ghosts of Wellington and Sandhurst had been finally laid to rest.

He glanced round the dining room with its motley collection of silver cups, candelabra and the amateur watercolours on the walls, always held in such affection. It was heady stuff, with so much of the regiment's history in this one room, as if the paths of glory were ever-present: 'the graves on the banks of the Euphrates, in the Afghan snows, under the poplars beside the pavé to Neuve Chapelle, on the Russian steppes, in the seas and the mountains and the hills.' Tradition, such as this, was at the core of army life. The decanters circulated. Masters, as the guest, had to be the first to leave. He went to the anteroom; the others soon joined him, a party in the making, but prudently he left now rather than later. It was the right move; 'I thought I saw a momentary gleam of approval in Murray-Lyon's eyes as he said, "Goodnight, Masters."' He lay in bed hearing the party going on till 3 a.m. but did not feel left out.

A newcomer had to watch for clues about how to fit in. James Fairweather, still his mentor, told him the secret of command was to 'walk around at a pace slightly faster than normal, carrying a bunch of papers, and working your lips as though thinking aloud.' This seemed good enough advice, and he stuck to it.

The military year for a battalion at base was really a training cycle divided into two halves: from March to October, the hot season, they stayed up in the cooler air of Bakloh, but from November to February they went down to the plains to train and march. He had joined them in October, and they were about to leave for the plains. Camels had already started the long trudge down the hill, snaking round the hairpin bends, laden with tents, boxes, bales and stores.

Their training day would start at seven in the morning with a march across the plain until lunchtime, when the heat became oppressive. After every 3 miles, or every fifty minutes, whichever came first, the march called a halt for a ten-minute rest. For baggage, each British officer was allotted a camel, which had an invaluable piss-pot hanging from his neck. Masters's relationship with his commanding officer was all-important at this stage. Murray-Lyon became a sort of father figure to him, watching over him, never staying too long or showing him up in front of his company. Masters needed this sort of guidance, despite his avowed aim to go it on his own. The need for a good father was deeply embedded in him. Once he saw Murray-Lyon angrily tell a major off for committing a transgression, which Masters had not felt was entirely justified. The way the major took it like a man and did not answer back in his defence was a further lesson to him in the code of loyalty. The ability to put up with misfortune with equanimity was all part of the English public school spirit of 'pulling one's weight', inculcated from an early age. Public schools here functioned as a prelude to Empire.

For Masters such notions were not as obvious, nor as easy, as they were for many of his contemporaries. They involved the question of belonging and the intrinsic linking of moral qualities with class. The fact that he preferred to assess each situation on its merits showed that he did not share these same basic assumptions. His moral boundaries were often of his own making.

Gaining full acceptance with Gurkha troops always took time. Masters started off, like many another before him, by imagining they always understood him, but often it was not true. Having assembled them once to congratulate them on the way they had carried out an exercise, he then found the subadar rounding them up again to explain, in a much shorter and more succinct manner, what he had just told them. They had looked attentive before, but it was apparent they had not taken in a word he had said. None of the men, not even the recruits, accepted a British officer until he had been there several months and they had had time to adjust themselves to his presence. However well he spoke – and Masters soon spoke very fair Gurkhali, a simplified version of several Nepali dialects – they would not 'understand' him until they decided to accept him. Acceptance was less dependent on personal qualities or military prowess than on some undecipherable factor when suddenly the outsider became a member of the family, of the blood. Gurkha regiments always reserved the right to get rid of British officers whom they considered unsuitable: 'A good officer, sahib, but not a Gurkha officer', they would say to their commanding officer, and the offending officer would be transferred.

Masters reckoned it took him nearly two years to gain this acceptance. Often when he was speaking to a Gurkha, the man would look woodenly to the nearest Gurkha officer for a translation. His jokes, even if they were made in Gurkhali, fell flat. Then suddenly one day he made what he thought was a rather lame remark, half in jest, about someone's large feet and his whole company exploded in paroxysms of laughter. Word of what he said was passed down the column and repeated over and over again. From that moment on he was in.

His relationship with Murray-Lyon seemed to be on a sure footing, but, in echoes of Sandhurst, there were 'stirrings of dislike' among his fellow officers. He asked Moke Murray what was wrong and was advised, gently, not to 'offer your opinions quite so often or so definitely.' It was the old problem again, his relentless need to 'shine', matched by an impatience with others who were slower than he. His was a driven and restless temperament, constantly striving to get on, to keep things moving. If matters stood still for too long, then what? There was always the risk of the downward spiral of self-doubt. At times his forcefulness and his abundance of energy were too much. Moke Murray's message got through to him, though, and he changed tack, discovering to his surprise and delight that 'it was as much fun to listen as to argue.' He was still only twenty; arrogance was part of his armoury in taking on the world, but his ambitious side was still keen to learn as a means of making his mark on the world.

His induction into the regiment heartened him. Body and character were toughened up by the long marches in the plains and in the mountains. It made him lean, hard and fit. Gurkha regiments prized above all steadfastness, loyalty and directness. This was moulded into an esprit de corps that ultimately produced the selfless courage needed in war, at moments when regimental ties counted for as much as the wider abstractions of King and Country. The moments a good officer – a successful one – was to find troops responding to his commands unquestioningly were what they were all striving for.

The 'white towers and ridges of the Himalayas' formed a permanent backdrop to life at Bakloh. Masters was captivated by them and took any opportunity he could to walk there. He loved their changing aspect, how, in their upper reaches, he could find what Kipling had described as 'the appalling sweep and dispersal of the cloud shadows after rain.' This quotation was from *Kim*, long Masters's favourite book and, in his opinion, Kipling's best book on India. The tang of the mountain air and the silence in the hill held him spellbound. The Gurkhas, a highland people, were just as appreciative, singing their jaunris (songs) as they came up from winter manoeuvres on the plains: *'Kati ramro jhyal bhunyo bhane makura-le,'* ('How many beautiful webs have I made?' said the spider).

As a bachelor, life at Bakloh had its restrictions. There were few women there, other than wives or daughters of other officers. Up at

Dalhousie, the hill station 15 miles further on, there was more choice. The club there was typical of many in India, with its cheerful young men drinking in the men's bar and not so cheerful middle-aged men soaking it up in nearby armchairs. It had an easy comfort, with its *Spy* cartoons on the walls. The lounge, where women congregated, was known familiarly as the snakepit, a hunting ground for 'lounge lizards' and 'sofa cobras'. The card room was soon filled in the afternoon with bridge players, while, in the cool of the evening, tennis would be played outside. Masters took part in all this and relished the conviviality and made what amatory conquests came his way. There was a dance every week in the ballroom, where, despite its seedy air of forgotten splendour and its potted plants and faded curtains, romance of a sort could flourish.

When he came to write *Bugles and a Tiger*, he made a point of observing how different the life of the ordinary British soldier in India was. His leisure activities were restricted to 'a flyblown bar and grill on the outskirts of the bazaar, where he was robbed of his scanty pay and given adulterated drink and skimped food; sand-harlots, riddled with every type of venereal disease; old-fashioned barracks and the sour smell of sweaty socks and shirts; a cinema a mile away; and close at hand boredom, loneliness and despair.' The life of the officer was far apart, and Masters was conscious of these differences.

It was really only on leave periods at places like Srinagar in Kashmir that Masters could meet the female company he sought. Here most English visitors to India came at one time or another, together with the wives and daughters of service families. Unattached young women, nurses or secretaries, from all over India flocked there too, but sexual mores in India between the wars were not as relaxed as was often imagined. Rumours that the so-called 'fishing fleet' of girls out from England to search for a husband would play fast and loose were also largely unfounded. The serious philanderer's best bet was a brother officer's wife, and Kashmir was as likely a setting as any, as this favourite summer venue was regarded by some as a Saturnalia where ordinary rules did not apply.

Legends used to proliferate about 'grass widows'. Masters cites a classic story of Captain A who comes up to join his wife in another hill station at Mussoorie for a month's leave. 'The station forms a wordless conspiracy never to let him know of the existence of Mr B, a resident official who has, they all know, spent most of his days and nights with Mrs A for some weeks past, and will resume the practice as soon as Captain A has returned to Sweattypore.' There was a tacit understanding that such liaisons were tolerated, so long as they didn't go as far as divorce. In an officer's case, being named as co-respondent might require that he resign his commission, a situation that was to confront Masters later on.

Social life for the British in India was a goldfish bowl. The servants usually knew what was going on, Gurkhas especially. At the annual celebrations for Dussehra at Bakloh in October, some of the imitations the Gurkhas put on were horrifyingly accurate caricatures of English tribal customs, as observed by the former through ballroom windows and on mess verandahs.

Masters liked going to Srinagar and spent his leave there whenever possible. It offered rare delights: lunch parties on Dal Lake under the awnings of houseboats, with women lying on deep cushions and gramophones playing the latest Noël Coward tunes; cocktails were served at 11.00 in the morning and lunch ended in a 'drowsy repletion of brandy and ice souffle' at 4.00. Houseboats lent themselves to such dalliance; the sensual delight of the green, cool water and the distant view of the snow-clad hills, and the sight of girls 'trailing their fingers through the curtains into the rippling water' were all an irresistible prelude to amorous carousing. Masters revelled in this atmosphere and engaged in brief affairs, none long-lasting, for it was still not part of his plan to embark on a permanent relationship. His motto was still *Carpe Diem.*

Kashmir offered the closest thing to an English country house tradition in India. House parties on Dal Lake were numerous, particularly as foreigners were not allowed to buy land or build houses in Kashmir. Most colonials in India, and elsewhere in the Empire, aspired and contrived to lead a higher level of social life than would have been available to them in their own country. The Indian Army did not always look favourably upon this and sometimes dissuaded its members from going to Kashmir because of its rather dilettante reputation. Leave there was known, in the vernacular, as 'poodlefaking' and was considered rather unmanly and sybaritic, in comparison to the more robust tiger shooting, fishing and mountain walking pursued by other officers.

Leave for an Indian Army officer was basically two months' 'privilege leave' for which he got full pay each year, or three months if he was serving on the frontier or in a non-family station. Every fourth year he got an additional six months' leave on reduced pay, which if he combined with his privilege leave meant eight months altogether, enough for a decent trip back to England. Masters was not due for such leave, or long furlough as it was called, until 1938, but in 1936 after finishing his small arms course at Pachmarchi – his shooting hardly improved – he decided to use up his two months' leave to return to England on a quick visit.

He had been away from England for two years and was immediately struck by the contrast with India. Gone were the openness and friendliness; people 'looked neither to left nor right but scurried in their thousands down the underground at Waterloo station', then sat pale and hunched in the train compartment. It was a shock returning to England after an absence and having to adjust to the insular and small scale.

Masters's visit was a success and a boost to his self-esteem. At home in Uplyme, he felt more confident than before. He recognised inside himself 'a more fearsome censor' made in India. The censor was more than just conscience and tact; it was a way of accommodating all that he had learnt through trial and error. 'I didn't have to live with anyone but myself – and my regiment.' The addition of the regiment was significant, as his identity was clearly linked to it now. He felt as if a weight had been taken off his shoulders. He could be himself more; he did not need to jump in brashly to impress people before they had a chance of sizing him up.

Returning home was a way of having these changes mirrored back to him, reporting back to base as it were: 'Jackie's back, look how he's changed'. There is a photograph of the family reunion with them all standing on the doorstep of Bailey Gate. Masters stands out and up, his role within the family as the bright hope validated; he was the carrier of the family's aspirations, fulfilling their unmet ambitions. His success in the Indian Army seemed destined to reach beyond anything his father had achieved.

His other reason for wanting to get back to England was to see Lois Jervis and maintain the strength of their relationship. They spent as much time together as they could. In her spare time they would go off together to the Downs for a picnic, or up to London. Her zest for life was as strong as ever, a little near the edge at times, but they enjoyed each other's company; it was exciting and dramatic and, aged twenty-one, he was looking for little else.

His leave was soon up, and he set off for India again, the same way he had come, the well-known quick overland route via Paris and Marseilles, a boat to Suez and on to Bombay. At the Gare de Lyon in Paris, he ate in the station buffet, where the attendants must have known half the Indian Army officers by sight. When he landed in Bombay and boarded his train up to Pathankot, it was August 1936.

Six months later Masters was on the move again; his battalion was

being called down to the the North-West Frontier. Trouble had started
in November 1936, when an ambush by tribesmen at Biche Kaskai in
the Tochi Valley in Waziristan had inflicted severe casualties on the
Bannu Brigade. Nineteen had been killed and over a hundred wounded
in a two-day battle, and there had been the usual seizure of rifles and
ammunition. It was clearly a prepared and thought-out attack and a
signal for an escalation of hostilities. Tribesmen seemed to be restless
again after a period of relative peacefulness.

In fact the Frontier had been ominously quiet for more than six
years, hence the resurgence of war. A generation had grown up that
had missed it. War for the Pathans was an honourable, exciting and
manly exercise, in which each succeeding generation needed to prove
itself, but war was also ruthless; no mercy was shown and none was
expected. Neither side aimed to take prisoners. The Pathans customarily
mutilated and then beheaded any wounded or dead who fell into their
hands. Women often carried out these operations. A well-known torture
was called the Thousand Cuts, whereby flesh wounds were newly made
and grass and thorns pushed into them so that they would hurt
horribly. A prisoner might be pegged out on the ground and his jaw
forcibly opened with a stick so that he could not swallow, then women
would urinate in his mouth until he drowned. Frank Baines, who
served on the North-West Frontier and later with Masters in Burma,
put it more crudely: 'If you got captured, you were not only killed in a
lively and imaginative manner, you were carved up and quartered and
had your cock cut off and stuffed in your mouth, for good measure.'
Masters admits that the British also 'took few prisoners at any time,
and very few indeed if there was no Political Agent about.'

War in the Tribal Territory had its own rules and conventions. In the
warming-up days of a Frontier campaign, the troubled area was called
the prescribed area, outside of which no action could be taken by
British or Indian Army soldiers unless they were shot at. This was an
obvious excuse for guerilla warfare, at which the Pathans excelled.
Always elusive and mobile, they were almost impossible to pin down
on their own hilly terrain, and, then as now, superior firepower meant
little in these surroundings. Yet for all its ferocity, war had its own
strong, rather brutal, sense of humour. When a particular episode was
over, and the political agent had imposed his fine and the kidnapped
hostages had gone safely home, Pathans would meet with the opposing
side and happily discuss the mistakes each side had made, in the spirit
of a friendly football match. Even though they might have tortured
and killed the wounded and mutilated the dead, afterwards they would
come to this tikala, or feast, and would end up telling the political

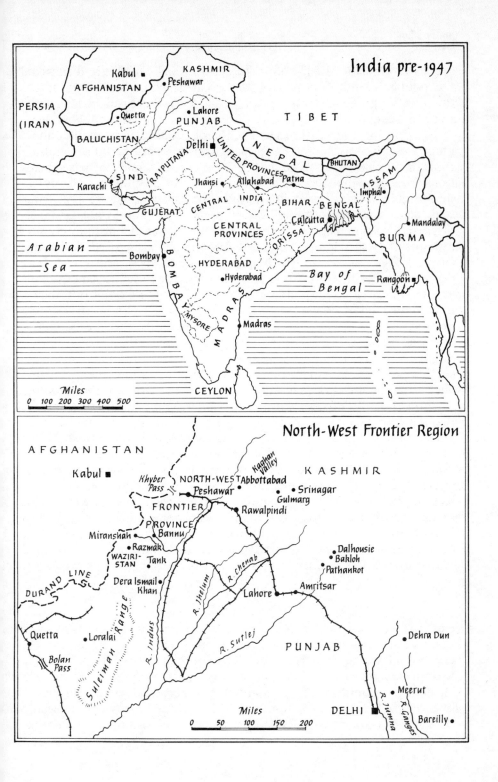

India pre-1947

PERSIA
(IRAN)

AFGHANISTAN
Kabul ■

KASHMIR
Peshawar ●

Quetta ●

BALUCHISTAN

Lahore ●
PUNJAB

T I B E T

SIND

Delhi ■

RAJPUTANA

NEPAL

BHUTAN

Karachi ●

UNITED PROVINCES

Jhansi ●

Allahabad ●

Patna ●

ASSAM

Imphal ●

GUJERAT

CENTRAL INDIA

BIHAR

BENGAL

Arabian
Sea

Bombay ●

CENTRAL
PROVINCES

ORISSA

Calcutta ●

Mandalay ●

BURMA

HYDERABAD

Hyderabad ●

Bay of
Bengal

Rangoon ●

BOMBAY

MYSORE

MADRAS

Madras ●

Miles
0 100 200 300 400 500

CEYLON

North-West Frontier Region

AFGHANISTAN

Kabul ■

Khyber
Pass

NORTH-WEST

Kaghan
Valley

Abbottabad ●

KASHMIR

Peshawar ●

Srinagar ●

Gulmarg ●

FRONTIER

Rawalpindi ●

PROVINCE
Bannu ●

Miranshah ●

Razmak ●

WAZIRI-
STAN

Tank ●

DURAND LINE

Dera Ismail
Khan ●

Suleiman Range

R. Indus

R. Jhelum

R. Chenab

Dalhousie ●
Bakloh ●
Pathankot ●

Amritsar ●

Lahore ●

Quetta ●

Loralai ●

Bolan
Pass

R. Sutlej

PUNJAB

Dehra Dun ●

Meerut ●

DELHI ■

R. Jumna

R. Ganges

Bareilly ●

Miles
0   50   100 150 200

agent he was their father and mother. After one campaign, they asked the political agent for medals, the same as had been given out to the army opposing them – after all, they were all part of the same campaign.

The Pathans adhered to their own highly developed code of conduct known as Puktunwhali. Its two main features were badal, or revenge regardless of cost or consequence – blood feuds could last for generations – and melamastia, the obligation to offer hospitality and protection to every guest. The Pathans abided by this code vigorously; it was both strict and honourable. To allow a guest to be killed was as disgraceful as to leave unavenged the murder of a kinsman, as this example shows: a sentry, inflamed by religious zeal, suddenly shot a British officer as he lay sleeping in the open because his feet were disrespectfully turned towards Mecca. Everyone – British and Pathans alike – agreed that the sentry must die. So that it should not start a blood feud, there was also agreement that the Pathan's brother should fire the shot. When it was put to him, the murderer also agreed that this was fitting, so the episode ended decently and with order.

Tough, hardy, fiercely independent, the Pathans resolved issues like these at a jirga, a communal tribal gathering where everyone was allowed a say and decisions were reached by the 'sense of the meeting', as closely resembling the Athenian original of democracy as could be found anywhere.

Masters, like many a Frontier hand before him, was drawn to the Pathans, 'these fierce men – physically the hardest people on earth, rangy and hawk-nosed, made of whipcord and steel', with their long, loping strides and manly bearing. They were formidable warriors but had a softer side. Men held hands and wore roses in their hair. Their sexual preferences were often homosexual, echoing the well-known Pathan proverb 'a woman for business, a boy for pleasure, a goat for choice.' There is a memorable Pathan song, 'Zakhmi Dil' (Wounded Heart) that expresses this:

> There's a boy across the river with a bottom like a peach,
> But, alas, I can't swim.'

Responsible for much of the present trouble, in British eyes, was the Fakir of Ipi, a name easily and readily mispronounced by the British. His real name was Haji Mizra Ali Khan, a mullah from Tori Khel. He had quickly emerged as a leading figure after the notorious Islam Bibi incident. A young Hindu girl, a minor, had been abducted from Bannu by a Wazir student, a Muslim, and taken to the hills, where allegedly she had been converted to Islam. Her Hindu relations brought a charge against him and attempts were made to get her back, but the Wazirs refused; she was now a Muslim and had to stay. On 7 April 1936, the day set for the trial, a huge crowd of two thousand Muslims gathered in Bannu blocking the approaches to the court and causing the trial to be postponed. Agitators whipped them up into a frenzy; prominent among these was the Fakir, hitherto a moderate but now implacably anti-British and a fervent champion of Islam.

On occasions like this, the usual procedure for defusing trouble was to send the British political agent up to parley with the tribesmen. He always had free access to them and was usually trusted by them. He would try to arrange a settlement at a jirga. If this failed, khassadars were called in. Khassadars were an irregular force of tribesmen, who, as one new Viceroy remarked, guarded you by day and shot at you by night. Even then, as a last resort, the Frontier Scouts would be called in – a special and highly disciplined force made up of British officers and Pathans, from different districts. The Scouts were an impressive and disciplined corps. 'Scouts on the move were a magnificent sight', Masters wrote, 'all brown as berries, all wearing khaki turbans, grey shirts flapping loose outside khaki shorts, stockings and nailed sandals, British officers were indistinguishable from the men.' Their patrols were called gashts; a hundred and eighty men, with their single British commander, 'swept along the ridges and past the loopholed towers, loping ceaselessly at five miles an hour, returning after a circuit of 25 or 35 miles to their fort'. On a barampta, a punitive patrol, the men pounced before dawn on a fortress, 'arrested the startled headman, and whisked him lightfoot to HQ, there to explain just what hand the young men of his village had taken in last week's mail robbery, and why he had not come on his own in answer to several polite summons.' The present situation had developed beyond the control of the Scouts and hence the army had been called in, with reinforcements brought from further afield. There were now all the signs of a full-scale Frontier war – the first since the big campaigns of 1919–23.

The Fakir of Ipi had made his base at a complex of caves at Arsal Kot – another name that led to much ribald mispronunciation by British troops. All that winter of 1936 the Fakir's troops harassed the opposing army, killing and marauding over a wide area. By March 1937 retaliation was called for, and Masters's battalion was sent down to join the large expedition mounted against the Fakir; in all some 32,000 regular troops were employed.

Masters arrived at Bannu on 29 March, just as things were hotting up. The Frontier was the real thing and a proper testing ground for his recent training. Bannu was alive with the bustle of war and 'war's nervous, incessant gossip'. Transport columns came down from the hills and their drivers were questioned anxiously about the fighting. Mostly they shrugged their shoulders; they had heard firing but had seen nothing more. Masters was in charge of A Company and set off in a convoy of lorries towards the front, sitting beside the driver, a loaded revolver on his lap. They were going to Miranshah, about 15 miles short of the battle zone, now centred on the road to Razmak.

Miranshah was a small fort with an airstrip, right in the middle of the Waziristan plain. T. E. Lawrence had been stationed there in the 1920s, incognito as Aircraftsman Shaw. He had liked its isolation; 'the station of a dream, as though one had fallen right over the world and had lost one's memory of its troubles. The quietness is so intense that I rub my ears, wondering if I am going deaf', he wrote at the time. Brown and white tents were lined up on the aerodrome, and Masters reported to the mess, a dug-down pit with a tent roof and petromax lamps, and saw familiar faces, among them James Fairweather ('You're early').

Their initial task was to carry out road protection, i.e. to make sure the lorry convoys coming up from Bannu got through safely. This meant piquet duty again, changing their routine each day, an essential frontier principle. Tribesmen were always on the lookout for a mistake, a single act of carelessness; their 'infinite, murderous patience' enabled them to wait indefinitely. If the piquet commander had been careless in his search of ground, or sited the sentries badly, the tribesmen would get dangerously close. A retreating piquet member might be shot and the piquet would then have to go back to get him, which meant retaking the hill and more loss of life. 'All this happened because one jemadar put one sentry one yard too far back, because one man walked when he should have run, because one machine-gunner pressed his thumbpieces one second later than he should have. War on the Frontier was not only very dangerous, but it was exacting, personal, and merciless.'

Commanders such as Murray-Lyon tricked the Pathans at their own game. A typical ploy would be to tell the men on piquet duty to pretend to be careless and move around heedless of the enemy, chatting and talking, then get them to move off the hill seemingly in no hurry. Fifteen seconds later, reverting to their true skill, they would sweep back up again and meet the confident, rushing tribesmen with a blast of fire at point-blank range.

The time at Miranshah, apart from road protection duty, was a period of waiting. Masters wrote on 25 April to his brother Alex, now in the Indian Army with the 1st Gurkhas in Poona, having been through Wellington and Sandhurst:

How are you getting on in your sloth station down there? We are cut off from the world here officially, as no convoys are running for a fortnight ... The war as such is definitely a quiet one here in Miranshah. We have been sniped at here four times since I arrived at the beginning of this month but with no damage to anyone. The flies here are perfectly awful and the only time they let up for an instant is in a dust storm, which is if anything worse. The Fucker of Ipi has announced his intention of leading his men in unison against the 1st Division today but although they will very probably be attacked between Jalei or Biche, I doubt if the Fucker will move very far from Arsehole Koti, where he is living. I saw a most frightful crash here about ten days ago when an Australian from Kohat stalled a Wapiti as he was taking off. He crashed and a 250 lb bomb went off, then the whole thing caught fire and the other bomb went off, the pilot and observer had to be swept up, poor buggers.

Masters kept up a regular correspondence with his brother, as he did with his parents; weekly letter-writing in those days was very much an accepted part of his, and others', life. Masters's tone is still very much that of the elder brother, with its hint of slight superiority, but there is warmth and friendliness too. The quiet period he describes was no more than a lull before the storm, and before long he was in the thick of action.

It was to be his blooding in war. His battalion was ordered out late one cold, moonlit night in search of a party of Pathans who had been reported slipping away from the battle area and were now in their vicinity. His company stood bunched and shivering in the cold before setting off. Night was the enemy's friend, allowing them to disappear into the surrounding landscape. Masters sent men to scour ditches and culverts by the side of the road en route, but they found nothing. Then, as dawn rose, they climbed a hill overlooking a valley and suddenly Masters's field glasses picked out a thin straggle of people on the other side of the Tochi valley – a group of nearly thirty men moving unconcernedly along a river bank, convinced that no one else was nearby.

For a moment he found it difficult to focus his glasses in his eagerness and excitement. It was his first sight of an enemy that he knew that he would have to shoot to kill – a heart-wrenching moment. So much flashed through his mind: might he be mistaken, were they friendly Scouts returning from a barampta nobody had told him about? No, on second sight they couldn't be, but they looked so human and unsuspecting. They were already within range of his light automatics.

If he waited much longer he might never give the order to fire. He hesitated and the emptiness in his stomach grew. Finally he gave his order; even so, he had been too hasty and had given it too soon, and many of the Pathans escaped among the rocks. Murray-Lyon later mildly reprimanded him for this, but congratulated him on his speed and ability to spot the enemy. Later he learnt they had killed eight out of a party of twenty-seven tribesmen, but he was left with a mixed feeling of elation and sadness.

At Miranshah, a new arrival was Major Joe Lentaigne from Staff College at Camberley. Masters and he got along famously. Lentaigne was an Irishman, a great talker, voluble and fond of his whisky. He was full of the newest thinking of the army and of the military hierarchy at home. John Strickland noted how similar they both were in build and facial expression and how they spoke 'fast and furiously with something of a nasal twang.' It was the beginning of a formative and important friendship for Masters.

At the beginning of May the 4th Gurkhas moved further south into Mahsud territory and the battle zone. Masters wrote to Alex:

> I was in Tocol's famous night march from Dosalli on to the Sham Plain over the Iblanke Spur on May 11/12 – and I hope I'm never in anything like that again. Mules were falling down the khud all over the place and we advanced two miles between 8.30 p.m. and 5.30 a.m. When dawn broke and I heard the rattle of firing ahead, and found myself on an exposed ridge, with two unheld ridges to right and left at a range of about 600 yards or less, I felt distinctly nervous. Especially as there was a hell of a mob of people carrying mule loads to the top of the hill and waiting for spare mules to be sent back to take them over. Later on I became advanced guard and actually we were the first troops on to the Sham Plain. We were fired on while attacking across the plain to get to some low ridges on the other side.

They rested in Coronation Camp, so named after the Coronation of George VI, which had taken place in England on 12 May. Their task was road building and road protection, but it was dangerous. 'We were sniped at all hours of the day in that bloody place, two bullets landing quite near me while I was falling in a battalion road fatigue at 9.00 a.m.!'

Eventually the Fakir of Ipi's hiding place in the caves above Arsal Kot was discovered. It was blackened with cooking fires, but he had left some days before. The war was getting rougher and Masters was feeling the pace. Masters wrote to Alex: 'We've been shot at for twenty-three days continuously, and we had lice and worked nineteen hours a day for five days and I want a rest. One of these days I suppose they'll open leave and then I'm off like shit from a duck.'

Masters had been on active service for two months, but was now transferred back to Bannu, which he described as 'this bloody oven' – it was 120 degrees in the shade – before going back to Bakloh where he had been delegated to look after the depot and take charge of training new recruits. It had been Murray-Lyon's decision. He felt Masters had seen enough active service and was ready to take on other responsibilities. From a military career point of view, he was shaping up well. In his annual report, Murray-Lyon described him as a 'very capable officer' who had done well in the war, though the old bugbear of his 'impetuousity' was mentioned as well.

His new post was quite a responsibility. Being in charge of the depot at Bakloh, with sixty new recruits, various old soldiers, storemen, clerks, instructors and bandsmen, women and children, was a tall order for a twenty-three-year-old. His predecessor handed over to him and he felt momentarily overwhelmed. He was on his own, and he would be judged by his performance. Determined as ever, he entered into his work with gusto, devising a meticulous timetable for the new recruits and making sure he kept on top of his administrative tasks. In the evening, with few fellow officers in the mess, he read in the well-stocked library; his favourite books were Gibbon's *Decline and Fall*, which he liked reading every morning at breakfast, Frazer's *Golden Bough*, Machiavelli's *The Prince* and Hakluyt's *Voyages*, and anything he could find about the American Civil War, which he was studying for his promotion exam. Promotion was much on his mind as he thought about his army future during the long evenings sitting on the verandah with the Punjab plain below.

It was a lonely existence though. When John Strickland passed through later that year in the cold season, he found Masters swaddled in a brown dressing-gown, made out of an army blanket, reading by the light of a hurricane lamp. Masters mentions this in *Bugles and a Tiger* and states that Strickland advised him to go and get 'a damned great fat woman' – which he did, but he omits this from *Bugles and a Tiger*. He went down to Lahore, and came back satisfied, but with a dose of clap, and then had to submit to the very painful so-called 'umbrella treatment', devised by a Japanese doctor for such a contingency – very painful too. He recalled the experience in his novel *Far, Far the Mountain Peak*, when Peter Savage slips away to the old city of Lahore to 'attain a physical release in these affairs', even though this is 'at the cost of a gradually increasing mental tension, because he was always

moved to try to put more into the relationship – in this case the mere
act of union – than it could in those circumstances contain. He felt,
and strove for, an increasing wild kind of lifting up.'

Female company did exist in Bakloh. The wives of officers engaged
on the frontier were still there. One of these women, Barbara Hughes,
became a close friend and her domestic knowledge – checking babies
for health for example – was very useful. Masters's contribution to the
troops' welfare was a thorough and detailed forty-eight page pamphlet
in Gurkhali on the correct care of Gurkha children, with an appendix
on running a household.

To counter the often long and monotonous days, and what he
enjoyed most, was taking the recruits trekking in the mountains. He
took them up past Dalhousie to Chamba, where he stayed with the
Rajah while the recruits camped in the grounds. Mountains provided
him with some of his happiest moments. 'Inside me my spirit sang, the
body and the spirit, the lonely mountains, running water. The Himalaya
had breathed its breath into my nostrils while I lay asleep.' There was
almost a quasi-mystical feeling about it, the elation and oneness with
surroundings that mountaineers sometimes experience. As he went
back over a high pass, with the Himalayas 'blindingly blue and white
to the north,' past meadows 'blinking with the flowers of early summer',
a feeling of utter content came over him. Hills, mountain air, Gurkha
troops under his command – what more could he want?

In February 1938 his tranquillity was shattered by an unexpected
happening. Just after 3.00 in the afternoon, his orderly knocked on his
bungalow door to report that a grass cutter had just seen a leopard, or
a panther as they were called locally, in the scrub below the squash
court. It seemed to be hiding near one of the unoccupied bungalows.
Leopards were not all that uncommon in Bakloh, so he set off with a
.303 rifle, collecting beaters on the way to roust it out. They approached
its hiding place and spread out in a line to throw stones, and beat the
earth with sticks to get it to move. Suddenly a huge roar broke from
the branches as they cracked and snapped, and a great blur of black
and gold stripes sped past at full speed. The tiger, for such it was,
lunged at one of the beaters, a lance-naik, whose face was half torn
away by the impact. Masters quickly went to attend to the wound and
started applying a tourniquet. The tiger doubled back on its tracks and
raced past him to hide in a thicket some 10 yards away and then set off
downhill. Masters, never confident of his shooting prowess, followed it,
rifle at the ready. A crowd had gathered once the news spread like
wildfire round the depot, as people dropped what they were doing to
hurry over to see what was going on. Masters got a shot at the tiger as

it lurked in the bushes, only wounding it in its off forepaw. As it scampered away for cover, more dangerous than ever, it roared ominously. Masters had to move towards it, anxiety now at fever pitch, to reach a vantage point with his back to a rock. He peered ahead to see the animal. Its natural camouflage merged with its surroundings. Then it moved and the white fur of its neck ruff showed. He took aim and fired; the animal leapt convulsively and then lay still. He approached, now surrounded by even greater crowds. He had shot it just above the left eye, killing it instantly.

The tiger was slung on poles and carried up, amid much jubilation, to the mess. It was put with grim humour in the guest room, with a circle of kerosene laid on the floor to keep away ants. Celebrations were now going on all over the camp. The Gurkhas brought him rum, and he played his record of 'Tiger Rag' on the mess gramophone, the Gurkhas standing outside roaring rhythmically in unison. Later they made up their own jaunri to commemorate the event and sang it wherever Masters was with them:

> In '38 in the month of February
> Masters-Sahib killed the tiger.

The tiger turned out to be a young male about 9 ft 4 in long; it was never clear why it had come to Bakloh, where no tigers were usually seen. Still, Masters had shot it, and had lost neither dignity nor face in doing so. His contemporary, George Orwell, had been presented with a similar situation in Burma when called upon to shoot a rogue elephant and had loathed every moment of it. For Orwell it only reinforced his feeling of the gulf between East and West, whereas for Masters it had the opposite effect and strengthened his bond with the Gurkhas. He wrote an article about it that was published in *The Field* in England.

Thoughts of his first full home leave – due at the end of September 1938, four years after he first arrived in India – now occupied his attention. At Bakloh he had time to plan it. He had chosen, characteristically perhaps, to go back to England the wrong way, i.e. via Japan and America rather than the normal route through Suez and the Mediterranean. America had held a fascination for him since his youthful friendship with the Odlums. He liked jazz – he often played his records of the sensual trumpeting of Bix Beiderbecke in the mess – and he longed to go to New Orleans, where jazz originated. He was drawn to American literature, the powerful realism of Steinbeck and Faulkner being favourites, and at Bakloh he had kept in touch with things American by subscribing to *The New Yorker* magazine, where he could savour, in anticipation, the latest shows and nightclubs in New York listed there. Another reason for going was to visit the American Civil War battlefields, part of his special topic for his promotion exam. America held a magnetic appeal for him; it represented glamour, novelty and adventure.

He had it all planned, and by late September 1938 was on his way to Bombay, where he was due to board ship. He was aware of the deteriorating international situation in Europe and he bought newspapers at every station en route to get the latest news. Chamberlain had been to see Hitler at Berchtesgaden on 15 September, but Hitler left him in no doubt that he was going to annex Sudetenland. By 27 September, the situation was worse. In England, the Royal Navy had been mobilised and trenches were dug in Hyde Park. Chamberlain went back to Germany. By the time Masters got to Bombay, a military policeman was posted by the gangplank of his ship at Ballard Pier, with a list in his hand. Even before Masters reached him, he heard his name called out on the loud hailer telling him to report to the station-master's office. A message was waiting for him: 'Leave cancelled. Return at once to your unit.'

He duly returned to Bakloh. A week later, Chamberlain returned from Munich with his 'Peace in our time' promise, and leave was reopened. Masters was on his way again, this time via Jullundur, where he stopped off to celebrate his twenty-fourth birthday with the 1st Battalion of his regiment stationed there on their cold-weather training. It was an all-night thrash, which he could sleep off in the silence of his coupé on the Bombay train next morning.

He had a few hours to spend in Bombay before the ship sailed and he looked up his old friend, Reggie Sawhny. Sawhny, the same age as he, ran a successful motor car company, and had once sold Masters a bull-nosed Morris. Sawhny was an Anglo-Indian; his English mother had come out as ward to the governor of Punjab and had met his Cambridge-educated Indian father when he romantically rescued her from a fire. They talked about the political situation in India and abroad. Politics had not entered Masters's life much in India. In common with the military generally in the between-war years, he had been more or less insulated from political goings-on in India. The Indian Army always steered clear of politics, rationalising its position by claiming that it was the servant of the state. It was a self-protective policy as well, since Indian politics at the time probably meant sedition. The 1935 Act had seen the first signs of democracy in India, with a federal structure introduced and Congress government taking over in eight out of eleven of India's provinces. Nationalism, under Gandhi's influence, was strengthening all the time. Officers tried to make sure that the men in the ranks were kept away from what was felt to be the corrupting taint of politics. It was a case of 'see no politics, hear no politics, think no politics'. They behaved as though loyalty to anyone but the King Emperor simply could not arise, and political discussion was pushed aside.

Part of the problem was that there were still relatively few Indian officers in the Indian Army; only ten Indian officer cadets were sent each year to Sandhurst, and even then an Indian officer in the Indian Army might never, or rarely, be invited to his commanding officer's house. Paradoxically, less discrimination was felt towards the men. This was where the British Indian Army officer often felt happiest and drew much of his self-esteem from, confident of his relationship with the Indians and the way he handled 'his' men. He felt a deep affection for the Indian soldier – and peasant – more so than for the townsman or politician. Indeed, many a British officer felt he knew the true India better than many of the Indians who spoke for her. It was an idealised master-servant relationship. Hence the wish – conspiracy even – to keep politics, with its horizon of unrest, out of it. Native soldiers were undoubtedly aware of political change taking place, but were told to put the interests of the regiment first. As Philip Mason wrote in *A Matter of Honour*, his account of the Indian Army:

> To read any political account of India between the wars is to picture a scene of constant turmoil and agitation, one campaign of civil disobedience succeeding another, national leaders in and out of gaol . . . After this, to read the regimental histories of the same period is to blink in astonishment. The infantry regiments record the prowess of their regimental hockey teams, the cavalry their successes at polo. The regiment puts on a beautifully rehearsed musical ride at the Delhi Horse Show or sends a contigent to London for the Coronation. There is some fighting in Waziristan and some battalions have the unpleasant experience of being posted to Bengal. But there is only the most occasional mention of political events and hardly a hint that there might be a strain on the loyalties of sepoy or sowar.

Masters himself was no different in this respect and went along with the majority view, but he drew the line always at racial intolerance.

Reggie straddled both worlds, the Indian and the English, and Masters could, in part, identify with that; he could talk frankly with Reggie when they met. Reggie was quite willing to give the British credit where credit was due, and his view was that the quickest and best way of getting independence was for Indians to prove that they would be capable of handling it when it came. The spread of Congress government had shown signs of this already. But Masters, like so many of the British, was mistrustful of Congress, and felt a hostility stemming from Congress's long history of challenging British rule in India, decrying its past and privileges. Masters took the view that Britain had forged modern India out of a collection of warring states and brought unity and cohesion and, those essential British factors, discipline and self-denial. This was its historic mission, but Masters was pragmatic enough to realise that a transfer of power from Britain to India must one day take place. Masters was, at heart, a romantic imperialist, keen to preserve much of the British presence in India – the sense of justice and fair play, and order that the British had brought. He saw the future as a passing-on of the imperial baton to the best the other side could produce. Reggie and others like him represented this. The Congress Party, he felt, was too iconoclastic. As he later wrote, 'they seemed set on proving only that they could never be trusted with anything more delicately adjusted than a crowbar.'

7

USA

1938–1939

Reggie drove Masters down to his ship in his red Bugatti. The good ship SS *Canton* lay on the tide, bound for Hong Kong out from London. Masters went straight to the purser's office and asked to be put on an 'interesting' table. The purser duly obliged and the next morning at breakfast he found himself sitting next to an English girl travelling alone to Hong Kong. She was Norah Collins, still unattached, and this was her first time abroad. Aged thirty-two, she was going to stay with relatives in Hong Kong. They soon became inseparable companions, and she found him 'most attractive, a very good dancer, fun-loving, the best companion you could find.' Indeed, she was swept off her feet by his charm and vivacity. Masters later described the trip in evocative terms: 'nothing was missing for a tropic voyage – a soughing wind, phosphorescent seas, flying fish, good food, good wine, a stout ship, and a slim girl, with whom I promptly fell in love.' But, in the manner of shipboard romances, when the ship got to Hong Kong she never expected to hear from him again. She told herself he was simply out for a good time; besides, she was eight years older than he.

He kept an album as a record and souvenir of all the stages of his trip. The Canton pages show groups of passengers in white Bermuda shorts playing deck quoits or leaning against the deck rail, a high-spirited fun-loving group. He said goodbye to Norah in Hong Kong and then boarded the *Empress of Japan* bound for Shanghai, Japan, and eventually Honolulu. The Japanese, no longer well-disposed to Westerners – they had withdrawn from the League of Nations on 2 October – insisted that every passenger provide not just a urine sample but a stool sample as well; embarrassed passengers bumped into each other as they hurried along to the doctor's cabin with their little cardboard boxes. At Kobe where the ship docked, customs officers insisted on stamping each of Masters's cigarettes individually in its case. The revenge against Europeans for their arrogance in nineteenth-century Japan had started and was a contributory factor to the forthcoming war. Despite this, Masters paid a quick visit to Tokyo, and rejoined the ship at Yokohama. The long journey across the

Pacific meant new fellow passengers. He got to know a tall, dark-haired, leggy American girl, Barbara Dunn, and joined up in a male foursome with Herman Geschwind, Tubby Edwards and Denys Slater. Pictures of all of them feature prominently in the album. Herman Geschwind's business was importing human hair from China which he made into hairnets in New York.

Masters was in an exuberant mood on board the ship. He talked to old China hands and to Mormon missionaries returning to Utah, but Barbara soon took most of his attention. When they got to Honolulu, he invited her and Herman and another girl from the ship to explore the island. They picnicked by the surf beach, and danced to jazz music and played Paul Robeson records from the old wind-up gramophone that Masters had originally brought out from England in 1934. American girls, he claimed in *Bugles and a Tiger*, were a novelty to him: 'simultaneously as wild as coots and as virginal as – as wholesome American girls.' I wonder.

Honolulu appealed to him and he decided to stay longer, eight days in all; Herman stayed with him. 'Honolulu is a hell of a place', he wrote back to Alex at Razmak. 'I never got to sleep really.' He bought an Aloha shirt and took time off to visit Schofield Barracks, the US Army base on the island. Finally, he and Herman left on 2 December on SS *Lurline* for Los Angeles. To save money he travelled tourist class, sharing a cabin with three others. Dancing at night took place in the first-class section. He expected to be allowed in, as would be the case on an equivalent British ship, since he was an Indian Army officer. To his shock, he was refused admission. The ship's American officers explained that here what you paid was the deciding factor. If you were travelling second-class, then second-class you stayed – there was no special 'privilege' of a class system. It was an eye-opener to him, and a lesson well learnt. He went down to the tourist class and, not to be outdone, proceeded to teach his fellow passengers the Lambeth Walk, then newly in vogue. This failed to please some of the staider ones, notably two American ladies from Virginia, who were appalled at such 'vulgar' behaviour from a British officer. He could not win either way.

At Los Angeles, on the quayside he met his erstwhile friends from the *Empress of Japan*, Denys and Tubby, and Barbara. The four men all clubbed together and hired a U-Drive Ford V8 in Los Angeles. 'For four days we beat hell out of Los Angeles. We saw the MGM studios and Joan Crawford and Rudy Vallee at the Coconut Grove and Gene Krupa at the Palomar and Louis Prima at the Hollywood Jitterbug House.' Denys, Tubby and Herman then left for New York. Masters's original plan had been to cross the continent by train, but he now wanted to spend more time with Barbara. Herman had convinced him that the best way to see America was by car, so he bought his own vehicle, a 1932 Dodge. 'On Tuesday we drove down to Balboa and Laguna and back and we went dancing at night', he told Alex. 'Los Angeles is a wonderful city. You suddenly wake up in the hotel at night and hear those sirens you hear on the flicks screaming as fire or police cars rush by in the streets. They always seemed to be on the go. The first time one passed me I didn't know what to do. You've got to stop dead wherever you are until it's passed.' Driving round Los Angeles was terrifying. 'Traffic moves so fast that if you put your hand out to make a signal you're liable to have it taken off.' But he enjoyed it enormously. Los Angeles was his first taste of America, and its great boulevards and neon signs and lights 'soaring down Wilshire Boulevard trying to jump the traffic lights with the best of them' was exciting and memorable. He was sorry to say goodbye to Barbara, 'a superb girl', but the great, wide continent of America beckoned.

He had christened his car Ol' Man Mose, a suitable name, he thought, for this epic crossing of the continent. His first night was spent at Barstow, east of Los Angeles, where he stayed in an auto camp, an early version of a motel – one room with all conveniences and a garage next door. Next day he moved on through the Mojave Desert to Las Vegas, then Boulder (now Hoover) Dam, 'about 500 ft high with a four track road over the top, the narrow rocky canyon of the Colorado River suddenly ending in this sheer wall of concrete, about twice as high as St Paul's, with the big lake on the other side', and on through the 'superb scenery' of Arizona to New Mexico, his future home, and Texas. He was covering some 300 miles a day, on a budget of a mere $2 a day. 'I live on Hamburgers, a typical American food – both good and cheap, but the helpings are so colossal you have trouble finishing them.'

He hoped to get to New Orleans by Christmas. Texas lived up to his expectations – 'Yippee, Texas, here I come!' In a bar in El Paso, he witnessed a fight with a bar stool being flung through the window, just as in the movies. Wherever there was excitement he was seeking it out. At New Orleans he was going to meet the Westfeldt family. Their daughter Alice was expecting him: 'Jack's arrival in New Orleans was heralded well in advance by a letter from my aunt Lulie Westfeldt, who lived in New York and had lived several years in England. He turned up one afternoon and the maid repeating exactly what she had heard told my mother that 'Mr Mahsters' was at the door. Being a Southern family, this caused much hilarity.'

It was Christmas Eve and they were having a family 'do', a very

festive family occasion, singing round the piano and drinking bourbon.
Jack joined in and ended up the evening dancing and singing a Gurkha
jaunri. Alice remembers that, 'if we had qualms about dealing with a
stereotypical reserved Englishman, Jack's exuberance and convivial
friendliness soon disposed of them. The exoticness – an Englishman
who looked unmistakably English even in a Hawaiian shirt – was
a bonus.'

Their house was small and Alice was making her debut, 'so we had
less money than usual. It was too bad because Jack was short of funds
too and had to stay in some tourist camp on the outskirts of town. We
introduced him to friends and family and started him off with dates.
He was much taken with Ann Kilpatrick, a petite and lovely brunette.'
Masters lapped up the atmosphere of New Orleans. 'I remember his
willingness to talk about anything and everything, and his ability to
match my father dirty song for dirty song. Once after the Twelfth
Night Revellers Ball, we all went in full fig, my fiancé with us, down to
Albert Martin's Bon Ton Café on Magazine Street and we stayed there
from one in the morning to daylight, drinking Ramos Gin Fizzes. It
was Jack's special elan that kept us there.' A photograph of him in full
evening dress at the Twelfth Night Revellers Ball also appeared in the
New Orleans Times Picayune, who commissioned an article from him
on Dussehra, the Gurkha ritual festival, and paid him half a cent a
line, putting $8.95 in the kitty and boosting his spending power.

The Westfeldts part-owned a 35-foot schooner called the *Vagabond*,
with the Waters, Watters and Witherspoon families – the four Ws.
Masters went aboard protected against the chill of a grey January day
by his poshteen, a Frontier garment, nowadays known as an Afghan
coat, and they set sail. His memory of the occasion was of 'tearing high
spirits when the sun was setting on Lake Pontchartrain, the wind filled
the sails and the boat heeled far into the racing water. I danced a
Gurkha jaunri on the deck and nearly fell off.'

Masters took in a Sugar Bowl football game, Texas Christian Union
versus Carnegie Technical; it was his first exposure to what was to
become a passion for American football. He left New Orleans on 13
January. 'I loved New Orleans but it was getting a bit too expensive for
my very limited resources. The food there was wonderful.' In true
fraternal fashion he advised Alex about current hits and incipient girl
friends. '"That's a Plenty" is the popular tune now, but the best new
tunes out are "You must have been a wonderful baby" and "My
Reverie" – get them both by Bing Crosby. I took a very beautiful little
girl called Ann Kilpatrick out three or four times. We saw Buddy
Rogers and his band at the Roosevelt Hotel. Ann has a beautiful

Southern drawl and speaks in a low husky voice – too entrancing.' As a thank-you he sent the Westfeldts an annual subscription to *The Spectator* and *Punch* – a more than generous token of gratitude.

Masters moved north through the Civil War battlefields and the scenes of Stonewall Jackson's campaigns, and suddenly realised, 'I had suddenly fallen in love with America, the land, as tempestuously as with any woman', a crucial and formative experience for him. He ventured further north to New England, bitterly cold, twenty-eight degrees below zero (Fahrenheit), with no heater in the car. In Manchester, Vermont, he visited an American lady who had once stayed temporarily with his regiment at Jullundur, when stranded in India at Christmas, and had offered reciprocal hospitality to any visiting 4th Gurkha officer. It gave him a week of skiing, but time was running out. He moved on to Poughkeepsie, New York, to sell his car, before taking a train to New York to meet up with Herman Geschwind.

His souvenir album is full of treasured mementos from a crowded week's stay: a matchbox cover from Jack Dempsey's Bar, an ink sketch made of him by a waiter at 3.30 a.m. at the Onyx Club on 52nd Street, a menu signed by Joe Venuti with a drawing of his violin at the Belmont Plaza, and photographs of Radio City, the Empire State Building and Times Square. New York's fast and furious pace matched his mood. He barely slept a wink the whole time he was there.

The album was put together once he was back in India. It bears the legend 'At the Sign of the Raised Eyebrow' with a jazz cornet player standing on one side, and the shapely legs of a young woman, with the message 'Do Not Disturb', on the other. His USA adventure was encapsulated for him in that and was something more too. It had come at exactly the right time. He was twenty-four, outgoing, manly, sexual and keen to make his own mark. The choice of the 'wrong way' home through America was no surprise; it was asserting his difference, his rejection of the rather inert conventions that characterised much of British India. America had shown him a new world, a multifaceted and stimulating one, where each individual could make his way. It was fast, slick and glamorous. The Wellington schoolboy who had played his 78s louder than anyone else felt at home there. He treasured his memories of America and stored them away for future use.

In England, in February 1939, the mood of the country was apprehensive at the prospect of war. It contrasted sharply with the buoyant atmosphere in the USA, still fresh from Roosevelt's New Deal. He went down to Uplyme, where his parents remarked on the American accent he retained. He met up with Lois and they went off for a weekend together in Paris, in those days a surreptitious event. Attractive as she was, Lois was proving to have too volatile a temperament for Masters. Their stay in Paris seemed to confirm this, and Masters did not feel he could offer her the necessary stability. He did not want to settle down yet, especially after the excitements of his recent trip. After they got back to England, their relationship cooled; before leaving England, Masters found himself writing to Norah Collins in Hong Kong asking her to meet him when he got back to India.

8

INDIA AND QUETTA
1940–1942

Masters's home leave coincided, intentionally, with the publication of his father's book, called *The Compleat Indian Angler*, published by Country Life Books in 1938. His father had always been an excellent draughtsman and a keen fisherman – putting these two talents together, he produced this, his only book, with many fine drawings of Indian fish, mahseer and barbus particularly. The text, as the title indicates, is a take-off of Izaak Walton's masterpiece. Walton has travelled in a time machine ('one of James Jeans's coaches') to the modern age and joins the author on an angling expedition in Kashmir and the Himalayas. It is an entertaining book, with its deliberate archaicisms, though at times these become almost too fashioned and self-conscious, the product of the author's quirky humour.

His home leave over, Masters took a ship back to India from Marseilles, the SS *Corfu*. Shipboard romance was in the air again. A young lady doctor was also heading out for India. Wasting no time, he took her to Bandol, for the two hours before the ship sailed, to a waterfront bar, where a pianist was playing Fats Waller tunes, and their relationship continued on board. He enjoyed these sea journeys out to India. Unattached bachelors such as he always had a good time, and his American trip encouraged him to make the most of things.

By June 1939, he was back in India, not to Bakloh where his tour of duty had finished, but to rejoin his regiment, now stationed at Loralai in Baluchistan. Baluchistan, the southernmost part of the North-West Frontier region, is wider, more open country than further north, a predominantly arid and desert landscape of mountains and plains, thinly populated. The Baluchis have always been fiercely independent and gave the British a tough fight when they first met in 1841. Mostly nomadic, they preferred living in tents or small mud huts on the plains. The British built towns – a major cantonment at Quetta and garrison forts at Fort Sandeman, Loralai and Chaman – linked by a network of roads. These roads, arteries of the Empire, were partly designed to bring a more settled way of life to local tribesmen. Loralai was more of an outpost than a frontier station. It was 120 miles east of Quetta, with a small fort and cantonment, pleasantly tree-lined and green from the deep-linked wells.

Having left a Europe on the verge of war, it all now seemed so distant to Masters, even though his battalion was put on a war footing. Mobilisation regulations had been ordered and pored over, and exercises drawn up to ready men for the future contingencies of war. Masters was now adjutant, the colonel's personal staff officer, a key position in the battalion, responsible in peacetime for making sure that all matters concerning dress, drill, discipline, military law and ceremonial were properly adhered to and in wartime for carrying out his battle plans. Adjutants thought they ran the battalion and a wise commanding officer would let them feel they did. It was a valued, not to say prized, appointment and was usually held for four years.

Masters was gaining promotion quickly and here was a chance to demonstrate his meticulousness and attention to detail. The adjutant had to run a tight ship, and Masters was no exception. Proverbially his watch had to be right to within one second and when he strode on to the parade ground, his privileged sword flapping long and loose by his side, he exhibited a self-assurance that meant he was never expected to look down, round or about, and never trip nor stumble, yet keep an eagle eye out for what was going on. Masters fitted the bill almost exactly, though he did not always enjoy riding across the parade ground to give the parade state to the colonel. He never was a confident horseman.

Small outposts like Loralai had their annual Week when festivities took place. Masters was made master of ceremonies for this one by the new Colonel, Billy Barstow, who had taken over from Murray-Lyon. Masters was the obvious candidate for this: extrovert, convivial and fun-loving, and a good organiser. Remembering his recent Pacific sojourn, he designated the Fancy Dress Ball 'Tahiti Today'. Gurkha troops were set to work making garlands, or leis, from coloured paper, to be draped around the neck, and grass skirts in similar fashion. Loralai was small, so 'spare' girls had to be imported from Quetta. Paddy Massey of Hodson's Horse, also stationed there, was detailed to go across to find them.

The ball started at 9.30 p.m. with a cocktail made by Masters and called the Bakloh Bombshell (six parts of champagne to six of champagne cider to two of brandy, the whole iced). His newly-acquired American records of Red Nichols, Jack Teagarden, Joe Venuti and Bix Beiderbecke made up the music, with an impromptu group of officers called the Tahitian Beachcombers. Guests entered into the spirit of things: Paddy Massey rode his bicycle round the floor because they would not let him bring in his horse; the 'Sailor' cut off most of the girls' grass skirts, leaving them in panties or wearing curtains borrowed from the tall windows; Ted Royds was hanging upside down by his knees from a tree on the lawn, a position he regularly used in times of stress. Such jolly japes were typical of celebrations at any Indian outstation of the day, as much as their subalterns' games of climbing around the four walls of the mess without touching the ground or vigorous games such as high-cockalorum.

One of the Quetta girls was Valentine Roberts, whose father was stationed there as a brigadier. She remembered the evening well, and above all Masters's

> tremendous zest for living. It was largely due to him that the Loralai week became magic. My most vivid memory was after the evening's entertainment, when we young ones would crowd onto the mess lawn, squeezing ourselves into armchairs and sofas, Jack would teach us songs he had learned in the USA on his recent visit, like 'Casey Jones', 'Dinah', and 'Blow Your Horn'. He would sing the verse, we would join in the chorus. After the American songs we would always end with 'I dreamt that I dwelt in marble halls', and it became our theme song. Even now when I hear it, it brings back everything so vividly, the warm Indian night, all of us clustered together, Jack in the centre of the circle leading his choir. I'm sure I wasn't the only girl who was a little in love with him – he was attractive, he was fun and above all he genuinely seemed to LIKE women and enjoy their company whether sex came into it or not.

The uneasy summer drew to an end on 3 September when war was declared. India was brought into the conflict by the Viceroy, Lord Linlithgow, without consulting Congress, on the basis that since India was not yet a dominion, when Britain was at war, India was at war. It was seen by many Indians as treating India as a mere dependency, and Congress retaliated by resigning its government in eight provinces, though the Punjab, where most soldiers came from, remained loyal. Civil unrest in India was to be a backcloth to the war. Here it was still the phoney war, though, and life in India went on much as usual.

Norah Collins wrote to Masters from Hong Kong saying she was heading back to England to be with her family. They arranged a week together in Delhi, staying at the Hotel Marina and visiting the sights, including the Taj Mahal in Agra. Their relationship grew stronger and her level-headedness and reliable nature offered a different sort of relationship to the more effervescent ones he found on his travels. After she left, they corresponded regularly. He became the man in her life.

Christmas came and Masters's regiment still awaited news of their destination. They were moved to Quetta, in readiness, so they thought, for transfer to a war zone. There was an unspoken rivalry between the Gurkha regiments to see who would be the first to see active service, but the 4th Gurkhas may have been kept back in case of civil disturbances in India. Congress's support for the war was still less than wholehearted. Masters's battalion, having brought itself to a crest of technical efficiency and spiritual unity, was keen to get into action. The men were fast, flexible and fit. 'Nothing ever had to be said twice and no word could be recalled.' It was a moment of fusion between officers and men, the sort of empathetic bonding that regiments aspire to and which particularly pleased Masters, with his sense of order.

At Quetta, Masters's battalion came under the command of Lt-Col Willie Weallens. They had met on the frontier in 1937 and had not got on. 'Weallens kept persecuting me, as he thought I was a shit and he kept needling me in order that I might cease to be a shit. He disapproved of nearly everything about me, my dress, attitude, lack of manners, addiction to jazz.' Masters, for his part, had shown him a 'poorly concealed insubordination'. Now they had to get on with each other. Weallens was of the old school, an Edwardian at heart, with his look of 'insulted bloodhound'. Just before war was declared, he had been languishing unhappily in a desk job in Delhi, with little prospect of command again. His new appointment had thrown Masters and him together again, but they found that, beneath the surface, they shared more in common than they had previously realised. Both were deeply committed to the Gurkhas, sharing regimental pride. Scratching the surface a bit more, Masters could see the sensitive side of Weallens, the inferiority complex he still felt at never having attended Sandhurst. Masters had always been something of an outsider himself, but had counteracted this by his determination, his hard work and his boisterous behaviour. On parade Weallens was formality itself, 'his face cold and set', but at home his geniality shone through ('when I fumbled for a cigarette, he was halfway across the room with a match').

Rumours circulated that the battalion was to be sent to the Western Desert, since their training was for desert warfare. The war in Europe was now at its height, with the Battle of Britain and the Blitz at its strongest, yet out here they were still waiting to be drawn in. It was a strange life. The social life in Quetta went on in much the same way as before the war, with dances at the club, women wearing long dresses and men in dinner jackets, and picnics by Hanna Lake. A brief scandal flared up when someone found a camera there with a loaded film, developed it to trace its owner, and found only photographs of naked bodies in amatory poses by the lake shore. However, in a haunting passage in his autobiography, Masters shows how the menace of war was never far away: '. . . and it was all a game except when suddenly it wasn't, when the satin skin moved differently under your hand and the low voices, your own among them, tried to ward off with jokes the unexpected assault of love, unexpected and unwanted because earlier that day you had already been caught in the same way, when the clacking roar of machine-gun bullets dipped suddenly close on the field firing range, and war showed its face, violent and demanding behind the play of the manoeuvres.'

War and love were awkward bedfellows, as Tolstoy discovered. But the passage hints too at Masters's wariness of love, of its unexpected assault. Better by far to ward off its sudden inrush, the unbearable promise that all would be all right now and not to worry heard distantly by the child with parents in a far-off country. Marriage and the permanence of relationships had not yet seriously entered his considerations. He was still playing the field. His many affairs with women were not meant to be serious. He intended to go on living on that basis. Moreover, in the Indian Army you were expected to remain a bachelor until thirty; only then were you entitled to a marriage allowance and a separate bungalow. Up to that point you were expected to remain 'married to the Regiment'.

For much of 1940 they were 'like firemen trying to find our shoes and socks while the alarm jangled even louder and more hysterically in our ears.' It was a frustrating wait on the periphery. They awaited orders from Indian Army headquarters at Delhi.

Letters arrived from home recounting the experience of war there. His father was in charge of the Uplyme Home Guard, stalking the Dorset hills in a tin hat and rifle watching for signs of invasion. Masters learnt that his cousin Marjorie had been killed in the Café de Paris in London by a bomb which had fallen straight down the chimney and exploded in the basement night club, killing many people, including the bandleader 'Snake-Hips' Johnson. Marjorie was the daughter of his mother's favourite sister, Cis, and the cousins had grown up together.

In April the regiment finally got their marching orders – to Iraq. A military coup in this country, Britain's most pampered ally, had installed a government headed by General Rashid Ali. Iraq had been a British mandate since the First World War, and had close treaty rights with Britain. Rashid Ali's new regime was pro-Hitler and as such menaced the route to India and the Persian Gulf oil installations at Abadan. Treaty rights were invoked to justify a British-led invasion to reinstate the ousted government, despite the risk of alienating Arab sympathy elsewhere. The route to India and the protection of the oilfields over-rode such considerations. The 8th Indian Division was despatched, with the 2nd Battalion 4th Gurkhas among them. They left Bombay in the troopship *Devonshire* for the port of Basra and went into action immediately, fighting to clear away opposition in the town so that other troops could land behind them. They then moved up country and established their base near Baghdad at Habbaniyah, an air base that had fallen into Rashid Ali's hands. After an initial skirmish, it was recaptured along with Mosul in the north, where German fighters and bombers had been stationed. Then they headed off west to Syria, now hostile under a Vichy French Government command. The French forces there were eventually compelled to surrender.

Two moments stood out for Masters in these campaigns. One was when Bill Slim arrived as their new divisional commander and spoke to them assembled in an aircraft hangar, impressing Masters with his calibre as a commander when he spoke of the dominant feeling in a battlefield being loneliness, hence the need for morale as the foundation for victory. These were lessons Masters took to heart.

The second was a characteristic episode with his Gurkhas that he later described in *Road Past Mandalay*.

> There, standing in an open field, I saw two riflemen of B Company. They had been moving their Bren gun, on its anti-aircraft mount, from one site to another when the attack came in. The Moranes [French fighter planes] were not firing at us now, but at them. Unhurriedly the two Gurkhas set up the tripod. One took the gun, the other stood ready with the reserve magazines. The fighters screamed down on them – CRRRRRUMP. The Bren began to fire back. I began to cry with pride. The earth boiled round and behind the two men, both nineteen years old, and they stood there, completely in the open, upright, and always sending that thin stream of fire back at the multi-gun monsters. This was what we were fighting with, and, by God, this was what we were fighting for, too – survival, and self-respect, a refusal to be terrified by sheer force. The attacks continued for five minutes, and the last plane climbed away very slowly, black smoke pouring from its engine nacelle. Riflemen Deba and Ghanbahadur picked up the gun and tripod and marched on to their new position.

It is Masters writing at his best: precise, visual, dramatic, using the 'lightning flash' technique so beloved of Kipling. It displays his admiration for the Gurkhas, their peculiar obstinacy and devotion to duty. He is caught up by their sense of purpose, taken by surprise ('by God') as the sudden realisation of their almost foolhardy valour dawns on him.

Eventually his battalion was ordered across to the Western Desert, but without him. He had been recommended for the Staff College course at Quetta by Weallens, testimony to his promise as an up-and-coming officer. Such a promotion needed the personal recommendation of his senior officer. Despite the kudos of being selected, he was sad to say goodbye to his battalion, envious of them too, now that they were heading for real fighting in Africa. His battalion had been his home for six years and he had got to know and value every man under his command. He felt he had a part in moulding their esprit de corps. Weallens, too, he would miss. He was surprised at how emotional his parting from him was. 'I shall be sorry to lose you,' Weallens told him, echoing the words of his Wellington headmaster. They had worked well together and Weallens had come to admire and rely upon his efficiency and enthusiasm. Not having any children himself, he may have looked upon Masters as a son, a feeling probably reciprocated by Masters, whose search for a father figure to emulate underpinned much of his ambition.

These brisk campaigns in 1941 had served their purpose and taught Masters valuable lessons. He had developed a greater all-round competence, monitoring himself with self-criticism when necessary. The Staff College was a definite move up the ladder; a pass there and he would end up a field officer, altogether a more senior post, the equivalent in civilian terms of becoming a responsible adult. He was twenty-seven years old, and as Quetta beckoned for a second time, his life looked full of promise.

He took ten days' leave in Persia, in Teheran, and then at a resort called Babulsar near the Caspian Sea. It was in Russian hands and the consulate in Teheran had issued him with a laissez-passer and told him to be careful. As the only guest in his hotel the hotel owner invited him to dine with him before going up to his room. He noticed the pretty chambermaid was hanging around, dusting a picture, though it was late. Remembering the consul's warning, he stood a long way off from her and said in a neutral voice in French, 'I would like to be called at six, please. That is all.' His account continues: 'She nodded pleasantly, lay down on the bed, and hauled up her skirt.' It is a typical Masters's vignette and probably happened like he said, though the added touch of faux-naïveté lends a not uncharacteristic exaggeration to the proceedings.

Masters arrived in Quetta in February 1942, coming up by train through the Bolan Pass to the plateau on which Quetta stands, some 5,500 feet above sea level. Snow lay on the surrounding mountains and it was bitterly cold, yet his mood was one of exhilaration; he was excited at the prospect ahead.

The Staff College, a Neo-Gothic building, had been founded in 1905 by Kitchener as the 'Camberley of the East' shortly after the 1902 reorganisation of the Indian Army had revealed a dearth of properly trained staff officers. Wavell, Auchinleck, Montgomery had all been there. Quetta was the biggest cantonment in the Indian sub-continent with a population of thirty thousand, and was the Headquarters of Western Army Command. By 1942 it was still recovering from the 1935 earthquake, which had devastated the town in the middle of the night of 31 May, killing twenty thousand people in thirty seconds, most still in their beds. No warning had been given, only the persistent barking of dogs in the hours beforehand. The cantonment itself, to the north of the native town, was hardly damaged, being built on higher ground and on a rock and gravel base, whereas the town stood on alluvial soil. Indeed, many at the Staff College four miles to the north of the town slept through the night unaware of the disaster nearby.

Masters was given rooms in the bachelor quarters inside the Staff College. There were about ninety students on the course, with an average age of just over thirty. Some he knew already, like Paddy Massey from Loralai, Philip Mortimer, Beetle Lewis of the 4th Gurkhas, and Mohamed Usman of the Baluchi Regiment, but he was to make special friends with Goff Hamilton of the Guides, already the proud possessor of a DSO, gained, aged twenty, when as a second lieutenant he had momentarily commanded his battalion when all other officers had been killed in a frontier engagement. Also in Quetta at that time was Goff's wife-to-be, Mollie Kaye, the future novelist.

The Staff College course had been cut from its peacetime two years to five and a half months but with very little reduction in the syllabus. It would mean hard work. The essence of the course was to equip its students to be staff officers. A staff officer must have two loyalties: first to his commander, helping him to exercise command by pointing out how any task can be done better or less expensively, in terms of money, lives or time; and then to the troops below him. The instructors were all of the rank of lieutenant-colonel and known as Directing Staff, or DS. Here again the marginal comment on students' essays assumed great importance: 'Careless' in red ink echoing the 'Idle' of Sandhurst days. Accuracy was emphasised more than speculation; the principles of each subject and theory were thoroughly ground in. They went over the former campaigns at Gallipoli and Suvla, learning from their mistakes as a means of devising future strategy. Some of those on the course had already fought in the present war and could throw a different, and more relevant, light on modern warfare than these First World War campaigns offered. They were divided into syndicates, of about eight students each, who worked together collectively. Masters was the outstanding member of his. A fellow syndicate member, Bulgy Leach, recalls how they regularly left the more difficult solution-finding and decision-making to him. They were kept on their toes. At times students would be woken up in the middle of the night and made to carry out an exercise. Overall, it was widening Masters's perspective, showing him the intricate and complex nature of a modern army, and, in the Indian context, its role as an instrument of civil power.

Masters was undoubtedly one of the brightest and quickest of the students. Five weeks into the course 'even the red ink on my work often expressed a grudging admiration.' Mollie Kaye recalls how 'Goff had to work hard throughout, whereas Jack seemed to get by with no work. He would go off on the toot, be back at 3 a.m. and put his head in a wet towel, and get to work. He could do it straight off the cuff, better than anyone else. He had a very quick brain, and knew how to cut through the woffle.'

She remembers asking him who he thought would come out top of the course. Masters proceeded to list the first ten. 'I shall be first', he announced unabashedly. Then he gave the name of the second, and those listening protested. Mollie Kaye said, 'You can't beat him possibly', because this other student was 'good-looking, one of those real bootlickers and smarmers. He used to stay behind after every lecture and go up to the lecturer and say, "I hope you don't mind me saying so, Sir, but there was a point that you made that really interests me, I wonder if you could just . . ." We all thought the DS had come to the conclusion that this chap was a very keen student. But Jack said, "He'll be second. Yes, he's fooled the whole staff but he won't last, just you wait. He'll get one of the plum jobs and fall down on it." And he did. I wouldn't have guessed it but Jack was shrewd enough to know that.' Students were 'graded' at the end by the importance of the posting they were then given.

Mollie Kaye found Masters very amusing and interesting to talk to. Once, he confided in her about his misgivings, his fears of being out of his depth socially with some of his upper class fellow students. He told her in confidence: 'I keep putting my foot in it. I don't know what the right thing to do or say is. All these others have been at Eton and so forth and it's easy for them.' She was surprised at this, but he really meant it. Despite his bravura, he was still conscious of his social inferiority, just as he had been at times at Sandhurst. That he cared shows that the chip on his shoulder was still there.

She and Goff and he shared a liking for classical music. At first glance he did not seem to her to be the type to be 'really bitten by it', but she noticed he obviously had an ear for it, 'which I suppose gave him the ear for writing.' Every Sunday night he used to give a musical evening in his rooms. Music would be provided on his old wind-up gramophone, still going strong since he first brought it out to India in 1934. One week it would be serious, Beethoven and wine: the next jazz and beer, with the sensual Bix Beiderbecke to the fore. Mollie Kaye and Goff were regular attenders. If Masters caught them, or anyone else, talking during a classical evening, he would make a loud shushing sound to keep them quiet, but he could not stand the atmosphere becoming over-reverential. Mollie Kaye recalls one particular evening when, with a room full of people taking the music a bit too piously, all sitting with cast-up eyes showing they knew what was coming next, Masters suddenly got very impatient and, pulling Goff alongside him, announced to the assembled company, 'We're now going to sing a madrigal.' This caused a lot of raised eyebrows, but the audience waited, expecting something Elizabethan. Instead Goff, Masters and Paddy Massey, who was roped in, sang 'They're digging up father's grave to build a sewer' in full Cockney verve. Mollie Kaye recalls, 'I can still see the faces. There was dead silence afterwards, then a few muttered words of annoyance as the guests rose and swept out. Jack used a sort of chopping or washing motion with his hands once they had gone and said, "Well, that's got rid of that lot. No more phoneys, thank you."' For Mollie Kaye it was one of the high spots in her stay in Quetta.

Field sports featured in the life at Quetta, the British once again imposing their own favourite pastimes regardless of surroundings – a pack of hounds that chased jackal, shooting in the hills after chukor and a racecourse – but these held little appeal for Masters. He liked walking and would often take himself off into the surrounding mountains; but for him the main attraction of Quetta was the rich and varied social life it offered. It certainly was not dull. 'It was electric. Something in the air produced pregnancy in the childless, nymphomania in the frigid, larceny in the respectable, and scandals of wonderful variety.' The crisp dry air seemed to sharpen people up and refresh their libidos. It was a bit like shipboard life, with the same air of impermanence from so many people passing through. For many it was the chance to relish an active social life after years at a tiny station or outpost. For a bachelor, it offered rich pickings. Women were plentiful:

nurses from the hospital run by the famous eye surgeon Sir Henry Holland, daughters of army families, grass widows and now, with wartime, wives of soldiers away fighting at the front. 'From all over India abandoned women were sent to Quetta for the duration. Good girls grew lonely, naughty girls grew naughtier.' Reputations were made and lost. There was the so-called Passionate Haystack, and her competitor, the Lilo, not to mention the redoubtable Vice Queen, 'who collected other ladies' husbands and cut a notch in her bedstead for every conquest. No one knew why the bed was still standing.' It was a milieu he thrived in.

The hub of social activity was the Quetta Club a quarter of a mile down the road from the Staff College. Masters made a point of attending the dance there every Wednesday and Saturday night. He would pedal down on his bike from the Staff College, pushing against the icy cold Khojak wind. He knew some of the girls there from his previous visit. Now there were newly-arrived WAACs (Women's Army Auxiliary Corps), who, the morning after, had to go through the rigmarole of saluting their cheek-to-cheek dancing partners of the night before if they passed them on the street. Being gregarious and fun-loving, Masters entered into the spirit of things, so much so that, unknown to him, a plot was being hatched behind his back to introduce him to someone whom it was felt sure he would get on with.

She was Barbara Rose. She had noticed him already at gatherings at the Quetta Club. Whenever a Paul Jones took place at a club dance, she kept willing the music to stop opposite him, but it never did. Now a mutual friend, Basil Knott, who had been at Loralai with him in 1939, was setting up a meeting. He had invited them both to a Saturday night birthday party at the Quetta Club. When Masters arrived, he walked into the sitting room and saw Basil's party at a table near the fireplace. Then, by his own account, 'One of the women in the party was looking at me with an expression of utter astonishment. She was about 5 feet 5 inches, a good figure, with wonderful green-brown eyes, classically set. She was wearing a flowered silk dress in a pattern of dark red roses on a dark green background. Her hair was a bit of a mess. She managed to control her surprise but by then we were looking straight at each other, and it had happened.' It was a *coup de foudre*. They fell for each other straightaway, and spent most of that evening together, sensing that it was the beginning of a long relationship. 'Things didn't go further than that in those days. That was all you needed,' Barbara recalls. 'I knew when I first met Jack that this was it, it was special.'

She knew there were other contenders, 'but they were probably keener on him than he on them. I knew they were a couple of rivals in Quetta at the time, sort of overlapping. He was a very happy butterfly, just out for dabbling with the other sex, very attractive, amusing, a good dancer. He wasn't quite making nesting noises yet, but was on the brink of it.' Their attraction was mutual. She found him a breath of fresh air, able to bring out the unorthodox in her, while he was immediately attracted to her sense of fun and adventure and her maturity – that counted with him.

He had noticed almost immediately that she wore a wedding ring, and enquired about this. Her husband was Hugh Rose, a captain in the 3rd Gurkhas, also stationed in Quetta. He had not been invited to the party as their marriage was not going well, indeed, it was virtually over. Most of their fellow partygoers knew this, and Barbara herself was quite adamant, 'I was sick of Hugh, everybody knew it.' When she and Masters parted that evening they agreed to meet again soon.

If something was to become of their relationship, it immediately raised complications for Masters. A brief fling was one thing, but getting involved on a long term basis was another. There was an unwritten rule in the Indian Army that you did not go off with a fellow officer's wife. If it led to divorce, you would have to resign your commission. Although Hugh Rose was not in the same regiment, he was a fellow Gurkha officer, which amounted to much the same thing.

As they spent more time together, their attraction to each other increased and yielded deeper layers. Barbara had never felt at home with the conventional side of Indian Army life. Her own upbringing had been in England. Her parents' marriage, seemingly respectable on the surface, was full of undercurrents; her father effectively led a double life, which her mother seemed to condone. Her father had kept up a second ménage, even after losing much of his money in the Clarence Hatry crash in 1926. Somehow he had contrived to keep up this high standard of living, including a yacht, which the rest of the family knew nothing about. It was a trap she was determined not to fall into. She had come out to India, hoping to get away from that sort of world, only to find herself, ironically, in almost the same set of circumstances she had left England to escape from. Now, with Hugh Rose, Barbara found the social pressures of cantonment life stifling, and full of humbug and false pretences.

Earlier, as an adolescent, she had shown a rebellious streak and had left home at the first opportunity. After going to a finishing school in Lausanne for a year, she insisted on staying on and then went to Germany in the early 1930s, an enjoyable interlude cut short by the rise of Hitler. Returning to England, she took a job at an art gallery in

Cork Street and it was through the gallery owner that she met Hugh Rose, a cousin of the owner. He was good-looking and personable; she fell for him and they were soon engaged. He was about to set off for India, an exciting prospect to her, and they married. But the world of protocol and precedence (with endless discussions about who sat on the colonel's right) held little appeal for her. Hugh Rose liked this and fitted in well, always keen to ascend the social and military ladder, but it made her feel at times that she was little more than an appendage to his military career.

With Masters, she sensed an immediate difference. He was unsnobbish, lively, humorous, adventurous, unconventional, ambitious certainly but in a different way. He was determined to get ahead by his own efforts, on merit, and, in doing so, was likely to take her with him and treat her as an equal. In going places, she would be part of the adventure, part of the enterprise. This joint viewing of the world was an immediate attraction and was to form the basis of their relationship. For Barbara there was excitement, too, in seeing this uncharted territory ahead, and Masters exuded for her a magnetism that she found irresistible; the physical and sexual attraction was there from the beginning.

Masters liked her spirited individuality. In his book *Far, Far the Mountain Peak*, his main character says 'his wife must have vision and will and courage equal to his – equal but independent.' It could very well have been a description of his relationship with Barbara from the start.

The fact that Barbara already had two children, aged four and two, by Hugh Rose, was a worry and a complication. Whatever else, Masters knew that their continued relationship was going to cause the family pain and disruption. But they were in love, it was war, it was Quetta, and with so much uncertain, why not enjoy themselves while they could? This live-for-today attitude was something they both shared, and there was an element of youthful defiance in it, of challenging the gods, as if deep down they both had a feeling that the complications would eventually sort themselves out. Others saw it less charitably and, despite the imperfections of Barbara's marriage, criticised Masters's actions as being those of a bounder, a cad, in so swiftly taking Barbara away from the unfortunate Rose.

Masters invited Barbara to his music evenings. When they ended at midnight, he would take her home on his bicycle, she sitting on the crossbar, her hair blowing in his face, just like his brother Alex had all those years before on the Wiltshire Downs. Seeing Barbara in an unfulfilled and unsatisfactory marriage brought out a restitutive side in Masters, an urge to put wrong to right. He had seen his own parents' marriage hit rocky times with his father's philandering, and his strong affection for his mother had pushed him to take her side. Injustice, wrong-doing, was something that often motivated him to speak up, as had happened before in the army, and often out of turn, but here there was a double incentive, for he wanted Barbara to be happy, and he wanted her to be his.

However, the situation with Barbara put him in a serious quandary. He had his army career to consider. Being involved in a divorce case and resigning his commission were extreme matters. By now he was fully committed to his army life, having pitched himself wholeheartedly into it. 'Soldiering was all to me. I had no other training, skill or aptitude, as far as I knew. Every day the horizon was broadening and greater vistas becoming apparent to my view.' To give all this up at this point would be an enormous sacrifice. He took himself off for a long walk on Chiltan Mountain high above Quetta to think it over.

Tugging away at his heart-strings was the awareness 'for the first time of a different kind of happiness, which I had never known before.' His other relationships with women had been mostly short-lived, or so arranged as not to lead anywhere. Part of him resisted becoming too caught-up or ensnared. This was something different. He and Barbara were drawn together intensely. 'We loved, and there's an end', he wrote of it later, and pithily, the romantic in him preferring to leave its mysteries unexamined. His dilemma was heightened by his performance on the Staff College course, where he was clearly doing well and was going to pass out at the very top. That then was one avenue ahead. The relationship with Barbara offered him a further, but not necessarily complementary route. Standing back momentarily, high on Chiltan looking down on Quetta below, he realised that the next two to three months were crucial.

At the Staff College ball to celebrate the end of the course, he and Barbara danced together and drank champagne 'under heavy shadows, for we were both frantic with love, and oppressed by the decisions we must make sooner or later.' At about one in the morning, a group of them walked up the Hanna Lake road. Barbara suddenly caught hold of his hand without warning and started to run up the dusty road in her high heels. They ran on together, leaving the others behind, until they were alone in the valley. It was a symbolic gesture indicative of their joint wish to be free and unencumbered.

The course ended in July 1942 and the day of their reports came round. Like other candidates, Masters was summoned to the office of the Commandant, Brigadier Geoff Evans. As he walked up to his desk he saw a square of white paper on the front of it and was told to read it –

a moment all the students dreaded. His report was full of praise. He made a mental note of it and later jotted down its salient features: 'military knowledge: very good. A cheerful officer with personality. He possesses very marked qualities of command, leadership and initiative, with an exceptionally quick, active and shrewd brain. Clear and incisive in everything he does. Unlikely to get flustered in an emergency.' This was heady stuff. Brigadier Evans told him that that would go on record, but, privately, he warned him to be more careful about his dress, and to curb his tendency to be so 'self-opinionated and above himself in appearance'; he might get away with it at the Staff College where contemporaries could answer back, even argue with him, but more senior officers elsewhere would not tolerate it. He took note of this and made a private memo to himself: 'I must work on this.'

He had indeed come out top on the course, as he had accurately forecast. Back in his rooms he put on his favourite record, Beethoven's *Eroica*, and stretched his legs and reflected on Evans's comments. Perhaps it was not as bad as it seemed. Within each of his 'faults' lay its opposite: his self-opinionatedness concealed determination, his drive hid sensitivity – perhaps even possessiveness shielded love.

His posting came through, as brigade major of the 114th Indian Infantry Brigade. This was part of the 7th Indian Division, then training in northern India. It meant parting from Barbara, a difficult and a painful moment for them both as they had reached an intimacy and reliance on each other that was hard to break. She came to see him off at the railway station. As the train left and he lay on his bunk during the long journey north, his thoughts kept returning to Barbara. Deep down his mind was already made up. She would have to stay in Quetta, for the time being, with her children to look after and the complications of her marriage still unresolved. As he saw it, their relationship was fully launched, however unclear their joint future was, with him returning to active service and almost certainly going to a war zone.

Family news came through about Alex, who had gone missing in one of the first battles of the Malaya campaign and was now a prisoner of war. Another bad bit of family news followed. His Aunt Cis, his mother's favourite sister, had died in Rawalpindi of a broken heart just over a year after her daughter Marjorie had been killed in the Café de Paris. To compound matters, he now heard his own Gurkha battalion under Weallens had been overwhelmed by German Panzers in the Western Desert, and Weallens himself had been taken prisoner. War was bringing its customary harvest of bad news, and it contributed to his need to keep his plans short-term.

114 Brigade was stationed at Bakarial, near Abbottabad, north of
Rawalpindi, near the foothills of the Karakoram Mountains. It felt good
to be up in the mountains again. The camp was in pine forests, dotted
about with hundreds of brown-dyed tents. His commanding officer was
Brigadier Michael Roberts of the 10th Gurkha Rifles, aged forty-eight.
They had met before in Quetta when Masters had taken his daughter
Val out to a dance. Roberts was an ideal commander for him, with a
quick and decisive mind. For a first-time brigade major, this helped
enormously, and Masters set about his duties looking after all general
staff matters at brigade headquarters with alacrity.

He was given a Gurkha orderly, Rifleman Daljit Thapa, from the
4th Battalion 5th Gurkhas. Smart and alert, like so many of his kind,
the sight of his Mongolian face made Masters want to embrace him. 'I
had been too long away from him and his peerless like', was his
comment. Daljit was to stay with him for quite some time, and later
achieved a fictional reincarnation as Jagbir in *The Lotus and the Wind*.

Keen to show his mettle to Roberts, Masters's chance came not long
afterwards. One evening Roberts had mentioned a plan for a training
exercise, saying he would draw up a draft the next day which Masters
could then 'whip into shape'. Instead, Masters stayed up all night,
preparing it along the lines Roberts had indicated. He kept his staff
clerk on standby for midnight and, helped by the staff captain, had the
whole thing ready by 2 a.m. and placed on Roberts's table first thing in
the morning with a pencilled note 'For Approval'. It was a typical
Masters's tour de force and one that his senior officer could not fail to
be impressed by. The quasi-filial relationship with his commanding
officer was once again being established.

His zeal sometimes outran Masters and didn't always make him
popular. He drove his staff hard in what he called 'bouts of military
ferocity', and arranged for long and arduous exercises to make them
the equal of any other battalion. Roberts oversaw all this, pointing out
mistakes as they occurred and praising when praise was due. Val
Roberts recalls:

> My father grew to have a great regard for Jack as an officer and liked
> him immensely as a man. My parents were always delighted to
> welcome him, somewhat to my surprise as I hadn't thought he was
> the conventional type of army officer of whom they would normally
> approve. We were all living in tents, in the pine forests near Bakarial,
> and life was somewhat primitive. My mother ran the mess catering,
> with my help, which was more in the line of moral support. I was in
> the throes of a doomed love affair. So when Jack arrived to join the

Brigade I was delighted. I noted in my diary that it was marvellous to see him again but that he seemed much quieter than he used to be. I didn't know it at the time, but he was having to face the separation from Barbara in Quetta. We had many pleasant evenings before the time came for the Brigade to move on.

He and Barbara kept in constant touch by letter, he, so she recalls, writing 'the longest letters to me each day.' She wanted to spare him anxieties about her own situation and rarely mentioned the strain she was under. She was facing monumental decisions, and it says much for her own strength of feeling and personal courage that she was prepared to risk so much. If she left Hugh Rose, she really was burning her boats. Masters might easily get killed in action and then she would be left high and dry with her children.

On a quick visit down to Rawalpindi, Masters ran into an officer they had both known in Quetta. He told him that Barbara was not at all well and was suffering from dysentery. Alarmed by this, Masters telegraphed her to come on a two-week walk with him in the mountains. She replied that she would. He asked Michael Roberts for leave, not revealing his true intentions, but telling him he was going trekking up the nearby Kaghan Valley, towards Nanga Parbat and the high Babusar Pass.

It was early October, three months since they had met, when he went down to Rawalpindi to meet Barbara. The town was seething with unrest following that autumn's disturbances throughout India after Gandhi's arrest with other leaders of the Quit India movement. Trains had been derailed, and he feared for Barbara's safety on her own lengthy trip from Quetta. When she arrived, she looked haggard and tired, but she assured him her dysentery had stopped the day she left Quetta.

They hired a car with a driver for the 120-mile drive north, along what is now the Karakoram Highway, but then was a dusty, pot-holed road – it is still not much better. They reached Balakot, the town at the head of the Kaghan Valley. From then on, they proceeded on foot, accompanied by porters with ponies carrying their food and bedding. Daljit, Masters's orderly, had come with him and oversaw the practical arrangements. He valued Daljit's presence. By now theirs had developed into a typical relationship, full of respectful wariness of each other and humour. They both shared a feeling that the other might be a bit foolish, a bit obsessed. Masters's characteristic greeting to Daljit, 'Don't you understand, O one pubic hair?', were words that serenely passed him by, though they inevitably brought a smile to his face.

He had chosen the Kaghan Valley both for its accessibility and its remoteness. Accessible for him as being within reach of Abbottabad, the nearest town to Bakarial, and remote enough for them to be free of other people. The Kaghan Valley, then and now, is famed for its tranquillity and beauty. Dervla Murphy on a trip there in 1964 commented, 'The Kaghan Valley is so beautiful that one has to stop every hundred yards to sit and look.' Ninety-six miles long and 3,000 feet above sea level, it lies between steeply-rising terraced slopes, where miniscule fields of rice are cultivated. Torrents flow down into the icy Kunhar river below that leads eventually to the Jhelum and Indus rivers. Like most enchanted spots it has its own legends; at Lake Saif-ul-Muluk the fairy Princess Badri Jamal lies buried in its depths, banished there by her father as punishment for marrying a mortal with whom she had fallen in love. Could this be an omen for them?

This was to be their first experience of being wholly alone together over a protracted period of time, a true testing ground for their relationship. These were surroundings that suited them both, so their compatibility could be put to the question. From his Bakloh days, Masters had always felt a sense of wonder at mountains ('There is nothing so remote, so calm with the calmness of original creation, as the side of a Himalayan mountain towards evening'), while for Barbara the details, the flowers and thriving animal life mattered. She readily pointed to the colonies of marmots announcing their presence with shrill cries and the rare Himalayan pheasants whenever they came across them.

Masters waxes lyrical in his autobiography about this episode, as well he might, for it was a turning point in his life. With this space and freedom, he describes how they were able to 'relearn the essential harmonies, to breathe easily, and step with a delicate rhythm, to rise with the sun and eat by the fire.' Primitive perhaps, and evocative of the sort of communion with nature that inspired Romantic poets, but what better setting than the foothills of the Himalayas for this? Each day was a sensual pleasure, the feel of the short, springy turf underfoot, the fragrance of the forests of oak, pine, fir and juniper, and on the harsher ground what he called 'the uncompromising work sound – stone on steel.' Mountain walking as he did it was a serious business, a test of stamina and endurance. He would plan the day's route ahead and make sure they kept rigorously to his schedule. Barbara would be required to fall in with this, but she was up to it; her own stamina and endurance were just as formidable.

They stayed the night at Forest Rest Houses, interspersed through the length of the valley and normally used by the district forest officer on his tours of inspection. The caretaker in the village below would see smoke rising from the chimney and come up to attend to them. At night, with curtains drawn, their cook would prepare a meal of rice and dal, and they would drink sweet cocoa laced with rum. Outside the wind roared across the roof of the world. It was an exhilarating experience feeling so secure in their own lost valley, their Shangri-la. A later traveller, V. S. Naipaul, visiting the same valley in the 1970s, felt similarly enchanted: 'The tent, the cooking fire, the mountains, the river, the tea and the roti: I felt momentarily I could surrender to the life.'

Occasionally they met other people, nomadic shepherds mostly: free-striding men and boys with reed pipes tending their flocks, and veiled women, whose 'dark eyes now smile at my companion, because she too is a woman, and they can see she is in love.' All the time they were sounding each other out, getting to know more about each other, peeling away the layers of discretion and concealment.

On the third night Barbara related to Masters the story of her journey from Quetta and its difficulties. Travel restrictions had been imposed in Quetta, and the Indus had been flooded, making it virtually impassable, but she was determined to go. Her sister, due to go to Bombay, accompanied her. A slow twelve-hour train journey took them down to the flooded plains, but the train then stopped. They managed to find a tonga, a horse-drawn, two-wheeled carriage where the passengers perch, uneasily, on the backwards-facing rear seat, which took them on a further six-hour journey through the relentless heat to the banks of the Indus. There they commandeered a dhow and crossed with sundry other passengers; on the other side a ramshackle bus took them to the station at Rohri, which connected with the mainline trains to Rawalpindi. It was a journey of epic endurance, showing not only her determination to join him at all costs, but also her readiness to make sacrifices on his behalf. He was deeply moved by it. It only confirmed to him what he was already beginning to suspect, that the basis of their relationship was well grounded, and any doubts he may have had at the start of this trip were now resolved. In retrospect he commented on these nine days with Barbara, a woman, Daljit, a Gurkha soldier, and the mountains, which he loved, as being decisive for him. 'My life, my love, my work were all here and the answers had taken shape out of that union.'

It was true, this conjunction of the three abiding interests of his life meant that his searching was now over; he would seek to consolidate and recapture this moment time and again. The development of his relationship with Barbara had taught him several lessons. It had helped modify his ambition. It was all well and good to aim to become General Sir John Masters, but not if the cost was to lose touch with what the Kaghan Valley had taught him, an appreciation of the here and now, 'the delight in each day, the lyrical enjoyment of each hour', and, above all, the value of personal relationships, embodied in his relationship with Barbara. 'The wonder of living lay not in the abstractions of command, as such, but in the direct personal relationship . . .'

The hidden agenda of this episode was the question of marriage, of converting their relationship into something permanent. Barbara had shown herself willing; it was clear from the enormous effort she had put into getting there. In his rhapsodic mood again, he wrote: 'she had walked beside me in the whistling wind, and rested with me among the wild flowers.' It had been a trial by ordeal for both of them and the love they felt for each other had only grown as a result.

On their penultimate evening, over dinner in the rest house, he asked her to marry him. She said yes. Ahead lay many problems, the separation of war, the complications of divorce, even the potentially damaging effect on his military career, but they knew now they could face it together. 'We can see it through' was their motto and guideline.

They returned down the valley as the snow clouds pressed in, passing on their way other nomadic shepherds bringing flocks down from the high summer pastures to the plains below; the upper reaches of the Kaghan Valley would now be closed off until April. It was time to return to civilisation and day-to-day concerns. Masters accompanied Barbara to Rawalpindi where she took a train back to Quetta to await developments, while he went back to Bakarial. There he confided in Michael Roberts. Momentarily taken aback by the question of divorce, Roberts then came to see how genuine his feelings were. He warmly commended to him the idea of a good marriage. It was 'worth ten times this', he told him, fingering the red brigadier's band on his hat.

Barbara spent a difficult month extricating herself from Quetta, and then came up with her children to Rawalpindi. She had taken the decision to leave her husband and all semblance of security. She got a job on the general staff at army headquarters as a WAAC. Over the next two months they only managed to meet up twice, for a day at a time, whenever Masters could make the 75-mile journey down from Abbottabad. Their clear understanding with each other – and what kept them going – was the plan to get married as soon as the opportunity arose.

Then in January 1943, news came through that 114 Brigade were to start jungle warfare training, and would then proceed to the Arakan to fight the Japanese. Barbara's heart sank; the casualty rate there was higher than anywhere. She knew deep down that getting a divorce from

Hugh Rose was going to be difficult. They had offered themselves as guilty parties, and adultery was then the only ground for divorce, but Hugh Rose was still extremely vexed at her running off and was not going to accede easily.

As 114 Brigade prepared to leave Bakarial, there was a final 'unforgettable' farewell party that Val Roberts attended, 'Jack as usual at the heart of everything.' Then the brigade moved to Chindwara in Central Provinces for their final training, which lasted from January until April 1943. As they were about to set off for the Arakan, Masters asked for some last minute leave and went down to see Barbara, with her children in Bombay, staying with her sister. They spent a few days together at Juhu Beach 15 miles north of the city in a beach-front hut. Barbara told him that the question of divorce had become more complicated, as Hugh Rose was asking for financial guarantees to cover the upbringing of the children as a pre-condition. He was also asking that Barbara should alter her will, leaving him the bulk of her inheritance. Only then would he agree to start proceedings. They talked it over endlessly, trying to find a solution. The weather at Juhu was sultry and overcast; a copper-coloured sky hung over the beach. Daljit, who was still with him, was restless, never having seen the sea before and complaining of its unpleasant taste. Violent tropical storms blew up and they decided to leave and go up to the hills again, back to the Kaghan Valley. Masters stopped off in Bombay and visited a lawyer to make his own will, leaving all his possessions exclusively to Barbara and opening a joint bank account in both their names. That at least would give her some security, if anything happened to him.

Two days later they were climbing the slopes above Balakot, Daljit still in tow. They kept to the high ground now, walking along the crest of the ridges, in this peaceful and spectacular valley. On the third night, Masters was hurriedly woken by Daljit. A telegram had come through from Balakot summoning him back to Chindwara. His brigade was clearly about to move to the front. Barbara accompanied him down to Rawalpindi and took the same train, before parting at Delhi. When he reached Chindwara he found his brigade had already gone, but a sealed envelope awaited him in Michael Roberts's handwriting. Inside were two pieces of paper, the first a short order from the military secretary at general headquarters in Delhi posting him as brigade major of the 111th Indian Infantry Brigade to report forthwith to Ghatera, Central Provinces – a sudden and unexpected transfer. The second was a personal note from Michael Roberts deeply distressed at this appointment splitting them up after all the training and co-operation together. Masters's transfer had been specially requested by

Joe Lentaigne of 4th Gurkhas. He was to be his brigade major for a mission still shrouded in secrecy. Mention of the phrase 'Long Range Penetration Group' was made, whatever that might mean. Masters was flattered at being chosen; it was a move up the ladder, but he felt bad at letting Michael Roberts down, and it meant more training. He looked up Ghatera in his well-thumbed copy of Bradshaw's *Indian Railway Guide* and found it, a six-hour train journey away.

CHINDITS
AND BURMA
1943–1945

When Masters got to Ghatera, Joe Lentaigne met him at the station. They had last met in 1937 at Miranshah, where their similarities of manner and appearance had caused the Gurkhas to call him Lentaigne junior. Lentaigne was then forty-three, tall, Irish, a twinkle in his eye. He told Masters to jump into the Jeep and drove him at breakneck speed to their encampment. He explained that the Long Range Penetration Brigade was part of the forthcoming Chindit operation into Burma. He himself had been on the first Chindit expedition that February and was now to take a leading part in the second.

The Chindit idea was the brainchild of Orde Wingate, one of the strangest figures to emerge during the Second World War. Wingate had been born in 1903 at Naini Tal in India, of parents who were strict Plymouth Brethren. Educated at Charterhouse and the Royal Military Academy, Woolwich, Wingate first made a name for himself in Palestine where he was a strong supporter of the Zionist cause in the mid-1930s, organising Special Night Squads to protect kibbutzim during the Arab Rebellion in 1936. Later in 1940, in Ethiopia, he led a guerrilla group, 'Gideon's Force', against the Italians, which helped restore the Emperor Haile Selassie to his throne. In 1941 his underlying instability came out and he suffered a nervous breakdown in Cairo and attempted suicide in a hotel room there. Wavell, now commanding the Indian Army, had been his former commander-in-chief in Ethiopia and remembered him for his unorthodox methods. Such an approach might well be needed in the Burma campaign, where the Japanese had swept through the country and were now at the gates of India. It called for desperate measures, and Wingate's methods and personality – abrasive, fanatic, unconventional – seemed to offer possibilities. Wavell summoned him to India and gave him free rein to organise the first Chindit operation, much to the annoyance of many Indian Army officers. This took place in February 1943.

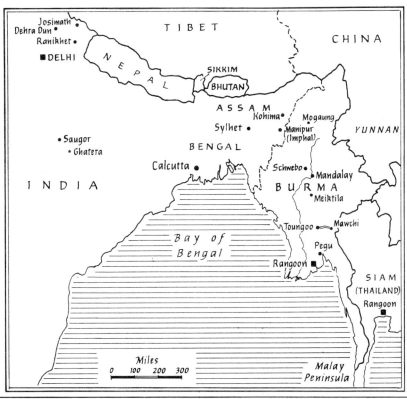

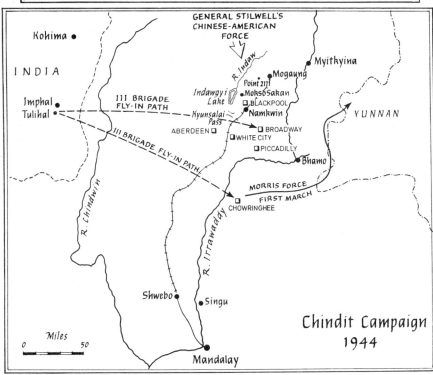

Chindit Campaign
1944

The name Chindit derived from the 'chinthe', the winged, lion-headed dragons that guard the entrance to Burmese pagodas to ward off evil spirits. The Chindit principle was to send specially-trained airborne troops far behind enemy lines to operate as roving bands. Their function was to disrupt the enemy's lines of communication rather than confront them in battle. Wingate had formulated this concept – a development of the guerilla warfare he had tried elsewhere – in the belief that air power and improved wireless communications offered radically improved ways of conducting a modern war. The sudden burst of activity and then retreat fitted in with the manic depressive side of his temperament.

The first Chindit expedition had dropped some three thousand men behind enemy lines, and they had succeeded in destroying part of the main Mandalay-Myitkyina Railway. They were then forced to scatter, returning to India as best they could. About a third of their men were lost on the way – a heavy casualty rate – but the expedition nevertheless had served as a great morale booster, and showed, crucially, that in the jungle, where hitherto they had reigned supreme, the Japanese were not as invincible as had been previously thought.

The reverberations of this expedition reached the highest level. Wavell, pressing his advantage and aware of the stalemate of the set-piece battles in the Arakan, favoured the Chindit approach as a bold and imaginative way to unlock the situation. He told Wingate to send his report of the first expedition back to London, where it ended up on the desk of Leo Amery, Secretary of State for India. Amery showed it to Churchill, who seized on it. The glamour of Wingate's romantic, bearded Chindits appealed strongly to Churchill. It fitted in with the tradition that Churchill so admired of derring-do, of Zeebrugge, Gallipoli and T. E. Lawrence, and he saw it as a way of infusing new spirit into the 'forgotten' 14th Army. Wingate was summoned back to England and accompanied Churchill to the Quebec Conference when he met his American allies in August 1943. Wingate thrived in these surroundings, able to communicate his ideas at the highest level and with such conviction and assurance that the Americans were won over and pledged crucial air support for his plans. It fitted in with their war aims as well, as they desperately needed to open up the Burma road and build a pipeline route through northern Burma to China, to enable them to bomb mainland Japan from airfields established there.

Wingate was promoted to major-general and allowed to select the troops and equipment he wanted, much to the chagrin of GHQ in Delhi, who resented both his intrusion and his unbureaucratic way of doing things. With the ear of Churchill, he knew he could go over the heads of Indian Army command, which infuriated them even more. Wingate was no lover of the Indian Army and once called it 'a system of outdoor relief'. It was hardly surprising, therefore, that he chose his old column commanders from the first expedition for key positions in this; Joe Lentaigne and Mike Calvert were among them. It tended to be an all-British show with few Indian troops or officers involved, except for the Gurkhas. Soon Wingate had mustered the six brigades he needed, something over twenty thousand men, plus the promise of American air transport. In assembling the elements of this operation he used every trick in the book: impassioned pleas to Churchill, tantrums, threats to resign.

For the second expedition, Wingate had introduced the concept of strongholds, fortified base camps set far behind Japanese lines. Airborne troops would be dropped to establish these and then use them as a base to sortie and disrupt Japanese supply routes, then in danger of being overstretched from south to north Burma. These sorties would be made by 'floater' columns, acting rather like submarines emerging from a safe harbour to harass the enemy. Their success would depend on mobility and surprise, and they would avoid bringing the Japanese into any head-on conflict as before.

Wingate knew his impact would be best served by personal exhortation. For the stronghold concept he used a Biblical quotation from the book of Zechariah, 'Turn ye to the Stronghold, ye prisoners of hope.' Wingate himself, bearded, small, sharp-featured, with piercing eyes, had the looks of an Old Testament prophet. Troops soon became infused by his oratory. Each stronghold in the depths of the jungle would have an airstrip built alongside it into which supplies would be flown and out of which the wounded would be flown. The latter was crucial; morale depended on it. In the first expedition some of the wounded had to be left behind. Mike Calvert, a column commander, had left his in the care of Burmese villagers, with a note to the Japanese commanding officer: 'I leave these men to your charge. They have fought bravely for King and Country. I know you will, with bushido, see they are properly looked after.' They were, but it was not always the case.

Wingate's concept was bold and daring and the Chindits sensed this and saw themselves as an elite corps. 111 Brigade then consisted of two battalions: the 1st Battalion Cameronians and 4th Battalion 9th Gurkhas. The Cameronians came from Glasgow and the surrounding Lanarkshire mining districts. Tough and hardy, they had always got on famously with the Gurkhas. Both had Highland connections and used bagpipes, and had a similar idiosyncratic sense of humour. They could be guaranteed to help each other out in emergencies. For training each battalion was divided into two columns, of four hundred men each, to duplicate how they would operate in the Burmese jungle. Masters was pleased to be working again with Gurkhas, though he hardly knew the 4th Battalion 9th Gurkhas, who were higher caste, taller and thinner than those of his regiment.

Conditions at Ghatera were somewhat primitive, the mess 'a most inadequate little tent with a table made of dried mud and bamboo.' Other tents lay dotted about in an air of abandon. The Chindits were allowed to look scruffy, part of the preparation for the jungle conditions ahead.

The area around Ghatera had been chosen by Wingate for its similarity to the Burmese jungle. Masters knew it from his reading of Kipling – it was the setting for *The Jungle Book* – and he was later to use it himself for his book *The Deceivers*. The surrounding villages had hardly been touched by the war and many had never seen a soldier before. The eye of the future novelist picked this out: 'I saw a young nubile girl's eyes droop with sheer sudden love at the face and form of a handsome soldier striding by, rifle in hand.' But this was 1943 and elsewhere in India conditions were bad, the appalling Bengal famine had started, largely, and reprehensibly, caused by foodstuffs being diverted to the war zone in the north-east. Gandhi's Quit India movement was mobilising public opinion, reinforced to some extent by the belief that Britain was unlikely to win the war. Yet here in this backwater, a strange, disengaged atmosphere prevailed, and political goings-on further afield seemed very remote.

Wingate came down to give them a pep talk, which provided a chance for Masters to take a closer look at him. He was wearing his familiar Wolsey helmet, and he seemed ill at ease, gruff and awkward, but the moment he started speaking, he was mesmerising. His high-pitched, rasping voice held the audience spellbound. At one point he called together a group of Cameronians who formed a tight mass around him. Typically he fixed one of them in the eye and said, 'You're going to die', then moved on to the next and gave him another piercing look, telling him, 'Many of you are going to die, or suffer wounds or near starvation. All of you will meet hardship worse than anything you have imagined.' It was deliberately theatrical; his way was to over-dramatise the situation to bind the men together into a special force, co-opting them with his zeal. Not all of the officers liked it; some felt his insistence on personal loyalty to him undermined their own efforts. Masters remained in two minds about Wingate and still had to be convinced that his message of sacrifice was justified.

Accompanying Wingate on this visit was Colonel Philip Cochran,

joint commander of 1st Air Commando, and later to be the model for
the famous 'Flip Corkin' American strip cartoon hero created by
Milton Caniff. He told them the welcome news that thirty Mustang
fighters, twelve Mitchell B25 medium bombers, one hundred L5 light
planes and gliders, as well as the C-47 Dakotas needed for supply
drops, would be available for them. His parting remark, an offer of
further help, 'Just dream it up', soon became a catch phrase for the
Chindits. For many, it was their first glimpse of the American fliers
whose fearlessness and daredevil spirit contributed so much to the
Chindit operation.

Wingate stayed on to attend an entertainment laid on that evening.
Its broad farce and sexual innuendo provided by two ENSA girls went
down a treat with most of the brigade, especially the Glaswegian
Cameronians, and with Masters, but Wingate sat through it with a
sickly smile on his face, feeling distinctly ill at ease.

The training was intentionally tough, and the fall-out rate high.
Their day began at 6 a.m., with bayonet drill and unarmed combat.
Breakfast was followed by jungle craft lectures and demonstrations.
During the intense heat of the middle of the day, they rested, but
fatigues were carried out between 3 p.m. and 5 p.m. Jungle training
was meant to prepare them for acute hardship and often they were
worked to the point of exhaustion. Some men found they simply
weren't fit enough, and fell by the wayside; others were afflicted by
heatstroke and malaria.

It was Wingate's show and as a frequent visitor to the brigades in
training, he was making sure they lived up to his exacting standards.
Some cursed him; others admired him. To his superiors, he may have
been arrogant and insufferable, but to his juniors he was often an
inspired military genius. His eccentricities often appealed to them: he
was found stark-naked scrubbing himself down with a stiff hairbrush;
he consumed buffalo milk and devoured raw onions, the virtues of
which he preached to all and sundry.

Mike Calvert was a prototype Chindit and survivor from the first
expedition. He was now in charge of 77 Brigade. He was brave,
thorough, and full of panache. He visited 111 Brigade to be questioned
about his experience on that first expedition. 'Jack welcomed me and
listened attentively to all I said. I hit it off with him straightaway. He
was a man full of ideas, eager to learn, questioning the right sort of
things, so I probably learnt as much while talking to him as he did
from what I told him.' Another brigade commander to visit was
Bernard Fergusson, temporarily allocated to 111 Brigade, pending
being given his own brigade. His reaction was quite different. 'My

reception was inevitably chilly, and the Brigade Major was Jack Masters. I thought him conceited and coarse, but in all likelihood a brave and competent soldier. After ten uncomfortable days I was appointed to command a brigade of my own.' Fergusson and Masters were to cross paths and swords at other times. Both men were strong characters with their own way of doing things. They never hit it off and disliked each other intensely, though they retained a grudging admiration for each other's soldierly qualities. Fergusson, with his patrician background – when he lost his monocle in the Burmese jungle he had a replacement flown out specially for him – moved easily among the higher echelons of the British Army, and this exacerbated a rivalry already felt by Masters as an Indian Army officer.

The training soon intensified. Marches of 10 to 20 miles carrying a pack weighing 50 lb were common. Silence had to be observed in preparation for the jungle; mules' vocal chords were cut accordingly. Masters was in his element under these conditions. On an 80-mile practice march to Jubbulpore, a fellow officer recalled how Masters 'as usual dominated and scintillated, having a crack at a particularly weary officer or starting an argument on the relative merits of Bix Beiderbecke and Harry James.' Special Force, as they were now called, needed to be a close-knit group to function properly, and camaraderie and esprit de corps were all-important. They were allowed some breaks and on one of these Masters found time to go off to Dehra Dun to see Goff Hamilton at the Indian Military Academy there, hoping to persuade him to join the Chindits. Masters drove over in a Jeep. Mollie Kaye remembers it: 'They got absolutely tight as newts and had a hilarious afternoon. Then Jack drove the Jeep all over the CO's garden, not popular at all. Jack said a Jeep could go anywhere – it was new in those days – and he made a very determined effort to climb a palm tree. Goff was on the mat next morning. "Ghastly friend of yours."'

A new arrival at Brigade HQ was Richard Rhodes-James, their cipher officer. Masters made a deep impression on him: 'He was one of the most extraordinary people I have ever met. I got to know him extremely well. Brigade HQ was a very intimate place, there were just half a dozen of us living on top of each other. In a funny sort of way Jack made a deeper impression on me than almost anybody else I have ever met, an extraordinarily acute brain, a mind like a razor, any problem that came to him he could solve quicker than anyone else. As a Staff Officer he was supreme.' But he noted that Masters made enemies. 'A lot of people didn't like him. He was classed by some people as too clever by half, too much of a thrusting egoist, a person who imposed himself, sharpening himself on other people. People in the Army didn't always like this, and he was something of an outsider.'

Rhodes-James found his earthiness, 'a crudeness that hovered round the conversations in the mess', only just bearable; it did not accord with his principles as a committed Christian. Even though they were 'poles apart', he still found him a 'compelling person' whom he valued for his warmth and personal friendliness.

All along, Barbara and Masters had kept up a steady correspondence and now she wrote, 'Hooray, Hooray I'm pregnant.' It dated from their time at Juhu together. Masters read the letter over and over again, elated and apprehensive at the same time. He was thrilled at the thought of becoming a father, though they had not planned it, but his anxiety was raised at the thought of going off on this secret and potentially dangerous mission into Burma. A child, though, gave him something to fight for – a shared and enhanced future with Barbara. She told him too about her work with the British marines in Bombay and how some of the officers there were helping her with her divorce; this child legally would be Hugh Rose's. Masters told Lentaigne about all this and they sat up late into the night drinking whisky and talking about marriage; Lentaigne's own marriage was in difficulties, and there was much they could discuss together.

The time was nearing for their departure for the front. 111 Brigade was now up to full strength and consisted of Brigade HQ and two new battalions, so that in all they comprised:

> 2nd Battalion King's Own Royal Regiment (Lancaster)
> 1st Battalion Cameronians (Scottish Rifles)
> 3rd Battalion 4th Prince of Wales's Own Gurkha Rifles
> 4th Battalion 9th Gurkha Rifles.

Their intelligence officer was John Hedley, an Old Etonian with a large, booming voice, who had pre-war experience in the Burmah Trading Corporation; he was fearless and as steady as a rock, so too was their medical officer. 'Doc' Whyte from Northern Ireland was tireless, and always whistled 'Moonlight becomes you'.

Early in January 1944 the brigade set off on the six-day train ride to Assam. Each morning they breakfasted by the side of the track, and the officers shaved with hot water from the engine. At one point, Masters, fulfilling many a childhood ambition, drove the train himself. Eventually – even in wartime India, trains seemed to go no faster – they reached their destination, the little town of Sylhet in the tea-planting district. From there a 120-mile march lay ahead through the Manipur Hills to Imphal. The Chindits were geared up for their task ahead. Masters had grown long sideburns on his cheek, a personal form of camouflage as he jokingly told his signals sergeant. Chindits were encouraged to develop idiosyncratic touches. At this stage their mood was high, euphoric even: they were marching to war, the Gurkhas singing their jaunris. Masters had taken his copy of *Paradise Lost* along and would read aloud from it at night, by the light of the campfire, to his group of officers.

February brought a halt and a long wait at a camp 33 miles south of Imphal, a delay that took some of the edge off their enthusiasm. Slim visited them and Mountbatten too, now Supreme Allied Commander South-East Asia. His pep talk, in characteristic fashion standing on an upturned crate, made them all feel understood and needed. Meanwhile, Masters used the waiting period to draw up a thorough Brigade Operation Order, co-ordinating the various elements of the fly-in, signallers, doctors, mules, specialists and so on. Its bewildering series of appendices and loading tables were a tribute to his logistical skills.

At the beginning of March they moved on again, up to Tulihal airfield. At the first full moon they would commence their fly-in. First in was to be Mike Calvert's 77 Brigade, followed by 111 Brigade. A date was set for 5 March, but there was a last-minute hitch when aerial reconnaissance photographs showed the chosen landing site to be covered in what seemed to be logs. These later turned out to be ruts in the ground from winter tree-felling. A hasty revision of their plan was made, while the gliders and troops stood waiting on the runway. Wingate, Calvert and US Air Commander Allison hurriedly picked an alternative site. It was a brave decision to go ahead, though if they had not, the whole expedition might have had to be called off. Wingate and the others watched anxiously from the ground as the first gliders, tugged in pairs by American planes, soared high into the night sky, momentarily visible in patches of moonlight before disappearing over the hills to Burma.

Their landing site was codenamed Broadway, a familiar name to give troops in a distant land a sense of belonging. This first fly-in to Broadway was a near disaster: only just over half the sixty or so gliders reached their destination, seventeen landed in various parts of Assam and six came down in Japanese-held territory.

Three nights later, on 8 March, it was 111 Brigade's turn. Masters wore for luck the thick woollen socks Barbara had knitted for him, and carried, as they all did, a yellow silk handkerchief with its map of Burma imprinted on it, plus two condoms in which they could wrap watch, compass and matches when the time came to swim or ford a river. Each man carried his own backpack on to the gliders. For the small-framed Gurkhas these packs often weighed more than half their body weight.

It was the culmination of all their training. Like any soldier highly tuned to do his job, Masters was itching to get into battle. Behind him lay the months of theory and the grand strategies; now it was the immediate group that mattered. Here were the men he was going to live and die with for the next three months: Lentaigne, Hedley, Whyte, Briggs, Macpherson, Baines, Rhodes-James, Jennings, Turner and the rest. Shortly before take-off he was handed a telegram. It was from Barbara and had taken three weeks to reach him. She had given birth to a girl, Susan, on 17 February. Both mother and child were well.

111 Brigade had two dropping zones, Chowringhee and Broadway. Masters's half of the brigade went to Chowringhee. Coming in to land at night, it presented an eerie sight, a brilliantly lit flarepath in the midst of the Burmese jungle, bright beams shining up to give landing directions amid the lights of planes taxiing to take off again in an intense hive of activity. They were 150 miles behind Japanese lines. Disembarking, he met Lentaigne, who told him the operation was going well; there had been no real accidents. They scattered for the night and hid in the jungle. Next morning, glancing up anxiously at the sky to see if the Japanese had located the spot, they waited for others to arrive. It took three nights and six hundred glider sorties to fly in the rest of 111 Brigade. The operation was ably directed by Commander Allison on the ground using the cockpit of his C-47 as his control tower.

When the twenty-five hundred men and fourteen hundred mules had been safely landed, Operation Thursday, as it was called, was launched. 'Our first task is fulfilled,' wrote Wingate in his Order of the Day, 'all our columns are inserted in the enemy's guts.' Wingate went on, 'This is a moment to live in history. It is an enterprise in which every man who takes part may feel proud one day to say "I was there".' His Nelson-like touch was deliberate. The Japanese were indeed largely taken by surprise. Looking up at the night sky on 5 March, a Japanese commander of the 214th Infantry Regiment saw what he assumed were transport planes passing overhead and thought they were on their way to bomb Rangoon.

111 Brigade split up. Two columns of 4th Battalion 9th Gurkhas under Jumbo Morris headed off to operate to the north-east in Yunnan Province; the rest, including Masters, were to move west and rendezvous with the Cameronians and King's Own who had landed at Broadway. The rendezvous point was 130 miles away and would take an estimated

twelve days to reach through dense teak jungle. They marched off and soon heard Japanese Zero fighters overhead. Using their well-rehearsed routine, standing rock-still, not a man looking upwards, they remained undetected, and the planes passed on to bomb the now unoccupied Chowringhee.

At night they would 'harbour' at a likely spot. Lentaigne would point to a tree and say, 'That's Brigade HQ for the night'. Masters then took charge, giving precise orders like, 'There's the brigade tree. Axis of advance 270, BHQ radius 70 yards, perimeter radius 150 yards, fires until 1800. Brigadier's orders at 1800 hours. Any questions?' The rest of them would then fan out in a circle and pitch their tents. Each night they reported their position back to base by cipher signal. Cooking was done on individual small fires lit from wax-impregnated paper from their American K rations, which were packets of dried food divided into three packets per day and providing 4,000 calories from 'terrible' dried ham, chocolate and eggs.

Every five days a supply drop was made consisting of further food rations, animal feeds for the mules, ammunition, equipment, medical supplies and, most welcome of all, mail. Letters out had to be censored, as this was still a secret mission, but inward letters were plentiful. Masters heard more news of Susan, now weighing seven and a half pounds. He sent off his own letters, cramming as much as he could on every inch of the thin yellow-surfaced paper.

111 Brigade's first major difficulty came with their attempt to cross the Irrawaddy at night, a plan backed up by air support. First, gliders brought in the rubber boats and outboard motors needed for the crossing, but these landed too far away and had to be manhandled back across sand dunes to the crossing places. The skill of the American C-47 pilots was a marvel to behold. Once the gliders had been emptied, they were strung up on a tow line between tall bamboo poles and then snatched up by the pilots in their planes. Mountbatten, when he first saw this daring manoeuvre, exclaimed, 'Jesus Christ all bloody mighty.' As they sped away, the intrepid pilots would even veer off course to slice in two with their wing tips any telephone wires they saw.

This crossing of the Irrawaddy was to prove a nightmare. Many of the outboard motors refused to start and the mules, normally the fastest and most reliable of swimmers, refused to swim the whole way across and kept turning back halfway. Mike MacGillicuddy of the Reeks, a young Irish officer in 111 Brigade and well-used to horses, took charge and tried again and again to lead the mules across, mounted on the strongest swimmer. Lentaigne was soon worried. They had the cover of night, but it was a very exposed position and daylight

would soon reveal it. He waited until the last possible moment. As
morning broke only half of them had got across, with one fifth of the
mules. He, and Masters, had seriously underestimated the difficulty of
this sort of river crossing. Lentaigne was forced to call a halt and those
troops and officers remaining on the far side of the Irrawaddy were
ordered to head off and join the other half of the brigade under Jumbo
Morris further east. Their own, now depleted, force, with insufficient
mules, had to jettison some of their valuable heavy equipment, including
wireless sets. It had been a long night and exhaustion was creeping up
on them; it was more than thirty-six hours since many of them had last
slept. Indeed, once they were in the jungle, exhaustion was to become
as important a factor as the as-yet-unseen enemy.

They headed off for their rendezvous point. Lentaigne was clearly
unsettled by the aborted river crossing, and the stillness of the teak
jungle was not making it any easier for him. He kept seeing the enemy
where none existed. On the second night he roused them all out of their
sleep at 4 a.m. and told them to move on. The 'enemy' turned out to be
Burmese villagers going about their early morning business. At forty-
three, he may have already been too old for this type of soldiering, and
it was beginning to tell. Masters later took the view that no one over
thirty-five ought to have been sent into Burma as a marching Chindit
and, as much as he liked Lentaigne on a personal level, he now had
doubts about his fitness for the job in hand.

By 24 March they reached their rendezvous point with the
Cameronians and King's Own. It should have been a moment for
celebration, but that same night the astounding news came through
from Force HQ that Wingate had been killed. His plane had crashed
into the side of a mountain. The cause of the crash was never
satisfactorily explained; it was probably bad weather, though sabotage
could never be ruled out. Sixteen days into the Chindit operation and
just as it was about to get going, its leader and prime mover was dead.
They all – officers and men alike – felt shattered.

A successor needed to be appointed quickly. Calvert seemed the
obvious choice, as he had been closest to Wingate both in temperament
and experience, but he was now fully occupied with establishing his
stronghold at White City, and could not easily be withdrawn. To many
people's surprise, Lentaigne was chosen instead. He had been on the
first Chindit campaign, was relatively senior and was also a Gurkha,
which must have counted to his commander, Bill Slim, a fellow Gurkha
whose decision it ultimately was. Overall command was taken by the
American General 'Vinegar Joe' Stilwell, and he decided to change
their priorities. The American interest in this campaign of the war had

always been to open up a road into China through northern Burma. This now became paramount, and all else was subsumed to that aim. Worse for the Chindits was that Stilwell was an unmitigated 'limey-hater', as his diaries amply testify. As a result, he persistently under-rated the Chindits, even doubting their willingness to fight.

Stilwell was a tough diamond, a folksy general who identified with his men and was rough-cut in comparison to the more upper-class British officers. He refers constantly, and critically, in his diaries to the British as still 'colonials' and to Mountbatten as 'Glamour Boy'. American senior officers often shared the same background as their men, unlike their British counterparts, whose sense of superiority was inbred and often irritated the Americans. Stilwell was no exception and being an old China hand from pre-war days, with Chiang Kai-Shek's forces now working for him, felt he knew what he was talking about.

It was a pity that Wingate had been killed, because in a curious way he and Stilwell shared certain similarities: both were spartan in their personal habits, idiosyncratic and difficult to get close to. Stilwell had his field headquarters in a bamboo shack and he insisted on always eating the same rations as his men. Now that Wingate was gone, Lentaigne was spokesman for the Chindits, but he was no match for Stilwell. The Chindit cause wilted and their status as a Special Force gradually diminished.

With Lentaigne's departure, the command of 111 Brigade was vacant. The senior officer was Jumbo Morris, but he was far away on the other side of the Irrawaddy. Masters was promoted on Lentaigne's decision. Morris was put in overall charge, but the effective day-to-day running of the brigade was now fully in Masters's hands. This sudden promotion meant he would have precedence over officers senior in rank to himself. He was still only a major while his column commanders, Hennings and Thompson, were lieutenant-colonels. Not wishing to offend them, he opted to wear no badges of rank for the time being and signed his orders with the de facto rank of commander.

This unexpected promotion was a tremendous boost, the high point of all he had been working for since his days at Sandhurst. Command lay before him. Lentaigne had needed someone he knew well and could trust, who could read his mind and interpret his orders. To some of the troops, the appointment was less of a surprise. To them Masters had already seemed to be 'running' the brigade, even before Wingate's death. They had nicknamed him Chota Wingate (Little Wingate) for the way he infused them with his energy and gathered them round in the evening and read the Bible to them, or lectured them on the resilience of the Japanese, as Wingate might have done. Masters was popular and mostly well-liked by the men; his lack of pomposity and earthiness were in his favour.

Most of the other officers in the brigade liked Masters too, and felt it was the right decision to promote him. Now that they were engaged in the earnestness of war, his abrasive side was less in evidence. Tim Brennan, then second in command of the Cameronians, approved of his elevation and saw Masters as both 'a highly trained staff officer, and a first-rate man manager with a natural ability to get on with people, able to go into the Sergeants' or Corporals' mess and be readily accepted by them.' Brigade HQ under Masters's control soon became, in Brennan's memory, a welcome place to go: 'tremendous fun, informal, convivial, a happy ambience. As soon as you arrived you were offered a drink, usually of rum, and Jack was at the centre of things.' Once the implications of his appointment had sunk in, Masters revelled in the prospect. Command nourished him; he grew with it, and he knew he had a tough job on his hands, but at least he was among men he had trained with and knew well.

They continued their march north, nearing the Japanese supply zone where their lines of communication met. Chance encounters with the Japanese were frequent. Once, rounding a bend, they met four Japanese troops, apparently lost. Each side just stood staring at the other, the Japanese making no attempt to run away. Another time they lay resting by the side of the road and a Japanese commander drove past, sitting bolt upright in his car. Both sides were too stunned to react and by the time the Chindits did so, the Japanese car was out of sight. Even in the midst of a war, the Burmese villagers kept on with their traditional life as if nothing was happening. The sight of a young Burmese girl in a wide-brimmed straw hat looking up suddenly from her paddy field stayed indelibly in Masters's memory.

A Japanese supply dump at Kyaungle was found and destroyed, including some 220 tons of stores and twenty vehicles. It made a good start to his Chindits performing their real function as a marauding group behind enemy lines. The rapport between himself and his men grew stronger. One night he decided to let them relax. After the hours of vigilance and silence in the jungle, they were suddenly allowed to light fires, to shout and talk and sing and make as much noise as they liked. The enemy were far enough away to be forgotten about. He gave them each an extra tot of rum, and went among them, listening to them talk and drinking the rum they offered him, a bit like Henry V on the eve of Agincourt. Next morning, without fail, they were all up and ready to move at the crack of dawn.

A message came through that Stilwell had switched their objective to the capture of Mogaung, a strategic necessity for his plans. Masters immediately felt the effect of this change of direction. 111 Brigade was ordered to establish a block, a watered-down version of a stronghold, close to the main north-south rail and road supply routes to Mogaung and to disrupt these. The siting of the block was much closer to Japanese lines than they had been trained for. This was not a wise move in their case, as the Long Range Penetration Brigade was only likely to succeed if it was remote from the front, with quick sorties to cut supplies and communications. Doc Whyte, part of Masters's immediate entourage, wrote later, 'When we received orders to establish the block, we were fully aware what this meant. Our lightly-armed force, trained in mobility and quick action of the jungle commando type, could not expect to take on a static role, encountering infantry and artillery assault, with any chance of survival.'

Masters privately felt in a quandary. Not wanting to show his unease, he flew to inspect the block at White City where Mike Calvert and 77 Brigade had operated successfully before they, too, had been ordered out to attack Mogaung. Eager to see what it looked like, Masters summoned a light L5 plane and visited the abandoned site, which got its name from the numerous parachutes stuck in nearby trees. He made a close inspection of its layout and defensive arrangements. The gruesome sight of bodies in an advanced state of decay on the perimeter wire told him where and how the Japanese had attacked. He returned in a thoughtful mood.

An air drop gave him aerial photographs of possible sites. Studying them closely, he selected one near the village of Namkwin, 20 miles south of Mogaung. He decided it would be quicker and easier to split 111 Brigade into two groups, each following roughly parallel routes. He marched with Brigade HQ in the left-hand group with the King's Own and 3rd Battalion 4th Gurkha Rifles. Their route took them along the pretty, twisting Meza River, which they must have crossed and re-crossed forty times or more.

They made their rendezvous at Mokso Sakan, near Lake Indawgyi, only a short distance from their destination on the other side of a short range of hills. Thinking ahead to possible eventualities, he left part of his brigade there – his trusted 30 Column of 4th Gurkhas – to guard the back entrance to the block over the hills. The site itself was 10 miles further on. Going ahead, he and his chief RAF officer, Chesty Jennings, disguised themselves as Burmese villagers and went forward to 'recce' it. They worked out a position for the airstrip next to the paddy field just below, and started to move in that same night, immediately digging trenches and putting up a defensive perimeter of barbed wire. Ammunition was stacked away and the paddy fields levelled out for the airstrip, in readiness for the first gliders bringing bulldozers, ammunition and other supplies for the block the next morning. Once Brigade HQ had been set up and the signallers had made contact with base, the code name Blackpool was given to the site.

By now it was late April 1944 and 111 Brigade had been in Burma for forty-five days, half the length of time Wingate reckoned was feasible for Chindit troops to remain in the field. Both men and officers viewed this ninety-day limit as a sort of contract, and its known duration was a key factor in sustaining their morale.

The layout of Blackpool seen from the air resembled an animal splayed flat on the ground with its four legs at right angles to its body. Masters named its salient features after the fielding positions on a cricket field – Cover Point, Midwicket, the Deep and so on – which would be familiar names for his troops in a distant land. Masters's best qualities came out in setting up the block – organising, ordering, foreseeing – but the isolation of command was never far away. As the gliders came in, one suddenly nose-dived, killing all its occupants. 'I shall not forget the sudden lurch in my own stomach, and the bitten-off cry I gave as the tail went up and the nose straight down', he later wrote.

The Japanese, having learnt a lesson from their White City experience, were quick to locate 111 Brigade's position, and started their offensive on the second night, taking up positions close to the wire and launching attacks from 10 or 20 yards away. At times it meant bitter hand-to-hand fighting. The next morning casualties were counted; the Japanese dead were festooned on the wire, while their own fatalities were slight. Battle raged almost continually, giving them little time to settle in. Masters stayed at his post, directing operations from Brigade HQ, anxious that the perimeter wire should not be breached at any point. At times it meant issuing orders that might mean certain death. As the enemy came close at the Deep, he ordered the King's Own to clear the way. 'Send your best man', he told Thompson; it became a haunting refrain for him, as the best man was quite likely to be killed. However intense the fighting, the worst was the shelling which seemed to be non-stop.

Their own casualties mounted after five nights of incessant bombardment. The men sat in their dugouts, counting the shells as they came over. Once they counted three hundred shells within the space of thirty minutes. It was distressing to watch the standing mules being hit one by one. Masters soon knew that this was a different kind of operation from the one they had been trained for. It was a challenge to his powers of resourcefulness and he was determined to do his best to meet it. Being shelled was the worst experience of all; often it went on from dusk until an hour before dawn.

Then the monsoon, which they had been half expecting, broke. It filled the trenches and weapon pits with water. The aircraft found it almost impossible to land, as the airstrip was like a quagmire. Now they could not take off the wounded and supplies were running short. Air drops were becoming more difficult. It was only the incredible bravery of the pilots that kept them supplied, though inevitably some supplies landed in the Japanese zone. The attempt to cut the railway line in the valley below became less and less practicable as only a few sorties could be made, so tightly hemmed-in were they by the Japanese. Now their task became primarily defensive, holding on until further support arrived. Masters looked to Lentaigne to send reinforcements. The latter had promised that 14 Brigade, another Chindit detachment, would be brought up as soon as possible. Until they arrived, Masters knew that his brigade were sitting targets, and could only try to minimise their losses.

In *Road Past Mandalay* Masters describes this anxious time evocatively. Ten days at Blackpool and he had reached his lowest point. Where, he cried, were his promised reinforcements? Why was Lentaigne not doing more to support him? 'My men' he wrote, 'were being worked and fought into the ground while twenty bloody battalions, forty flaming columns of Chindit bullshit sat on their arses and drank tea and wondered how we were getting on.' The tone may be exaggerated but it captures the desperation of that moment. He had been thrust into an increasingly impossible position, unable to operate in the way he had been trained as a Chindit, and had to learn defensive tactics on the spot. All eyes were on him as their commander, and he felt under intense pressure; his fury was the result of his own impotence in the situation.

Yet, whatever his private thoughts, he knew he had to keep up an optimistic front. He made sure he looked calm. A fellow officer, Major Larpent, remembered his 'complete confidence . . . he seemed to be on top of the world thoroughly enjoying himself and ready to cope with anything.' The rain worsened and the Deep began to look like Passchendaele. They were well and truly stuck. Masters stayed most of the time in Brigade HQ, directing operations from its nerve centre.

As the Japanese stepped up their bombardment of the Deep, Masters ordered the Cameronians under Brennan to relieve the King's Own position there. The King's Own came past him staggering, 'their eyes wandered, their mouths drooped open'. Many were wounded, others carried wounded men; it was like a scene from Goya's *Desastres de Guerra*. 'I wanted to cry, but dared not.'

Tiredness was universal, and as debilitating as fighting the enemy; they were lucky to get five hours' sleep a night. Masters reckoned that on most nights he had three. Their nerves were put on edge by the Japanese habit of screeching like jackals, gibbering and screaming to frighten the young soldiers. Two more battalions did arrive, the 2nd Battalion King's Regiment (Liverpool) under Lt-Col Scott and the 3rd Battalion 9th Gurkha Rifles under Lt-Col Harper. The sight which greeted them was of 'thin, determined ghosts'. One of them, Fred Holliday in the King's Regiment, remembers seeing Masters for the first time when he visited them shortly after their arrival, 'a rather gaunt looking individual, unkempt in appearance, with a minimum of clothing, but armed with carbine, revolver and grenades. I asked my platoon commander who he was, as he wasn't wearing any badges of rank and he said "Masters". I began to ponder upon our eventual fate – he didn't look up to much, but time would tell.'

They learnt over the radio that Stilwell's plan for the capture of Mogaung had been held up. They would have to stay put and endure two more weeks of this hell. Masters flew up to meet Lentaigne, justifiably annoyed that the latter had not been down personally to see his old brigade. He went in an American L5 plane. The pilot, Jack Gallagher, had to lend him a shirt for the meeting as Masters had arrived for the flight dressed only in his everyday wear of a pair of shorts – cut-off trousers, in fact – his issue boots and a nondescript hat. Lentaigne told him about his difficulties with Stilwell, a hard man for someone as essentially conciliatory as Lentaigne to stand up to. Masters met Stilwell, who 'looked just as the photos showed', and was asked tersely if he had managed to stop all traffic in the railway valley. Masters replied he hoped to do so once 14 Brigade arrived, to which Stilwell grunted brusquely. Stilwell's anglophobia was unmistakable and Masters went back with no misapprehensions about his attitude.

At Blackpool they had been under unremitting attack for two weeks. It was 22 May and the Japanese had brought up heavy anti-aircraft guns, making air supply even more hazardous. Inwardly Masters was near despair. Everything seemed to be piling up. The Japanese advanced closer to the wire; the shelling got worse; air supplies became more infrequent. Then, after incessant shelling during the night of 24 May, followed by tropical rain, the Japanese broke through the perimeter fence at 5 a.m. and overran an outpost. How it happened no one knew. The battle rapidly spread over the eastern half of the block and the main dressing station filled up with casualties. The situation was becoming untenable. Masters ordered all troops to withdraw from the eastern sector, guns to be spiked and abandoned.

Now Masters was faced with the hardest decision of all: whether to abandon the block altogether or to attempt to hold the position to the last man and the last round. No commander in the field likes to withdraw. Masters's better judgement told him that to sacrifice the lives of his men for the sake of honour and military reputation was uncalled for. He sent a signal to HQ stating that retention of the block would entail the loss of the entire brigade. Rhodes-James, a witness to these events, describes this moment: 'Having failed to eject the Japanese, without food and with sufficent ammunition for only another twelve hours' fighting, with no prospect of getting any more, with a large number of casualties and with no means for evacuating them and with utterly exhausted troops, Jack Masters gave the order to withdraw.'

There was no time to consult Lentaigne, though he dictated a signal to be sent to base, which never arrived. The number of wounded was mounting: they now had about ninety who could not walk unaided and another thirty who could not walk at all. The organisation of this withdrawal was to tax Masters's resourcefulness to the limit. He had a mind well-stocked with expedients for such a military emergency. His training on the North-West Frontier could be put to use and he remembered the method used there to withdraw piquets. Now he set about organising a similar system of laybacks, gradually thinning out the number of troops in actual contact with the enemy and then using those men to set up a series of covering positions while others withdrew, each layback successively covering the last and then leapfrogging forward. By mid-morning they were beginning to head back over the hill to Mokso Sakan in some sort of order. The Chindits, trained to be adaptable, handled this rearguard action with great ability, despite the confused circumstances.

The problem of what to do with the wounded dominated Masters's thinking at this point. It needed four to six men to carry one wounded man on a stretcher, a very slow and risky undertaking that put the stretcher-bearers at great risk. Some lay so appallingly wounded that they could hardly be moved. Masters went down to the dressing station to see for himself. His own words convey the horror of it: 'the first man was quite naked and a shell had removed the entire contents of his stomach. Between his chest and pelvis there was a bloody hollow, behind it his spine. Another had no legs and no hips, his trunk ending just below the waist. A third had no left arm, shoulder, or breast, all torn away in one piece. A fourth had no face and whitish liquid was trickling out of his head into the mud. A fifth seemed to have been torn in pieces by a mad giant, and his lips bubbled gently.' Nineteen men lay there in front of him, hardly conscious. A brigade doctor told him there were another thirty ahead who might be saved if they were carried, but the men here had little chance of survival. In the brutal atmosphere of war it called for a quick decision. He was responsible overall for some two thousand or more lives besides these. As he wrote, 'one small mistake, one little moment of hesitation and many more would be dead.' He issued the toughest order he had to give all through the war and told the doctor to shoot them. In years to come, it was to haunt him as a recurring nightmare.

The Cameronians were last to leave and Masters, like the captain of a ship, was the very last of all. 'At about noon, fifty minutes after giving the first order, after seventeen days, having been defeated, I left the Blackpool block in the rain.' It was a dismal moment, but in the thick of battle, he kept himself going, charged up on borrowed energy. As they retreated they kept looking back, expecting the Japanese to follow and press home their advantage, but they did not. Why they did not has never been satisfactorily explained, but the probability is that they were just as exhausted themselves and just as relieved that this horrendous episode was over for them too. It transpired after the war, when Japanese documents were available, that they were older troops, from Kyoto, and their casualty count had been much higher than previously thought, higher than that of the Chindits, with a thousand Japanese men lost as opposed to 111 Brigade's two hundred.

As they climbed away from Blackpool one section took the wrong fork in a path. It led directly back to the Japanese and a hail of murderous fire. Masters, summoning up all his reserves, came striding up the track from the rear, armed with carbine, kukri, pistol – and a Japanese officer's sword. He passed men and animals struggling uphill in the mud, walking wounded supporting each other, soldiers who seemed to be sleepwalking. Doc Whyte had arranged for those who were blinded to be tied together with bandages and led in file. He came across a man on the edge of the path with his wrists blown off, but could not stop to help. From people behind came cries of, 'Move on, move'; if they did not, a mortar might land on the path and they would all be blown up. Sometimes the mud was so thick and the gradient so steep that men were reduced to crawling uphill. Exhaustion and incessant rain added to their misery.

Masters knew he had to keep his men's spirits up. Momentarily buoyed up by organising the technicalities of the withdrawal, once they reached the higher ground, he felt suddenly deflated and on the verge of collapse. He had held the psychological impact of these traumatic events at bay for three days, in which he had hardly slept at all. The men of his escort offered to lift him along but he insisted on remaining part of the moving rearguard. Exhausted or not, he went on mentally planning for alternatives in the event of a Japanese attack. The first night in their makeshift harbour they were relieved, bewildered even, that no shells were about to fall on them. Their relief was tinged with a slightly unworthy joy, and guilt at being the survivors when so many had perished or been left behind.

Masters forced himself to keep functioning as commander. This was his show and he was going to see it through to the end. His mind raced back to Staff College days. What was the rate of collapse of walking wounded once shock began to take effect? 'Ah yes, that was it' – eighty per cent unable to walk after twenty-four hours. He kicked himself for leaving his staff officer's notebook behind in the confusion of departure. Self-recrimination began to take over. He should have led the last counter-attack himself, Mike Calvert would have done so. But he was too conscientious a commander to allow himself to wallow in the sadness of defeat. He knew his primary task was to keep the morale of his men up and the sight of a disconsolate or demoralised commander would have had untold ripple effects.

It took 111 Brigade four days to reach Mokso Sakan. They climbed for most of the time, one man often clasped around the neck of another, 'his legs trailing, the khaki bandage soaked with rain and blood and foul with mud where he has fallen a hundred times.' One Gurkha soldier carried another on his back for 3 miles. Near the top of the ridge, they met troops from the 6th Nigerian Regiment sent to meet them and already cutting steps into the trail to make their climb easier. The Nigerians tenderly took over the work of carrying the wounded. For Masters the encounter was less amicable. Their commanding officer, Gordon Upjohn, a friend from Sandhurst days, told him he had been ordered by Lentaigne to take over command of the 'scattered remains' of 111 Brigade. Masters was furious at being supplanted in this way with the implication that he was no longer capable of being in control. He wrote out a bitter signal to Lentaigne. All the frustration and pent-up fury he felt about the failure of Blackpool, and the non-arrival of 14 Brigade, were expressed in it. He later apologised, and Upjohn agreed to place himself under Masters's command until the situation could be sorted out. By 28 May, Masters was able to signal to Force HQ that he had with him '130 wounded and 2,000 men properly organised and under arms.' He had turned the 'rabble' into an organised unit and was fully in command again.

111 Brigade met up with the Gurkhas he had thoughtfully left behind at Mokso Sakan and moved on to Lake Indawgyi, where at last they rested. Blackpool was over. Could Masters have acted differently; could he have prevented the debacle? He has both critics and supporters. Most agree, though, that the siting of Blackpool was at fault. It was too close to Japanese lines. In *Road Past Mandalay*, Masters claims that he was hamstrung by waiting for 14 Brigade to arrive, as if, like Blücher at Waterloo, this would have turned the battle. Perhaps it would. The Japanese, after their White City experience, were much more adept at attacking a block, and were not going to let up on Blackpool. Rhodes-James's view confirms this: 'He was given an impossible task really. The site he chose had serious drawbacks to it, I don't think he could be blamed for that – his options were very small. Being asked to cut the road and rail communications to the north was always going to be difficult with 25 lb shells, and we couldn't get near it across open country.'

Rhodes-James also takes the view that Masters directed the brigade and the battle as skilfully as anyone could. It was fair comment. He was facing a hopeless task once supplies failed, and his brigade was ripe for encirclement. He managed the operation of withdrawal from Blackpool with great skill, under circumstances that were horrific.

The opposing view argues that he should have conducted the defence of Blackpool more vigorously. Instead of sitting in his foxhole or in Brigade HQ issuing orders, he should have shown himself more and led from the front, as Mike Calvert might have done. These critics see him as 'a brainy soldier who scribbled messages', not a warrior-type at the centre of action. The Chindit style was all in favour of an active profile and an aggressive one, but as Shelford Bidwell acknowledges in his account of the campaign in *The Chindit War*, Masters was ambitious and knew that fame could be won by a successful defence of Blackpool, 'but he was also a realist. His military perception was too detached and too clear to be blind to the weakness of his position if he was left unsupported.' Hence his waiting for 14 Brigade to arrive was a realistic appreciation of the situation.

In an unsuccessful operation criticisms are bound to fly and ultimately the commander has to bear responsibility. Masters did all he could under the circumstances. He had little room for manoeuvre and his hand was forced by outside factors: the monsoon had destroyed support and the constant bombardment by the Japanese took a heavy toll. He remained the staff officer par excellence: encouraging where he could, gaining the confidence of most of his officers and organising to the best of his ability. He was aware of the hallowed Chindit tradition of derring-do and bravado, leading from the front more, but Masters knew what he was doing. He needed to stay in his HQ and make his decisions there as reports came in from a continually fluid and changing situation. The verdict the historian Louis Allen reaches in *Burma, The Longest War*, namely that Masters was 'competent, flamboyant and ruthless', seems to be borne out by events.

Flamboyance and ruthlessness were there in the way he conducted the 'siege' of Blackpool. His competence was never in question, though it was in evidence mostly in his handling of the retreat, which many consider his finest achievement. At no stage did he shirk full responsibility for his actions. He hoped wherever possible to save unnecessary loss of life, even if this meant shooting the wounded. These were very tough decisions to make, but he took them and got on with it. Certainly, so far as Masters was concerned, Blackpool was not what he had been trained for. That he showed himself capable of taking over command at such short notice and conducting much of the siege of Blackpool and its final withdrawal with such skill was testimony to his personal qualities and his growth as a military commander. For him it was a good episode in the war and he subsequently was awarded a DSO for it.

At Lake Indawgyi the Gurkhas built bamboo shelters, known as bashas, as protection against the monsoon. 111 Brigade were exhausted and battle-shocked. Sunderland flying boats landed on the lake to ferry out their wounded. The chaplain wanted to carry out a service of thanksgiving. Masters, angry still at the lack of support, at first refused to let him, but later relented and agreed it could take place.

111 Brigade had now been eighty days in Burma, ten short of Wingate's ninety-day time limit. The sight of the flying boats encouraged the men. Once the wounded were away, their turn would surely be next. Rhodes-James describes how officers of all ranks would surround him as he deciphered messages from HQ. They were expecting the order to be flown out. They would then walk away disconsolate, with long faces, when none came. Masters chivvied them along. A fellow officer remembers attending a conference at Mokso Sakan where Masters was 'sitting stripped to his shorts on a sort of bamboo throne his Gurkhas had made for him. We were rather solemn and depressed until he began: "Well, chaps, let's get this next phase over and then we can go back to India for some proper peacetime soldiering."' His irreverence and facetiousness on these occasions were a deliberate attempt to lift their spirits.

By Lake Indawygi, the physical toll of Blackpool – shock, a severe all-round decline in health and general debilitation – delayed until now, began to make itself felt, so that even a small cut on a finger would quickly go septic. Malaria, amoebic dysentery and scrub-typhus all increased. With the tension gone, even the smallest exertion became an effort. Doc Whyte (in Masters's eyes the under-recognised hero of the campaign) informed him that a large proportion of the troops were suffering from acute exhaustion, undernourishment, exposure and strain. Morale was low, and not even the news on 6 June of the D-Day landings on the French coast managed to uplift them.

Then on 8 June came the astonishing news that 111 Brigade was to move out and attack Mogaung from the west. It was Stilwell's decision. He had taken the less than charitable view that Blackpool had been abandoned unnecessarily. Lentaigne came down to relay it and got a rude reception. The troops, mimicking his words, subsequently referred to him as 'Let's-get-cracking Lentaigne'. Pawns in Stilwell's game since Wingate's death, they had no option but to obey. Masters was placed in an invidious position. As commander he was obliged to obey orders, but he was aware of the poor state of health of his men and their sinking morale, the Cameronians especially. He had fought and struggled with them and felt indebted to them.

Mogaung was 25 miles almost due east. On 9 June 111 Brigade set off on a slow and laborious journey through mosquito-infested terrain and across streams where leeches clasped themselves to the skin. The days dissolved into a 'blur of cloud and rain, of fog and mist, and clay-coloured faces, dying eyes.' Their first objective was Point 2171, a hill occupied by the Japanese and overlooking the valley and the railway line to Mogaung.

Their assault on this hilltop lasted from 20 June to 5 July and was, in Masters's view, 'as hard on the soldiers as anything in my experience.' During it they lost many men, including prized officers, such as Mike MacGillicuddy, and Jim Blaker, who was awarded the VC. The battle itself was more like a slugging match between two heavyweight boxers: 'we were falling against each other, spent, drugged, crazed fighters, bare knuckles, pawing at each other, falling down.' The Japanese were as battle-weary as themselves. Masters, in a sort of doppelgänger effect, felt as if his and the Japanese commander's moves were running in tandem, their minds linked together.

Casualties mounted on both sides in this war of attrition. The 'fit' men from two Cameronian companies went out sixty-three strong. The next day four were able to move. Unsurprisingly there were signs that the men were not prepared to go on fighting. Acts of conspicuous gallantry took place, sometimes born of desperation. Masters records such moments in *Road Past Mandalay* in a suitably staccato style: 'All the men sleepwalking. Mules struggling up with wire just received by a supply drop down on the plateau. Ammunition needed. A Japanese counter-attack, heavy and well-supported. Destroy it. Again. Same. We are supposed to push on down towards the valley. The King's do so. Meet more Japanese, are stopped. Where the hell are they coming from? Sapper havildar runs into position, hands at throat, blood pouring out. Was setting booby traps, a grenade went off. David Wallace, sapper captain, kneels beside the writhing, dying body, weeping tears of love and rage.' Its relentless, all-consuming aspect was the rough edge of war.

The struggle for Point 2171 ended when an assault by 3rd Battalion 9th Gurkhas under Alec Harper captured it. Almost immediately afterwards they got orders to pull out, in spite of its costly acquisition. Masters, keenly aware of his brigade's deteriorating condition, kept sending in requests to Lentaigne to have it medically examined, as disease and foot-rot increased. Masters's request was refused initially. He sensed Stilwell's hand behind this and, livid at the inference they were malingering, threatened to hand over his command. His brigade, he affirmed, had a dietary deficiency of over 800 calories per day, its average weight loss was between 30 and 40 lb. All men not fit for action should be evacuated at once.

Masters never lost his grip, however much he may have 'bellyached like mad.' He went on giving orders, like the highly professional soldier he was. The realist in him knew how his men were feeling. Rhodes-James remembered: 'We just staggered around and I think it is to Jack's credit that he kept on pressing HQ and saying "We can't do any more."' Loyalty, especially when his back was to the wall, was a trait he understood and shared with his men. It never wavered.

A week later his demands for a medical examination were granted, and were carried out over the next three days in the jungle. Out of two thousand men, those judged fit for further action numbered one hundred and eighteen: Masters, seven British officers, twenty British soldiers and ninety Gurkhas. Those unfit were permitted to move west towards Kamaing where they would be picked up and flown to safety. Masters, in keeping with his punctilious sense of duty and partly out of pique, requested orders for the remainder, now reduced to a company. Whether Stilwell recognised the sarcasm or not, he promptly signalled Masters to join and cover a battery of Chinese medium artillery at Pahok. When they got there, the Chinese were not interested or pleased. Not to be bested, Masters insisted on reorganising their defences for them, and keeping guard for the next ten days. Mogaung eventually fell and with that, orders for 111 Brigade to leave Burma came through. They marched through Mogaung to be flown out from the airfield there. It was 1 August. They had been in the field since early March, five months in all and two more than was originally agreed.

No episode in the whole war in Burma has given rise to as much controversy as the second Chindit operation. Was it worth it? Did it achieve its aims? In terms of loss of life and materials, it could be deemed a failure. In terms of morale, it was clearly a success; it gave heart to British soldiers and politicians alike. In military terms, it paved the way for later airborne operations in the war. The crucial factor was its change of use after Wingate's death, when it came under Stilwell's direction. Most commentators now feel that had Wingate lived he would have pulled his Chindits out rather than see them deployed in this inappropriate – and opportunistic – way.

Post-war evidence from the opposing Japanese commanders shows that the Japanese were, in fact, much more inconvenienced by these 'airborne troops' than was originally thought. Their supply lines to the crucial battles at Kohima and Imphal were badly dented, a factor which may well have contributed to their subsequent defeat there. According to Mutaguchi, the Japanese commander of their 15th Army, the whole of the 53rd Division had to be diverted to confront the Chindits away from northern Burma, which may have 'swung the balance' against him when those major battles started.

Much of the controversy surrounds the enigmatic and abrasive figure of Wingate, whose eccentric and unconventional approach infuriated most of his colleagues when he was alive, just as it may have infuriated official military historians subsequently, reluctant as they often are to praise mavericks. Masters was later to think of writing a biography of Wingate, part in admiration of his 'striking mental power' and what Mountbatten termed his 'wild enthusiasm' and part in criticism of 'the intolerably aggressive confidence of a prophet' and questioning some of his military judgement. However, he could not get authorisation from the family and it came to nothing.

From Burma Masters went to the army base at Dehra Dun in India. He wrote his Battle Report. The unkind said this is how he got his DSO. He took great trouble sending letters to relatives of the dead, a personal letter to the next of kin of every officer killed under his command, agonising over the wording, which was doubly difficult when some had been killed by crates of 'flying fruit' on supply drops. Then he went straight to join Barbara in Gulmarg, Kashmir. She had been there since July, partly to meet her husband to discuss details of their divorce, which he had finally agreed to. Masters took his fellow Chindits Douglas Larpent and Doc Whyte with him. He saw his six-month-old daughter Susan for the first time. Barbara had her other two children with her, Liz now aged six and Mike aged four. She looked fitter than when he had last seen her, tanned by the mountain air, which had put colour into her cheeks. He was thrilled to see her. He hugged his daughter tight, but he was still too pent-up after the Chindit campaign to allow a full release of his emotions. It was a poignant moment for Larpent and Whyte, who had children of their own in England whom they had not seen for four years.

Gulmarg, 31 miles north of Srinagar, was an attractive and much-frequented hill-station, whose name means 'meadow of flowers'. Masters breathed in great lungfuls of fresh, invigorating mountain air and preferred to stay outside the house as much as possible after the claustrophobic atmosphere of Burma. He was glad Doc Whyte and Larpent had come with him. They had been through so much together; now they could unwind in each other's company, talking about the campaign. It provided a necessary safety net.

Yet often, in the middle of the night, Barbara found him waking up, shouting out names and calling out orders. His mind still had not freed itself from the war. Memories came flooding back, particularly 'send your best man' or the dreadful images of the wounded. Barbara, supportive as ever, tried to calm him down, but it would be months, years even, before these recurrent nightmares disappeared. His weight during the campaign had gone down to 9 st 10 lb and his appetite, usually so good, was patchy. Doc Whyte diagnosed jaundice. The best remedy seemed to be the long walks or rides along bridle paths in the pine forests above Gulmarg. Masters even attempted a round of golf, not a game he ever excelled at, but it was exercise none the less. Gradually his tension eased and he began to relax.

In his quieter moments, sometimes when he could not sleep at night, Barbara and he talked. They thought back to their time in the Kaghan Valley and his vow not to lose the personal touch. Had his being thrust into command diminished this in any way? He was a better soldier, he knew that, and his closeness to his men and his empathy with them had been a crucial factor in the orderly withdrawal from Blackpool. He liked to think some of their selfless courage and willingness to endure had rubbed off on him, and he felt a bigger person as a result. It had enlarged his sense of humanity. War for all its horrors brought with it a certain nobility of spirit. Yet nothing could erase the pain of the needless deaths. Each time a man under his command died, he felt he died a bit too. 'No man is an island entire of itself', he repeated over and over again to himself.

Barbara had made sacrifices on his behalf and had shown herself willing to make further ones. She had given him a child and a sense of future. Having a child gave him the feeling that 'in an odd and special way I felt I had physically absorbed something of all men and all women.' We can see here the beginnings of the novelist, participating and registering the full drama of events but retaining that 'splinter of ice in the heart' that Graham Greene spoke of as a necessary detachment.

The month's leave in Gulmarg sped by and early in September he returned to 111 Brigade at their base in Central Provinces. He was promoted to lieutenant-colonel and was put in command of 3rd Battalion 4th Gurkha Rifles, after the previous commander, Monteaith, was killed near Myitkina in June. They were now training for 'another show', the proposed next Chindit operation in south Burma. Barbara came down from the hills and found a bungalow at Saugor nearby. The training went on for some three months. Then, in January 1945, Mountbatten called the top Chindit officers together at Latipur Airfield and told them the Chindits were being disbanded; the resources needed to support a Chindit operation would be better diverted to the main army. Their formations were to be broken up and they were to be returned to their regiments. However, Masters was too valuable a commodity to be let go and five days later he got a telegram posting him as General Staff Officer, Grade 1, to the 19th Indian Infantry Division, then part of 33 Corps operating in Burma.

It meant that he would be parting from his Gurkhas. Their gentle and touching ceremonial of leave-taking moved him deeply. Flowers were strewn in the dust and every jemadar and havildar came forward with a garland to hang round his neck. It revived the old conflict between loyalty to the call of a higher command and human warmth. Masters, now just over thirty, was undoubtedly making rapid progress, already having commanded a brigade of over two thousand men in the field. His new appointment looked to be a chance to prove himself further. It was bound to be a tough assignment as Major-General Pete Rees, under whose command he was being put, had the reputation of a 'ruthless fire-eater'. He had managed to get through no less than thirteen GIs in the previous year – not the most reassuring piece of news to start with, but Masters was ready for the challenge. Deep down he knew his relationships with Weallens, Roberts and Lentaigne had shown he could work closely and effectively as a number two.

He set off by train from Saugor. Leaving Barbara, after this reunion, was almost more difficult than at any other time. The war in Burma

H.Q. Fourteenth Army,
S.E.A.C.   9 Sep 44.

Dear Major Masters,

    I am very pleased to hear that your gallant action has been rewarded, and send you my warmest congratulations on a well deserved honour.

          Yours sincerely,

Offg   General Officer Commanding-in-Chief,
                Fourteenth Army.

was in full spate and, although the Japanese were on the run, the outcome was still uncertain. Japanese resistance was unpredictable and the war might prolong itself indefinitely. After so much sacrifice on her part, it would be cruel indeed if he were to be a casualty at this late stage.

From Calcutta he flew into Burma, to a point some 100 miles south of where the Chindits had operated. He found Rees typically close to the front line, a striking figure only 5 ft 2 in tall, but a human dynamo. He was wearing his Gurkha hat with its gold general's badge prominently displayed and a huge red silk scarf; both items were clearly visible to the enemy some 200 yards away. His divisional pennant with the dagger after which the division was named fluttered just as prominently from the top of his Jeep's radio mast. But Rees seemed to lead a charmed life, and had the luck of all successful generals. He always led from the front and was famed for his conspicuous bravery, determined not to repeat his experience of the First World War, when he had watched generals order men into battle from safe positions far behind the lines. He was, so the story went, all set to win Burma single-handed. Masters was instantly drawn to him; Rees's panache and flamboyance touched off a latent chord in himself.

19th Indian Infantry Division were at Singu on the Irrawaddy bridgehead making top speed south for Mandalay, approximately 40 miles away. Rees liked to improvise tactics on the run, rarely abiding by the rule book. Quick and incisive, intolerant of fools or shirking, he demanded instant loyalty from his subordinates. Masters knew where he stood. Once again his competence as a staff officer was being called into play. He felt fit and healthy again, having recovered sufficiently from his Chindit ordeal some five months back. He was now eager for action and was encouraged to find around him men who were fired up by Rees's dashing leadership.

Rees called him to his quarters one night, and, sitting on a stone platform by a small pagoda on the banks of the Irrawaddy, went through the details of the next stage of their advance towards Mandalay. A bottle of whisky was produced and a huge cake, both items which were regularly sent out from England at fortnightly intervals by Rees's wife. Masters put forward a suggestion to use side roads, cart tracks and village paths as quicker than staying on the cluttered and dusty main highway. It was 3 a.m. by the time they had finished. Rees went to bed but Masters stayed up to put the plan into coherent shape. The beam of pleasure from Rees that greeted him in the morning and the alacrity with which Rees seized upon his plan showed Masters he had been readily accepted.

As they neared Mandalay, Rees was told to slow down, as he was getting too far ahead of the rest of Slim's 14th Army. Rees flew out to protest. He would be away for six hours. Masters assumed that a senior brigadier would take over in his absence. Not a bit of it. Rees, with a twinkle in his eye, told him he was in command of the whole division during his absence, some fifteen thousand men.

'Those six hours were the summit and culmination of my military life', Masters was to write later. By now he had an intimate knowledge of how Rees's mind worked, and knew what to do when the few occasions demanding positive decisions came up. But it was a supreme moment for other reasons. This time he really had been entrusted with command, in a way that was different from Blackpool. It was not just the size of the command that mattered, but the feeling of trust that went with it. At Blackpool, unexpected events had dictated his sudden elevation, and his frustration with Force HQ and Stilwell had kept him charged up. Here Rees seemed to value Masters for himself and for his ability, and had handed him his mantle, albeit temporarily. Masters, consciously or not, notes the symbolism of this moment. He refers to Rees's shaping of the 19th Indian Division as being 'like a sword in his hand', and 'it was Pete who had made and tempered it', and after Rees returned, 'I handed it back to him with pride that he had allowed me to wield it.' The Oedipal, and phallic, overtones are unmistakable. He continued, 'Twice the dialled face of the radio tempted me in moments of petty crisis. I had only to pick up the microphone and ask for Daddy, and all would be well.' The implication here is that Rees was the sort of father figure he had been seeking all along.

Rees won his fight with Corps HQ, and the advance continued. At one point they were held up by an unfordable stream. Rees made his sappers heave some three-ton tanks on their sides so that other tanks could drive across them. The engineer officer protested at such a waste of materials, but was vividly rebuked. Soon the 1,000-foot high, lion-like bulk of Mandalay Hill appeared, with its wreath of pagodas on the summit. On 10 March the main assault began. Rees told a Gurkha battalion under Hamish Mackay to lead the way. Mackay knew these buildings from his pre-war days in the Burma Rifles. All night they fought up the steep ridge, honeycombed with hillside temples linked to underground cellars and passageways, and filled with Japanese snipers. It took two days to flush them out before they finally cleared the summit. Rees and Masters stood on the highest point of Mandalay Hill, looking down on the city and the palace of the ancient kings of Burma, battered by three years of war. Below was the massive Fort Dufferin, with the wide yellow Irrawaddy to the right. Rees, conscientious as ever, made sure that as little damage as possible was done to sacred buildings.

At Mandalay Masters collected his mail. Barbara wrote with relief that her divorce had at last been made final at the beginning of March, even though she had to agree to give up the care of her two children by Rose, who had gone to England. This was Hugh Rose's condition for letting her keep Susan, who was legally his child. It had been a long and drawn-out struggle. Rees asked Masters why he was looking so moonstruck. He explained about the divorce. Rees told him to go and get married, and be back in ten days' time. There was a lull in the campaign and the big battle would be at Meiktila further south in about two weeks. Masters took him at his word and set off back to India, hitching a lift in Corps Commander General Stopford's plane which took him to Shwebo. There he got another lift on a USAF C-47 to Chittagong in India, and then another USAF plane to Barrackpore, this time through storms and lightning, followed by a night flight to Allahabad arriving at 3 a.m., just in time to pick up the Calcutta mail train that stopped conveniently at the small junction of Katni, a few miles from Saugor. Altogether it was a remarkable forty-hour journey from Mandalay to Saugor, 'from the smell of death to the smell of a drowsy, startled woman.' He was repaying Barbara for her own epic journey to Rawalpindi across the Indus three years before.

They were married four days later in Saugor on 18 March by the deputy commissioner. Two battalion commanders from 111 Brigade, still waiting to be disbanded, were witnesses, and their daughter Susan attended too – as Masters put it, not realising the unorthodoxy of her position – and enjoyed the occasion enormously. They held a small party afterwards and a three-day honeymoon was all they had time for, staying in the bungalow Barbara had taken in Haig Road and content to be with each other at last. They discussed future plans more confidently now, with the end of the war seemingly in sight. For Barbara this was the culmination of all the risks she had taken. She and Masters had their own child, but Barbara was still heartbroken at having to yield up the care of her two other children, without knowing for sure whether she might see them again. In the heat and pressure of war she felt she had little option. It was a sacrifice for love. With Masters by her side, she felt better and confident that things would work themselves out in the long run. She recognised that few people would have taken so bold a step as she had in walking out on Hugh with few prospects ahead, but for her that was infinitely preferable to staying in an unhappy marriage. Other Indian Army wives might have acted differently, and, as she put it, cried silently at night into their pillows. For her, life was too short and she had to seize her chance. As she said recently, looking back to those years, 'I drive cars that way. I see an opportunity and I take it, driving through a narrow gap. I make up my own mind very quickly and stick to it. Jack was like that too, which is probably why we got on so well.'

When Masters returned to Rees's division in Mandalay, the last phase of the Burma campaign was under way – the race to Rangoon before the monsoon broke in May. It was known as SOB ('Sea or Bust'). Slim's 'forgotten' 14th Army had been transformed into a vivid extension of his own personality. 'Brilliant, bold, publicising himself only to his troops and then only so that they should have confidence in him, he seldom made a mistake or missed an opportunity through the war and when he did he said so', was how Masters summarised him after the war. Slim was definitely one of his heroes. They had met briefly in Iraq in 1941 and were to meet again during this phase of the campaign. Slim and Rees were both exceptional leaders, and Masters counted himself lucky to be serving under them both. There is an attractive vignette of them shortly after the fall of Mandalay when Slim visited Rees and found him vigorously singing Welsh missionary hymns with a group of Assamese soldiers. 'The fact that he sang in Welsh and they in Khasi only added to the harmony', Slim commented, admiringly. 'My generals had character. Their men knew them and they knew their men.' It was true, every fighting man knew Rees by sight and admired and trusted him.

Rangoon was still 30 miles further south, thirty days to go before the monsoon. Meiktila was taken and the Japanese retreated further, putting up pockets of resistance wherever they went. Suicide squads waited in foxholes in the middle of the road with bombs held between their knees ready to blow up any passing tank. Sometimes the Japanese rearguard lagged behind and was overrun. In Pyinmana a Japanese traffic policeman was still on duty when the British tanks rolled in and the leading tank simply ran over him.

Masters was at the forefront and was memorably present at the historic moment when Slim let slip the final advance to Rangoon. 'I stood back wishing I had a camera as Slim, 4 Corps Commander, Frank Messervy, and three divisional commanders watched the leading division crash past the starting point.' Masters gives it the full treatment in *Road Past Mandalay*. 'The dust thickened under the trees lining the road until the column was motoring into a thunderous yellow tunnel, first the tanks, infantry all over them, then trucks filled with men, then more tanks going nose to tail, guns, more trucks, more guns – British, Sikhs, Gurkhas, Madrassis, Pathans, Americans, most of the soldiers were on their feet, cheering and yelling. The Gurkhas, of course, went by stiffly to attention, whole truckloads bouncing four feet in the air without change of expression . . .'

It was a picture that encapsulates both the final stages of the war in Burma and a unique moment both for Masters and the Indian Army. His description of it is as vivid as any he wrote: 'This was the old Indian Army going down to the attack for the last time in history, exactly two hundred and fifty years after the Honourable East India Company had enlisted its first ten sepoys on the Coromandel Coast.' It was a moment for him to savour, and was especially significant because of his family's long link with India. This was the last show of the war, the last time that he would be part of this 'band of brothers'. 'I and my forefathers, and hundreds like us, had worked for generations in India. Certainly we had been masters, and imperialists, but we had not been afraid to die with these men and we had always loved them and their country, usually with an intense, blind passion which could ignore all theoretical considerations of right and wrong.' Here was the very heart of Masters's attachment to India, the emotional, in-the-blood, tie.

As he watched the troops go by, he could only feel that the British presence in India had been justified. Domination was 'almost immaterial' to the heart of the matter, which was 'love and understanding, or loyalty to each other, or faith in each other's intentions, or whatever you like to call an almost mystical sense of dependence.' To our post-imperial ears such sentiments may seem unduly romantic, bordering on the paternalistic, but they are a distinct clue to Masters's viewpoint. His attachment to India was a deeply-felt and passionate one, not always clearly understood by him, nor even consistent, but intense, and long-lasting, and informing so much of what he believed in. India was full of ambiguity, and so was his response.

The 'mystical sense of dependence' constituted both the fascination and enigma of India for him. War and his experience of soldiering had only strengthened this. Now as he stood watching these 'twenty races, a dozen religions, a score of languages' passing by, it became a sort of valedictory farewell: 'India stood, at last, independent, proud, and incredibly generous to us, on these final battlefields in the Burmese plain.' The imperial days of 'miraculous sympathy' and 'brutal folly' were over, not necessarily forgotten, but also not likely to come back. The Indian Army had been Masters's home and he had valued it like a prized possession. He had reason to be proud of it. The Indian Army was bound together by its unique code of honour shared by Christian, Hindu and Muslim alike, and arguably it has been the most durable and remarkable of Britain's imperial creations. For all its apparent dissimilarity of peoples, it had survived through this special combination of love, distance and misunderstanding. For Masters the Indian Army had been his lifeblood, and here he was witnessing its demise. 'My India went down the road to Rangoon.'

The fighting went on and 19th Division pursued the Japanese down the Mawchi Road and to Toungoo. The war competed in his thoughts with Barbara. The repercussions of her divorce were still with him. Being named as co-respondent might still jeopardise his military future. He talked about it to Pete Rees, who gave him his support, and then decided to write a confidential memo to 19th Division HQ. His memo read:

> As I might be called upon to resign my commission unless there are good reasons to the contrary, I beg to give the following reasons:
> (a) Lt-Col Rose 3GR is the petitioner.
> (b) Separation had been discussed by Lt-Col Rose and his wife before I met either.
> (c) As can be appreciated there are many aspects in such cases, including cruelty.
> (d) I am now married to the lady who was Mrs Rose and as far as I am concerned the case is closed.
> (e) At this stage of the war it is impossible to foresee the future of any officer, particularly post-war, and I have every desire to continue in the service at present.

Rees backed this up with his own testimonial: 'In view of the uncertainty, due to war, of the future both as regards individuals and the Indian Army as a whole, also the difficulty of obtaining full facts in such cases, particularly in present circumstances, I do not recommend that Lt-Col J. Masters be called upon to resign his commission. He has rendered, and is rendering, valuable service to his country.' There were anxious times as Masters waited for a response. He had clearly contravened the prevailing code, but it had been a peacetime code. Whether it would be the same in war, he would have to wait and see. An encouragement of sorts could be got from the fact that Auchinleck's wife was about to be involved in divorce proceedings. Eventually a message came back in July from HQ 4 Corps telling him that 'this matter has been before HE C in C INDIA [Auchinleck] who has decided that Lt-Col Masters should not be called upon to resign his commission.' It was an enormous relief, and Masters approached the end of the campaign in Burma with a much lighter heart.

Rangoon fell at the beginning of May. The monsoon had already broken and the Japanese had fled, as a pilot reconnoitring in advance of the troops discovered. A slogan on the roof of Rangoon jail which served as a POW camp read: JAPS GONE PULL FUCKING FINGER OUT. The fighting now concentrated in the hills to the east, the Pegu Yomas, from where the Japanese hoped to escape to Siam. They fought a desperate rearguard action, with much loss of life.

The statistics for July alone show the Japanese had eleven and a half thousand killed as against ninety-six in the 14th Army.

Masters was tiring. He had been on the go for four months, with only a brief break. He told Rees he feared he might soon make a serious, even costly, mistake. Rees agreed to give him three months' leave as soon as his G1 replacement could be found, but he asked him to be sure to come back to 19th Indian Division afterwards. Masters agreed, aware that he had grown in stature and in outlook through Rees's influence. He knew now that he counted and was worth something in his own right. 'This mattered, this above all, always. It had taken a long time, and I had waded through seas of blood to learn it, but I had got it now, once and for all.' Now in his thirty-first year, he stood back for a moment's assessment. He had achieved much of what he had set out to do, was high-up with a promising military career ahead and, as he entered his thirties, was embarking on an era of responsibility, and of family ties. This seemed right.

Just before he left to go on leave, he received a signal asking if he was available to command a parachute brigade about to be sent to Malaya. His Chindit experience stood him in good stead for this, though he had no love of parachuting. The Far Eastern war looked like it would be prolonged; the European theatre had already ceased with the German surrender on 7 May. Masters thought about this offer, flattered and secretly pleased at being chosen by high command, but he declined it. He knew it would be a mistake, as he desperately needed to rest and, besides, he had given his word to Rees to return to 19th Indian Division.

Two days later he was in Rangoon harbour aboard the troopship *Devonshire* – coincidentally, the same as had taken him to Basra in 1941 – bound now for Calcutta. On the ship's radio mention was made of the General Election in Britain which had taken place on 5 July. Churchill had been defeated in a landslide victory for Labour and with him much of the old imperial idea had gone, especially so far as India was concerned. Churchill represented the old order. Had he not said in 1937: 'I want to see the British Empire present for a few more generations in its strength and splendour'? But the electorate were clearly tired of such attitudes, representative of the officer class they knew during the war. They wanted a change and the incoming Attlee government promised to 'do our utmost to promote in conjunction with the leaders of Indian opinion the early realisation of full self-government in India.' All that lay ahead, but for the moment Masters's thoughts were all for his wife and child.

*

Barbara was up in Ranikhet, a hill station near Mussorie at the foot of the Garhwal Himalayas, up in the cool air of the hills again. Masters wrote to his old Chindit colleague, Tim Brennan, of the Cameronians, describing his mood.

> I am on ninety days' leave at the moment, hence feeling pretty good and carefree, what with no damned telephones and miles of Tibet and my honey's loving arms stretching before me – it's almost like reliving. I had a damned hard job getting away from Burma, not physically but mentally – as two days ago I was offered a chance, a 90 per cent certainty, of a job that would have suited me down to the ground, with a little promotion thrown in. But I'm taking this leave because I think I need it, and after an awful mental tussle I refused to be considered.

This was the Malaya offer, and the letter shows once again the conflicts between ambition and personal satisfaction.

Barbara and he stayed at the Hotel Norbus in Ranikhet. Their plan was to walk in the Garhwal hills above, leaving Susan with her ayah at a friend's house in Ranikhet. They set off on 6 August with fourteen porters and enough pack ponies to carry food, clothing and tents. 'This was the life. No one here but Barbara and me, and cool air and weary legs.' The Garhwal mountains are among the most impressive of the Himalayas. Trisul, the three-peaked mountain, stands some 23,000 feet high, above the famed Valley of Flowers described by the mountaineer Frank Smythe, who wrote of the region: 'in scenery and climate Garhwal is comparable to Switzerland at its best and no district in the Himalayas can show scenery combining such tender beauties and savage grandeur.' Beyond Trisul lie the holy shrines of Josimath and Badrimath dedicated to the Hindu God Vishnu, and beyond them Gangotri, revered as the source of the Ganges. This was their ultimate destination.

It was a repeat of the Kaghan in many ways, especially the combination of exercise and outstanding natural beauty. It might have seemed strange that Masters wanted to spend his leave walking when he had done so much time on his feet in Burma, but what mattered to him was the absolute peace to be found in the mountains and the welcome distraction of occupying his mind with planning their route and looking after the porters. For all that, the war would not leave him alone. Around each bend in the track he imagined a potential enemy; each hill was sized up for its tactical value. They stayed, as they had in the Kaghan, in Forest Rest Houses, redolent of seasoned wood with their ever-present yellowing copies of *Punch*. Then, as they moved higher, they slept under canvas, Barbara admitting somewhat ruefully that she had never slept in a tent before. Masters, protectively, was pleased to show her. Their first objective was a small hidden lake on the western face of Trisul some 17,000 feet up. The black lake, or tarn, turned out to be full of skulls, the legacy of ancient burial rites. To Masters this was an oppressive reminder of war and they hurried away. Then one of the porters fell into the fast running river from a swaying suspension bridge and was swept downstream and only just rescued in time. Death was, it seemed, stalking them even here.

It rained much of the time that August but they kept up their schedule on the walk. They were relieved to be away on their own, far from everyday worries. They lived on tins of sardines and bully beef, and a sort of spinach dish their cook made out of tomato tops. Once Masters shot a pheasant and they made a special meal out of it with wild raspberries plucked from the hillside. Occasionally nomadic shepherds from Tibet, laden with salt, borax and jade, and whistling their haunting songs that sounded like a mixture of hawk and flute, passed them.

As he walked Masters reflected on his last few years. Fleeting snapshots came to mind:

> Willy Weallens walking down the road, the shells bursting round him, smiling encouragement. Michael Roberts alert on the mountain, quick of voice – 'There, we'll hold that.' Joe Lentaigne, eyes agleam, riding a Jeep like a bronco; grim and tired against Stilwell. At the Staff College, the harsh opening chords of the *Eroica* melting into the first theme, the faces soft in the dim light and the wind from Central Asia rattling the windows. Desmond Whyte, Douglas Larpent, Tim Brennan, his thick hair tousled, running down into the Deep positions at Blackpool in the dusk, Mohbat Singh going up to 2171. General Pete's suddenly hard voice, 'Who's winning this war?'

Such flashbacks punctuated the calm of their walks, and he was storing them away as experience. His impressionistic evocation of them appears later in *Road Past Mandalay*, yet these images were already taking shape as part of his keen observation of his surroundings.

On 19 August they reached Josimath and looked for the Government Rest House. They knocked on a door to make inquiries and it turned out to be the house of a south Indian rawal, or high priest, who lived there in retirement. He ushered them in and offered them tea. Glancing at a newspaper lying on the table, they saw the astounding headline ATOMIC BOMB DROPPED ON JAPAN. It was the first they heard of it and it took them some time to digest the news properly. For

Masters it held a special irony. Here he was a professional soldier and practically the last person on earth to hear about it. The prospect of the war ending brought mixed feelings: relief certainly that he and Barbara could be together and with Susan, but also a mingled sadness at having to give up the close comradeship of colleagues he had got to know so well. They thought of celebrating, but it all seemed so far away and distant, and this was such an unlikely setting. With so much uncertainty, they knew they ought to cut short their walking tour, and they headed back to Ranikhet.

There was mail waiting for them at Josimath. Pete Rees wrote describing his recent visit to England, where he was acclaimed as the hero and captor of Mandalay. Rees had returned to 19th Division and Masters's replacement G1 was about to leave. He wrote: 'We miss you very much – I particularly. And this will only too inadequately carry you my very, very real thanks for all you have done for the Dagger Division and for me personally. I think you know how much I appreciate it all and how grateful I am. Here's hoping I'll yet soldier with you again and that you'll go on as you so deserve. Again thank you very much! I shall always look back with pleasure at working with such a thruster. God bless! TWR'. High praise indeed from so senior a commander, and it moved Masters deeply. Their paths were not to cross again. Rees was to take charge of the Indo-Pakistan border at the time of Partition in 1947 at a crucial and volatile moment in Indian history.

Rees also mentioned in his letter that he had run into Masters's parents in England, at Charmouth in Dorset where he had gone down to make a speech on the Far Eastern situation. 'And who should be in the front row but your father and mother? So I had to be pretty careful not to tell any lies different from yours! Your mother was very nice to me and she sends you all the motherly greetings you can imagine.'

By the time they returned to Ranikhet, it was 7 September. Masters calculated that their walking had covered 203 miles in thirty-two days and they had climbed a total of 52,000 feet. He noted this in a log he kept of the whole trip, the first of many such logs he was to keep on future journeys.

DELHI
1945–1946

In Ranikhet, a few days later, an express letter dated 14 September arrived for Masters at the Hotel Norbus from GHQ Delhi: 'T/Lt Col Masters requested to report to DMO GHQ NEW DELHI on expiry of his leave to assume duties as G.S.O. 1, M.O. DTE GHQ.' This new appointment was a staff posting and a very good one at that – GSO1 (General Staff Officer, 1st grade) to the MO (Military Operations) DTE (Directorate) – pretty much at the centre of things in the Defence Department in Delhi. He was to start at the beginning of October.

The Japanese had surrendered on 14 August, and news now reached Masters of the release of his brother Alex from the notorious Changi Prisoner of War Camp in Singapore. Alex was at Bangalore in a resettlement camp. Masters invited his brother to stay with Barbara and him once they got to Delhi. In best fraternal fashion, he tells him not to be 'too enthusiastic about the beautiful nurses in Bangalore' since he felt sure that 'Ma has a nice girl lined up for you at home', adding that she is probably the same one she had lined up for him before the war, 'but I expect you'll do even better, being at least four inches longer!' Penile advantage was on Alex's side. Masters promised that in Delhi, 'Barbara, whom of course you haven't yet met, will feed you up and you can make yourself useful by taking Susan to pee when she says "Soo-Soo" and looks a bit worried.'

In Delhi they were able to share a house with Peter Cane, a fellow Chindit and an old friend from Sandhurst days. The house was too big for him on his own and centrally-located, and he was quite happy for them to move in too. Cane was also working in the Defence Department at South Block in the Mall, part of the massive, pink sandstone buildings designed by Lutyens that housed the government offices in Delhi. Masters's immediate boss there was Roddy McLeod, a 'bald, burly youngish Brigadier of Royal Artillery, with bulging forehead, magnificently incisive intelligence, markedly abrasive personality, and a total inability to suffer fools.' He was the Director of Military Operations. Masters's main tasks were concerned with the post-war military rearrangements as they affected India Command.

The Defence Department overall was under Auchinleck, Commander-in-Chief of the Indian Army, a popular figure with a deep love of India. McLeod soon put Masters to work and would ask him at very short notice to draw up a detailed note for the Commander-in-Chief. This meant compressing information on a single sheet of paper. Sometimes he had no more than a six-hour deadline. These reports became an object lesson for Masters in accurate and precise writing. He developed a technique of going straight to the point, editing the first draft rigorously, moving on to a second rewrite, then submitting the finished product to Roddy McLeod. 'Having my papers gone over by Roddy was rather like being bombarded by a howitzer at five feet range.' McLeod would pick out a sentence and tear it mercilessly to pieces. Words had to have exact meanings. Masters was told, 'the Chief doesn't have time to work out your meaning, you've got to make it clear.' Soon he learnt to dispense with excessive adjectives and adverbs. Verbs were what counted. McLeod's words stayed ringing in his ears: 'Don't ask the C-in-C questions, Jack. Tell him the military alternatives and the probable consequences of each, with a single clear recommendation.' It was an ideal proving ground for the future writer.

Topics of the reports included the future composition of the Indian Army and its reduction to a peacetime establishment. This was no easy task, as during the war the Indian Army had increased twelvefold from one hundred and fifty thousand to one million eight hundred thousand men – each one a volunteer – and there were nearly sixteen thousand Indian commissioned officers, as opposed to less than a thousand at the outset of the war. The war, understandably, had given the Indians a taste of running things their own way and they were keen to continue to do so. Wavell, the Viceroy, had foreseen this. The termination of the war and general demobilisation would create large scale unemployment and discontent, hence his efforts to bring together the leaders of Congress and the Muslim League to work out, co-operatively, the problems of Independence.

As Independence loomed, though its exact shape was still unclear as late as 1946, the military were drawn more and more into the political arena. The beginning of 1946 saw the Royal Indian Navy Mutiny in Bombay in February. Auchinleck faced a tricky task of keeping the Indian Army out of threatening situations, while preparing for the handover of British formations to Indian ones, as the former were repatriated. Masters, though no clearer than anyone else about what precisely was going to happen, was luckier than most in that he was able to observe the development of events from close up, and it gave him an indication of where his own military future might lie.

Alex came to stay with Barbara and Masters in December. By then they had moved into their own house at 90 Lodi Road, New Delhi. This had a good sized garden, which pleased Barbara, and more than adequate servants' quarters. It was close to the Lodi Tombs, which Masters would bicycle past on his way to work. Alex, with his weight loss from his four years of captivity, was worried about being medically downgraded and not being able to continue with his regiment, 1st Gurkhas. Masters tried to give him as much reassurance as he could, but Alex had missed out on the war and on his chances of promotion as a result. It must have been hard for Alex to be with a brother who had done so conspicuously well, when he had suffered so badly during the war. Fortunately, his worst fears were unfounded and he rejoined his regiment at Razmak in April 1946, after a spell of leave in the UK.

The dominant issue in all their minds was what shape the forthcoming Independence of India would take. Attlee's Government sent out the Pethick-Lawrence Commission from England in March 1946 to consult and put forward its proposals. For one of their meetings, Masters was asked at short notice to produce a five-page paper on the strategic military implications of splitting India along partition lines. Masters went through his by now habitual all night routine, keeping his G2 majors on standby and his office clerks at the ready until his paper was completed. At the crack of dawn, he submitted it to McLeod, who then passed it up the line, where it received favourable commendations.

Masters's own view was that partition was militarily possible but unsound. The Indian Army had always managed to absorb its disparate groups and function as an integrated whole, with Hindu and Muslim troops serving in the same regiment. Masters's personal experience as a soldier told him this too. The Indian Army was a magnificent instrument that he hated to see broken up – a view shared by Auchinleck. Furthermore, India had always solved its problems historically through unity, which it had been part of the British achievement to perpetuate. Partition might be possible, but it needed time and careful planning. Masters sympathised with Wavell's argument that it would need at least two years to effect any such change and that it should be done gradually.

For Masters things seemed to be going well. His annual report for 1946 was written by Roddy McLeod.

> This officer is occupying a position of considerable responsibility and has shown unusual balance and common sense. He is young to be holding this appointment, but his comparative inexperience has proved no handicap. On the other hand his enthusiasm, energy and drive

have been welcome, and his progressive outlook on tactical and strategical problems has been most stimulating. He is occasionally apt to be over-critical of existing difficulties and to express himself on paper in a way which is inclined to irritate the recipient. This is solely due to reluctance to suffer fools gladly and is a fault which he is overcoming . . . He is constructive and practical and expresses his views very clearly. His relations with his subordinates are most satisfactory and he runs his Section as a happy team. He is always cheerful, whatever the pressure of work, and has a keen sense of humour. A very competent, loyal and progressive young staff officer.

But Masters's cheerfulness and sense of humour could go over the top. Not long after his arrival in Delhi, he had accompanied Auchinleck and a group of military high-ups to South Persia, to visit the Indian Long Range Desert Squadron still stationed there. The squadron was commanded by an old Quetta colleague of his, Tim Waddilove. Dinner that evening had the 'makings of a good regimental night.' At the end of the meal, aided by the mood of post-war euphoria, Masters and an American major danced uninhibitedly on a table top while giving a spirited rendition of 'Casey Jones'. Masters followed this up with his solo version of 'Who'll take the mail to Dead Man's Gulch?' The vodka continued to flow. 'The Auk' sat there watching all this, only just amused. Later he beckoned Masters over to talk to him and they reminisced about Wellington, where 'the Auk' had been in the same house, Beresford. His comment, so Masters reported, was 'You're the most extraordinary Old Wellingtonian I've ever come across.'

The incident shows Masters in an interesting light. With his new and responsible position in Delhi, he might have been more circumspect, especially in front of his commander-in-chief, but some of his lifelong need to shine in superior company came out. His behaviour was close to being outrageous; it certainly was not 'the done thing'. He seemed to need to push his performance to the edge of decency as a sort of challenge. There is a world of difference between singing Cockney songs with Goff Hamilton in the privacy of the Staff College and performing in front of his superiors. The former stayed within the tradition of becoming acceptably, if temporarily, déclassé, but in this instance his bawdiness came out partly from his urge to shock and partly to stake his difference. He was not going to be conventional and with the war over, he may subconsciously have been beginning to separate himself from established codes of behaviour. Yet the uneasy laughter which greeted his performance may have been, deep down, an echo of his own unease at not quite belonging.

It is an example of how he managed to arouse both resentment and envy in others, not just because he was cleverer than many of his colleagues, but because of his irrepressible uppishness. Fellow, often senior, officers looked down on him at times. They rarely forgot the 'country-born' legend, and for this Masters seemed to be singled out in a way that many others, in the Indian Army and elsewhere, who also had Indian ancestors, never were. Envy works insidiously, and in Masters's case the fact that he seemed to be getting away with it, and was showing himself to be a cut above, was not easily forgotten or forgiven.

For all that, such incidents never stopped him from getting on with his job and succeeding at it. In Delhi, part of his duties was to assess the implications of the eighty thousand British troops still in India from India Command's point of view. His counterparts in London complained that his reports seemed to be treating Britain as a hostile power. He saw his task differently. 'We were simply pressing India's interests, as we saw them, against anyone else's, including Britain's.' He did not find this difficult. On a personal level, India seemed as much home to him as Britain did. Moreover, Masters's family had worked there for over a hundred years, and, as part of the fifth generation to live there, he could be proud of the fact that he was now at the centre of power, at a time when power was important.

Masters's work continued to take him far afield. In April 1946, he went to Rangoon accompanying an India Office representative from London, Mo Mayne, who wanted to confer with the governor. Burma, for all the hard-fought campaign, was rapidly seceding from British influence. 'I was backed off at short notice and I am doing very little conferring but a great deal of drinking. The climate here in Burma is pretty bloody – hot and very sticky'. This was in a letter to Alex. Masters had re-established a regular correspondence with his brother, writing once a week. Further trips took him up to Assam to assess the effects of the war there and to the North-West Frontier, still as unpredictable as ever. With the war over, and prospects of more settled times ahead, Barbara had become pregnant again and the baby was due in mid-1946.

However uncertain the mood in Delhi, Masters was tempted to imagine staying on, even in a civilian capacity: 'Sunday lunches of lamb pilao, dal, curried vegetables, pink gins before; and afterwards a sleep on the grass under a tree while Susan crawled all over us and the kitten crawled over Susan; dances at the club, old jokes, old friends, British and Indian ... long leave to England, short leave trekking in the Himalayas.' His attachment to India was as strong as ever.

Meanwhile, events were closing in. At the beginning of June the

Cabinet Mission left India, having conceived a plan for a united India based on a federal structure. All that summer the political leaders of the Hindu and Muslim communities, Nehru and Jinnah, argued back and forth. At one point Congress, putting aside their suspicions of British intentions, had almost accepted the plan; at another, the Muslims nearly gave their consent. Wavell did his best to reconcile their differences, but distrust was in the air and both parties were intent on bolstering their own positions as much as negotiating for a settlement, and the shadow of a divided continent continued to fall over India. The two sides drew further apart. Communal hatred increased, culminating in the dreadful killings in Calcutta in mid-August when at least five thousand died in civil riots.

Masters's expectation at this stage was to stay on in the Indian Army. His Gurkha regiment was very much his emotional home. However, he knew from his job near the centre of power that nothing was safe, and thought it wise to look around for alternatives. Philip Mason was working near him at South Block in the Defence Department. He had just published his first book, *Call the Next Witness*, about a murder case in rural India. Mason showed him a copy and told him that he had decided to go back to England to become a full-time author. The thought may have crossed Masters's mind. He kept the dust jacket of Mason's second book, *The Wild Sweet Witch*, in his personal scrapbook in later years. The book was published in 1947, so it is possible its insertion in the scrapbook was an afterthought. Masters felt his best chances were to stay in the army one way or another. With the present turmoil in India, perhaps it would be better to return to the UK for a spell first. After all, neither he nor Barbara had been there for more than seven years. They could look around in England and then see how India fared after that. He made inquiries and discovered the post of Indian Army instructor at the Staff College, Camberley, would be vacant at the end of the year. It would be a prestigious appointment and, in career terms, a definite rung up the ladder. He put in his application for the one-year post.

With Delhi getting more oppressive by the day, Barbara, now very pregnant, went up to the cooler air of Ranikhet. The birth of their second child was due in July, and Masters planned to join them. As the time approached, he was suddenly sent to England on a short liaison mission, carrying confidential documents from Auchinleck to Montgomery, the new Chief of Imperial General Staff in London, about the transfer of power. His RAF plane flew a circuitous route, via Cairo, Gibraltar and then across Spain, a country he had never seen before. As he looked down out of the plane window, he noted the arid plains and mountainous regions below, and thought it looked good walking country and was struck by its resemblance to India. That flight became lodged in his memory.

Barbara gave birth to a son, Martin, on 21 July, while Masters was in England. He got a cable telling him the news. Once back in India he described it to Alex in a letter.

I got back here to Delhi last Monday evening after a most interesting but very wearing trip. Long distance flying is very tiring, especially as I am constitutionally unable to sleep in a chair. The cable to me was the first inkling that Barbara had produced. I got it on the 27th at Claygate [where he was staying with Barbara's mother, Mrs Allcard, whom he was meeting for the first time]. Well, they always say the husband is the last to find out. I had a pleasant time at home but no beat-ups. Mrs Allcard is very nice and looks surprisingly young – she is sixty-five. Pa and Ma came up and they all seemed to get on well together. Even Daddy went down with a swing and was calling her Kate by the time we had a drop of brandy in the evenings. I didn't see any shows or flicks as I was working too much by day and trotted back to Claygate in the evenings.

Masters was delighted to hear that he had succeeded in getting the appointment at Camberley. No doubt he was helped by his many favourable reports, as this was a coveted and much sought-after post among Indian Army officers, especially those forcibly seeking a new future. This meant the Masterses had to leave by the beginning of September. They started packing their possessions into crates and tea chests, sorting out the children's belongings, arranging for their cat Gladstone to come with them. It was a hectic business, and a saddening one in their few moments of rest. He was leaving India at a time of unrest and uncertainty, and could not be sure when he would be back again. A round of goodbyes followed in a general atmosphere of excitement, anxiety, fear and hope.

On 5 September, the Masterses took the train to Bombay. The heat there was appalling and the two children cried all the way. They then had to wait for two days, staying at a small and uncomfortable hotel near the docks, until their ship was ready to sail on 8 September. The heat and humidity increased and Masters was distressed to be leaving India in this inglorious way. Their ship was the *Empress of Scotland*, and was, in fact, the former *Empress of Japan* which had taken him to Japan in 1938, now understandably renamed. It had become a grim troopship, and conditions were cramped and uncomfortable. Men and women were separated, and Barbara had to stay with the children in second class. The men on board got far better treatment. The colonel in charge on the ship seemed to take the view that fighting men needed pampering. Masters had his first-class cabin with two others, while Barbara, Susan and Martin were squeezed into a second-class one with umpteen others. There was a constant shortage of hot water to wash nappies in, and since it was mostly only available at lunchtimes, Barbara usually had to miss lunch.

Susan fell ill briefly and her temperature soared at one point to 106°F. That was bad enough, but Barbara felt so worn out that, with the strain of trying to feed Martin under these conditions, her milk gave out. To compound matters, the ship's officers turned the boat's clocks back one hour each day as they headed west. The babies naturally could not adjust to this and cried and howled at the wrong times of day and night. All in all it was a horrendous journey. Even the decks provided little recreational space, cramped and crowded as they were with returning soldiers.

The ship headed through the Mediterranean and past the Rock of Gibraltar, non-stop to Liverpool. Their thoughts turned more and more to England. Masters, now aged thirty-one, had spent relatively little time in England, twelve years as opposed to the nineteen years in India.

They steamed up the Mersey, where the weather was more wintery. A yellowish fog hung over Liverpool. It was raining. On the quayside, there was no one to greet them and their train was visible a long way from the pier. They had to carry their own luggage to it; Masters made five trips in all, while Barbara consoled the upset children. The train then set off for London, but was soon held up at Addison Road Station for an hour or more. No food or drink were provided and the floor looked unwashed. By now it was midnight. The train finally started slowly to move; the seats were mostly full. 'I got the message and, mentally folding my medals, my rank, and my beautiful record away into a trunk, went to sleep on the floor.' They had arrived back in post-war England, hardly a land fit for heroes.

ENGLAND
1946–1948

The Masters family went to stay with Barbara's mother, Ethel Allcard, at Greystones, Red Lane, Claygate, until their accommodation at the Staff College in Camberley was ready in December. Their bungalow was a long wooden shack originally built as a hospital ward, with a central passage and rooms leading off it, which they soon filled with second-hand furniture bought locally. German POWs, still not released, were on hand to paint the exterior and dig the garden for them.

As they settled in to their first English winter, with its severe frost and burst pipes, they caught the mood of post-war England, not just the austerity and the enforced hardship of rationing and food shortages, the weekly queues for the few ounces of meat allowed, but the boxed-in feeling. After the width and expanse of India, England was small-scale and insular. Contrasts were apparent in every sphere. In India, food and domestic help had been plentiful, here both were in short supply. And the class system, which the war had done so much to eradicate, seemed to be falling back into place.

Masters took some time adjusting to life in England. It felt, he told Barbara, like having the rug pulled from under his feet. She remembers him feeling very lost for a while and they both felt like 'strangers in a foreign land'. Both of them had been away for more than seven years and much was unfamiliar to them: practical matters such as how to buy rail tickets, what to order in pubs, how to drive in traffic. Minor irritations were irksome, such as the limited opening hours of pubs and shops. 'After the geographical space and freedom of India, I felt that I was in prison.' In some senses Masters felt he was back where he started, expected to conform to the requirements of dress and the behaviour of his class, with its 'hard rules and infallible punishments'. Gone were the shared camaraderie and excitement and adventure of war. He was impatient with this life; the war had fired him up and, like many of his contemporaries, he did not want to settle back into a humdrum existence.

However, he was better-off, with such a good post at the Staff College, than many of his ex-Indian Army colleagues. England was full of discharged army officers shuffling their feet and looking for somewhere to go. Part of his longer-term planning had been to view Camberley as a chance to have a good look at England before deciding what to do next.

The Staff College was a large, ivy-covered, square building, a mile through the woods from the Royal Military College at Sandhurst. His post meant that Masters was a member of the Directing Staff, or DS as they were called. He gave lectures and conducted seminars on 'Indian' soldiering, i.e. mountain warfare and situations typically met on the North-West Frontier, for instance. He was a good lecturer, concise, always to the point, enunciating his words clearly, and with humour. He formed quite a strong rapport with his students, most of whom had fought in the war, and were often not much younger than he. He enjoyed the challenge of teaching and turned his seminars into lively debating forums, encouraging the ten to twelve students to use their recent experiences of the war rather than rely on textbook answers. Remembering his own student days at Sandhurst, he marked their papers with particular care, knowing how important this could be for their future.

Being at Camberley meant that he could spend more time with his family, after the many wartime separations. He valued watching Susan and Martin growing up. He was a good father to them, romping and playing with them and reading them bedtime stories. He made visits to his parents at Uplyme and introduced Barbara to them. His parents had been worried when they first heard the news that he was marrying a married woman with two children in India. They both hoped for a more orthodox match, but once they had met, their objections disappeared. Barbara remembers Masters's mother as a hugging type who greeted her affectionately, while his father was friendly but more distant. Alex, too, was a frequent visitor to Camberley. He was now engaged to marry Joan Ingleson in the following June. Masters kept up with his Chindit colleagues and in May attended the first Chindit Reunion dinner at Claridge's. He kept his copy of the menu long afterwards, its surface studded with the signatures and high-spirited drawings of his fellow diners, Mike Calvert and Tim Brennan among them.

He took up former pastimes such as the England v Wales rugger match at Twickenham, lunches in pubs, walks in the country, and was always on the look-out for steam railways still proudly displaying their pre-nationalisation insignia, LMS, LNER and so on. Yet, however much he liked his Staff College job and his forays into traditional English life, underneath he felt a growing restlessness, a need to find

CHINDIT OFFICERS REUNION DINNER

1947

MENU

LES SUPREMES
DE TURBOTIN VICTORIA

• • •

LA POULARDE DE SURREY
A LA BROCHE

LES PETITS POIS FRAIS AU LAITUE

LA POMME PRE-CATELAN

LES CHAMPIGNONS ET TOMATES
GRILLEES

LE GRATIN DUBARRY

• • •

LA POIRE DU COMICE
ABRICOTINE

LA CHARLOTTE GLACEE
SICILIENNE

• • •

LE CAFE

something else. The egalitarian society the Labour Government was set on introducing meant little to him. He found post-war England colourless and flat. People he met in the street had grey, exhausted faces. It did little to lighten his mood. Barbara had become pregnant again, not intentionally, and the child, a daughter, was born in July and lived only one day. She had spina bifida. It was a heart-rending moment for them both. Things simply were not working. They decided to get away, and went to the Auvergne in France for a brief walking tour, living frugally since they had little money to spend with the harsh foreign exchange controls in force.

Masters continued to keep a watchful eye on events in India. Mountbatten had replaced Wavell as Viceroy in March 1947, determined to speed up the progress towards Independence. Partition into the separate countries of Pakistan and India was the order of the day. The Indian Army was being speedily 'Indianised'. Its British officers were being repatriated and fitted into the British Army; fewer were being seconded to the Indian Army than had been hoped. Masters had guessed as much from his time in the Defence Department in Delhi. The position of the Gurkhas was still unclear. Their special relationship with Britain put them in a different category. For their 130-year association with the Indian Army, they had never been fully part of India. They had been commanded by British officers. It was a tradition and historic arrangement that not one of the ten Gurkha regiments wanted to break.

Masters kept it in the back of his mind all through his year at Camberley that he would rejoin his old Gurkha regiment once the year was up. Independence was set for 15 August. A week beforehand, very much at the last minute, and indicative of the scramble that was taking place to get Independence through on time, news came through of the future of the Gurkhas. They were to be split up. The 2nd, 6th, 7th and 10th Gurkha Rifles were to join the British Army, while the other six Gurkha regiments, including the 4th Gurkhas, were to become part of the newly-formed Dominion of India. It was a shock and an immediate cause of dismay. The 4th Gurkhas had historic ties with Britain and a royal connection, yet all this was being discarded. Masters, like many others, felt aggrieved and abandoned. Indian officers would now take over and there was no place for Masters or his like. Suddenly a whole chapter in his life had come to a close.

On the day of Indian Independence Masters happened to be on a cross-Channel steamer, returning from a battlefield tour of the Somme with a group of his Camberley students. Glasses were raised to toast India in the bar, but he felt out of it, overwhelmed by sadness. 'I was cut adrift from my past', he wrote later. The double loss both of his regiment and of India was a bitter blow. He did not show it at the time, but the wound went deep. Back in Camberley it only added impetus to plan what to do next. He had the choice of transferring to the British Army – the 'opt' as it was called – where he would keep his rank and seniority, but the pay was lower and there was no certainty of getting in to the regiment of his choice. Besides, 'how could Aldershot, Suez, Nairobi and the rain-swept Ruhr – the places where most of the British Army was stationed – replace the Himalayan home of my regiment in Bakloh?' The romantic in him still yearned for 'the wild high jungles of upper Burma or the raw challenge of the North-West Frontier'.

British troops had none of the magic of the Gurkhas for him, none of their warmth, robust individualism, idiosyncratic humour and reliability that he had grown so attached to. British officers in a Gurkha regiment spent much of their time with the men, and the bond between them was very close. This was especially true in Masters's case as he had always got on very well with his men, a feeling that was reciprocated by them. He was fluent in their language, shared their food, and enjoyed an intense feeling of family. He could not see this happening with British troops.

He knew in his bones the British Army was not for him and, over time, never regretted his decision. Somewhat facetiously, so a colleague relates, he put down on his 'opt' form of regimental preferences first the Royal Army Service Corps and then the Coldstream Guards, neither of which he was likely to get into. In fact, he never made a serious attempt to get into the British Army, as this letter some four years later to his wartime colleague, Alec Harper, indicates:

> It sounds as if you've got into a better corner than some of the luckless buggers who were thrown out of our army in 1947 and succeeding years. I wake up at night screaming when I think of company commanders of Gurkhas counting boots for the Royal Army Ordnance Corps. I think you and I and those like us were right in not taking service with the British Army; personally I became antipathetic to the British troop some time during the war – this was not a personal thing because the Cameronians, for instance, were magnificent in that 1944 campaign. It is just an impersonal thing that I would rather not deal with the institution.

The British Army was too class-bound, too much part of the Establishment for him, and he knew he would not fit into its hierarchy.

Hardly suprising, therefore, that when a few days later he ran into a fellow Indian Army officer in Piccadilly, he told him, 'They've taken my India away from me.' It was a heartfelt cry, but the truculent edge makes it seem as if he had taken the de-selection of the 4th Gurkhas personally. He wrote later, 'If they don't want the 4th, they won't get me. To hell with them. I was bitter at the time, foolishly so.' His pique was compounded by the failure of the British Government to recognise the unique contribution of the Gurkhas over many years. To any serving Gurkha officer the loyalty of the men had been paramount, and Masters later felt aggrieved, as did many of his fellow Gurkha officers, at the way successive British Governments after the war disregarded the qualities of the Gurkha. Masters saw it as another nail in the coffin, only increasing his determination not to stay in England.

Barbara had her own worries. Ever since she had come back to England, she had been hoping to see her two children by Hugh Rose, Liz and Mike, now aged nine and seven, who had been in his custody since the divorce. The complication was that he was no longer in England, but was with his regiment in Malaya. The children, meanwhile, were in a children's home in Devon that took in children of army officers serving overseas. She enquired about seeing them and hoped she might be allowed to take charge of them at Camberley, at least until Hugh came back from overseas, but it was not to be. Hugh Rose would not budge; the rancour from the divorce was still too strong. Barbara was placed in an invidious position. If she went to see them at the home for an afternoon, say, and then went away again, it would cause them pain and suffering, more so than the relief at seeing them again. She was forced to agree to let them be, but it hurt her deeply and undermined much of her stay in England.

By now Masters was set on going abroad. He was only thirty-three, his ambition far from expended, and still brimming with energy generated by the war. Both he and Barbara saw their life together as just beginning, neither had any wish to settle into the comfortable, conventional English way of life of their class and milieu, epitomised by 'cottages in Devonshire, meetings at the Berkeley Buttery, prospects for the Grand Military at Sandown.' Being back in England underlined his feeling of not quite belonging, and in characteristic fashion he responded, as before, by becoming more determined to rise above it. The longer he stayed in England, the more he realised that class strictures still predominated; there was the constant reminder of his mother's working-class background or of his father's Anglo-Indian looks.

Both he and Barbara shared an adventurous streak, and England seemed less and less the place for adventure. They considered the Dominions where many ex-India hands were emigrating, Kenya especially, where colonial life could be replicated, with white supremacy and plentiful servants, but it wasn't them. Canada did hold some appeal and Masters went to the offices of the Canadian Pacific Railways near Trafalgar Square to enquire about openings with them. With his liking for railways, and as a well-trained staff officer, able to deal with the intricacies of railway movements and timetables, there were surely abilities they could put to good use, but their only offer was a job at the bottom, as a lineman, and he would have to work his way up.

The thought of Canada brought the USA to mind. He had never forgotten his pre-war trip there in 1938, the big skies of the West and the pace and excitement of New York; and in Burma his encounters with American airmen and officers had revived his favourable memories of their country. It was a place for young men, a land of opportunity and of space that offered a sense of future that was different from the England he saw around him. He liked the way its people radiated enthusiasm and openness. This was what he needed, he told himself, a contrast to the old order and the conformity of England. America's culture was forever being renewed and remade and it would be a challenge. Another increasingly important consideration was money. In America, if you were lucky and worked hard, you could make good money. For Masters, money represented not only power and status, but also a way to compensate for the shortcomings of his father and grandfather, both of whose later years had been bedevilled by a shortage of money.

He thought hard about it and discussed it with Barbara; she agreed. They both liked the notion that America was a country where you either had to pitch in or leave, as if the country had no time and was too preoccupied with its own tumultuous present to make a special fuss of foreigners. Everyone was expected to contribute. Other Englishmen had gone there and made a success of it. Raymond Chandler, an Englishman whose books he enjoyed, had written of America's 'warm-hearted vulgarity, with none of the irony of the English, none of their cool poise, none of their manner. But Americans did have friendliness. Where an Englishman would give you his card, an American would very likely give you his shirt.'

He was building himself up to an American frame of mind. Much of his own cultural trappings came from America. Favourite songs of his which he played on his ukelele and sang at parties were 'Casey Jones' and 'The Hills of West Virginia'. He knew all about American railroads and reputedly knew off by heart the name of every railroad station from Kansas to New Orleans 'because each of them has a blues named after it.' Another timely coincidence was that one of his colleagues at the Staff College was Bill Dodds, the USA liaison officer. They got on well together, possibly because each felt a bit of an outsider. Masters asked Dodds about job opportunities in America and Dodds suggested they look through the classified ads section of *The New York Times* together, spreading the newspaper on the floor of his bungalow.

America now became his definite target. Emboldened, he wrote to David Niven, based on the tenuous connections that Lois Jervis's father had conducted Niven's wartime marriage ceremony and he and Niven had both been at Sandhurst in the early 1930s. He asked him about openings in the movies. Niven wrote back telling him to try it for himself and that in the USA it was no use planning things in advance, but best to go out there and sell himself on the spot, as Niven had done. It proved to be useful advice.

He re-read his Sandhurst-prize copy of H. L. Mencken's *Selected Prejudices*, its iconoclastic mood matching his own. He took Barbara to see *Oklahoma* at Drury Lane. As his objectives became clearer, he sat down and, using his army training, wrote out an appreciation, an exercise in defining the aims of a situation in one sentence. He came up with: 'To live as a family unit in a place that offers space, liberty, and opportunity to all of us and, to me, independence in a work that I like.' He showed it to Barbara, who supported it.

Having made up his mind, he typed out his formal request to resign his commission from the army, to take effect in a year's time on 31 December 1948. With Indian Independence, he was the last Indian Army instructor at Camberley. It was a momentous decision: 'the idea of launching my family into a rootless future, with no special protection, no adequate pension, and almost no savings' was, he freely admitted, 'quite appalling'. Security had been a byword in his family's financial arrangements up till now and they had all relied on the eventual promise of a pension, but he did not want to become trapped by it. He had a second chance to break free, just as he considered doing before going up to Sandhurst. He wanted to challenge the family pattern. He thought of his father now living in Dorset on his reduced Indian Army pension, trying to keep up appearances as a retired Indian Army colonel, going out snipe shooting on the hill opposite. He thought, too, back to his grandfather, who had sacrificed so much for his children's education only to die prematurely and unhappily in India. Something else had to happen. Money was important, as he told Alex: 'If I stay in the Army and go on as now, I'll end up as a Lieutenant-General in twenty years' time. I want the money now.'

As he searched around for employment opportunities in America, the solution came, as it so often does, where he least expected it – on his own front doorstep. He still followed his Indian habit of going off for long walks to think things over. He had done this at Quetta on Chiltan Mountain, for instance, after meeting Barbara and needing to consider all the implications involved. Now on one of his woodland walks, the germ of an idea came to him. He could take people back to India on walking tours to the foothills of the Himalayas, and he would be their guide and tour leader. The people would have to be Americans, as they were then just about the only people who could afford it. It was a double coup, getting him across to America and back to his beloved India in one fell swoop. Excited at the prospect, he soon set to work planning his programme and devising possible itineraries. He gave his scheme the name Himalayan Holidays and created his own logo for it based on the three peaks of Trisul.

Things were beginning to take off. Enthusiasm mounted. He worked day and night on the details, contacting BOAC to inquire about discount airfares, visiting the Indian Deputy High Commissioner for visa requirements, inquiring about accommodation, and even the number of porters and pack animals required. He reckoned that a group of fifteen to twenty people, taken twice a year from New York, for a six-week round trip, costing nearly $3,000 per head, would make it financially viable.

Taking stock of his own finances, his pension of £300 per annum and the lump sum 'career loss' gratuity of £3,000 would be just about enough to launch the new project. Buoyed up at the prospect, he told his parents about it. They had misgivings; his mother particularly was upset at losing him to America. When his former Chindit colleague Richard Rhodes-James rang his home number to ask his mother for his address, she told him, 'He wants to go to America, can't you stop him?' But nothing was going to stop him now. Indeed his parents' resistance only strengthened Masters's resolve – he had something to prove to them and to himself.

The Staff College course ended in December 1947 and he made his farewells to the army. This was a definite moment of sadness, which was felt both ways, as his final report written by Brigadier Lambert, the Assistant Commandant at Camberley, testifies. It speaks of him as a 'most intelligent officer with a wide outlook on life. Considerable personality and a firm character. A very good brain supported by practical experience of military affairs. A good judge of character. An original thinker with energy and drive. If he were remaining in the Army he would be a very suitable candidate for the Joint Services Staff College.' It recommended him for 'accelerated promotion on the staff and for the command of troops.' This was high praise indeed, an all-round commendation of his abilities. But if he could succeed so well in the army, why not in civilian life?

Still in a buoyant mood, he put the finishing touches to his trip to America. Just before he left, a fellow DS at the Staff College who had heard of his Himalayan scheme mentioned an invention his wife had made for a special brassiere for women after lactation, and indeed for any woman with heavy breasts. Why didn't he take it with him to the USA and see if he could market it there too? Masters was amused at the thought of becoming a bra salesman and, game for anything, he agreed to do it.

To fit the role of visiting Englishman, he ordered a Harris tweed suit in Savile Row. When he went to the US Embassy to get the required immigration visa documents, he filled in his application form expecting little trouble. The British quota stood at sixty-five thousand per year. A week later, to his horror, he was told that, as he had been born in Calcutta, he had to be placed on the Indian quota; there was a waiting list of four and a half years. Masters immediately wrote back protesting and insisting he was British. It had no effect, a would-be immigrant's status was decided by country of birth and nothing else. Furthermore, the Embassy officials informed him that as he had applied for an immigrant's visa, he could not now change it to a visitor's visa, since too many 'visitors' had used this device to stay on as illegal immigrants. The Greeks, apparently, had a waiting list of eighty years as a result. The regulations were quite specific. Masters, suddenly seeing his whole plan threatened, did everything he could to get round it and finally persuaded the US Embassy officials that he, as a British officer and gentleman, would stick to his word, and not become an illegal immigrant. He was, after some hesitation, granted a six-month visitor's visa, but in time this was to cause further headaches.

Masters booked his passage on the *Queen Elizabeth*, due to sail from Southampton on 4 February 1948. Barbara and the children would follow later, if things went well. Barbara had supported Masters's plans throughout, more so now that she was resigned to the fact that her other two children would not be able to join her. It simply would not be fair to Susan and Martin to wait around on the offchance that the situation might change, but the anguish at having to leave Liz and Mike behind remained.

USA
1948–1952

Barbara drove Masters down to Southampton and he set off on a wintery journey. He managed to get first class accommodation by using up the spare money from his last Indian Army assisted passage. Among his fellow passengers that he spoke to were the Prime Minister of Nepal, with whom he chatted about the Gurkhas, and the Marquess of Linlithgow, the former Viceroy, now Chairman of the Midland Bank. They reached New York on 9 February, nine years to the day since he had last been there in 1938. Alice Westfeldt, his prewar friend from New Orleans, met him at the pier and drove him to the apartment on Morningside Heights, where she lived with her husband, Troup Mathews, an adviser to foreign students at Columbia University. Troup had a European background, and had been brought up at Le Havre and educated in England; Masters and he took to each other right away.

After a few days, although grateful for their hospitality, Masters wanted to be independent, and moved to the Hotel Le Marquis on East 31st Street. He set up office on the seventh floor in a room costing $19 per week and bought a typewriter for $18. Himalayan Holidays and the bra were launched into business. He gave himself a time limit of three months to see if they would work. He ate mostly at the cheap diner next door owned by two Greek brothers who worked from 5.30 in the morning until 3.30 the next, and slept in turns under the counter during the night. The determination of these brothers, fellow immigrants like himself, impressed him. New York seemed to invite such enterprise.

He started visiting travel agents, picking his way across the snow, still packing the sidewalk after the big Christmas fall, and walked up to fifty blocks a day. The travel agents were sceptical for the most part, and not too interested in India. They could not make him out and looked at him with ill-concealed suspicion; an Englishman with an upper-crust accent and manner, introducing himself by a senior army rank, did not seem right. In England such attributes would be considered signs of probity and honesty, but here his tweed suit and unfamiliar accent only aroused mistrust. What was the deal, what was his racket, they seemed to be thinking, as if he was a character straight out of a Damon Runyon play.

The recent excursion trips to India did not help the situation. A travel agent told him of a woman tour guide who had taken a group to Bombay recently and left them stranded there while she ran off with the money. Other agents were less well-informed, asking him whether the Himalayas were north or south of Miami. He visited the better-heeled Explorers' Club and explained his proposed itinerary to its affluent members: a flight to Delhi, a light aircraft up to the Gauchar in Garhwal, and then, three days out from New York, they would be walking in the Himalayas. The route was similar to the one he had taken with Barbara near Trisul in August 1945. Yet there were drawbacks. India was still in the throes of upheaval, Gandhi's recent murder and the newspaper reports of daily Indo-Pakistan massacres tended to scare off potential visitors, and the legacy of anti-colonialist feeling was still prevalent in America.

Travel editors in magazines and newspapers gave him a better deal by inserting snippets about his project in their publications. The *New York World Telegram*, the *Post* and the Sunday edition of *The New York Times* all came up with items. Each night he would return to his room in the Hotel Le Marquis and plan his campaign for the next day. The bra idea was not making much headway either. He went round major department stores, unashamedly touting its benefits, and went down to the 7th Avenue garment district, a tough area for any outsider to break into, an incongruous sight in his tweed suit. He was given some excellent kosher lunches and a colourful résumé of life in New York, but still no business.

He wrote home at the end of February: 'Life alternates between being very rushed and very boring. It would never be boring if I had plenty of money of course, but to save money I have just to sit tight here in my hotel room very often with nothing special on. Last Monday was a holiday and I spent the day out on Long Island with the Mathews in a house someone had lent them for a fortnight – it's very pretty out there, with the rolling hills and Long Island Sound, even though it's all under snow.'

The elegant, fifty-year-old Vyvyan Donner, a cousin of the inventor of the bra, gave a cocktail party for him at her apartment in the Osborne, which led to further introductions. She was fashion director of Movietone, and tried to arrange a travelogue documentary on the Himalayas with Masters acting as narrator. Troup and Alice Mathews were constant supporters, always ready to strengthen his flagging moral fibre.

Masters looked up his old boyhood friend from Wiltshire, Stanley Odlum. He had been shot down over Germany during the war and had spent two years as a prisoner. Now married and wealthy from the money inherited from his millionaire father, he seemed desperately unhappy, an 'embittered alcoholic' at the age of thirty-one. Their periodic meetings hurt Masters, because Stanley had represented much of the glamour of America in their youth. Yet seeing him in such a state now only reinforced his determination to succeed.

For all his lack of commercial success, the longer he spent in New York, the more he liked it. Its pace, its energy, the clash of nationalities, all competing for their bit of space, their slice of the American dream, uplifted him. It was a far cry from the woes of post-war England. In a curious way he felt at home here. He liked the city's obstinacy, its 'don't yield' attitude. But, two months on, his money supply was running low and he had to decide what to do. Characteristically, he went for a walk to Pelham Bay Park in the Bronx to think things over. It was cold and fresh, but sunny. He wished Barbara was there to help him. The house in Camberley was due to be vacated in June, so he had to hurry if he was to pull something off. Momentarily he was tempted to chuck it all in and go back to England, but 'walking along the edge of the grass while the cars whizzed by on Sunday excursions to the country, I knew that I did not want to leave New York at this time. The city had excitement and wonder, and my opportunity was there somewhere. I had heard it scratching behind the wainscot in a hundred interviews, in the reading of a hundred newspapers.'

Newspapers, or rather magazines, came to his rescue. A reporter on *The New Yorker*, Rex Lardner, had read one of the newspaper clips about him. Intrigued by stories of this tweed-suited Indian Army colonel marching around Manhattan, Lardner suggested a piece on him for their Talk of the Town section to his editor, William Shawn. Lardner invited him for lunch at Lucca's, his local restaurant. Masters takes up the story:

> Lardner was a good host and a good journalist. He stood me two Martinis and a decent lunch, none of which I could then afford, and accomplished the interview with rapidity and no pain. Who was I? (Lieutenant-Colonel John Masters, D.S.O., O.B.E., p.s.c. [passed staff college] 4th Prince of Wales's Own Gurkha Rifles, on leave pending retirement; thirty-three years of age.) Where had I come from? (India, by way of England.) What was I doing? (Trying to find a niche in civilian life, after fourteen years as a regular officer of the Indian Army. At the moment – organising a conducted tour to the

Himalayas.) How was it going? (It wasn't.) Why had I come to the
United States? (Land of opportunity.) His duty done, Lardner turned
the conversation to more general subjects. We discussed films, and the
two Martinis gave me a biting eloquence. I described that very
specialised and peculiar world, the Hollywood Orient, with examples
and apt illustrations. Lardner laughed quite a lot, and said, 'You tell
stories so well, why don't you write that up? It's pretty funny.'

Disciplined as ever, Masters went back to his hotel room and wrote the
article Lardner suggested that same afternoon. He had a special motive,
since he felt Hollywood's presentation of India was one of the reasons
why he had failed to interest people in trips to the Himalayas. He could
not get them interested in seeing the real thing. His weeks of frustration
now found a vent in barbed prose about these Hollywood images of
British India: 'We enter an India where motives are never complicated
and the thermometer stands steady, rain or shine, at 114 degrees',
where Englishmen are either 'sweating heroes or sweating cads' and
Maharajahs wear 'an outcaste's turban, Sikh trousers and Mohammedan slippers', and females 'laden with nose rings and bangles,
disport a Mohammedan yashmak to cover part of their faces, wear
Hindu caste marks, and have the forehead, eyes and nose of a well-
tanned Pasadena cigarette girl', and so on in similar satirical vein.

He sent the article, now called 'Hymn to Hollywood', to Lardner
who forwarded it to his magazine, but *The New Yorker* was not
publishing articles on Hollywood at that time, nor did their Talk of the
Town piece appear. Lardner sent it instead to his agent, Jacques
Chambrun. Chambrun rang almost immediately to say how much he
liked it and that he was sending it off to the *Atlantic Monthly*. Three
days later he called Masters into his offices on 5th Avenue and handed
him a letter from *Atlantic*'s editor Edward Weeks, saying he was
delighted to take the piece and would pay $100. They published it as
'Through the Films Darkly'. Masters kept the cover of that month's
issue framed in his house for life. It was a tremendous boost to his
sagging self-esteem, but, more importantly, it was pointing him in a
new direction. When Chambrun sent him the cheque three days later,
he commented, '*The New Yorker*'s loss is my – and another magazine's
– gain. I should like to see anything else you have written.' Suddenly a
whole new vista opened up for him and he began to think seriously of
becoming a writer.

Back at the hotel he thrust his Himalayan files under the bed and
settled down to think. He thought back to the few things he had
written which he could feel proud of: the papers for McLeod in Delhi

JACQUES CHAMBRUN, INC.

745 FIFTH AVENUE, NEW YORK 22
WICKERSHAM 2-9464-9465-9466
CABLES CHAMBRUN NEW YORK

9 April 1948

Dear Mr. Masters,

I must tell you how very much I enjoyed your "Hymn to Hollywood." The New Yorker's loss is my--and another magazine's, I hope--gain.

I should like to see anything else you have written; and may I, after the New Yorker and Mr. Lardner, have first chance at anything new you write?

Sincerely yours,

[signature: Jacques Chambrun]

Mr. Jack Masters

D. W. HALL, *Editorial*   BRENT KENYON, *England*

JACQUES CHAMBRUN, INC.

745 FIFTH AVENUE, NEW YORK
PLAZA 5-9464-9465-946
CABLES CHAMBRUN NEW YO

25 May 1948

Col. Jack Masters

"An Englishman's Hymn to Hollywood" sold to The Atlantic Monthly	$100.
Less 10% commission	10.
	$ 90.
Less typing charges:	
"The Bones of Rupkunda" "Dussehra" Two chapters of book	19.25.
Check #9232 herewith	$ 70.75

D. W. HALL, *Editorial*   BRENT KENYON, *England*   ALFREDO CAHN, *South Ame* and ones on mountain warfare at Camberley Staff College, a pre-war article on infantry dress in India that was published by the *United Services Journal* in 1937, and his shooting a tiger article for *The Field* in 1938, and, even further back, the essay on the early Christian Church at Wellington that had merited Malim's much-prized marginal comment, 'Very good'. Not much to go on, admittedly.

Writing, if he could make a go of it, certainly offered the 'space, liberty and opportunity and independence in a work that I like' that had been the mainstay of his appreciation at Camberley, but from a professional point of view, it was precarious and insecure. That $100 was a lot of money, far better than the equivalent rates in England where *Blackwood's Magazine*, for example, would only pay a half of that, or less. The more he looked at it the more he realised it was a possibility. Ultimately it was up to him – a personal challenge. 'As long as I remained my own master, my scope as a writer would depend only on my scope as a human being.' The army in his day was also an uneven occupation; at times he worked very hard and then slackened off. He would be given responsibilities, but how he discharged them was his business. Yet there were differences, as he knew. Writing was essentially a sedentary and lonely job, whereas in the army,

> I had dealt with men as well as words, with physical as well as mental hurdles. There had been hours at a desk, but there had also been hours in the open air, under the sun, in snow and rain. When I, or my superiors, or Fate, set me a task, I could exercise my whole personality in the achievement of it. I could write explanations and orders: I could harangue and debate and argue and plead; I could go out and physically prove my point by demonstration or example. All my senses were engaged in my work – I could smell sweat and blood and cordite and oil. I could see dawns and dusks and the look on a tired man's face. I could hear bugles and the voices of men at play – the men to whom I was bound in a common purpose. I could taste rice and dal and dust and the rum ration. I could feel the pack on my back and the texture of a soldier's hand, helping me up some steep place. All this I must give up, to work only through words on paper.

It was a risk but that only added to the incentive. It matched his post-war need to generate adventure, to recapture some of the excitement and uncertainty of the war years. He thought of Nelson's dictum: 'Something must be left to chance. No captain can do very wrong if he lays his ship alongside that of the enemy.' And it did mean he could stay on in the USA.

He made some provisional calculations and reckoned his family could live on his existing pension and his loss of career gratuity for about two and a half years more, until 31 December 1950. He wrote to Barbara telling her of this. If she was in favour, she should plan to come over with the children. At the back of his mind he knew that if all else failed, there were other opportunities. He would not mind taking on a menial job, shovelling snow or running a petrol station, when such jobs would have little of the stigma they would attract in England. America was blessedly free of such class considerations.

He went to see Chambrun and told him he would give writing a try. Back at his hotel, he sketched out possible themes to write about. India was foremost; it was what he knew most about and he could use the wealth of material from his family background too. Writers he admired, such as Faulkner, had created their own territory, why should he not do the same with his India novels?

In a subsequent newspaper interview Masters described this moment: 'At that point I sat down and started to make a list of what I could write about. I've heard of so many writers who've done one book and then just vanished. Also I didn't want to waste time on something I couldn't make a living at. I knew about men in action; I knew about India. I skimmed that country's bloody history and inside an hour I had thought of thirty-five events which might make novels. I decided to become a professional novelist.' This list of thirty-five novels became famous. Agents and publishers were astounded when he produced it and assured them that he would write that number of books. Its very boldness captures something of his forthright and forward-looking mood of the time.

His list started in 1600 with the arrival of the British in India and the formation of the East India Company and it went up to Independence in 1947. He drew on his own remarkable memory, always a strong point of his in his army days and why he was such a good staff officer. Thinking of his own family's history, he decided to create his own literary family and called them, not without irony, Savage; a hint, too, at the wildness and sexuality repressed in British India that his novels would seek to bring out. The Savage family would provide a continuity in all the novels, paralleling in that way his own family's continuous stay in India since the early 1800s. Each member of this Savage family would, in every succeeding generation, act as a kind of measuring rod to the major historical events happening around him, and the way he witnessed and reacted to these events would be in a manner typical of British India at that time.

He thought back to writers he had been influenced by: 'Both John Buchan and C. S. Forester interested me and affected me as a writer because they were writing about men of action, men of energy, men who were doing things particularly in the open air. Buchan's heroes of clubland were men with heads, hearts, brains and muscles but I thought they didn't have bowels. The things that happened to them were always rather proper things and their emotions were also proper. I have seen enough of action to know this is not always so.' He wanted to improve on this, get closer to the feel and agony of the battlefield and the harshness of life on the North-West Frontier, for example. India had 'bowels', its history, as he well knew, was shot through with brutality and violence.

Kipling appealed to him for his spirit of place. As his biographer, Angus Wilson, wrote of him, 'there is no introspection, no looking into oneself. You must only weave tapestries when an external observation has set up a shape or a story in your mind.' C. S. Forester had this ability too; Masters had always admired his 'gritty realism', especially in his early books about Spain, such as *Brown on Resolution.* 'There was the feeling of the sea, of the spray. You could feel the stones of Spain underfoot, as if you could smell the sweat in the ranks, you knew what it meant to be a rifleman in the Peninsular War.' He knew personally and from hard-earned experience what it was like to be a soldier in India and he would bring this to bear on his writing.

He had mapped out his grand design quickly. It was, in his own words, 'just as I would do if my objective was to take a certain hill by dawn.' He went to see Chambrun, who put his affairs there in charge of Desmond Hall. As a first step he wrote two short stories, both on Indian themes, one entitled 'The Bones of Rupkunda' and the second on the Gurkha festival of Dussehra, where buffalo are sacrificed. Chambrun placed them both with *Esquire*, which bought them for $300 – an encouraging start. He continued with his short stories, but their violent action put off editors. Selling the mood of a Gurkha soldier or a British colonial was a different and difficult proposition in America with no colonial past of its own.

India had not featured much in the American book world but the one really successful book in recent years on the subject had been Yeats-Brown's *Bengal Lancer* (1930), a semi-autobiographical account. Masters had not particularly liked the book, feeling that it had an excess of 'mystical' content. Hall felt there was now room for another book on that theme. He had spoken to Dial Press who seemed interested. Masters agreed to defer starting on his first novel and write up his autobiographical experiences in the Indian Army instead. They were, after all, still fresh in his memory.

He was learning the tricks of the trade all the time, aiming to write with more objectivity, implying his characters' thoughts and emotions rather than explaining them, but he still lacked the technique to choose which acts would carry implication as well as fact. He knew he had to shift his ground and become more involved. No one could write well unless he was deeply involved in his work.

In the meantime, Barbara had written back in full support of his plan. She would bring the children over as soon as she could arrange it. He had to decide where they were going to live. New York was clearly too expensive, yet he needed to be within easy reach of agents, editors, and publishers. Alice Mathews suggested looking through the house-rental advertisements in *The New York Times*. Most were too expensive or were in the commuter belt of Connecticut and New Jersey. The cheapest he saw was one in New York State, in Rockland County, about 30 miles north of New York City. Alice knew its location and offered to drive him there. It was now early summer, it was a fine day, and the journey took an hour. Passing across George Washington Bridge they reached the apple orchards of Rockland County and came to South Mountain Road, where the house stood. It was two storeys high, with an upper balcony, a large sitting room and a log fireplace, and lay cut into the side of the hill, with trees behind. It looked just right for them and Masters took it on the spot from its owner, Eleanor Hope, who lived nearby.

As Masters drove back with Alice, she told him something of South Mountain Road, a famous artists' and writers' colony started up just after the First World War by such luminaries as the playwright Maxwell Anderson and the architect Henry Varnum Poor, and now populated by other notables such as Kurt Weill and Lotte Lenya, John Houseman and Burgess Meredith. His initiative in chancing his arm as a writer really did seem to be paying off, for these looked to be ideal surroundings for a novice writer.

He moved into the house to get it ready for Barbara and the children. They arrived, with their nanny, on 22 June on the *Queen Mary*. He had borrowed the Mathewses' car for the occasion, and it was a rapturous reunion. Barbara was thrilled to be in America, remarking on the occasional similarities of the landscape to parts of the Central Provinces in India, as if she wanted to take up where they had left off in India. A new life beckoned for them. Susan and Martin seemed excited too, though Susan's stammer, the product of too many moves in recent years, had come back. Masters knew they should settle down now. As they unpacked, they found some of their crates had remained unopened since Delhi.

South Mountain Road straggled along just below a hillside for 3 or 4 miles, with houses on either side mostly hidden by trees. As they got to know their neighbours, they began to feel welcomed; they were gregarious and friendly, but respected individual privacy. At a summer garden party, the contrasts with England were evident. Here were fifty to sixty people drinking on a maple-shaded lawn at 4 p.m. on a Sunday. Slightly taken aback at this, since in England 6 p.m. was the recognised starting time, they nevertheless joined in. People were dressed more informally – even bohemian in appearance – with ladies in raffia dresses with huge beaded necklaces. As they caught snatches of conversation, they realised this was a talented group, the intelligentsia of the New York theatre, music and publishing worlds. As new arrivals, the Masterses were welcomed and shown a pleasant offhand courtesy. Masters felt at home in these surroundings and found them immediately agreeable.

He soon made a work-study for himself out of a back bedroom at Hope House, as their new home was called. He did not like too many distractions when writing, and this room had no inviting view. He soon began a disciplined and rigorous work-day, starting writing at 8.00 a.m. promptly and continuing until lunch at 1 p.m. Then he would work all afternoon, and even into the late evening. But after the first few months, he would feel dizzy once he stood up and have to hold on to the table for support. So he moderated his regime with a short nap after lunch, then a walk, before starting again. He was always a fast writer, writing in longhand in pencil, sometimes achieving 6,000 words per day. Barbara typed his manuscripts for him; she was an expert typist from her pre-war days as secretary to a Tory MP. At other times she took charge of the domestic side and helped the children acclimatise themselves, shedding their British accents and grappling with the confusing notions of jam meaning jelly and gas, petrol.

The nearest shopping town of any size was New City, five miles away. Once, in the exuberance of the early days, he and Barbara walked there and back at midnight, Barbara dancing in her bare feet in the road. It was part of the sense of liberation they both felt, but walking was not always so easy. Masters frequently used to take his afternoon walk along South Mountain Road, but local residents kept stopping their cars to offer him a lift, unable to comprehend that he was doing this for pleasure – walking was considered an emergency activity.

Within a month, working at high speed, he had finished the first draft of his autobiography. Some 125,000 words lay in front of him. He gave it the working title *Brutal and Licentious*, an indication of his wish to emphasise the realism, the 'bowels' of a soldier's life. His technique had been to block it out chapter by chapter, pinning these up on the wall above his desk. Now, looking at the completed first draft, he was dissatisfied. It seemed uneven and patchy. To remedy it, he used a procedure from his military days, drawing up further charts to evaluate the text according to Action, Explanation, Colour and Characterisation. He then graded each chapter accordingly. His conclusion was that the book needed more colour and more action to keep the reader's interest alive. It had to have a Second Level, as he defined it, so that the underlying emotions came through. 'I rubbed my hands gleefully. My new-discovered Doctrine of the Second-Level would infallibly lead me to the heights.' He was learning the craft of writing on the job, as it were, fuelled by his great energy, attention to detail and ambition to succeed.

He rewrote the first two chapters, but the many corrections to his original typescript led him to use another army method, namely dictating directly to a typewriter. For this, he and Barbara worked together at high speed. He sent these chapters off to Desmond Hall with an outline of the rest of the book. Hall passed them on to Dial Press, who seemed enthusiastic and summoned Masters to their offices in Manhattan. Without a car, this was a lengthy two-hour journey: by bus to Haverstraw, then the rickety, grimy West Shore Railroad to Weehawken, a ferry across the Hudson, and two more buses across Manhattan. Dial told him an offer might be pending. He returned home in high excitement. Then, just two days later, one of their editors, George Joel, rang to say there was no deal. He had run into the English publisher Victor Gollancz at a party in New York and Gollancz had advised against taking the reminiscences of yet another Indian Army 'curry colonel'. They were two a penny in England, he had said. Masters, momentarily taken aback, reread what he had written to reassure himself and, seeing that it was better than Gollancz's prediction, finished it, telling Hall to continue circulating it to publishers.

Among the Masterses' Rockland County neighbours were Keith and Emily Jennison, who became among their closest friends. Emily was tall, slim and dark, Keith taller, blond and strongly handsome. A humorous, hard-drinking type, Keith was from Vermont; his brusque bonhomie appealed to Masters. They lived a mile away up South Mountain Road and in the basement of their house was a drinking den named the Toad and Throstle, which had once been a bar. The cash register was still in place, and whenever they gave a party, gatecrashers would soon be given away when they offered to pay for their drinks. There Masters met Frank Laskier, another English resident on South

Mountain Road, an ex-naval man and self-taught author, whose novel *Unseen Harbour* had been published shortly before, recounting his wartime experiences; he had had a leg blown off in the battle with the German battleship *von Scheer*. Laskier had no formal education other than 'what British reform schools had taught me.' He was a rough diamond and his writing seemed to have an in-built grasp of rhythm and force that Masters would have liked to emulate: he wrote that Laskier 'could put teeth into a phrase much better than I could.' As drinking companions they developed a bar routine together. An 'argument' would start and Masters would suddenly thrust a knife into Laskier's foot as he 'shrieked' with agony, to the horror of surprised onlookers, unaware that the leg was artificial.

Keith worked for the publishers William Sloane Associates and was interested in Masters's writing plans. Soon he found Masters asking him a whole series of questions about his prospects as a writer: how much could he earn and so forth. It was, as Keith recalls, 'the goddamnest interview I ever had with an author.' The Jennisons were invited down for a meal, a curry with dal cooked by Masters, and Keith was shown his workplace. Keith was immediately struck by the professionalism and thoroughness of his approach. On the wall was a large-scale map of India into which Masters had inserted pins at all the key geographical locations of important battles and events. Then he had placed a sort of transparency on top of it, with the birthplace of each successive generation of the Savage family, marking the places where they lived and worked. On the adjacent wall was his chart listing the outline plans for the full thirty-five novels. Keith remembers thinking, 'My God I've never seen anyone organise like that.' It seemed more like a battle headquarters.

Keith advised him not to waste too much time waiting to hear back from publishers about the autobiography, but to start on his novel projects. In the long run it would be better to have made his name first as a novelist and then the public would be curious to know more about him – that would be the time to publish an autobiography.

At the top of his list of thirty-five events, and the subject matter for his first novel, was the Indian Mutiny of 1857, or the First War of Independence as Indians call it. It offered tremendous scope for narrative which he already knew was his strongest suit. His only doubt was whether he was ready to tackle so important a subject. 'I would have preferred to leave it until I was more assured and, I hoped, better. But a man in my position is not free to choose his ammunition; he must use the best available, the first time, or he may not survive for another shot.' Masters saw the Mutiny as 'the physical and psychological hinge of all relations between England and India. The resulting explosion had destroyed much of the good and some of the bad in the British-India relationship', and it had opened up a 'gulf of hatred and disgust' between the two nations that ultimately led to Independence.

Masters set about writing with a method that was at once practical, efficient and thorough:

> My approach to writing a book begins with something from my military habit – writing appreciations, appreciations of situations. If you have six hours to do an appreciation, you devote half of the time to defining your object, in one line. It may take three hours to think exactly what you want to do. For instance, in a military situation, the first thing that comes to mind is that you want to capture that hill or want to defeat the Germans or something. That really isn't your object. Your object is to get a better peace than before, to wipe out some threat that caused the war – this is the sort of thing you have to think about. I define my object – in every book I write – in one sentence.

In this case it was: 'To tell an exciting story about the Indian Mutiny which will give an accurate feel of the time and underline that hatred breeds hatred.' He wanted to show that good and bad existed on both sides. Then he spent some time finding a title that would combine the ideas of action, mystery, India, and his theme, and he came up with *Nightrunners of Bengal*.

His aim was to look deeper than previous historians who tended to see it as the Sepoy Mutiny, an affair of disgruntled soldiers, or as a half-hearted attempt by the fading Indian aristocracy to regain its lost power. In the end, he dedicated the book to the Sepoy of India 1695–1947, which shows his orientation and, in the explanatory foreword to the American edition, he described how 'England – Victoria's pompous, stolid Christian England – sprang up in an ecstasy of outrage, to answer mass murder with mass murder, and hate with a demoniacal fury of hate. This was at once the noon of courage and the midnight of barbarism.' India had become a 'flaming wreck', and good and evil were wrought on both sides.

His central character, the first of the Savage family, Captain Rodney Savage, is a typical British officer serving in the Bengal Native Infantry, married to a typical memsahib, Joanna, and they have a son, Robin. He represents the British at that time, slightly overbearing and out of touch with native feelings 'like men in an upstairs room, secure, cut off'.

In the book, a visitor from England, Caroline Langford, has come out to India and notices strange signs and portents in the villages, such as the chapatis being symbolically carried from one village to another. She asks Rodney about these at the 1857 New Year's Ball they are attending. He tries to reassure her it means nothing, and deters her from further involvement: 'an English girl had no business to involve herself with gurus and fakirs and the edges of magic.' He goes on, 'If you want to feel India, you must become Indian, gain one set of qualities and lose another. As a race we don't do it – we can't.' This is really the main theme of the novel, the extent of the 'dialogue between races' and how far it can go – a theme he was to explore in subsequent novels.

Trouble breaks out in a neighbouring princely state, Kishnapur, and Rodney is despatched to restore law and order. The Rajah has been assassinated, and his widow, the Rani, is a formidable character and passionate nationalist, who tries to seduce Rodney: 'I killed my husband for India; I pretended to be a whore for India; I lied for India. I am an Indian first and woman afterward.' Sex gets an early mention in the novel, as it does in most of the books that followed. Once the Mutiny proper has broken out, appalling atrocities occur on both sides, sepoys are blown live from cannons or hanged on the branches of trees and finished off 'artistically' in a figure of eight, and Indians retaliate likewise. Rodney stands in the blood bath around him, overcome with shame at the British failure in India, and Masters spares us few of the gory details. His wife Joanna is killed, but he manages to escape with his son, helped by Piroo, the Indian carpenter of the regiment. Caroline Langford joins them and they head off across country for Gondwara, where a British garrison is holding out.

It is an epic journey across central India, a region Masters knew well from his Chindit training, and this 'retreat', so convincingly described, may have borrowed something from Blackpool. Threatened by death, Rodney and his followers are given hospitality by villagers, at great peril to themselves. Masters is making the point that the simple villager is the essence of India, capable of showing the love that he sees as India's saving grace. Rodney eventually reaches Gondwara and, reunited with the British forces, marches back to capture Kishnapur, driving the Rani to suicide. Her last words are 'the rebellion will go on until I and those who follow me are wiped out'.

Rodney's viewpoint remains only partly modified, mirroring the relationship Britain then held to India. His eyes have been only half opened. He still takes the view that 'The Company is not going to lose India . . . and if it did, do you think Indians are fit to rule themselves,

or protect themselves yet? There'd be a year of anarchy, civil wars
between the Rajahs, mad for power. And who would suffer in all that
but the ordinary people of India? And afterward Russia.' Here Masters
was laying the theme for a future novel, *The Lotus and the Wind*. The
Mutiny is described as a temporary aberration to British eyes, who
'seeing much, believed nothing.'

Masters managed to keep the narrative running at a fast-moving
pace; it reads like an adventure told with gripping intensity, confirming
his strength as a story-teller. The underlying theme of the book, as he
saw it, was the 'inherent melancholy of power', the point at which
power – here, pride and an abiding arrogance – heads towards its own
destruction. The Mutiny brought the demise of the East India
Company. The 'chains of hatred' forged on that Sunday afternoon
when the Mutiny broke out in Meerut in June 1857 remained in place
until Independence. The cure, if a cure were possible, was love. 'The
chains could have been broken by love, but there was no love.' Love, in
this context, resonated in the bond he had held with his Gurkha
troops, for example. In *Nightrunners of Bengal* he wrote: 'for most of
us it's a sort of giving; we give all we have, and we don't keep accounts
... it's only trust that matters, and we do trust each other, we and the
native officers and the sepoys – completely, unconditionally.'

Masters worked on the principle that it was better, and preferable, to
do the research after the first draft was written. Too much preliminary
research got in the way of a strong narrative. Once the first draft was
completed, then he could check it for details, such as what crops were
in the fields and whether he had got the phases of the moon right, or
whether his calendar for the year 1857 was accurate and he had got the
Sundays right – Sundays being the day the British went to church,
leaving their arms behind. He already had a near-encyclopaedic
knowledge of India, much of it gained from his days in the Bakloh
library, and a phenomenal memory which he could now draw upon.

The best bits in the book are the descriptive parts, such as Rodney
overcoming danger and hardship to rescue himself and his son, but an
added dimension of psychological insight comes from Rodney's efforts
to rescue himself from the bitterness of heart and mind that these
experiences engender in him.

The book took six months to complete and three drafts. While
writing it, Masters's dizzy fits became more pronounced and he usually
had to lie down for twenty minutes in the evening before eating;
sometimes he lost his appetite altogether. He was spurred on by the
interest Doubleday were showing in the book. When the final draft was
finished, he completed it by writing on the last page the words he

always wrote at the end of every book thereafter, a sort of private
talismanic injunction to the future: 'Nunc dimittis'. He also started
what became another regular custom: at the end of each book, before
getting up from his writing desk, he inserted a fresh sheet of paper in
the typewriter, and on it typed the title of his next book, or a few
words describing what it was going to be about, followed by the
hortatory words 'by John Masters'. It served as a combined reassurance, threat and promise, and kept his momentum going.

The draft was sent to Doubleday. Though the editor liked it, he
could not persuade the rest of the editorial board. Masters's reaction
was one of disappointment. In a move which he claimed was not quite
as illogical or unfair as it sounded, he decided to change agents. He felt
that Desmond Hall and he had too similar values and he wanted a
fresh approach. He needed an agent 'of dyspeptic mien, uncompromising pessimism, and vanilla-American views'. On the recommendation
of his neighbour A. J. Balaban, he went to the Paul Small Agency and
his affairs were put in the care of Miriam Howell.

A. J. and Carrie Balaban lived opposite; he was a movie mogul and
part-owner of a nickelodeon cinema chain. Originally impoverished
immigrants themselves, the Balabans knew what it was like to be
struggling to make one's way in America. They used to send their
butler over with left-overs from their kitchen. The Jennisons were
present once when surplus duck casserole arrived and was hastily
converted into a delicious meal. At the end of their parties, uneaten
hors d'oeuvres were left on their back porch for guests to take away
with them.

On South Mountain Road their circle of friends was widening and
now included Alan and Nancy Anderson – he was the second son of
Maxwell Anderson and about the same age as Masters – and Fernand
and Laura Auberjonois, he worked for the Voice of America and she
was originally a Princess Murat. South Mountain Road was, as Keith
Jennison defined it, a horizontal society, where what mattered most
was how well you did something. If you were a good workman, serious
and committed to your craft, you would be respected. At parties the
local stonemason rubbed shoulders with the movie star. The Masterses
welcomed this openness and lack of pressure or condescension, and
compared it favourably against England.

America had its own rules though. The Masterses learnt not to hang
clothing out on a washing line in front of the house. This simply was
not done. No one locked their door at night. A car mechanic might
wave away an offer to pay for a small repair and say 'forget it' but
charge heavily for a major one. The Masterses became avid listeners to

the radio and followed World Series baseball. It was all part of their self-imposed induction into the American way of life – their discovery period – and they began to understand the greater American sense of communalism. Life for the moment had a few worries, though Masters's unsettled status as an immigrant troubled him, his visitor's visa had been extended for six months, until February 1949.

He wrote to his brother in England in November 1948: 'Life continues to be hazardous but exciting . . . we can cook with real things instead of invisible meat and fat', and he reassured them of his prospects as a successful writer, looking forward to the time 'when I'm a millionaire and author of *Dead Seagulls* or *Fifty Years with the 4th Gurkhas and other Tales.*' In line with this, he designed his own colophon, an emblem for the title page of books. Kipling had his swastika, Maugham his arch, so why should he not have one too? He chose twin snow-topped mountain peaks, above the five rivers and rising sun crest of the Punjab. Later it was to appear in all his books.

The 1948 presidential campaign that autumn was sharply fought between Truman and Dewey, with accusations and counter-accusations flying back and forth. It forced Masters to query his own political standpoint. Although not yet an American citizen, he was a civilian and no longer protected by the neutral stance of the military man. Now he sided with Truman, admiring the 'essential guts and quality of the man'. When the election took place early in November, he and Barbara sat up all night listening to the returns of Truman's victory.

America so throbbed with energy – there was so much 'doing, talking, acting, planning' he wrote of that time – that he was swept along by it as well. It suited him. They joined in typical American diversions, such as softball with the Andersons, and started exploring nearby Bear Mountain Park. Masters kept up his interest in railways, driving over to Westchester to watch the New York Central steam-hauled expresses speeding by the Hudson: 'at night I could hear the distant breathing of West Shore freights making the long climb from West Nyack, and the mournful minor key moaning of the whistles for the level crossing at Congers.' It was a re-creation of his childhood memories at Bottlesford, the romance of trains going somewhere, always running on time.

Money was still tight that first winter; the whole family kept their underclothes on overnight when it froze and used the central heating sparingly. To get extra money Barbara started typing for Carrie Balaban for $3 per hour. She was writing a book about her Aunt Hattie, a pioneer of the Wild West, who lived in Colorado mining towns at the turn of the century.

American football caught Masters's interest, with its strategy that seemed to combine a mix of chess and armoured warfare. They drove up to West Point, 20 miles further north, for the Army-Columbia game. It was a bright, wintry Saturday afternoon, and they brought the required sandwiches and all-important flask with them. The crowd seemed good-tempered, more of a family outing than the equivalent in England. He ran into Bill Dodds there, his old Camberley Staff College friend. Being at West Point took him back to a military environment. At first he was surprised by the poor standard of the cadets' drill; they appeared to be slouching along on the grass with none of the 'crisp crack and crash of British drill'. Then he understood that this was how it was meant to be; their aim was to create 'grace in an effortless unhurried step.'

Meanwhile, *Brutal and Licentious* was doing the rounds of publishers. Macmillan, Harpers and John Day had all turned it down, usually with a terse 'No comment'. Little Brown liked it and found it 'eminently readable', but could not put it in a category. Doubleday, Putnams, Alfred Knopf, Farrar Strauss, Holt all followed suit and rejected it. Keith Jennison told him not to be disheartened, and listed the successful writers who had had difficulty with their first book.

The end of 1948 marked the end of Masters's army career. His resignation was to take effect from midnight on 31 December. He decided to celebrate it in style and went to a local New Year's Eve party in the full-dress military mess kit of his regiment, with miniature medals – an impressive sight. As the party warmed up and became unmistakably raucous, one or two of the guests decided it was time to debag the proud Gurkha officer. Suddenly he was not at all amused and got very huffy when he saw they really meant it. Keith Jennison was there and saw him freeze. 'When Jack went cold on you, you could really feel it.'

Midnight came and symbolically he changed into civilian clothes. The party went on. Emily Jennison put her arm round him and said, 'You know when we first met, I thought you were going to be the only sort of Englishman I don't like. But you're not so bad and Barbara's marvellous.' By the time dawn was peeping through, Masters was singing his Gurkha jaunris and doing a nautch dance.

No longer a fighting man, but now a writing man, he had crossed a threshold. What lay ahead was still uncertain, decidedly so. His total net earnings for the past year had been a paltry $402.

He had other worries too; with February looming, his visitor's visa was due to expire. Desperate now to stay on, he engaged the services of a specialist lawyer, Kahn, whose tactic was to claim that Masters, with his Staff College background as an instructor, was a 'privileged academic'. Next Kahn claimed that, as he had been born on British territory within India, i.e. a British military hospital in Calcutta, Masters had to be a British citizen. Neither tactic worked. His neighbours, notably the Balabans, began collecting signatures on his behalf for a petition to Congress, testifying to his worthiness. One hundred and thirty-seven of them signed. Their district representative in Congress, Mrs Katherine St George, promised to introduce a special bill on his behalf and Senator Kilgore said he would do the same in the Senate. Masters was leaving no stone unturned.

In January 1949, the sublease of Hope House ran out. Troup and Alice Mathews stepped into the breach again and put them in touch with an actor friend, Tony Palmer, with a cottage outside Milltown, New Jersey. They could rent it free for three months, provided they looked after his two-year-old son, as the Palmers were going on tour with the Lunts. A Crossley car was there as well. They accepted with alacrity, grateful for the offer. The cottage, small and rather dilapidated, was in a predominantly Hungarian and Polish-American neighbourhood. The Masters children seemed happy playing in the sand with the Palmer boy, but whenever they misbehaved, Masters would smack his two, and the Palmer boy looked on surprised, unused to such stern methods. Soon he would queue up for his smack and Masters would give him a sweet as consolation.

Money was still tight, so Barbara went to New York twice a week to continue working for the Balabans, now at the Dorset Hotel on West 54th Street. Masters could keep up his writing as they still had their nanny with them. When their time in New Jersey came to an end, they were relieved to find Hope House available again for the same reasonable rent, $980 per annum. It was like coming home. They liked the lack of social pressure on South Mountain Road. It made few demands on Masters's life as a writer, and they were both relieved to be free of the dictates of class in England, where people of their type usually had to follow set patterns of behaviour and keep up appearances as a priority. Americans, he noticed, took each occasion on its merit and were much less judgemental. Conduct which in England might lead to social ostracism would be shrugged off here. Social life was much more mobile, much more fluid and Americans would 'tell all' on early acquaintance, believing in this social shorthand as if it was their story that counted rather than establishing their class background.

Masters was less happy about the upbringing of American children and the lack of guidance for them. It seemed too lax and permissive, though he had noted that the two Jennison sons, then twelve and ten, had a natural politeness and goodwill towards strangers, despite their somewhat undisciplined upbringing. Most American parents of the time were guided by Dr Spock, whose book *Baby and Child Care* had come out in 1946. Its opening line, 'Trust yourself. You know more than you think you do', was an invitation to parents to follow their instincts in bringing up their children and to respond instantly to the demands of babies. Such an approach was a reaction against hitherto prevailing attitudes, such as Dr Watson's *Psychological Care of Infant and Child*, whose text advocated: 'Never, never kiss your child. Never hold it in your lap. Never rock its carriage.' Masters was more old-fashioned in his views, and sought to combine being a hard taskmaster for his children with warmth and affection as a father. Susan and Martin remembered the excitement as he counted them up to bed at night, standing at the bottom of the stairs, and they had to be in bed by the time he counted zero.

Education was becoming an issue now with Susan aged five and Martin three. There was no question of shipping them back to England for boarding school, a repeat of his own schooldays. America was their home, and they were being brought up as American children and educated at American schools. Susan soon started at the local state school just down the road. Barbara and Masters attended PTA meetings, another eye-opener for them. They were amazed at the tolerance shown to speakers, however long-winded and off the point. It seemed to be part of the American respect for individualism and for freedom of speech. In England such educational discussions tended to be much more abrupt and heated.

Television now began, after its wartime lull, to intrude more into family life. It was still in black and white; colour was not introduced until 1952. Masters was not keen on television and restricted his children's viewing to one hour a day at their neighbours', the Auberjonoises', house, the matter to be reconsidered in a couple of years when his 'children, and TV, had grown up a bit.' He preferred them to discover their own resources, 'the solitary confrontation of oneself against the fact.' Too much outside entertainment was counter-productive and enfeebling, in his view.

The lawyer was still working on their immigration difficulties and came up with the suggestion that Barbara, who had been born in the UK, should go to Canada and get her own immigration permit and then come back to the USA and establish her legal domicile, which Masters could then be attached to. Meanwhile, he kept up his pressure on the authorities, with the express aim of convincing them he would make a worthwhile American citizen. He even offered to enlist in their army as a reserve officer and wrote to his old Burma commander, Field Marshal Slim, for a testimonial and to the Head of the British Military Mission in Washington to support his application. The US Army politely declined his offer.

In September 1949 the Masterses' money situation took a nosedive when the British Government devalued the pound by thirty per cent, thus reducing Masters's career gratuity by the same amount. This meant cutting even further back on expenses – the 'darn socks' syndrome, as they called it. In America, no one darned socks because it was cheaper to throw them away and buy new ones, whereas in England in times of hardship, people darned socks. All in all, Masters liked the way Americans viewed money – first working out how much they needed and then going out and getting it – a more enterprising approach than the penny-counting of England. Barbara's earning power at the moment was greater than his and she arranged to take on a secretarial post in New York at the rate of $60 per week. It meant she had to travel in each day, leaving Masters in charge of domestic chores, such as the cooking and ironing Susan's and Martin's clothes for school.

In November 1949, a year and a half since he had come across to the USA and started writing, *Nightrunners of Bengal* was still doing the rounds of publishers. Sticking to his schedule, he started on the second novel on his list about Thuggee. It was based on the historically true story of the Thugs, gangs of religiously-motivated men who had strangled and robbed travellers in central India undetected for centuries, before the English, in the person of William Sleeman, a 19th-century British administrator, had eventually discovered them. Masters was attracted to this highly dramatic theme because of its narrative strength and because it meant he could take his 'dialogue between races' idea a stage further. His aim here was to show how an ordinary, unsuspecting Englishman, William Savage, father of Rodney, could get himself involved in arcane and mysterious Indian rituals. Masters planned for him to disguise himself as an Indian in order to penetrate their secret society and ultimately reveal these secret goings-on. They were devotees of the goddess Kali, goddess of destruction and death.

Masters was exploring hidden Indian life in this book. He was also examining the extent to which the British were justified in intervening in local customs. Thuggee, evil as it was, was a practice that had been going on for centuries, and it must have been secretly approved of, and colluded with, by local populations. The British had clearly been unaware of Indian religious sensibilities at the time of the Mutiny, and here was another East-West divide that Masters was wanting to highlight. The book's title, *The Deceivers*, is a direct translation of the Hindi word for 'smilers', and hence refers to the smiling face of India, behind which much could go on unseen. The British, like people living in an upstairs room, would easily miss much of this.

Masters soon realised that William Savage would need to be characterised more subtly than his previous Savage family member, Rodney. William, very loosely based on the real life character of William Sleeman, would have to be depicted as an exception to the general run of district officer. Masters read Meadows Taylor's *Confessions of a Thug* in the New York Public Library as additional source material. Technically, he needed to make William interesting enough as a character in his own right and yet still credible when he joins the Thugs. Masters's solution was to make him a not particularly bright person, rather slow and hard-working, a loner, with enough of a liking for India to join the Thugs, and susceptible enough to take their communion and even murder on their behalf. The tension in the book comes from the acute moral dilemmas he faces. Should he kill as the Thugs do? Can he ever regain his former clear conscience? In line with the fascination and enigma of India theme, William soon finds that the longer he remains a Thug, the more strongly he is attracted to them. He even feels a competence as one of them that he never felt as a district officer. Masters seems to be hinting here at the potential for destruction within all of us and at the fatal attraction of India and the risks this poses for Europeans who, in succumbing to it, lose their identity in the process. Writing in this way was opening doors for Masters too, bringing out the 'Indianness' within himself. William's development as a character was like a journey into his own family past.

In November 1949, Barbara went to Canada as arranged. She and the children stayed with English friends in Montreal. At the US Consulate, they had to queue for hours, the children becoming restive in such unfamiliar surroundings. Armed with her precious immigration visa, she headed back to Rockland County, another lengthy and tiring train journey. When they got to the station, Masters was not there to meet them; his car, a Dodge given to them by a South Mountain Road resident who was buying a new one, had shed a gasket on the way. When he did arrive, Barbara was in tears. 'It was the only time she broke down during all these long and, in truth, nerve-racking years of literary rejection and official harassment', Masters wrote in *Pilgrim Son*. He had every reason to be indebted to her, as her forbearance had been the rock on which their relationship was founded.

Lippincott turned *Nightrunners* down, though their accompanying

letter spoke of 'a complete series of readings and a lot of discussions',
and the editor concerned was personally enthusiastic, telling Masters
that he could not help feeling that they were 'making a mistake and I
practically lost my voice saying so.' Things seemed to be looking up.

Rejections or not, there was still the Toad and Throstle to drink in.
Masters, always a keen drinker but never to excess, concocted his own
Dry Martini recipe based on House of Lords gin. In an idle moment
Keith and he devised the Martinicle, an iced Dry Martini stick that
could be sold to commuters at Grand Central Station to suck content-
edly on their way home. More practical considerations now interposed.
He and Barbara were using up money fast, no writing income was
coming in, other than the proceeds of an article about shooting a tiger
he had sold to *Field and Stream* for $300.

Keith Jennison had always kept a watchful eye on Masters's progress
as a writer. He was keen to help but Masters had put him off,
preferring to make his mark on his own rather than feel Jennison had
taken him out of friendship, which might not only compromise their
friendship but leave him never knowing how good he was. Jennison
had now moved from William Sloane Associates and joined Viking. He
asked to read the manuscript of *Nightrunners* but Masters always
refused. That autumn, in October 1949, he finally agreed to give
Jennison a copy. Jennison took it into his office, read it at one sitting
and, the next day, sent Masters the following letter: finished [your
manuscript] about an hour ago. Not to waste words – I'm crazy about
it. You're a born story teller, a very perceptive observer and a damn
damn good writer. It was one of the best reading experiences I've had
in many years.'

Masters was thrilled; it was a real breakthrough at last. When
Jennison called in over the weekend and confirmed what his letter had
said, Masters knew it was the beginning of something. Jennison
explained that he wanted to show it to a colleague at Viking, Helen
Taylor, and if she also liked it, they would put it forward to the
editorial board. Helen was interested and, after the next editorial
meeting at Viking, readers' reports were commissioned. They came
back in favour, even though there was still a feeling that it was not
quite a Viking book, which was then a very literary house. Jennison,
very much its champion, adopted Fabian tactics, bringing the book up
every other week, talking about it a little more, and, if he sensed that
the meeting was going to say 'no', he would then say, 'Let's forget it
for the moment.' Each time he filled in some more details of Masters's
background in India, a rich future source of material. Viking adhered
to the maxim 'We publish authors, not books'. Eventually the board

1914–1921

ABOVE Masters with his ayah, Calcutta, 1915. LEFT Mother and son. RIGHT On Eastbourne beach, aged seven, when he first arrived in England, with his nanny and her sister.

VE Fort William, Calcutta, aged CENTRE His mother at her home town of Scarborough.

ABOVE His parents at Eastbourne, 1921.

TOP OF PAGE At Cheltenham Prep School, a long way from India.
ABOVE School Prefects at Wellington, Michaelmas Term 1932. Masters is in the back row
extreme left; F.B. Malim, the Headmaster, is seated centre right.

ABOVE The two brothers in front of
Bailey Gate, the family home at
Uplyme, Dorset.

CENTRE In Sandhurst mufti.
ABOVE The Optimist.

LEFT Son preceding father.
RIGHT Masters's girlfriend, Lois Jervis.

INDIA

Top Left Family group at Bailey Gate before Masters set off for India, 1934.
Top Right Near Razmak in Waziristan.
Above With officers of the 4th Gurkha Rifles at Jullundur, December 1935. Back row: Fairweather,
Strickland, Goldney, Murray, Masters, Douglas, Lowis, Mills. Front row: Mackay, Murray-Lyon,
Graeme, Southgate, Madge.

ABOVE With the famous tiger he shot at Bakloh, February 1938; Gurkhas in attendance. BELOW With his regiment marching on column, and officers being served luncheon, on the North-West Frontier, 1937.

1945-1959

1974 –1980

CENTRE Chili and Marching Society members. From left standing: Chudd, Chudd, Unknown, Muchmore, Noyes, Overhage, Talley, Bogert, Kyger, Buresch, Masters, Masters, Attenburger, Casady, Bunker, Kyger, Bunker. Seated: Brennan, Shultz, Shultz, Scholder, Clark, Fuller, Jenks, Muchmore, Bontecue, Bogert (*Courtesy of Phil Shultz*).

ABOVE As sadhu, sitting naked und tree awaiting expedition memb near Platoro, Color

BELOW LEFT With Barbara at Santa Fe house. Masters is wea his favourite Navajo jewel.

BELOW RIGHT The warrior at

THE VIKING PRESS INC · PUBLISHERS
18 EAST 48TH STREET · NEW YORK 17 · NY
Cable: Vikpress   Telephone: PL 5-4330

Wednesday $\left(19\ \text{oct}\ 49 \right)$

Dear Jack:

Your manuscript arrived yesterday. I finished
it about an hour ago. Not to waste words — I'm
crazy about it. You're a born story teller,
a very perceptive observer and a damn damn good
writer. It was one of the best reading experiences
I've had in many years.

Helen will read it as soon as possible — I'm
reasonably certain her opinion will coincide with
mine, after that we will take up the matter
with Harold and Marshall.

My deep congratulations and rspect. I'll tell
you more over the weekend.

Yours,

was persuaded, not least the chairman, Harold Guinzburg, who had
had a hand in the publication of *Bengal Lancer* before the war and
liked Indian themes. As Jennison recalls, Guinzburg summed up the
decisive meeting, 'Maybe Keith knows what he's talking about. Let's
go.' An option agreement was drawn up and an advance of $350 was

offered with the balance of $650 due when editing was completed. Helen Taylor was appointed his editor.

Masters went into New York to meet her. She was a big, blonde woman, independent-minded, of liberal views, friendly but a tough editor, a true professional, firm but kind. They immediately hit it off together and she was to give him the sort of exacting encouragement that was crucial to his development as a writer. For the next six months they 'battled' over the book, by correspondence mostly, with Masters making a monthly visit to New York to see her and Keith at her office. Then the three of them would go for lunch at Louis and Armand's or to the Absinthe House.

Helen read through the first draft of *Nightrunners* and sent it back heavily corrected. 'Before you blow up in a cloud of sulphurous smoke at some of the hen-scratching, I'd like to reassure you, you are not a stumblebum of a writer, as many of the disfigured pages might indicate. Chapter 2 contains the most markings and this is fairly normal. Always, it seems, opening a book, a writer has the most awkwardnesses – something like stage fright.' She warned him about his 'tendency to overblow', the overuse of detail and adjectives, 'which often negates the impression you're striving for' and his use of repetitive phrases, such as 'ripe curve of the breast', 'eyes catching fire', or 'slumberous glance', which convey 'nothing real or telling'. She had, he admitted, recognised his main fault – 'hitting the same nail too hard, and too often'. She also warned him to tone down the explicitness of the sex scenes and scenes of rape and murder.

However, she had nothing but praise for his visual ability, a strength to outweigh the trying-too-hard attitude of a first-time writer. Masters accepted her criticisms – 'I have asked Keith to go on an adjective hunt' – but was upset by her adverse comments on his handling of 'blood and sex', and his use of explicit language. Here he hoped to be making an original and valuable contribution as a writer. 'I do not write anything indirectly – I do my best to say exactly what it is, in the plainest possible words.' This question of his use of 'raw' language was important to him. He felt it was authentic; it was what men of action used in such situations. In a drab post-war era he wanted to introduce colour and passion into books and his own version of explicit sex. He was also making a stand, a form of protest, against what he saw as the rather insipid and prissy writing then prevalent in England. His frankness and directness tied up in this way with his decision to leave England; here he was setting out to write in his own distinctive way and differently. India was like that, his argument ran, and men of action were like that too.

Helen explained that she was not asking him to go 'namby-pamby', but the Viking readers who had looked at the book so far all shared her feeling, 'and it's fairly safe to predict that it would be shared by the public.' He took the point, deferred to her professional judgement and toned down the relevant sections. By early April, the editing was done. Jennison called in again on his way home from work, a giveaway smile on his face, and announced, 'We're going to publish.' A date was set for January 1951. Masters felt 'weak with relief', for he had at last won a 'grim, wearing and painful' campaign.

Once the euphoria had subsided, a mixture of emotions set in: pleasure at this eventual moment of triumph over the many publishers who had turned the manuscript down; a momentary unease at what he was letting himself in for; and a characteristic determination to keep going, to prove his point and now to justify his publisher's faith in him. He took Barbara out to celebrate. Their two and a half years of struggle and ups and downs had paid off.

With *Nightrunners of Bengal* out of the way, he could tell Helen Taylor about his next book: 'I have started work on my next book, about the suppression of the Thugs. Period 1825; place – Central India; protagonist – William Savage, Rodney's father; tentative title – THE SMILERS; expected date of completion of draft for submission to publishers – 15th October, 1950.'

Summer was approaching and Barbara and he decided to get away. 'I have been doing desk work continuously and hard since September 1946, mostly seven days a week and often up to fourteen hours a day', he explained to Helen. The past two summers in the Hudson Valley had been hot and humid, enough for them to agree 'not again'. Besides, he wanted to give his own children 'the chiefest delight of my own childhood', a summer by the sea. He chose Maine. It was similar to the Cornwall of his childhood: rugged coastline, weatherbeaten fishermen, lobsters, Atlantic rollers, cliffs. He sent off for a list of rentable cottages from the Maine Information Bureau, and found a cheap and suitable one at Prince's Point, near Yarmouth. To pay the three months' rent of $150, they needed to sublet South Mountain Road and put an advertisement in the local paper, but there were no takers, so following the new American principle of acting first and finding the money afterwards, he booked the Maine cottage. Then, as if to confirm his theory, the bandleader at their local country club rang to take their house, offering $550 for the three months – a welcome profit of $400 on the two deals.

They left on 10 June to drive up to Maine, taking Marie-Laure

Auberjonois, then aged thirteen, with them as a companion for the children. En route they stopped off at Mystic, Connecticut, to visit the Whaling Museum there, and noted the look of this peaceful town with its old houses and broad-sheltered estuary ringed by elms. As they reached the Maine coastline, the air smelled sharply of fresh seaweed, and they lunched at the Westcustogo Inn on their first steamed clams and lobster rolls. Their cottage was primitive but perfectly liveable. Masters made a work place for himself at a table in their bedroom, and kept up a morning work routine. The afternoon was spent exploring their surroundings, the nearby cove with its small curved sandy beach, hemmed in by seaweed-covered rocks. No one else in sight, Maine was as they had hoped.

A daily routine was soon established. 'Jack seems to be able to work pretty well here. I take the children out as soon as possible in the morning and he comes down to the beach and fetches us back in time for a cold lunch mostly', Barbara wrote to his parents. Their mood was still buoyant and the euphoria of success released a lot of pent-up energy. 'We explored the White Mountains and scrambled up rocky streams in the Pemigewasset wilderness; we built sand castles and rode the surf at Higgins beach and dug up bushels of steamer clams and watched our children meet and play with our neighbours.' The feeling of a united family was something both he and Barbara treasured, and now his writing was running well. He wrote to Helen the following week: 'I have been trying to tell Keith how much his belief in *Nightrunners* and in me in this strange new profession meant to me. I think your own share in the book is just as big, and I want to thank you. I hope we shall continue in the same way for years to come; maybe in ten or fifteen years my prose will be entirely free from flowers and suet. Then, by God, you can stand me a drink.'

He and Barbara went for evening walks along the beach towards Half-Way Rock lighthouse, perched on the edge of the Atlantic. These were moments to savour. 'The transformation which we knew, theoretically, would happen when we left England had come to pass. We physically loved America. We had lost nothing of love for the English land, but the nostalgia for it had faded.' America was now very much their home; Masters had none of the expatriate's longing for the old country. Something seemed to have clicked into place, a realisation that they had crossed over a divide. 'This land under our feet, Maine or Rockland or Manhattan, was where our hearts rested. From now on, wherever we travelled, however much we thrilled to the journeys, it was these seas, this sun, this wind that would define "home".' He had acquired a new sense of belonging and he knew that he could thrive in

America in a way he was never likely to do in England. Unexpected gestures reinforced this feeling. A local store owner, George de Freitas, originally from Portugal, closed his shop for the day to show them and the children how to fish off Bailey Island. It was an example of the communalism of America, the melting pot of all nationalities, that he could feel part of.

A memorable event of their stay was a Maine clambake, organised by their neighbours, the Curtis family. They all met on the beach in mid-afternoon and collected driftwood and seaweed for the fire, which was then layered with lobsters, clams, corn on the cob, chicken and eggs; seaweed was placed between each layer, to a height of 3 feet. All this was then pressed down with a huge tarpaulin cover weighted with rocks. While the bake went on, they played softball on the beach and drank bourbon and beer. As evening fell, the tarpaulin was lifted off and a smell 'indescribably biblical and savoury' burst out, to sighs and groans of 'pure animal contentment'. There followed what Masters called the greatest eating experience he had ever known. 'Everything was done to perfection, each part distinctive in its own flavour, but welded by the savour of smoke and seaweed and the steaming juices of the other ingredients into one single, great whole.'

Their pleasure was greatly enhanced when a few days later Mrs Rounds, the wife of their landlord, hurried over to the cottage to tell them a long distance telephone call from New York had come through. Masters went over to take it. It was Keith Jennison, his voice trembling with emotion. The Literary Guild had chosen *Nightrunners of Bengal* as their Book of the Month for January 1951. Masters's share of the guaranteed royalties would be over $16,000. 'And Mr Beecroft of the Guild says you have written a damned good book.' It was the high point of the summer.

Keith followed his telephone call with a letter: 'It is difficult to describe the extent of our happiness over the sagacity displayed by the Literary Guild in selecting your book. We all send our congratulations. You will probably be asked to do a good deal of radio appearances around publication time. Before that time, if you would like your advance against the book increased, you have only to ask.' And Helen Taylor added her comments:

It was a wonderful thrill. I had to take a little white dope pill to calm me down. A break like this sets you ahead in your writing career to an incalculable degree. And it's a complete justification of the sturm and drang of the editorial process to which you so gallantly submitted yourself. You have been patient and understanding and intelligent

about the whole business over these many months, and now you've
been duly rewarded, not only for the perfectly workmanlike attitude
you've had, but for the talent and ability you bring to historical
fiction. I couldn't be happier about it.

Her and Keith's praise really mattered to him; they were now part of a
team and their joint professionalism spurred him on. In Maine he kept
up work on his new Thuggee book, aware as he wrote of other
interesting parallels: the similarity of Thug rituals to Christian ones as
both had a communion, and the fact that both Hindu and Muslim
followers had been devotees of Kali, a Hindu goddess. This surely
meant that a Christian such as his William Savage could be drawn by
her power as well. The Thuggee cult, a secret society, made him think
of Nazism: 'the mystique cutting across all other faiths; the ritual
necessity to kill, to wipe out; the sense of being God's appointed right
hand on earth; above all the arousal of a feeling in the non-Nazi, the
non-Thug, that cried, "How could these ordinary people be turned into
such monsters?"' As he went on writing and revising, Masters felt it
was a richer theme by far than *Nightrunners of Bengal.*

The Masters family returned to South Mountain Road on Labor Day
weekend in the first week in September. The traffic was so heavy that
they were held up 40 miles north of their home and had to spend the
night en route. The Literary Guild news had reached their friends
locally and greetings were plentiful, even tearful. Miriam Howell told
him that a prestigious English publisher, Michael Joseph, would take the
book. The manuscript had been taken across to London in proof form by
Ben Huebsch of Viking and put on his friend Robert Lusty's desk at
Michael Joseph 'as a present'. Lusty read the book and liked it and
Masters joined a distinguished list that included H. E. Bates and C. S.
Forester, among others. Miriam had arranged for his agents in London
to be Pearn, Pollinger and Higham, an equally prominent firm founded
in the 1930s. She told him that further afield two Swedish publishers
were competing for the rights as well. Success was snowballing.

'We got back home early Tuesday', he wrote to his parents on 8
September, 'dashing round madly that day, arranging for people to
look after the kids, picking up mail, fixing the departure of our tenants,
etc. Next day we went in for a celebratory lunch at 21 with Keith and
Miriam – smoked salmon, oysters, soft-shelled crabs – God knows
what it cost, probably about five pounds a head, but the publishers
were paying, so what the hell.' The mood of exuberance continued with

an afternoon shopping spree: a suit and dress for Barbara, a dressing gown and his first Brooks Brothers suit of 'excessive correctness' for himself. Their evening ended up with a visit to a night club, the Latin Quarter, to dance and see a girlie-show – 'a pilao show – all legs and breasts.'

At last he could afford a decent car and bought a pale green Plymouth convertible, and they decided to throw the first of what became an annual party in October, inviting everyone they knew – one hundred and twenty guests in all – and feeding them fried chicken and beer. Nevertheless he soon settled back into his writing routine, and by the end of October wrote to Helen: 'Heil, hi, and what-ballyho. It is my birthday, and I have finished the first fine narrative rapture of THUG.' 60,000 words, out of an expected 85,000, had been completed.

Masters went through anxious moments waiting for Helen's and Keith's reactions, the nervousness all writers undergo over their second book. Was it going to be as good as the first, or 'just the first with a different setting and all the original sap expended?' Then Keith rang up and said he liked it more than *Nightrunners*. Helen echoed him, 'The main characters are more real to me, than Rodney, Caroline or Joanna ever became. The writing is cleaner, freer and faster; the action develops naturally and never seems forced.' Masters was relieved and gratified by this response; it showed he was developing as a writer. Barbara conveyed this in a letter home to his parents: 'Isn't it grand about Jack's second book? We are thrilled to death – it really looks as if he'll make a great success of writing.'

The English nanny was beginning to play up, and they had to send her home. 'Nanny was mad as a hatter, we found out in the end. Suppressed sex. She used to watch through our bedroom keyhole when she thought anything interesting might be going on till I peered at her through it and blew violently. She used to wander through the house at midnight singing tunelessly. We sent her back with a chit advising no one to employ her except by the day and to send her back to her mother at night.' In any event, her services were no longer really needed with Martin and Susan growing up.

By now the Korean War had started, casting a gloom over their and most people's mood. Red China crossed the 38th Parallel on 28 December. It generated feelings of impermanence: 'More and more I feel what's the use of planning things ahead . . . if you have any money go out and spend it, and have a good time. God knows what is going to happen in the world. All the pale pinks like the *New Statesman* crowd blame MacArthur, who may not be the greatest man who ever lived, as he thinks, but in this case has only been doing what he was

told to do . . . right now things could not look worse, but what the hell
. . . let us have our boots on when we fall.' He rarely got involved in
politics but adhered to his military viewpoint, namely that if an army
was sent in, it had a job to do and should be supported.

Nightrunners of Bengal was published on 26 January 1951, and Masters
went in to New York for the day for lunch with Keith and Helen at 21,
where a 'rich but tasteless' curry had been specially prepared by the
chef. The book attracted much publicity and was widely reviewed.
Orville Prescott in *The New York Times* wrote that 'Few first novels
historical or otherwise are greeted by such a blare of trumpets as Mr
Masters has received.' The historical novelist, F. van Wyck Mason
added his praises: 'To me this is one of the most fascinating pieces of
historification I have encountered in a long while.'

Indeed, nearly all the reviews were gratifyingly favourable. Orville
Prescott saved some criticism for the 'violence for its own sake'; he
worried about the way the author 'piled on the horrible details of rape
and murder with an insistence close to relish' and thought the 'ripe and
gaudy prose spattered with purple patches' excessive at times, but,
basically, he was hailing a new writer with enthusiasm.

Masters himself always claimed not to put too much store by critics.
He took an aversion to what he called the American liberal establishment and their East Coast reviewers. He saw himself writing primarily
for a general readership, people who would lap up such high drama
and appreciate the gore and violence, which was justified, in his
view, by the subject matter he was dealing with. The sales figure
proved him right. *Nightrunners* stayed on the bestseller lists for several
weeks following publication and within six months had sold over
300,000 copies.

The English edition followed some four months later, in May – a
pattern usually followed for all his books. English reviewers were just
as laudatory. John Raymond in the *New Statesman* called it 'the best
historical novel about the Indian Mutiny that I have ever read. Mr
Masters is a specialist who knows how to arrange his material. He has
that intuitive sense of history that so many novelists of his type lack.'
Readers familiar with India appreciated it just as readily. They admired
his accuracy and the rightness of the 'feel' he gave of the country and
his insight into Indian character. Here, it seemed, was a new author,
knowledgeable and forthright, who was giving them back some of the
India they had just lost. He immediately built up a following among his
readers and they eagerly anticipated his second book.

Masters sent signed copies to all of the members of his family,

including one to Alex, who wrote back congratulating him effusively –
too effusively, as it turned out. In Masters's letter back, his hackles
were rising. He admonished Alex for putting no date on his letter:
'H'm, no date. What sort of p.s.c. did *you* get?' He goes on, keeping his
younger brother very much in place: 'I am glad you liked the book,
though you seem to have a rather higher opinion of it in the scale of
literature than most people and critics over here. It is not deathless
prose but it is all right at the level I wrote it – an adventure story.'

Then, comes the punch line: '*And*, my boy, whatever the defects of my prose style, you have developed an extraordinarily pompous style of your own! Parts of your letter sounded as if they had been written by the Suffragan Bishop of Nyasaland or Cameroons. The phrase about "brother love for the wog" is the sort of thing I would only put in the mouth of the most blimpish character I could imagine, except I'd think it was overdoing it.'

Clearly Alex had transgressed by using the term 'wog' and its conjunction with 'brother love' was too much for Masters. It revived the spectre of racism and their separate stance towards it. Part of his motivation for writing the book had been to highlight British racial intolerance in India. It was always an issue close to his heart. He had detested it in India when he came across it among British serving officers and soldiers, and here in America on an early visit to North Carolina, he had felt just as indignant. Alex and he had different perspectives on India and different responses to their Indian background. Alex had sought to distance himself by becoming more and more of an English gentleman and, implicitly in this letter, invites his brother to join him and disassociate himself from 'the wog'. Masters resists in firm but quite unequivocal terms: 'Personally I do believe in brother love for everyone, if you can manage it. If you or I, or anyone, can't manage it, as we often can't, the defect is in us, not in the "Wog", "Jap", "Chink", "Dago", or "Kike".' He reminds Alex that he left England and came to America because 'I do believe all men are created free and equal. This country does try and live up to that, and recognises its own fault when it cannot.'

It is a clear statement of where Masters stood on both the racial issue and some of the reasons for his 'exile' to America. His writing was in part to discover, or rather bring in, more of his origins, more of his family background, not leave it out. He wanted to explore its relevance to him. Writing in this way was like uncovering a text that had already been written, uncovering hidden messages from his past.

His letters to Alex, and to his parents, give a broad picture of his life during his time in America. Towards Alex he is still quite protective over the issue of settling into normal life after his harrowing prisoner-of-war experiences. Masters warns him against using these as a crutch. 'Being a prisoner of war in the last conflict was damned hard luck – but it's not a professional calamity. During the war I met some characters fairly high up in the Indian Army who had been prisoners in the first war, or in the early days of this one. It wasn't the prisonership that made them touchy, but the fact that some of them seemed to have spent the rest of their careers brooding over it instead of getting on

with the job and trying to forget it had happened. Verb. sap.' He
wanted to infuse Alex with some of his own go-aheadness.

The success of *Nightrunners* had put money in the bank and, for the
first time since they had come to the USA, the Masterses could choose
what to do. Their first priority, they decided, was to buy a house of
their own. They had been living in rented accommodation for too long.
The children needed a settled home. Martin, his father calculated, had
travelled 11,000 miles and lived in seven different houses by the age of
four. There might even be an outside chance of Liz and Mike coming
to live with them if they had a more permanent home.

Masters was in favour of a move elsewhere. He could not quite
believe that they had been lucky enough to arrive in the best place in
the world straightaway. 'A good, a very good place, yes – but the best?'
It was his restless side coming out again. This searching for something
better had a long history; it had to do with his eye for the main chance,
which went back to ditching the Waight children for the more glamorous Odlums. Barbara, reasonably enough, was in favour of staying,
arguing that the people on South Mountain Road were 'nice, fun,
intelligent – they read, talk and write. I don't see how we could do
better than here.'

Masters had a fear of getting stuck, of being dragged down. Moving
on was a way of combating this, just as his fondness for ordering and
scheduling was a way of covering the void and keeping depression at
bay. Alastair Reid, another exile, has written in this context: 'What
haunts a foreigner is the thought of finding, in the places where he
comes to rest, the ghosts he thought were left behind; or else of losing
the sharp edge, the wry, surprised eye that keeps him extraconscious of
things. Even at his most assured, he tends to keep a bag packed in
case.' Masters was, at this stage in his life, caught by similar conflicting
urges, whether to put down roots or to keep on the move.

As a family man, other considerations were prompting him, such as
the wish to recreate a 'lost' childhood landscape. Alastair Reid takes
up this point too: 'We spend a good part of our lives trying to find
these landscapes again, trying to lose ourselves in the sense in which
children are lost. We come away with no more than occasional glimpses,
whiffs, suggestions, and yet these are enough, often, to transform
suddenly the whole current of our lives.' Masters's childhood landscape
had been by the sea: his brief kingdom by the sea at Eastbourne before
the onset of school, and later of family summer holidays in Devon and
Cornwall. He now wanted to give his children a taste of this carefree
childhood existence.

They started looking for a house by the sea and turned once again to the classified ads in *The New York Times*. They thought first of Maine, but it was far from New York and its climate off-putting, as locals said, 'down here we have two seasons, July and winter'. Then they saw a house for sale in Mystic, Connecticut, the place where they had stopped off the summer before on their way to Maine. They went to see it and liked it: it was an old, white-painted lath house, not too large, with green shutters and sycamore trees on an acre and a half of lawn sloping down to a low sea wall. Masters liked it immediately, Barbara agreed and they bought it for $22,000. Viking provided them with a loan of $13,000, set against future earnings. The house was to the west of the town, but right on the sea, at Goat Point, West Mystic.

They arrived there early in April 1951 and Masters soon wrote to Helen Taylor to tell her about it. 'We have arrived after not much more than the expected turmoil, and we are settling in. The place is fine, the people – we will have to wait several months to make up our minds. There are masses of other kids for ours to play with, so they're enjoying it. I sprained my ankle the day before moving. Ha! Ha! It is a little better now, in fact quite a lot.' He soon got into his routine, working from 9 till 12 in the morning, then lunch and a nap, more work and letters and 'admin'' until 4 p.m., after which he would play with the children till 6, then, punctual as ever, have his first Dry Martini at precisely 6 p.m. But it was not long before he began to miss South Mountain Road, especially at moments like this. A letter to Keith Jennison at the end of their first month there conveys this: 'We are here and everything is fine but we sorely miss our Emilys and our Keiths and Carols and Amelias and all the other drunken God-bleeding damned bastards on South Fugging Mountain Road. I will not go into the sordid tale of our activities here, except that we have had tea with the vicar, who is English and browned-off, and seen little of anyone else, and painted and patched and dug and weeded and burned assorted garden junk and made a very fair unpleasaunce by the sea wall. Trains flash by on their way to and from great cities and we rout the fleas in the old chicken house by devious means.'

The truth was that they were both finding New England a little too staid, agreeable but lifeless. 'I am getting bored; I like things to happen – either to be working, or to be opening letters and cashing fat checks, or swearing at someone for not sending me the checks, or arranging overdrafts, or something', Masters bemoaned in another letter to Keith.

Masters asked for news of how the Thug book was progressing, now that the editing had been completed. The publication date had already

been set for January 1952, just a year after his first book. Viking was
hoping to make him a January author. Magazine articles were then
considered a valuable adjunct to a writer's career. Masters told Keith
that he was trying to persuade a magazine to send him off to the East
to write a series of articles on affairs in India, Pakistan and Nepal –

> the articles to be subjectized (angle-wise) in relation to the views
> (reader-interest-wise) of the publications concerned. At least, I have
> asked Miriam to get some action on this scheme. My point is that I
> have an unusual set of contacts in the three countries named; that
> world affairs are making accurate information about those countries
> more and more necessary to Americans; that I have a strong desire,
> and I believe some ability, to get in, find out, and write something
> interesting but true. If you can do anything to forward this plan,
> please do so. Come on Keith, catch hold of an unsuspecting editor
> and swing him round by the balls until he drops off, or coughs up.

All along Masters had nursed a desire to return to India. Meanwhile,
as he told Keith, he was doing the next best thing, writing about it. 'As
you know I do not consider myself qualified to write deathless prose,
or even the novel of our generation, but I do think I have as yet got
several things to say about people and events in the near and far past
which must be said.' A modest disclaimer perhaps, but he was getting
more and more into his stride and a month later sent Keith an outline
of his imminent writing plans.

Subject:- WRITING PLANS FOR JOHN MASTERS FOR
JULY 1951–1952.

1. After much thought I am reasonably sure that I ought to devote
    the next two years to writing two books simultaneously, viz
    another Savage novel and a biography of the late Orde Wingate.
    The novel would be completed about July 1952, the biography
    about July 1953.

2. The Savage novel:– This would be the centre on the actions and
    character of Robin Savage, Rodney's son, the small boy who was
    after so much hardship rescued from death in the Mutiny. The
    year will be about 1882, when Robin is twenty-eight. There will
    be two story levels in the book:– a story of secret service in the
    Pamirs on the borders of India, Russia, and Afghanistan, and a
    story of spiritual conflict between Robin and the world as
    represented by a young woman he loves.

I have no idea yet how the secret service tale will develop. It will take up about two thirds of the book's wordage and will involve Robin's exploring, searching, and fighting in the high and lonely places of Asia, 'the misty rooftrees of the world, where the wind always blows'. The second level is based on the fact that Robin's experiences as a baby have turned him, as he grew up, into a recluse, a solitary and mystic, a kind of pacifist. Nevertheless he is, by tradition, an officer of the Indian Army.

He then described how the book would open during the Afghan war of 1879–1882. Robin is suspected of cowardice in action. He is also about to become engaged to a girl. The girl is deeply in love with him. The second level of the story would describe the girl's struggle for Robin.

At first she is fighting for him against the world – she gets him the secret service job so that he can prove his courage; she becomes engaged to him in the face of all opposition. Later, she comes to realise that she is fighting with the world for Robin. It is in this part of the struggle that she marries him and bears twins. All the while, in high and lonely places, Robin is being forced to realise that even she and his children are parts of the violent and bloody earth which he hates. The climax comes when all these paths are converged. Robin's incredible courage in the secret service becomes known, and the world is eager to accept him; the woman has used every means and fought until she can fight no more; Robin has worked out what he believes and what he is.

The girl, THE LOTUS, has been fighting the thing that all women fight in all men, to the extent that they find it, THE WIND. A part of the book's impact depends on my ability to transmit THE WIND and why men will run away after it. Of course she loses and Robin goes, he disappears into the wastes of Central Asia, with the wind. (Actually he will become an archaeological explorer and mystic on the model of one of the greatest and bravest and wisest men who ever served India, Sir Aurel Stein). This book I want to call THE LOTUS AND THE WIND.

The biography of Orde Wingate appealed to him as Wingate was, in his eyes,

a very unusual man – animated by a daemon, shielded by the intoler-ably aggressive confidence of a prophet, armed with a mental power of a kind that could unbalance Winston Churchill; he did not come ready-made off the production bench of Charterhouse and Woolwich; unusual hands shaped him and unusual events finished him. He fitted into the peacetime regular army as Chinese Gordon had, i.e. not at all and violently so. He explored the Libyan desert and wrote learned papers for the Royal Geographical Society. He organised irregulars in Abyssinia and Chindits in Burma. Whether by nature or from art he achieved in his legend, while he was alive, a blend of Stonewall Jackson and Lawrence of Arabia.

Now with his own knowledge of Wingate, Masters felt he was well placed to write about him and his strange individualism, his Establishment background and his need to distance himself from it. 'His acts are a record of adventure, which should fill at least half of any biography of him. But here too there is a second level. Wingate had a daemon. Where did it come from? Why? Did he try to exorcise it, or decide to embrace it? Did he really believe that he was a prophet of the Old Testament?'

Masters was motivated, too, by what he considered to be the poor quality of the 'small spate of war memoirs, the majority rather poorly written', published about Wingate and the Chindit campaign, Wingate appearing in these stories as a 'sort of ready-made offstage genie.' His biography would, he assured them, be 'absolutely and ruthlessly accurate, tightly-written, and hard. Only so can I hit the reader in his living room with the force of Wingate's own personality. I doubt if anyone else is as qualified as I am to write this book. No one who had not known, heard and spoken to Wingate could write it with sufficient force of feeling.'

The biography would obviously depend on getting sole rights from Mrs Wingate and he hoped both his English and American publishers would come up with a two-book contract and a 'substantial' advance of about $7,000 to include his travelling expenses. In the end Masters's Wingate biography never came to anything, as Wingate's widow would not agree to his writing it. An 'official' biography did appear later, written by Christopher Sykes, in 1959.

The Lotus and the Wind soon absorbed him. Set in the early 1880s, its background was the Great Game, a subject explored by Kipling in *Kim*, but the book Masters had in mind as his model was Erskine Childers's *The Riddle of the Sands*, in his view 'the best spy story ever written'. By switching the setting from the sea background of north Germany to the mountain background of the Himalayas, and drawing on his own first-hand experience, not only of the North-West Frontier, but also his own passionate feeling for Central Asia, known to him partly through his 1940–1941 campaigns there, Masters hoped to evoke the mind of a loner and searcher after truth in such remote and spectacular settings.

There was something of himself in this. Indeed, each Indian novel was bringing out a different side of him. Here Robin keeps searching, rather like the Flying Dutchman, 'for what I don't know. I have to be alone, stripped of all that encumbers thought. I must be free to move like the wind across the earth. I love this girl but she terrifies me. The deeper she gets into my heart, with her need for love and a home, the more I fear her, because she will kill me. I am the wind. Hold the wind still, and what happens to it? It dies. She is the lotus, a flower. Tell the flower to follow the wind, throw it up in the wind, and what happens to it? It dies.' There was something of the 'wind' in Masters too, the restless mover reluctant to settle down, with that special British liking for the desert, for being a loner, where he might discover, like Alexander the Great in a favourite Shelley poem of his, the 'secret strength of things'. The novel, whether Masters was conscious of it or not, belongs to the tradition of quest narrative like Rider Haggard's *She*, Kipling's *The Man Who Would Be King* and Conrad's *Heart of Darkness*, all voyages into imperial darkness that exhibit a flight from woman and show the male dread of woman's sexual and generative powers. Robin in this book is fleeing from what he too sees as 'false pretences'.

The Great Game, so called after the threat of 19th-century Russian expansion into Central Asia, offered a suitable backdrop for this novel. The Great Game itself had become a 'tournament of shadows', as one of the Czar's ministers defined it, an elaborate chess game of spy and counterspy. The playing field was the vast uncharted territory between the Caspian and the Karakorams, its borders Afghanistan and Tibet. Much of it was desert or mountain, all of it inhospitable and dangerous. The players were the official, or unofficial, agents of Britain and Russia, who were usually a particular sort of young man, typical of the age – adventurous to the point of foolhardiness, first-rate linguists and geographers, possessing much intellectual ability. Masters was going to make his Robin Savage representative of this type.

It was proving technically difficult to write. Masters's proficiency as a writer was moving too fast. He liked to plan each book thoroughly in advance and map out each character's progress. Now his characters were refusing to stick to the channels he had cut out for them, and seemed to be acquiring a life of their own. He wondered if he might have been too ambitious in his original aims. 'I had set up a target and was now finding it beyond the range of my weapons.' Robin was like the haunting presence of an individual he wanted to understand. The peculiar affinity which develops between Robin and his adversary, the Russian spy Muralev, as they play out their own 'tournament of shadows', was an examination of the 'other' within everyone. Muralev is both the enemy and Robin's shadow side. It made it an intriguing voyage of self-discovery for Masters, as much as for his creation. When Robin goes into the desert, he says: 'I want something which I don't seem able to find among people... I've only met one man who can help me and he is an enemy. I don't know why he is so important to me, because I only spoke to him three or four times. But things happened that made me sure he is like me, only farther on, closer to finding what he's looking for.' It brings him to a recognition and understanding of opposites, 'that every human quality is balanced, there is no humility without pride, no love without hate, no courage without cowardice.' It was a theme Masters was to explore in later novels.

He took time off from his writing that summer and went camping with Barbara in the White Mountains of New Hampshire. They stopped for the night near Berlin, also in New Hampshire, pitching a tent in the woods near the Appalachian Trail. In the middle of the night they were woken by the sound of a locomotive labouring up the Androscoggin Valley, Montreal-bound. 'The exhaust beat grew louder, stronger, though always hollowed and blurred by our remoteness on the mountain above. We watched the searchlight creep up the valley, and at the unseen crossings heard the long mournful owl call of the whistle. That call has always cried America! for me, ever since I first heard it at Kingman, Arizona, on a Santa Fe express grinding in out of a Mojave blizzard in a winter night of 1938.' These moments of identification with the physical presence of America were clearly important to him, binding him to the earth around him, its physicality and landscape as powerful a force of attraction as the life he was leading. On their way back from New Hampshire, they made a detour through Brattleboro in Vermont to look, through the hedge, at Kipling's former house, Naulakha, just outside the town. It was a large, greystone building that could have come straight from Simla. Kipling had spent four productive years there in the 1890s and had written *Kim* while there. Kipling was Masters's mentor in many ways, and Masters's secret hope was to emulate Kipling or at least to follow in his footsteps. This glimpse of Kipling's former residence gave him added impetus to continue as a writer.

At Mystic Masters settled down to work again. He wrote to his brother in September,

> the writing business prospers pretty well, though one never knows from minute to minute what the hell is happening or going to happen.

Being a writer is like being a messenger boy in a hotel corridor; you knock on every door in sight, and then sit down and wait to see if anyone is going to open, or if they do what they are going to offer. Sometimes one seems to wait a lifetime, and no door opens – they all remain closed and blank; suddenly one opens – then one starts getting excited about that, then 20 more open . . . meanwhile chap #1 slams his door in your face again . . . and so on and so on. Right at this moment I have received payment from the *Ladies' Home Journal*, who have bought *The Deceivers* for one-shot condensation. I got $5,000 as my share and had to put $3,000 straight into a savings account to pay next year's taxes.

Alex was still unsettled. His arthritis, an effect of his wartime experiences, was troubling him, and he was still feeling hard done by. Masters took up the cudgels on his behalf.

What worried me, and what I wrote about in my last letter, was that sometimes people in your position get persecution complexes. I was convinced, back in 1936, that one Willy Weallens, was persecuting me – and I didn't have any such misfortune behind me such as the POW business. It turned out in the end that he thought I was a shit and was needling me in order that I might cease to be a shit; later when I was his adjutant we became great friends. I suppose my point is that from the angle of the Medical Service boys, and the bosses generally, everyone is allowed to get on the wrong side of someone, once; after that he becomes a bolshie. Privately I'm damned sure that's what happened to Daddy. I also feel that Daddy may have made a poor appreciation some time in the early 1920s. He likes fishing, shooting and riding; he couldn't get them anywhere in the world as cheaply or as much as in India; perhaps a little more bootlicking, or tact, or industrious militarism would have given him ten more years in India, ten more years of that life. I often thought of him when I was in Burma, on those lines. Your own Gehenna seems to be over and I hope you'll be able just to forget the whole thing and start again.

Masters's relationship with his brother was important to him, as his correspondence indicates. He was concerned for him, but impatient too. As he points out, his experience in Burma had taught him a few lessons. Command had nourished him and toughened him up, and he wanted Alex to learn from that. It was not easy for Alex to be the younger brother as he recently admitted. 'Jack was the great man, and always made me out to be a fool. I grew up thinking everyone was the same standard as Jack but they weren't. It took me a long time to realise I was a damn sight cleverer than most people I met. Jack always made me think he was normal, he wasn't, he was so superior, but he never encouraged me, or said "you're quite a clever boy, really" – which I was.' The childhood legacy stayed with them and here, as before, Masters urges Alex not to allow history to repeat itself. He saw himself as pacesetter for the family, and never let up.

At Mystic the rumble of disquiet started. On the surface, life seemed to be thriving. He was writing another potentially successful book, his children seemed fit and happy, browning themselves in the sun and wind, the house was nice, the New York Giants were on a winning streak. 'We settled back in our chairs and told ourselves, "This is it, this is what it's going to be like for the rest of our lives."' But it did not feel like that. Something was missing. Mystic was too good to be true, too 'right'.

The atmosphere in the town was certainly more formal than they expected. It was prim and stuffy, with an emphasis on gracious living for its own sake – the 'white gloves and hats brigade' Masters called it – that was new to them in America. They found Mystic people honest, generous and hard-working, but they disliked their snobbery, which was evident in such things as The Daughters of the American Revolution. It made Masters reflect, 'We had not come to the US in search of the aristocratic ideal; we had seen that system working, and pretty well, in England.' America was meant to be a fresh start rather than a repeat of old colonial ways transposed to another setting. Mystic seemed too close to that with its hierarchies and propriety. Barbara had been right, they really belonged in Rockland County.

After six months they had had enough. The last straw was when their neighbours asked them not to paint their shutters blue 'because that's the colour the Italians paint them.' They put out inquiries on houses available on South Mountain Road and Laura Auberjonois, who sometimes acted as a house agent, told them that a house had just come on the market at a reasonable price. It belonged to Helen Eustace, author of the bestselling *Horizontal Man*, whom they knew slightly. It was next door to the Jennisons and was a former farm house, with five and a half acres of land, and about 2 miles from their previous house and thus in the same school district. The poor quality of the schools in Mystic in comparison to Rockland County had been another reason for wanting to leave. It was too good an opportunity to miss and they told Laura there and then to reserve it for them, and they would send a cheque in the next post. They put their Mystic house on the market.

To make matters worse, when the locals saw the house was up for sale, they asked them not to sell it to a Jew or Negro. In the end, they sold it for a small profit and headed back to Rockland County. It was November 1951. 'Our experiment in Connecticut had failed. We had no regrets. We had learned a lot.'

In Rockland County they were greeted with 'affectionate badinage' by their friends, ribbing them for their foolhardiness in preferring New England. Their new home, Well Wheel House, was at the eastern end of South Mountain Road, in the hamlet of Centenary. It was formerly a farm, barn-red in colour, with white shutters and wistaria climbing up one wall. A maple tree stood by the front door giving welcome shade in summer and bathing the living room with autumnal golden light. The children immediately took to the house. It was roomy enough with a large lawn and an orchard of apple trees beyond. Barbara's green fingers set about transforming the 300-foot road frontage, planting it with forsythia.

A letter came through from England from an old 4th Gurkha colleague, Hamish Mackay, who had led the assault on Mandalay Hill in 1945, enquiring about coming over to the USA. 'We find the couldn't-care-less attitude of people here little to our liking.' Mackay was then fifty-two, a retired full colonel with DSO and bar. Masters, ever mindful of America as the land of opportunity, encouraged him to do so. Mackay and his wife found jobs as butler and housekeeper with a wealthy Long Island family, thereby earning enough money to put their daughter through her English public school.

Six months had elapsed and no order for his deportation had come through. Was he now a legal resident? A new lawyer working on his case, Simon Rifkind, rang the immigration bureau on his behalf. They confirmed that they would now consider him a resident and that they would record his date of legal entry into the USA as 9 February 1948, i.e. the day he stepped off the *Queen Elizabeth*. He immediately put in his application for US citizenship, something he had been waiting to do for some time. This, too, was backdated to February 1949, ironically ahead of Barbara's, whose legal immigration had been the only way he had managed to remain there in the first place! A tortuous saga was reaching its end. His British passport expired that April; the British Consul-General told him that as he had been born in India, he could only now get a Republic of India one, which he applied for and 'formally abandoned the idea, so long dear to me, that I was an Englishman.'

Keith Jennison liked the finished version of *The Lotus and the Wind* and called it 'an enormously good book, one of the most truly impressive books I have read in years', and went further by telling Masters that 'the privilege and excitement of being associated with the introduction and development of a writer such as you is what makes book publishing worthwhile for me.' Helen Taylor was just as enthusiastic. 'I finished *Lotus* over the weekend and I like it unreservedly. It's a curiously haunting and demanding book, one I won't be able to forget for a very long time. After the opening chapter I abandoned any editorial eye and just read for pleasure and excitement. The approach of the end gave me a real sinking feeling. I wondered if you were going to desert me, bring Robin back to wife and babies and make him a redeemed character and spoil it all. But you didn't, God bless you.'

With the money available from *Nightrunners*, Masters invited his parents over for Christmas. It was four years since they had last met and he wanted them to see how well he had done, proof that his gamble of leaving England and the army had paid off. They had never been to the USA before. Once there, they remained steadfastly English. American prices were compared with England's: 'very reasonable, not dear at all'; America seemed such a throwaway society – 'Are you really going to get rid of that nice brown paper bag and all that string?' – after England, still in the throes of post-war rationing. They remarked on the lack of privacy, on the novelty of advertisements on the radio and the habit of eating everything with a fork and of Christmas trees being clearly visible in the front windows and the curtains undrawn in neighbouring houses.

There was a lot of pleasure in the reunion though. Masters was genuinely glad to see his mother; the warmth of their relationship was as strong as ever. He could sense she was pleased by his success, and that pleased him too. They had a convivial family Christmas together, his mother giving him her usual present of a sponge bag. He took his father ice-skating on a nearby lake, and in *Pilgrim Son* describes watching him, 'in his old-fashioned suit and wool scarf and earmuffs, a cloth cap on his head, his hands clasped formally behind his back, small and dark against the white background, leaning slightly forward, circling alone on the large and empty ice'. It was the side of his father he could warm to, his endearing stubbornness and individuality. His father insisted on going up to Niagara Falls and Masters took him to La Guardia for the flight; the same small figure stumped up the airplane gangplank.

His parents' stay lasted three weeks and they returned to England on the *Ile de France*. His father's thank-you letter complained about the 'nasty ship, rude stewards, nasty French sauces on everything ... I couldn't get a decent fried egg for breakfast.' Seeing his parents again and hearing news of the rest of the family revived in Barbara and Masters a wish to revisit England and they planned to visit in the summer of 1952.

The Deceivers was published in the USA in April and received good reviews. F. van Wyck Mason called it 'intensely dramatic and gripping, a worthy successor to *Nightrunners of Bengal.*' Edison Marshall wrote, 'I know of no writer in English since Kipling who understands India as well.' *The New York Herald Tribune* reviewer commented: 'This is a frightening book, frightening in the ordinary sense and fit to produce the standard symptoms; hair stands on end, cold sweat damps the brow, a chill runs down the spine. But it is frightening in another way, taking the reader for an unbelievable moment into the intoxication of killing. A man may find that reading it reveals to him aspects of his own character which he did not suspect.' Masters felt pleased at this, as it showed his strategy had worked: his aim of getting readers to identify and get inside the skin of his main character had come off. Sterling North in the *New York World Telegram* also remarked on its suspense, 'the whirl-wind windup which will have most readers biting their fingernails down to the second knuckle.' This was a clutch of excellent reviews and made him feel he really had crossed the threshold to becoming a fully-fledged professional writer.

As summer neared, their European trip began to take shape. England was their first port of call, but at the back of Masters's mind was a wish to visit Spain, lodged indelibly in his memory since his flight over the country in 1946, when he had spotted its arid, mountainous landscape as good walking country and similar to India. He went to the Spanish Tourist Office in New York and asked for information on walking there, particularly in the Pyrenees. They gave him the name of a local Pyrenean climbing club, the Peña Guara in Huesca, which he wrote to. Meanwhile, never one to do things by half measures, he bought Holt's *Teach Yourself Spanish* and a full series of Spanish linguaphone records, and sat down with Barbara each night to listen to them and study the language. They felt it was time to learn another language and to see and get to know a different country.

They crossed the Atlantic on the *Mauretania* on 15 April. Both grandmothers were at the quayside at Southampton to meet them, slightly taken aback at the unfamiliar sight of their 'English' grandchildren in cowboy jeans and boots. Masters's emotions were more mixed, 'England, their England, I thought to myself, yet I felt a pang, for I still loved it and always would'. After a week seeing relatives and publishers, the Masterses left for Spain and caught the boat train to Paris from Victoria on Monday, 28 April. With time to spare, they took in a film at the station newsreel cinema, topically enough on bull-running and the corrida at Pamplona. At Dover the passport officials looked oddly at his Indian passport. To keep them guessing he spoke to them in Hindustani.

From Paris, they travelled third class to the Spanish frontier, changing trains to the wider Spanish gauge. Entering Spain they noticed an immediate change of atmosphere; passengers talked to each other and were friendly, civil and hospitable, sharing food and stories. Spain, still recovering from the Civil War, had been more or less closed to the outside world since 1939. Its traditional way of life had been largely unchanged under the Franco regime, but the marks of the Civil War were still there. A jarring note on the train was the presence of an unpleasant-looking secret policeman in a corduroy jacket with bulgy eyes, flashing his badge – a reminder of the repressive side to the Spanish dictatorship. In Barcelona they stayed at the Hotel Princesa, where Masters contacted his Spanish publisher, Luis de Caralt, who supplied him with pesetas from the recent Spanish translation of *Nightrunners of Bengal*. As they walked down the Ramblas, Barbara's trousers caused quite a stir and she was much stared at.

In Huesca they contacted Peña Guara and met two eventual lifelong friends, both keen walkers, Julio Nogues and Antonio Lacoma. Lacoma, who spoke English and was an avid reader of George Orwell's books, did most of the interpreting, though Masters was keen to try out his Spanish, but his parrot-like learning from records and grammar book meant mistakes were frequent, like confusing jabon (soap) for jamon (ham). Lacoma and Nogues recommended Sallent high up in the Pyrenees near the French border. The Masterses went to buy tickets for the bus, Masters in his Indian Army khaki and Gurkha hat, but were elbowed out of the queue by fellow passengers until a Spanish workman insisted on taking them to their rightful place at the front. Spanish civility and punctiliousness were making an impression on them both. Their ramshackle bus, with no tread on the tyres, its bare canvas showing through, and a driver who insisted on keeping perilously close to the outside edge, reminded them of India, yet was typical of the haphazard nature of the Spanish way of life.

Spain soon showed itself as a country of extremes: there was great poverty, but dignity and honour too. 'Everything felt vaguely familiar and I did not know why. The view was large. It was hot and uncomfortable, but we were at home.' It continually echoed India: 'the two countries touched the same chords in us – a sense of space, of poverty faced with courage, of man-to-man relationships that had nothing to do with the obvious class or caste systems, of indestructibility, of values quite different from ours, seeming sometimes barbarous, sometimes ethereal.' Their efforts to learn the language were beginning to pay off: 'we had learned already that there was one key to the riches of this country – the ability to speak Spanish. To the man who tries to speak Spanish, and is not afraid of making a fool of himself in the process, no doors are closed.' It was a pattern repeated wherever they went.

They liked being high up in the hills. Masters was never happier than when above the tree line, looking at a long view that stretched the eyes. They camped in the Ordesa on land belonging to a farmer, surrounded by spectacular scenery 'like a miniature Grand Canyon'. When they went up to the border with France by the snowline on the Puente de Navarros, the army insisted on escorting them as the border was still closed and exiles and undercover agents might be crossing over. Their camera and passports were taken away by nervous guards near the frontier – in those days passports had to be carried everywhere in Spain – but both were returned later, the sergeant coming in his bedroom slippers to return them, apologising for the 'stupidity' of his men. Masters made friends with the local military commander. Later on that summer, when Lacoma visited the area, he heard mention of this 'inglés simpático' who had been there earlier.

Spain was incredibly cheap, another point in its favour, and, in Barbara's words, 'nicely uncivilised'. Its aridity and space suited them. They liked the way people greeted them as they passed and the respect shown to rich and poor alike. Time, however, was running out and they returned to Barcelona. Sitting at a bar near the cathedral they watched 'females in tight-bottom skirts in fascination. Why do they do it? Tremendous va-et-vient. Kids up till eleven.' Spain was getting to them: 'everything about Spain was a matter of form, of inherent shape, not of decoration. It was the quality of the fish that mattered, not the sauce.' They went to a bullfight at the Plaza Monumental – Julio Aparicio booed for killing too soon – and bought the usual packets of contraband US cigarettes off bootblacks in the Ramblas and had their shoes shined by them. This was to be the first of many trips to Spain; it was soon to become a second home for them in Europe and an emotional and geographical replacement for India and the Himalayas.

By 3 June they were back in England. *The Deceivers* was published that month, two months after the American edition. Its reviews were just as favourable. C. P. Snow wrote in *The Sunday Times*: 'The central figure is an admirable piece of character-drawing on the Hornblower level [which will have pleased Masters] and the story is as exciting as any I have read for a long time. No more readable, vivid and spectacular novel has appeared for many months.' Marghanita Laski in the *Observer* emphasised the characterisation, the 'marriage between his hero and the cruelty and horror that surround him' and 'the ambivalence of fascination and disgust that obsess William Savage.' It was a perceptive comment, as this ambivalence with its implication of the darker side of the English character was something he was striving after. This succession of good reviews pleased him, especially in England where his severest critics might lie in wait. 'I seem to be in danger of becoming a "good" writer', he wrote not without irony to Alex, 'which means that I shall starve.' In fact, he had no intention of joining any literary milieu nor any intention of starving. He wrote partly out of conviction, partly to make money. He felt he had something to say about India and he wanted to prove to himself and to his readers that he could write a 'damned good' book in a professional and entertaining way.

The same letter gave an up-to-date portrait of himself: 'I have grown a couple of inches round the waist but the principal sign of change is that my face is no longer lean, hawk-like and divinely handsome. I have not got a double chin yet, however.' His face was to change noticeably over the years, as photographs show, filling out as time went on and pressures eased.

England meant catching up with his old friends and he went to the annual Chindit Reunion dinner that June. He found himself seated next to his old 'adversary' Bernard Fergusson. Fergusson made a speech which included references to the 'Calvert case'. Michael Calvert was the Chindit hero they all admired so much but had been recently had up on charges of homosexuality and was facing possible dismissal from the army. Masters felt sympathy for him and was prepared to contribute to his defence fund. After he had finished talking, Fergusson sat down and turned to Masters with a 'witty anti-Americanism'. This clearly annoyed Masters, already out of sorts because of the content of the speech, which he felt was treating Calvert in a patronising manner. The anti-Americanism was the last straw.

Masters might have been vaunting his American side earlier on that evening. Richard Rhodes-James, who was also at the dinner, recalls him going around saying words to the effect that England was a 'load of nonsense' and that America was much better, trying to persuade people to come over there. This pro-Americanism certainly would not have gone down well with Fergusson, who shared a then quite prevalent English upper-class antipathy to America and most things American. Envy may have been behind this, not just of American wealth and technical know-how, but the galling aspect of being dependent on Marshall Aid and the like. This envy was often disguised as contempt for American brashness, and here was Masters as a living example. He had gone to the dinner wearing his American Brooks Brothers suit, not the most tactful of gestures, but he had at least worn his Gurkha Brigade tie. Fergusson, conscious of superior British breeding and social mores, would have looked askance at this. Masters was an uneasy reminder of the divide, and as such was not easily forgiven. His rejection of the tribal loyalties of school and Sandhurst by skipping off across the Atlantic was seen as letting the side down and nearly tantamount to being a traitor to his class. No wonder he put many people's backs up; they did not like the feeling he was getting away with it.

One of the chief objectives of this trip back to England was for Barbara to see her children, Liz and Mike, and to see if more contact could be made. They were now living in Gloucestershire. Liz recalls the occasion:

> She came down for half an afternoon. I was thirteen at the time. I didn't realise they were trying to get us to live with them as they were completely out of our lives. Originally I had been told the story that a wicked man had stolen my mother away. Right from the beginning we did not know what was happening. We were told to say goodbye to our mother in India and that we wouldn't see her again and were put on a train and taken back to England with our father. When just after the war he was sent abroad again to Borneo in the Army, he was like a dog in a manger, he couldn't look after us, but he was equally determined Barbara shouldn't do so. We were without parents for five or six years. Father put us in a holiday home in Devon, more like an orphanage really, for children whose parents were abroad. There were about seventeen of us. My father would come home once every two years and we'd be told on the day, 'Get up, you're going to London. Guess who's going to be there,' and we'd spend a fortnight with him. Then one day he arrived out of the blue and said 'Pack your bags, I've found these people I'm taking you away to.' We said, 'For two weeks?' 'No,' he said, 'for ever.' I remember the shock as I had just built a Wendy House for myself. We went to live with Sir Bernard Pratt and his family in Gloucestershire. He had been head of ICI in India which was how father had got to know him. They became substitute parents for us; they had a daughter two years older than me and it became very much a country sheltered life for us. It was home but not quite.

Barbara managed a brief, joyful and tearful reunion. There was still no possibility of her children coming to live in America, but they were older now and therefore more able to understand what had been happening. She felt relieved to see they had grown up so well over the years, though there were obviously hidden tensions and an emotional distance between them.

Masters visited his family at Uplyme and went to see his grandmother in Torquay, the Mater, then aged ninety-one and still as vigorous as ever, as a front-page newspaper headline in the *Sunday Graphic* showed. It displayed a photograph of her, and the text read:

> She swims at ninety-one. Salute to an age of Great Women. Like you, we marvelled when we saw these pictures. We felt a little humble, too. It was a tough generation that nurtured such folk as Mrs Annie Masters, who, at ninety-one, still enjoys a dip in the baths at Torquay. That Mrs Masters should mother four distinguished soldier sons and three daughters was only to be expected. It was such women who made possible the Golden Age of Queen Victoria, and in this modern world she is still an example to younger people. We salute her!

Masters's reaction was more mixed; he still found her a bit of a menace, her appalling snobbery undiminished, which in its small way may have contributed to his wish not to live in England. She was, as he put it, 'an old gorgon who despite her devout Roman Catholicism equally despised Frogs, Jews, Natives, Niggers and the lower classes', but he had to admit to a sneaking admiration for her. She plainly had guts, and this was the last time he was to see her.

While he was at Uplyme that summer a surprise development came in the form of an offer via his London agent, Laurence Pollinger, from Sir Alexander Korda, the Hungarian film producer and head of London Films. Masters went to Korda's London offices at 146 Piccadilly and was asked to write two scripts, one a successor to *The Thief of Baghdad*, a film Korda had made before the war, and the other based on *The Thousand and One Nights*. Korda had read *The Deceivers* and was also considering this as a possible film. Masters liked Korda immediately and fell for his charm. He was a man with considerable flair, and more cultured and educated than the average film producer. These two commissions were worth £500 each, a sizeable sum and a useful entrée into the film business, something Masters had secretly hankered after. He had to reshuffle his summer schedule and delay his return to the USA as a result. Korda wanted him to work in London through the autumn. As compensation Korda agreed to pay for first-class tickets for the whole Masters family on board the *Caronia* back to the USA, with two luxurious sundeck cabins to themselves.

The *Caronia* was full of Republican supporters of McCarthy, with whom Masters, perhaps unwisely, got into heated discussions. He had few illusions about McCarthy, not least because his anti-communist crusade had damaged the careers of two close friends, Troup Mathews and Fernand Auberjonois at the Voice of America, hounded out of their jobs by his witch-hunt. Masters, being a European, probably underestimated the impact of McCarthyism on ordinary American citizens, whose anger at the Truman administration's failure to halt the communist advance in China in 1949 had found an outlet in their support of McCarthy. Much of the American war effort had been to safeguard China, as Masters himself knew from his time in Burma. China was America's friend and seeing the arrival of communism there led to a widespread feeling of betrayal among ordinary Americans. McCarthy capitalised on this and accused the government and its 'communist sympathisers' of being responsible. He became a rallying point that fed on this misplaced paranoia and patriotism in an America that had already lost some of its way after the war.

13

BHOWANI JUNCTION
1953–1954

After his return home, Masters moved on to the fourth novel on his list. It had been shaping up in his mind for some time; it was to be more personal than his preceding ones, as if he had been saving it up, like sending in his best batsman at number four. By early November he was writing to Alex, 'I am more than half way through the first draft of book no 4, *Bhowani Junction*, which is going to upend the critics – one way or another – so that they won't know what the hell to say next. It is modern and is about the Anglo-Indians; also about express trains and sex. I told my publishers that it was my hope to give them an orgasm in every chapter but I find I shall not be able to do more than one in every two chapters, though the pace hots up a bit towards the end of the book. The chief character is an Anglo-Indian girl, the daughter of an engine driver. It is going to be a very different and rather serious book in some ways.'

In *Pilgrim Son*, he put it more graphically: 'I could tackle it now. I was acquiring the technique ... trains, going somewhere – that fitted the requirement for movement, to interest the reader in where these people are going. That would apply to the Anglo-Indians, as a people, too. I would put Anglo-Indians in trains, where they belonged in real life, their English background perhaps trying to send them one way and their Indian background another like a junction' and then with a typical Masters flourish, 'Big drivers turning, hot wind blowing, sex in the sleepers behind. Great!' He knew he was sticking his neck out by taking on this theme, but he felt he needed to do it. 'If I bring it off you will freely hear me hailed as a genius; if I don't, there will be cries of tripe and heavens knows what. The readers are the people who will really say whether I pulled it off though, not the critics', he added in his letter to Alex. If his writing was taking him back into his family past, this theme was the nearest he got to the real skeletons in the cupboard. The treatment of Anglo-Indians was personal in terms of his own family, but at the same time Masters wanted to use their plight as a microcosm of British imperial history. The period he was going to describe was the one he had lived through – the last stage of the British presence in India – and its multiple cross-currents would underpin the book. Hence the acknowledgement to Alex that this would be a 'rather different and serious book'.

He had talked about the book the year before, in 1951, when he met an old friend, Wilfrid Russell, for lunch in New York. Russell's book, *Indian Summer*, had recently been published recounting his post-war experiences in post-Independence India. Russell was married to the sister of Masters's old friend Reggie Sawhny, and was chairman of Killick Nixon Industries in Bombay, a British conglomerate with extensive interests all over India. He was also Chairman of the Bombay Education Society for Anglo-Indian schools and a chapter of his book described the problems of maintaining an Anglo-Indian school in the years after Independence. Masters wanted to use material from this chapter in his own book, because he felt education had always been important for Anglo-Indians. They lunched at the Pierre, as Russell recalls. 'We knew each other from before the war through Reggie and we had corresponded more recently, but I was amazed to see how unlike an Indian Army officer he now looked, almost blatantly so both in manner and dress, but he was confident and relaxed. After the third Drambuie of a somewhat vinous lunch, we walked down 5th Avenue together and I listened with amazement as he outlined his plans for his epic-romantic series of books covering the whole history of the British in India – an extraordinary enterprise. I was impressed too by the knowledge he already showed of the Anglo-Indian Community.' Russell agreed to let him use the material and offered to correct his first draft.

Essentially the book was going to be a psychological study of the Anglo-Indian community at this cross-roads of their existence. Set in 1947 when the British decision to withdraw from India had thrown their lives into confusion, the book would tell the story from the point of view of three protagonists, each of whom would tell his or her version of the same events – 'presenting the characters from the inside, thus allowing the reader to understand a great deal which he could not otherwise have done.'

The main character was to be Victoria Jones, an Anglo-Indian girl in her late twenties, 'pale coffee skin, brown eyes, slender, just above average height, long legs, bedroom eyes,' and with a 'silkiness' that the Russells found quite typical. Her fiancé was Patrick Taylor, the traffic superintendent on the railways, also Anglo-Indian, 'in his mid-thirties, big, heavily-built, sallow, dull ginger hair, pale blue-green eyes, big hands, hoarse, loud voice, no sense of humour.' The third central character was Rodney Savage, the great-grandson of the hero of *Nightrunners of Bengal*, aged thirty-four, ex-Wellington and Sandhurst, a lieutenant-colonel with an MC from the Burma campaign, and now in command of 1st Battalion 13th Gurkhas, with 'thick, dark hair, thin moustache, 5″ 10″, pale blue eyes, long face, a pierced eardrum and war wounds to his neck and shoulders', and all the makings of a Masters alter ego.

Victoria was to be the pivotal character in the book, a catalyst for change, as women often are in Masters's books. During the war she had served in Delhi with the WAAC, and Masters may well have come across her prototype when he was working in Delhi in 1945-1946, though he always claimed Victoria was not based on a known individual. Her time in Delhi has changed her ideas, her eyes have been opened to the reality of the situation: 'I've been four years among only Englishmen and Indians. Do you realize that they hardly know there is such a thing as an Anglo-Indian community? Once I heard an old English colonel talking to an Indian – he was a young fellow, a financial adviser. The colonel said, "What are you going to do about the Anglo-Indians when we leave?" "We're not going to do anything, Colonel," the Indian said. "Their fate is in their own hands. They've just got to look around and see where they are and who they are – after you've gone."'

Reunited now with Patrick after the war at the railway town of Bhowani Junction (based on Jhansi), Victoria tries to convert him to her changed perspective. She wants him to have more confidence in himself, as she now does: '"I don't despise anyone now, and I don't fear anyone. I'm just me."' When Patrick protests that if the British leave he'll go with them, she cries, '"Home? where is your home, man? England? Then you fell into the Black Sea on your way out?"' Patrick represents the plight of the Anglo-Indians caught between two worlds, ultimately belonging to neither. '"We can't become English, because we are half-Indian. We can't become Indian because we are half-English. We can only stay where we are, and be what we are . . ."'

The story follows Victoria's self-exploration. Against a background of unrest and civil dissension as rival Indian political factions jostle for power, dominated by K. P. Roy, the communist agitator, and Surabhai, a liberal Congress representative, Victoria searches for her identity and tries to discover her roots and where she now belongs. The British forces are brought in to keep order, under the command of Rodney Savage. Victoria works for him and becomes his mistress, but he treats her harshly, repeatedly putting her down and reminding her that she is just an Anglo-Indian. Disenchanted both with the British in the guise of Savage and with the Anglo-Indians as typified by the clumsiness of Patrick, she veers towards her Indian past, and starts wearing a sari instead of Western dress and prepares to take on the Sikh religion and marry Ranjit, an Indian.

Just as she is about to be initiated into the Sikh religion, she changes her mind and realises that she does not belong there, and flees from the Sikh temple. She returns briefly to Savage, but can see she has no future with him either, and in the end goes back to her own people and to Patrick, whom she finally marries. Masters uses Savage to sum up the situation: 'She couldn't desert her people ... the great changes swept across India and the world, and she had searched, not by deliberate plan but because the wind of change blew through her too, for ways of escape ... she'd tried becoming an Indian – but she wasn't an Indian. She'd tried becoming English – but she wasn't English. An idea of the future, of herself as a dweller in India, had sent her to Ranjit. Sexual passions, the knowledge of herself as a woman, had sent her to me. But this was Bhowani Junction ... and from Bhowani Junction the lines spread out to every Indian horizon for them.'

The book seemed to be ending on a message of hope and optimism and sexual fulfilment. For this ending Masters had Wilfrid and Sheila Russell to thank. He had sent them the first draft of the book and Russell had written back advising him that he had been too harsh on the Anglo-Indian community, leaving them with a hopeless future, 'whereas, though bewildered in 1946, they have since in a curious way fitted into the new dispensation much better than any of us expected.' Masters welcomed these comments and adjusted the ending accordingly, introducing the notion of the Anglo-Indian school's continued survival as a symbol of hope.

Masters worked on this book all winter and by the end of March 1953 was able to deliver the second draft, including the Russell amendments, to Viking. He was due to leave soon afterwards for England on Korda film business. Helen Taylor set about editing, as she had only glanced through the earlier version. Her comments were communicated mostly by letters sent across the Atlantic. What was remarkable in view of the subsequent success of the book was that her first reaction was unfavourable. She wrote that she was 'not entirely happy with the book' and doubted whether it would further his writing career. She did not like the subject matter, though she admitted it might have more success in England. The reader's report Keith Jennison commissioned from Harrison Smith of the *Saturday Review* took a similar line. Smith spoke of 'sitting on the fence' and said, 'if I had to publish it I would have many doubts', though he called it an excellent novel and was 'astonished, knowing his two previous novels, that he has written as well as he has.'

Viking were seriously considering postponing it in favour of another book of his.

Helen saw Patrick as 'the unsure and unstable victim of an unfortunate societal environment, whose worst qualities come to the fore in any emergency, a man who has learned no protective coloration whatsoever,' as if he has fallen away from an approved standard of conduct. Equally she found Victoria's attitude towards men and sex 'somewhat strange and contradictory', and asked if an experienced woman of twenty-eight would use words like chest for breast and inter-fere for rape – missing the point of the deliberate evasiveness and false prudery of much Anglo-Indian language. She suggested 'removing the prudery and inserting a more knowledgeable attitude.' It was a difficulty that Masters knew he was going to face when writing the book. Helen was bound to be less aware of the subtleties and nuances of colonial life and of Anglo-Indian customs and of the peculiar status they held in the British Indian hierarchy. This comes out in some of her comments. It highlighted for the first time the difficulty of working primarily with an American editor. This time Masters did feel he knew what he was writing about and their correspondence charts their arguments back and forth across the Atlantic. At times he became very testy with her: 'the revision of Bhowani is going strong, only handicapped by high blood pressure brought on by the crass stupidity of editors. In the short intervals between these towering rages I am getting a lot of work done.'

The issue in question, which Helen hauled him up for, was Rodney's profane language.

> Some of Savage's language is offensive, and I speak for all readers, all of them male except me. His profanity and violence are pronounced and proper to his character, but the lewd words are too much. Avoid fuck and shit, and at least use the old dash dodge. I would hate to see this, a serious and ambitious novel, castigated by some damn investigating committee on charges of obscenity, especially since there is no artistic necessity for these extreme cases, the atmosphere of intent being perfectly clear without the words. Filthy words are no novelty any more, they do not sell books, and to intelligent readers they are stale and tasteless rather than shocking.

It was fair comment on her part, but Masters did not want to give in. He felt both coarse language and sex were necessary. 'Surely you realize that nine-tenths of the urge to write these books comes, in me, from a feeling that everybody ought to be told these things?' This was the side of him wanting to get beyond 'false pretences'. As for the various individual words, your comments have been uniformly unhelpful. The problems of coarseness and bad language are all mixed up into one thing you can call Taste, and I shall call Honesty, or Realness. First, it is amazingly unhelpful to write the message 'COARSE' in the margin opposite some sentence. You must believe me when I tell you I meant it to be coarse. It was a coarse man speaking in a coarse moment. Do you mean that you don't want any coarse people in any book published by Viking Press? You know perfectly well that many men use foul language. I know perfectly well that men who use foul language in a fox-hole would probably restrain themselves in a lady's drawing room. You are asking me to take the soldier or the railroader into the drawing room, first shampooing the smell of corpse off him, when I promised to take my readers into the fox-hole or the locomotive cabin.

In a letter to Russell he makes the point that 'Rodney is meant to be rather a tough egg and becoming increasingly bitter as the affair with Victoria leads to its inevitable conclusion and India starts sliding out of his reach. Furthermore he speaks deliberately in that way to Victoria (and only to her you will note) because he has been trying to show himself exactly as he is. The language is not, as a matter of fact, at all overstressed for a wartime officer though only in special cases would it be on display.'

Yet in the end, on reflection, he felt he could not sustain his attack and bowed to Helen's better judgement. 'Because I am a coward and because you are all cowards too I am going to eliminate these words.' Then comes his apologia:

If I sound a little upset about the matter it is because this case hinges on my inability to write as well as I mean to – in other words I plead not guilty to cowardice but acknowledge amateurishness. The case goes like this: – I write a book as well as I know how; I use the words that seem right to me throughout, thinking openly of rightness, not of taste, coarseness, investigating committees, or Senator McCarthy. Then I survey what I have written and try to estimate, with the help of outside opinion, the size and 'weight' of the book. Then, armed with a sense of proportion, I look at the words. Whether I like it or not there are people who will be hurt, shocked or disgusted by certain words – is the book 'big' enough for me to press on regardless? Obviously it would be silly and wrong to have a workman in a fairy tale using real workman's language. With regret, I decide that *Bhowani Junction* is not as 'big' as it set out to be. In summing up I think the whole question of these individual words – technical, American, bad and so on – can be disregarded. Fifty words never yet made a book good or bad (though they came damned near to it in Lady Chatterley).

It was a generous – and wise – move; the book was the better for it. Certainly Helen Taylor thought so.

> When I returned to the office on Monday, *Bhowani Junction* was here and I went right thru it. You handled everything wonderfully. I was struck again and again by the authority and clarity of so many fixes, even the smallest. Patrick is exactly right, Victoria, who seemed so unpredictable, is now quite a person. The love affair with Rodney, which was a difficult thing to understand below the surface, is now, at least to me, a very moving thing. Toning down Rodney's brutal side a bit and inserting some notion of what you call his complexes has done a lot to give it real emotion.

And she takes up the points he was making.

> I realize it was hard for you to yield on the obscenity, but it wasn't honesty I was talking about, nor McCarthy either. If you'd insisted on keeping the objectionable words, we'd have consulted the lawyers on the obscenity laws, and picked our way from there, weighing not only legal but practical considerations of book clubs etc. We can still do this if you prefer. You have not violated criteria of honesty in suggesting rather than being explicit. The whole argument of whether honesty must mean verisimilitude is one for the wee small hours, and this is a busy August working day so I won't run on about it. But the book has lost not one bit of strength or force by your deletions on this score, so don't feel put upon. On the contrary I think it has gained by the peculiar emphasis that restraint very often gives.

It was a good point, and Masters was unstinting in his indebtedness to her over this book:

> Your long and detailed review of the book was extraordinarily helpful. Here, as before, your real genius came out in your studies of the motivation of my characters. Often I have only a hazy idea of why my people do the things they do; this results in cumbersomely contrived situations and unlikely actions. You somehow understand them better than I do, and have the gift of being able to explain them to me. *Bhowani Junction* has, I am sure, been greatly improved by your dissections of Patrick, Victoria, and Rodney, all of which I have

accepted in toto. There was no real question of accepting or rejecting them, as a matter of fact. They were just right. Do please remember this, in future books – how much these character studies mean to me.

It was an example where their collaboration worked at its best and the end result was proof of it. The book still retained its strength of feeling, an indication of the author's close attachment to the subject, and the excesses had been ironed out.

The book had been through four drafts within the space of eighteen months. Masters sent the completed manuscript off to the USA at the end of July, and to celebrate he and Barbara climbed Cader Idris, the mountain near the cottage in Wales overlooking Cardigan Bay that they had rented for the summer. 'We are delighted to find we are not stiff or anything,' he told Helen, 'although we have done nothing but sit on our a***s and drink whisky since then. I am also feeling better now that *Bhowani Junction* is off my chest and in someone else's hands to get on with. I have been scribbling on bits of paper about the Coromandel coast, trying to get some meaningful shape into what at present is a mere collection of picaresque incidents.'

This was to be his next book, *Coromandel*, but meanwhile he had to go back to his Korda projects, currently a script which had been commissioned on a film about the love story behind the building of the Taj Mahal. Film work was less predictable, as he wrote to Alex: 'my planned trip to Scotland has been buggered up by not knowing for more than a few days in advance when I am supposed to be working, or where I'm supposed to be going.' He had to be at Korda's beck and call, and he did not always like it.

He liked Korda, however; he was a larger-than-life character, and good company. Masters went to a dinner party given by Korda at Claridge's that summer. It was meant to be a black tie affair but Masters had no dinner jacket. Instead, he wore a suit with a brocaded flowered waistcoat in gold, black and red, and his familiar Brooks Brothers suit. He describes the moment in *Pilgrim Son*. 'Alex paled and stepped back, a hand to his eyes. David Lean, the film director, was also there and called me the bravest man he had ever met.' Masters's dress sense at times was an odd mixture of defiance and bravado. Korda invited him down to Antibes to stay on board his yacht *Elsewhere* so that they could continue working there together. He was present when Korda married his second wife. By a strange coincidence his first wife had been Merle Oberon, almost certainly Anglo-Indian by origin, although she fiercely denied it all her life. Korda paid him well – Masters was earning $250 per month, all expenses paid – and life with

Korda was entertaining, but Masters's real interest was in his book writing.

It was October by the time he returned to Rockland County and he wrote to Alex that same month: 'the immediate future is an opaque fog as usual – I have no idea whether I'll have $500 or $15,000 this time six months hence, but what the hell. The weather's absolutely glorious, the colour is out in all the trees and the World Series is on.' The letter catches his mood of optimism at the time. As ardent followers of the New York Giants, he and Barbara would listen to every broadcast game on the radio. If the Giants won, they hugged each other in delight, the radio blaring in the background, a scene repeated in countless American households.

Coromandel was catching his interest. Set in the early 1600s when the British first went to India, it follows the fortunes of the first Savage in his family, Jason, a traveller and adventurer. As a young man in England, Jason had come across a map showing a treasure located in the Himalayan mountains in India. After several escapades in England, centred round Wiltshire where he was born, he ventures to the southern Coromandel coast of India and then journeys inland and to the north, accompanied by a blind Portuguese girl (perhaps Masters's version of Kim's lama), and eventually finds the site of the treasure, but the treasure is an illusion. It was really a journey into himself: 'the Golden Fleece was inside you rather than at the end of any road or map.' The blind girl had symbolised inner resources and when Jason concludes, 'I know now that the magic mountain is always the one you have climbed, the coast of Coromandel is always over the horizon', we get a glimpse of some of Masters's own changed perspective on the deceptive nature of ambition. Better, the advice seems to be saying, to be grounded and in touch with the 'wise, beautiful, understanding earth which knew which dreams were good and which were evil', and not to go chasing illusions in the mountains of Meru. As in *Bhowani Junction*, the book focuses on a search for identity. The inference is that the dream ultimately is always further on and contentment comes from acceptance of who you really are.

When *Bhowani Junction* came out in America in March 1954, the reviews were nearly all impressive and favourable. John Barkham in the *New York Times Book Review* called it 'far and away his best book so far; indeed, in this reviewer's opinion it is the best novel of India since E. M. Forster's *Passage to India*.' He admired the author's 'coiled power, so that you don't always realise his pages are filled with violence. His control of his material is superb.' Orville Prescott in *The*

New York Times called it 'immensely readable and considerably more ambitious in its concern with psychological subtleties than its predecessors.' *Time* magazine even added a photograph of Masters beside their review, but he was not entirely happy with it. 'The photo of me in *Time* was taken at the same time as the other one with the gold waistcoat at the NBA book award reception. It's not very good but I am not photogenic, and it is only once in ten years or so that I ever get a photo that looks like me in a flattering way, that is.'

The book was quickly on the bestseller list. It had been selected by the Book of the Month Club for April 1954, and this alone promised sales in excess of 100,000. He seemed to have hit a winner. He stayed for the celebrations and a radio broadcast on Mary McBride's radio show listened to by millions, and then he was off to South America on a trip arranged by his new agent, Helen Strauss of the William Morris Agency. She had come at the recommendation of Laurence Pollinger, when Masters wanted a change from Miriam Howell, someone with more bite and thrust.

Helen Strauss, whom Masters described as a 'real, tough business-woman' after their first meeting, had advised him to do magazine article writing. Besides being lucrative, it widened his readership. She had good contacts with Life International and they commissioned an article by him on Cape Horn, now strategically more important as the enormous US carriers such as *Forrestal* were too big to go through Panama. He could expect to get $1,250 for this article, all expenses paid.

He left for South America by plane on 15 March, flying from Miami to Santiago, and then on down to Puntas Arenas on the Straits of Magellan. It was, he wrote, 'the most spectacular flight down the whole length of the southern Andes and then over Patagonia on the Argentine side till we reached Punto Arenas.' There he boarded a Chilean Navy ship, the *Lautaro*, an ex-USA Navy tug, for a two-week cruise to the extreme south. It was awe-inspiring scenery. When they tied up at some remote outpost, he was reminded of India: 'whole scene – open platform, poorly dressed peasants, bare foot boys, smell of woodsmoke, steam engines hissing under scattered electric lights, clouds of luminous steam, cries of vendors of bananas, peanuts, very like India.' As a traveller he liked these out of the way places.

By the third week he had accumulated enough material for his article and was feeling homesick. 'Sitting in my hotel in Villarica, it's raining, low clouds, dull, cold. I pounded back down the black, corrugated, potholed road in pouring rain dodging cattle and being missed by a side-swiping bus by about two feet. I'm getting too old for this sort of thing and am now going to consider seriously whether to come home as quickly as possible. My hotel is full of a fishing party, all of Syrian descent – first generation immigrants. This explains their looks, which have been puzzling me.'

The next day, 10 April, was another dull, rainy day, with infrequent showers. Masters was about to go out shopping when the proprietor of the hotel, Herr Fritsch, stopped him and said a garbled telephone message had come through from Santiago, relaying a cable sent from 'William Strangeways' in New York. Masters guessed 'brilliantly' that this was William Morris Agency and waited in the lounge with four female Syrians until Fritsch could get through to Santiago again. 'Their lunatic fisher husbands had gone fishing. After a couple of false alarms he finally got through around 12.15 p.m., to receive a message that *Bhowani Junction* was sold to MGM for more than $150,000. This must be a mistake. But $50,000 is good enough to celebrate, so I ordered a couple of bottles of champagne and drank happily with the four Syrian females until and through lunch. I ate quickly and left, the ladies practically rolling around under the tables, before their husbands came back.'

He took the first train to Santiago still not believing the news. Confirmation then came through that the cable did state $150,000, and Masters was on the next plane home. Later, he was to tell Helen to follow the well-tried army custom of always putting figures in words. As soon as his plane touched down in Miami, he rang Barbara before she met him at Idlewild Airport in New York just to make sure the figure was right.

Helen Strauss had conducted the negotiations with the three film companies that wanted the book. They had started bidding against each other at $50,000 and finished a week later with Zanuck bidding $150,000 and MGM going up to $155,000, at which point Helen closed the deal. She had shown her mettle throughout as a tough negotiator. MGM wanted it as a vehicle for Ava Gardner, whom they had under contract.

Suddenly Masters was in the possession of more wealth than he had ever dreamed of; indeed, he would be financially secure for the rest of his life. Films were proving his ally, first with Korda and now this. His first three books, including *Nightrunners of Bengal* through its Literary Guild selection, had sold well enough to provide him with a steady income from royalties, but this was the real icing on the cake. His reaction, typically enough, was to spend some of it and then to include others in his success. He invited his parents over: 'Come over this year and next and just about as often as you want to.' Money had put him firmly in the driving seat and could now compensate for all those early years of missing out. He could afford a generosity that was free and spontaneous ('Here take one, take two'), with the resources to back it up. Straightaway he sent his father a cheque for £100, telling him to buy a decent TV set, and the promise of a new Rover if only he would get rid of his old one. He enclosed £25 for his grandmother adding, 'if she wants to give it to the priests, let her be happy her way. I know Granny is a terrible old woman but I can't help feeling sorry for her, sitting there alone and helpless, a widow for over fifty years.' For Alex, too, he promised financial help with the education of his children. As for himself, he was going to buy a new car to replace his present one, which, as he told Alex, was still not 'enormous enough yet to please me, not phallic enough.' He went ahead and bought a huge, white Cadillac El Dorado convertible, the fashionable car of the era, with its red leather upholstery and wire wheels, the 1950s status symbol par excellence and bound to impress his South Mountain Road neighbours.

Bhowani Junction was published in England in May and was a Book Society selection for the same month. The *Daily Mail* and *Evening Standard* both chose it as their book of the month too, causing Laurence Pollinger to comment: 'never before have I known two newspapers owned by rival press barons [Rothermere and Beaverbrook] choose the same book.' Masters thanked his two 'tiger-agents' on either side of the Atlantic for their part in the success of the book and added, 'I'm stinking rich, this week, but can't sleep wondering what I'm going to get my ****s chewed off for next.' Success still felt precarious.

The English reading public liked the book, and huge sales followed. It gained a *succès de scandale*, the notoriety of its subject matter, the Anglo-Indian issue, being fully exposed in English fiction for the first time. This controversial subject touched on sensibilities still attuned to the colonial past, more so in England than in America. The loss of the Indian Empire was still recent and the adjustment to its loss hardly begun. Victoria Jones's sexuality stirred up strong reactions. The active sex life of the seemingly uninhibited half-caste girl stimulated curiosity and an almost voyeuristic appeal. Masters was, to many English eyes, breaching a taboo subject, and not everyone was pleased. The Commanding Officer of his regiment, Sir Arthur Mills, felt he had gone too far; indeed, his status as an ex-Gurkha officer was to cause whisperings of discontent over the excesses of his writing. It was outlandish and risqué, deliberately so.

Reviewers liked the book. In the *Observer* the novelist Angus Wilson called him a 'very impressive writer. He organizes and controls the swift-moving, exciting narrative with the unobtrusive brilliance of a first-class military strategist' and made the point that he was a 'masculine' writer – 'intelligent rather than intellectual, his terms of reference are those of practical affairs rather than of any abstract culture, his feelings are tender, cynical or sensual, seldom sensitive, ironic or passionate. Good writers of this kind are increasingly rare in English fiction.' Masters was creating his own niche, carving out his own corner of the English literary scene – literate but not literary. Years later, a female guest at a party gushed rapturously about the literary merits of his books, especially *Bhowani Junction*. Masters retorted, 'Madam, it was about fucking on a train.'

Bhowani Junction was quickly high on the bestseller list both in England and America and remained there for several weeks. Masters felt pleased by this, and vindicated, too, for his courageous step in writing the novel. He felt he had got it right and the reviews and public reaction seemed to confirm this. The extra money meant they could make improvements to the house. 'We are beginning to knock hell out of this poor old house, now that Hollywood has spoken – making a study above the barn, giving the kids a decent playroom.' In the basement, Masters built a model railway that Martin and he shared. 'Martin has one end, I have the other but we give each other running rights over each other's rails.' All railway enthusiasts long to have such perfect control over operations, regulating signals and track speeds at will, but it was a genuine hobby they could both share, and it strengthened the father-son relationship. Masters was ambitious for Martin and had his sights set on a military career for his son. Masters bought another three acres of land – making eight in all – to expand the garden, and to prevent anyone else building next to them. The garden was soon looking at its best: 'peach and apple blossom everywhere, pink almond blossom, yellow forsythia, tulips, daffodils and narcissus out and the grass green.'

The *Life* article was not published. Helen Strauss said they always commissioned ten times more articles than they actually needed. Nor did his Korda projects get made, as London Films ran into temporary financial difficulties, but films still took up Masters's attention. He met Fred Zinnemann in New York, 'sandwiched between his lunch date with Montgomery Clift and his departure by air for Los Angeles,' and they talked together about a possible movie on the American railroad. 'It's pretty certain to go through as we are both very keen on catching the spirit of the steam engine before it disappears.' If so, another $10,000 was expected.

With the publicity *Bhowani Junction* attracted in the USA, Keith Jennison felt the time was right to bring out Masters's earlier autobiography. 'My publishers are making noises for me to brush up and produce the first volume of my autobiography *Brutal and Licentious*, the first thing I wrote. It was turned down freely on all sides in 1948. I am torn between two wishes, one to improve it as it is fairly amateurish, and two, to make the bastards publish it with acclamation in exactly the same state as it was refused six years ago. I shall probably rewrite it in the end, because Viking themselves didn't turn it down as they never saw it.' It became his next writing project.

For the summer, the Masterses planned a long family expedition across the USA together. Masters – a believer in going straight to the top – wrote first to the Governor of Wyoming asking him which would be the best camp for his children. The answer came back that the Heart Six Ranch at Jackson Hole would do. While the children were there, their parents could walk in the Grand Tetons nearby. They all left at the end of June for the Midwest, a reverse journey to the one Masters had made in 1938. Then the West 'had impressed on my very spirit a sense of space, of sweeping wind and far water.' He remembered the big sky stretching to the horizon, so reminiscent of India. He wanted to share this with his wife and children: space was a big ingredient in his attraction to America. The author Charles Olson has written: 'I take SPACE to be the central fact to man born in America – I spell it large because it comes large here. Large, and without mercy . . . the fulcrum of America is the plains.' It was here that America brought out something of the Empire-builder in Masters. In this spacious land an individual could make his mark and develop a lifestyle suited to his needs. He could become more himself while retaining certain British traditions, punctiliousness and 'honour' among them. America's drive and its ethic of entitlement spurred him on.

In Martin's memory, his father was at his best on these occasions, taking full charge of the planning and schedules and pointing out things of interest en route. They always followed a particular routine when travelling. If they were camping, the alarm would go off at 4 a.m., coffee would be made quickly on a small primus-type stove, and they would be on the road by 4.30 at the latest, before the first light, when the roads were still empty. Another 200 miles would be driven before breakfast, with Barbara and Masters taking turns at the wheel every hour and a half. After a full breakfast, they would drive another 200 miles before lunch, and would always get to their next camp – or motel every fourth day – by 3 p.m. to be sure of finding room. Then they would relax, swim, walk and see the local sights.

The children stayed at the ranch in Wyoming for a month. For some of that time Masters and Barbara went to California through Arizona. In Kingman they stopped at a café for a cold drink. McCarthy was speaking on the radio. The woman behind the bar said he was the only man who could save the USA from the Red menace. It led to a row, but Masters had to be careful. His citizenship hearing was near now that he had fulfilled the five-year residency requirement; a letter had come through to Wyoming to say it was fixed for 9 August at the New York Court House on Foley Square. Even out here, far from New York, he had to keep his mouth shut, or almost shut, since the McCarthy influence was so pervasive. As he wrote to Pollinger at the time, 'I shall become an American citizen soon, unless Senator McCarthy finds that I spoke to a Russian soldier in Persia in 1941'.

He flew back from Denver for the citizenship hearing. Armon Glenn and Keith Jennison were his sponsors. Glenn recalls how Masters's knowledge of the Constitution and of American history was 'amazing – much greater than that of the judge who conducted the hearings.' The judge asked him what organisations and clubs he belonged to – another effect of McCarthyism – and Masters replied, 'The 4th Gurkhas Officers Association'. The judge was immediately suspicious and asked, 'Is that a Communist group?' But it did not stop his US citizenship from being granted. Glenn, Jennison and Masters then headed off to 21 to celebrate.

Back in Wyoming Masters collected Barbara and the children for the long drive home. Unbeknown to them the ranchers had been Baptists and the children were taught a stern and disapproving attitude towards drinking and smoking. Their parents were viewed anew with suspicion. These lengthy drives across America were to remain a feature of their lives. That summer Masters calculated that they had motored 13,000 miles and walked 400 miles or more and climbed up and down 60,000 feet – statistics that give proof to Masters's recording zeal and to his propensity for exploration. There were added advantages as well, as he wrote to Helen Strauss: 'My time on the road and now an exceedingly strenuous eight days in the Tetons have cleared my addled mind considerably about what I want to do in the immediate future.' Walking often served this function for him. His projected Warner Brothers-Zinnemann film was still high on the list of future plans and he had spent ten days in Laramie, Wyoming, riding in the cabs of expresses and the cabooses of freights on the Union Pacific Line, as research for it.

Masters's parents took up his invitation and came to visit in October. 'We have had Pa and Ma here for a week now, and they seem to be enjoying themselves. They have both aged a bit since they were here last, but not much.' He drove them around sightseeing in his Cadillac; his father asked to look at the air traffic at La Guardia and pass under the Brooklyn Battery tunnel. 'Now we are slowly making preparations for the big event of their stay here, my party. There are going to be about 150 people present. We give this party every year – it saves me giving a lot of smaller parties and we're having fried chicken, beer and mulled wine.' A second but no less worthy reason for the party was to celebrate the New York Giants winning the World Series.

Masters describes this party at some length in *Pilgrim Son*. His mother is presented as a very English, almost a la-di-da type. Here she is made to say, 'It's a nice party. Such well-bred people', for Masters to retort, 'I don't know about that, but they're good people.' He seems to be wanting to distance himself from his parents and their English attitudes with their inevitable class bias, and align himself more with the American emphasis on individualism. Then his father comments, 'a bit socialist, some of them', a characteristic British remark of the time. Masters takes his father firmly in hand, acting now more like a father to him. He waters down his drink and then aggressively puts him down: 'not for nothing was he known during his twenty-six years in India as smell-of-a-cork Masters, the cheapest man to get drunk between Dera Ghazi Khan and the head waters of the Dibong.' By the time *Pilgrim Son* was written in 1970 his father had been dead for seven years, and Masters's portrait of him reveals the mixture of affection and exasperation that he seemed always to feel towards him.

To make full use of the MGM money, Masters had turned himself into a corporation, Bengal-Rockland Inc, at the suggestion of his accountant Allen Kaufman. The idea was to spread the money from *Bhowani Junction* over nine years to gain maximum tax advantages. All future income from books, magazines or whatever was paid in to Bengal-Rockland. The reality of his newfound wealth took some time to sink in, and there was no guarantee of financial security for ever; as he wrote in a letter to Alex: 'It depends on whether I continue for a few years making the stuff at the fantastic rate of this year and next, or whether the wells run dry on me. Anything can happen to a writer.' He gave Alex news of his parents. 'We are putting the old 'uns on the boat next Friday, 12 November, on the *United States*. Barbara is going with them, as I'm off to Los Angeles on film business. We spent the whole of last Thursday with Stewart Granger who is going to play Rodney in *Bhowani Junction*. He seems a nice chap, very keen on hunting animals in Africa. We took him to the Museum of Natural History.' Masters was to follow the making of *Bhowani Junction* closely and was kept in reserve by MGM as a script consultant.

He had now just turned forty and the changes he noticed in himself were important ones. 'As I had gone up the army ladder I had gained control over more things and people – including myself. An odd fact about my present situation was that I had begun to feel the process was going into reverse. I was gradually losing control over the destinies of people. The children, for example, over whose future I would once have held decided opinions and a strong hand, were now going to be ruled by other influences, at least as much as by Barbara and me.' This awareness of loss of control was a crucial shift for him, a mid-life turning point, allowing other sides of his nature to come forward. 'I was changing sometimes in spite of myself.' There was less need to be in command, to be on top of people and events. 'Events were going their own ways, with me shrugging on the sidelines where once I would have been in there over the centre, barking the signals.' The urge for domination was slipping. Perhaps his writing was having this effect on him. He was mellowing, his driven and authoritarian side was now less in evidence. He could state: 'A writer cannot create without understanding and he cannot understand without allowing, tolerating.' Such shifts of perspective would be reflected in his future writing.

14

USA
1955–1957

There continued to be times when he missed the old days of command, the 'incisiveness of decision', the presence of the Gurkhas and the 'woodsmoke-and-leather camaraderie of the Indian Army.' But so much had happened now to replace those memories. Writing about India was proving cathartic – a lengthy mourning process that needed to run its course.

As a fully-fledged American citizen, aware of his obligations, he became more involved in community affairs. Hours were spent at the local North Clarkstown Civic Association, defending his neighbourhood against potential real estate developers. His political affiliations at this stage were Democrat: he had supported Adlai Stevenson in the 1952 election. If he found faults with the American way of life, it was mainly in things like the judicial system – 'a farce, slow, inefficient and widely disrespected' – and the education system – 'good but too rigid.' At grade-school level it seemed more concerned in adjusting children, than in teaching them. Masters took the view that adjusting was the family's job. Teachers should instill the 3 Rs, and no more.

Masters was getting the sort of balance into his life that suited him. His roots were now in America, yet the pull of Europe, or those parts of it he liked, remained with him. He structured his year accordingly: the winter months from October to May were spent writing in the USA, and the summer months from June to September were spent travelling, usually in Europe, most often walking in Spain. Barbara complemented him in this way, as she shared the same interests and the same attitude towards the outdoors. 'I saw and pointed out the long views, the grand scenes, while she saw and identified the flowers among the rocks, the birds in the trees'. As travelling companions, they were very compatible, not just because of similar tastes in food, restaurants, sights and museums, but because they shared a sense of wanting to make the most of each day and not waste time. Theirs was active tourism, with each day being based on a proper walk.

The revamping of *Brutal and Licentious* was going ahead. The first reactions from the editors at Viking were good. He bought a new IBM electric typewriter, and recommended it to Mollie Kaye, then at the beginning of her writing career, when she came with her husband Goff to stay with them, 'They're like some women, they jump when you tickle them.' She had noticed when she had rung up from New York that he had answered the phone with an American drawl, 'Masters speaking.'

On the film front, J. Arthur Rank had bought the movie rights to *Nightrunners of Bengal* 'after a good deal of haggling on my part.' An initial offer of £2,500 was worked up to £12,500 with Helen's assistance. Selznick was also showing interest in *Lotus*, and in India the film of *Bhowani Junction* was about to be made. The Indian Government were worried that the film might unsettle the Anglo-Indians, whose position was still delicately balanced in post-Independence India. So MGM took the film to Pakistan and shot it in Lahore, using the railway station there. Ava Gardner and the rest of the film crew were billeted at Faletti's hotel with Pathan guards standing outside her door day and night.

The film did much to widen Masters's reputation as an author. Ava Gardner's powerful portrayal of Victoria Jones, reckoned among her best roles, under the sensitive tutelage of the director, George Cukor, certainly helped. MGM, showing a major Hollywood studio's caution about such controversial subject matter, arranged to have the rough cut of the film previewed by UCLA (University of California) students in Los Angeles. Blank cards were distributed at the door for their comments. Most were shocked by Victoria's promiscuity, and MGM executives quickly ordered the film to be recut. The film was reconstructed as a flashback with Rodney Savage as narrator 'excusing' Victoria's behaviour. Overt sex scenes were then taboo in the cinema and the more suggestive ones in the original version were toned down to make her character more respectable. For instance, the scene in the train where Victoria takes Rodney's toothbrush and cleans her teeth in front of him, first dipping it in a glass of whisky, was changed; it was felt that this scene implied too great an intimacy. The film's ending was changed to Patrick Taylor being killed, as the UCLA students objected to Ava Gardner 'being left with an Anglo-Indian.' Racial prejudice was having the last word.

Coromandel came out at the end of March 1955; as Masters told Alex, '*Coromandel* is now out to the usual accompaniment of fierce cross-fire from those who like it and those who don't. The latter category consist mainly of intellectuals who are driven mad by the thought of all the money the unworthy Masters is making. One of them in his review was perfectly furious with me because I am a "throw back, a pre-Freudian."

I shall have to bear it as best I can.' It could not have been that hard to bear and he made no pretensions to inner psychological analysis. In his view actions spoke louder than words and the inner life of his characters was expressed that way. In his own life, introspection, or self-analysis, played little part.

March was the end of the fiscal year. As Masters signed his cheques for his income tax, both Federal and New York State, he reflected, 'It gave me quite an eerie feeling to realize that the cheques I was signing for tax payments were for four times as much as I'd ever earned in the army.'

By the fall of 1955 it was time for his children to move to new schools. Susan was eleven and Martin nine. Somewhat surprisingly, they were sent to boarding schools. First Masters wrote to the appropriate editor of *The New York Times* who specialised in education, and got back a list of four or five schools, from which he and Barbara chose North Country, Lake Placid, New York State, for Susan. It was a private school that originally had been a summer camp, and it was friendly and forward-looking. Susan had missed out a bit on South Mountain Road, where there seemed to be more boys than girls to play with, such as the three Anderson and two Simon boys whom Martin had as playmates of his own age. She had become rather withdrawn and North Country was intended to give her more company and stimulation. It had a collection of small houses with eight to ten pupils per house, and everyone was on first name terms. Barbara recalls, 'What really sold us was that they had slides by the main stairs in the building and the kids would go down the slides with their arms full of books onto crash pads at the bottom which they bounced off. Any school that had the imagination to build that in for this age group had our vote. It had quite a lot of scholarship kids and some blacks and mentally retarded ones as well, about seventy in all, as well as children of Mellons and Rockefellers, and so on. Yehudi Menuhin's children went there as did Yasmin, the daughter of Aly Khan and Rita Hayworth.'

Martin's chosen school was Fay in Southborough, Massachusetts; modelled along British lines, it was an all-boys school in which the boys wore suits and ties. Even beating was permitted, and prefects gave pupils tickets for running. Masters was in favour of its disciplined approach. His eyes were still set on his son going to West Point. When Martin first arrived at Fay, he was not happy. 'I was miserable, fell in with outcasts, had some emotional problems.' He could not help feeling he had been pushed out because he was not wanted at home; being sent off to boarding school was not expected of American children as it was for English children of his age. He was bright, though, and soon did well academically.

Susan took to her school immediately: 'My first boarding school was a wonderful place. I never regretted going there.' It had an organic farm attached, a timetable that included foreign languages, even Russian – a brave choice in those days of the Cold War. Subjects such as woodwork were compulsory. There were only sixty pupils, dress was informal, and each pupil had a housemother, giving it a family atmosphere. With the children away from home, the house was much quieter and Masters set about finishing *Bugles and a Tiger* with undivided attention. This new title had been arrived at 'after some argument'. Viking did not like *Brutal and Licentious* since these were epithets associated with mercenary soldiers. This title was derived from Edmund Burke's 'rapacious and licentious soldiery'. Viking suggested *Indian Morning*, which Masters did not like; he then suggested *Concerto for Bugles and a Tiger*, which was shortened to its eventual title.

Helen, as usual, was providing solid editorial help. She made him, to his regret, delete the line 'camels, conceited and supercilious, looking like their human counterparts, the literary critics of *The New Yorker* and *The New York Times*.' But, facetiousness aside, this was a serious book. His aim, as he stated in the foreword, was to 'tell the story of how a schoolboy became a professional soldier of the old Indian Army ... and of what India was like in those last twilit days of the Indian Empire.' He made it clear that this was his account, not a factual history. 'Please do not pounce on me with scorn if it turns out that there were seven, not eight, platoons of Tochi Scouts on the Iblanke that night of May 11–12, 1937.' It succeeds in conveying the snap and feel of pre-war Indian Army life, the institutional flavour of being at Sandhurst and the pain and embarrassment and exhilaration of joining new regiments in India. Masters used it, too, to demonstrate his great love for the Gurkhas and for India, 'my lusty, disinterested mistress that would have a hell of a time getting rid of me'. The book is his real testament to India, and is as vivid and compelling an account as any he wrote, its reputation as sure to last. It captures a unique period in British Indian history and is still used on officer training courses in both India and Pakistan.

Bugles and a Tiger went down particularly well in England. A reader's report, commissioned by Michael Joseph, had already anticipated this: 'Overall I have rarely read a more engrossing account of life in an Indian Regiment'. The reader made the point that 'Masters is far more a natural writer than a "homme de lettres". He relies more on his facts and his natural vigour and vitality to impress his readers

rather than any elegance of style or charm. One is forced to compare it
with that one time bestseller *Lives of a Bengal Lancer*. That book with
its beautiful, descriptive writing, its rather phoney glamour and its
mystical hooey was just a natural and bowled one over at first reading.
Afterwards one realised that one had been tricked and rather disliked
the author, at least I did.' The favourable comparison with *Bengal
Lancer* would have pleased Masters. It brought to mind the problems
he had had in 1948 with Desmond Hall and the Dial Press and Victor
Gollancz's comments. It was confirmation of his development as a
writer. He felt all along that he could write a better book than his
predecessor.

  Bugles and a Tiger's publication date was set for early 1956. It had
already been selected by the Book of the Month Club. Meanwhile,
Masters was still working on his steam engine novella, provisionally
entitled *Horizon Freight*, and went to the HQ of the Union Pacific
Railroad in Omaha for a week's research. 'I had a wonderful time there
sitting in an office every morning for two hours with two senior engine
drivers. They got as interested in the story as I did in engine driving by
the time we finished.' His story would tell of the decline of the steam
engine in face of increased automation, and the feelings of craftsmen
when they find their pride and skills are useless. Perhaps at the back of
his mind were echoes of his own father facing similar difficulties in
finding an outlet for his skills once he was forced out of retirement
after the Stock Market crash of 1929.

  His train book was really more of a sideshow. His main writing
concern was his Savage novels and his next one, on the theme of what
makes a mountaineer, was set at the turn of the century in Switzerland,
where he and Barbara went in September 1955. They spent a week in
Zermatt, getting the flavour of the 1890s, and talking to Alpine guides.
Being up in the mountains was a real tonic. 'Walking is when I can feel
completely relaxed with nothing to think about but the scenery, the
map, where and when and what we are going to eat and drink next.'
From there they moved on to München Gladbach to stay a few days
with Alex who was stationed there in the British Army. It was a good
reunion between the two brothers. 'Barbara and I were really delighted
to meet you and Joan again after such a long time. We think you have
a wonderful wife and are of the opinion you'd be lost without her
(literally sometimes . . . or at least half your belongings would be lost!).
The boys [Alex's sons] are wonderful, and we do very much appreciate
the trouble both of you went to to make our visit as much fun as it was.'

  This year, 1955, with the fame resulting from *Bhowani Junction*, and
the acclamation from the film, Masters was much in demand. Helen

Strauss kept notifying him of offers coming in: a film company wanted to involve him in an 'Indian' film with their Indian star, Sabu; he was asked to write the script for an Alec Waugh novel for 20th Century Fox; and Sam Spiegel even approached him to polish up the screen play for *The Bridge on the River Kwai*. Helen Strauss had strong links with the movie business and they both knew this was where the real money was. His novels had been obvious candidates for films all along, with their strong visual sense and almost photographic quality of the writing and their powerful narrative, and most were sold for their film rights not long after they were published. In the end, however, *The Deceivers* was the only Masters novel to be made into a full-scale film, apart from *Bhowani Junction*.

Bugles and a Tiger came out on 4 January 1956. Keith Jennison sent a cable: 'All Vikings, in and out of solemn conclave, send you affection, regards and unbridled admiration on publication day.' The book met with very good reviews on both sides of the Atlantic. Harrison Smith in the *Saturday Review* wrote: 'it will be a long time before we have a better report on the last stormy days of the British in India', while in England Compton Mackenzie wrote in *The Spectator* of the 'flawlessness' of its presentation of the world of the Indian Army.

Bernard Fergusson was asked to review the book by *The Sunday Times*. He starts by giving Masters credit for his previous novels, which he says are 'superbly written, remarkably vivid, with the tang of India and a sound ring of authenticity both in characters and settings', and adds that Masters is 'steeped as well as learned in his subject; he has heard with his ears, and his fathers have declared unto him.' But then he picks on the way the novels are 'marred, to my taste, by a lurid vein of savagery.' He finds the same in the autobiography. 'The same notes are still struck, authentic even when they jangle in the discords of poor taste.' This question of good taste was a real bone of contention between them, as they fenced for the high ground: Fergusson as an aristocrat above the mêlée of everyday life and Masters as someone who had sought to detach himself from a humdrum existence. It is a mixed review, paralleling their mixed, and competitive, relationship. Fergusson ends with, 'his lapses are irritating, his flats flat; but his heights are very good', and he cannot resist a dig at Masters becoming an American citizen, stating that this book must be primarily intended 'for an American audience'.

Bugles and a Tiger made a wide impact and stirred up more fan mail than any of his previous books. 'I must have had a score of letters from people in the USA alone, telling me tearfully about their great uncles in the 98th Rumbletummi Lancers, and how much this book has meant to them.' In England the book had even wider acclaim. Indeed the reviews in England were so good that, as Masters told Alex, 'I keep taking the book out of the shelf and reading a few pages in puzzled astonishment, trying to see whether it really is that good. Except, as you say, the Preux Chevalier Fergusson; I came to the conclusion twelve years ago that Bernard was a pompous ass with two or three shallow talents, and I fear my manner at subsequent meetings allowed him to guess this: also he is jealous.' Fergusson had written his own wartime memoirs, *The Wild Green Earth* and *Beyond the Chindwin*, which certainly did not receive anything like the same sales or publicity as Masters's books.

The sales figures were encouraging. Five weeks after publication Laurence Pollinger was writing to him, 'the book continues to make magnificent progress – upwards of 2,200 copies sold last week. The total sales to date are over 34,000.' Masters wrote back: 'The success is nice; it is also good to feel that I have been able to make so many people listen to a story that needed to be told and never has been told yet. F. M. Auchinleck wrote the other day pointing out what Compton Mackenzie said too – that England would not have survived the last war without the Indian Army; and though that was not my theme at all, it does have some importance.'

After *Bugles'* publication, the Masterses went for a short holiday to Cuba, a regular haunt of theirs over the next few years, not so much for the exotic night life of Havana, but for the peace and tranquillity of Varadero Beach, 80 miles further east on the northern coast, which was 'quite wonderful – I have never seen such beautifully coloured water as the sea is there.' He took the manuscript of his new novel, *Far, Far the Mountain Peak*, with him and found it a good place to work: 'I got about 65,000 words of the novel written, and bathed three times a day in magnificent weather and water.'

His parents visited them in the USA in mid-March. 'Ma and Pa are here, actually they are getting older quite noticeably. Daddy's never very reliable memory is worse, and Mummy is telling the same stories even more frequently and they both get tired more readily'. He adds a homely vignette of their presence: 'Dad is taking his binoculars to pieces behind me and Hinny [Mrs Masters] is berating him for using a clean handkerchief to do it with.' It would be intriguing to know what his father thought of the portrait given of him in *Bugles and a Tiger*, but there is no record of his response. They were clearly on good terms at this point, so his father is likely to have endorsed it despite its rather unflattering criticism of him. He would have thought it a 'bit of fun.'

They all went up to Martin's school at Fay that month. Martin's progress was distinctly encouraging: 'At Fay they are in a tizzy about Martin; I told them he was bright but they thought I was just being a proud parent; now they are really quite frightened – he has done three years' maths in two thirds of a year; passed the 11th grade spelling and English exams (he is in 4th grade); and the headmaster says he is about the most brilliant boy he has known in twenty-eight years of teaching. Their problem is to keep him interested while also keeping him in his social group, as he is still only a little boy of nine in other ways.' Leaving aside parental bias, Masters was clearly proud of Martin's achievements, as he had high hopes for the boy.

For the summer the family was going to Spain again, taking the Jennisons' fifteen-year-old son Nicky with them. Their destination this time was to a lesser known region, the north-western Atlantic coast near Vigo. They left on 22 June, Masters collecting a ticket on Belt Parkway for doing 69 mph, 'which I damn well wasn't, merely 47', on their way to Idlewild airport, from where they flew to Lisbon and travelled by train to Vigo.

Bayona, where they ended up, was to become a place they visited regularly during future trips to Spain. A small fishing port, 12 miles south of Vigo, with its castle occupying a spit of land overlooking the harbour, was unspoilt, with no tourists, and was active and colourful. There was plenty to do and see for children. They watched, fascinated, as a pulpo (octopus) was killed by a boatman by squashing it against the sea bed with the end of his oar. On these trips Masters always set the day's routine at breakfast time. In the evening he made all the children write diaries giving an account of their day.

They had rented a house with four bedrooms, primitive but adequate; the front door had to be locked by taking the handle off. They ate all their meals at the Bar Moscón nearby, as the owner was their landlord. 'What meals, sea food! huge crabs, lobsters, percebes', Masters exclaimed. It was cheap too, full board and lodging costing the equivalent of $2 or about 16s a head. Days were spent snorkelling and speargun fishing, with Masters and Nicky in friendly competition. Any fish they caught was given to the Bar Moscón for their evening meal. They got to know many of the locals who became their friends as they merged into the life of the small Spanish community.

Masters undeniably got great pleasure out of being in Spain and the country became a real second home to him. He felt good there: it was a man's country and brought out that side of him that had been quiescent since Indian Army days. He wanted the children to enjoy it too. 'We will not stress culture as the children will do better to absorb it on the side, with the fishing and the food.' Martin remembers these holidays with particular affection. 'When we were together as a family we did great things together, it was very instructive and exciting.' Susan recalls how her father would tell them details of Spanish history at mealtimes, about Catherine of Aragon and how the Moors were repulsed from Spain and which Spanish words derived from Arabic.

Inland, the countryside resembled 'Devon, crossed with Cornwall and a bit of Maine – the villages are narrow, roughly paved lanes, tile-roofed cottages, some painted blue. The people are good-looking, and the picturesqueness is in the fish on the baskets, people carrying everything on their heads, ox carts, patched clothes.' The simplicity of these surroundings was important. The Spain Masters preferred was off the beaten track, where the essential Spanish characteristics of dignity, humour and honour, and a certain earthiness, could be found. From Bayona they went across by train, as slow and exotic as Indian railways, to the Pyrenees, another regular summer stamping ground.

Barbara and the children then flew back to the USA while he went to England for conferences with J. Arthur Rank about the filming of *The Deceivers*, whose film rights they had bought for $70,000. Rank never made the film, but the producer Ismail Merchant did in 1988, fulfilling an ambition he had nurtured since he read the book as a young man in Bombay, soon after it came out in 1952. Meanwhile, Masters attended the premiere of *Bhowani Junction* at the Empire, Leicester Square, at the end of August.

As an 'authority' on India, approaches were made, through Helen Strauss, to convert the book into a musical on Broadway. Another Broadway producer wanted him for the script of a musical comedy with an Indian background; in Hollywood his name was put forward to do an adaptation of the *Rāmāyana* for a film; and Auchinleck wanted him to complete the second volume of the Indian Army history which Compton Mackenzie had started. The ripples of success were spreading.

In December he was back in London for more 'hectic conferring' with Rank. Barbara came with him and she had arranged to see Liz and Mike, both in their late teens now. She invited them to the USA for Christmas, with their guardian, Bunny Pratt, and his daughter, Elizabeth. Masters paid for all their trips unstintingly. His generosity was often put to good use. When his old friends Troup and Alice Mathews were going through hard times, he lent them money and bought enough llama rugs, which Troup was importing from South America, to carpet his own entrance hall.

Liz much enjoyed meeting Masters, recalling, 'when he met me he was like a breath of fresh air and very sweet to me as my mother's daughter.' At first she found him 'daunting', but then he took her into New York and bought her some clothes, including red tights, which made her feel very grown up and accepted. This Christmas was the first time all four children had been together and it was strange for the half-brothers and sisters to meet and get to know each other. Strange, too, that they paralleled each other, an elder daughter and then a son, a second family in the making. They were inevitably a bit edgy, aware of how much they had each missed out over the years, and understandably there were moments of rivalry and hidden jealousy, and of sadness, too, at all the missed opportunities, but they were all keen to make the best of it. For Barbara, this visit had enormous significance and she could at last feel they had become a united family. It was the beginning of renewed, and lasting, ties between both sets of children.

15

FANDANGO ROCK

1958–1959

*F*ar, *Far the Mountain Peak* was published at the end of April
1957. Masters wrote to Pollinger: 'The book was published last
Friday, and has so far had about eight reviews that I've heard of,
all except one in *Time* magazine, being excellent.' Now Masters felt he
wanted to branch out from Indian themes and move on to something
different and more contemporary. India, he feared, was becoming too
narrow a designation for him and he did not want to become typecast
as the novelist who wrote only about India. He wanted to broaden his
field, an indication of his confidence as a writer and of his ambition.
He discussed this with Keith Jennison, who supported him. He still
nursed the notion, as he told Jennison, that he might have been a
major-general by now, and this was something to live up to in his
writing career.

Spain suggested itself as an obvious source of subject matter. It was
a country he now knew well and it also was undergoing similar
conflicts to those he had often described in his Indian novels: an old
civilisation was being confronted with the advent of the new, in the
shape of American air force bases being 'imposed' on Spain and
causing tensions. The parallel with colonialism was an obvious one.

He set to work and by mid-May 1957 he had finished the first
'unformed' draft of a novel on this theme, tentatively entitled *Valleys of
Spring*, which he sent off to Helen Taylor. The central character was a
respectable twenty-year-old American girl who stays with her family at
the air force base and is initiated into womanhood and love by a
Spanish grandee. She is shown to gain physically and spiritually from
the experience and returns to the USA a more fully developed person. It
is a theme of growth and development through the interplay of two
cultures. He wanted to make it as dramatic as possible, highlighting the
clash of American and Spanish values: the brashly new and materialistic
against the traditional and honour-bound. Equally dramatic events
were to symbolise this difference: the crash of an American bomber on
the town and the rape of a Spanish woman by, it is presumed, one of
the American airmen.

Helen's first reaction bowled him over. 'I am almost totally bewildered by my first reading of the novel. So much so that I must read it again to concentrate on the whys and wherefores of this helpless feeling. I'm taking it away with me on a short trip and will go through it again; then let's talk.' She had doubts whether the theme of the novel and the story and characters were real enough, 'all of which covers a lot of ground. So bear with me for another week?'

She did read it through again and wrote back less critically, 'perhaps the roughness of the script did, after all, obscure the reaction'. She admitted to liking the Spanish background, but felt the central female figure, the young American girl, was not at all convincing. She was 'not a very clear character, and I continually felt that she had no distinguishing personality, and very little atmosphere of even a typical American college girl, let alone a particular one.' She felt she was 'more of a tool at the hands of these people rather than a major participant,' and was being used as 'an implement to tell a story.'

It was valid criticism. In his eagerness to break new ground, Masters had allowed the novel to be too planned, too worked-out in advance. In his India novels, whatever else, he was always writing from the heart and this came through and informed his writing. Here Helen felt that even the sex scenes were 'too reportorial to be acceptable to a lot of readers', especially as 'one of the valid themes of the novel is the overwhelming experience of physical love, and it ought to come across that way, rather than clinically.' Masters did not like the criticism that his sex scenes were too mechanical, too formulated. Sex scenes had, in his eyes, been his strength. Mollie Kaye tells the story that when *Bhowani Junction* came out she wrote to him congratulating him on the book, but wondering whether quite so much sex was necessary. Masters wrote back, 'Don't be silly, Mollie, it's the only reason why the Americans read me, they chase through the book for the juicy bits. I'm so sure of this that there are times when I lie in bed at night and I can't get to sleep and I'm worrying about the bills and I get up and I dash downstairs at night and I write in another rape.' It usually worked, but at the moment he seemed to be off target.

His central female character was meant to be a catalyst. She was intended to be 'very much a guiding force', transforming the Spanish family she gets involved with 'to a strong and healthy character from the somewhat decadent or unnatural one existing before, and then she too could graduate from the College of Life, with Magna cum Laude. We ought to have tears of joy in our eyes as she comes down with the invisible diploma.' It was a tall order, and at this stage it did not work, not in Helen Taylor's eyes anyway. She remained unconvinced, the girl looked too much like a 'Little Miss Fixit'.

The best bits of the book at this stage and later were the descriptions of Spain, the paseo and the corrida, the interiors of cathedral and bar. Don Cesar, the Spanish grandee, was enough of a self-portrait of Masters to have a life of his own. Masters described him thus: 'don Cesar may certainly be a lover of life all the way round, and it is basically an overflowing energy, plus this zest for life, which governs what he does, and which makes his wife much more philosophical about his aberrations than she otherwise might have been.' Masters's own occasional aberrations outside marriage were becoming more frequent and, he would have claimed, were aimed, like don Cesar's, at 'spreading happiness and interest and a kind of enthusiasm.' Don Cesar was over-sexed, as was Masters. He liked and was attracted to women, a feeling that was reciprocated. At the same time, he did his level best to ensure his affairs never threatened his marriage. He saw, or rather rationalised, these extramarital liaisons as having an educative purpose. They were often with wives caught in an unsatisfactory and sexually-unfulfilling marriage, a point he takes up in his new book. 'One of the themes of the story is that sexual love is not a discreet, even thing that goes on behind closed doors, but confronts men and women with all kinds of extraordinary pains and rewards.' His advocacy of the beneficial aspects of sex and of openness about it was one thing, but it was hard for Barbara to put up with.

By this stage there was usually one extramarital affair on the go at any one time. Barbara could, to some extent, be philosophical about them, as she recognised that they were primarily a sexual outlet for him. The fact that Masters showed no compunction about carrying on such liaisons so openly, with Barbara's knowledge, tells us something about his very individual attitude towards sex, based on the paradox that it mattered a great deal to him on the personal level and little in terms of marriage.

There was a price to pay for this, as he has don Cesar say: 'his very dominance over his immediate family, and the way he has engineered his life with his wife, prevent him from going to her for comfort, and her from being able to give it, because both of them have erected barriers against each other – Cesar to preserve his freedom, Teresa [his wife] to prevent herself from being mortally wounded by his acts.' Barbara and he had not erected barriers, but his infidelities put a severe strain on their relationship. Barbara tolerated them, grudgingly, sensing that ultimately they were no threat to the marriage. Deep down they both needed each other, and nothing was going to change that. There may be a hint of self-portrait in the lines, 'this is an entirely new situation for Cesar [i.e. to need sympathy and comfort] for he has spent all his adult years providing these things for others and has persuaded himself he doesn't need them – he provides them.' For Masters this had a long history, dating back to the self-sufficiency of his early years. This denial of, or refusal to admit, his own needs made him a provider for others.

Masters sensed his novel might not be working when he wrote to Helen, 'supposing the mechanics were done perfectly, within the general framework given, would the final result, the novel, be worth the effort?' Helen replied on 11 June: 'I can't answer the question about whether the novel would be worth the effort – not at this point. There is too much undeveloped.' She still felt the American girl was not a 'palpable character' and the story lacked a 'point from which to tell it.' Their previously harmonious relationship was breaking down. Masters was so determined to see his new book through that he was beginning to pay less attention to Helen's comments.

Soon they had reached an impasse. Masters was not prepared to budge on the book and Helen, or rather Viking, was not prepared to take it as it was. It led to a split between them, and Masters began to look for another publisher. He told Keith at the time: 'I don't think a change of publishers will do me any harm and it might do me some good.' It sounds as though he was covering up the disappointment that he must have felt when Viking failed to support him in his new venture. However, he was not a person to dwell on such misfortunes and the military man in him quickly drew up another battle plan. Masters's last letter to Helen does convey some of his sadness: 'You will know most of all how much I am going to miss you. We have had a wonderful professional association and I do not suppose I will ever find as good an editor.' It was true; Helen had helped him enormously and his debt to her was considerable.

In October 1957, Masters returned to India for the centenary reunion of his regiment at Bakloh, his first trip back to India since 1946. There were four days of celebration to mark the occasion, but it poured with rain throughout, the outdoor spectacles and parades continuing regardless, in best Gurkha tradition. The weather only intensified the indoor celebrations, such as drinking rum and singing Gurkha jaunris. Being back in India and among the people he cared for most – his beloved Gurkhas – moved Masters. He kept a diary of this visit, but it records only events and factual details rather than his impressions and feelings. In a characteristic response, the emotions were not allowed to surface or be put on record. A small sign of his generosity was that he paid, anonymously, for the passage of a senior member of the Officers' Association in England, Col A. M. Harrison.

Masters completed his Spanish book, now called *Fandango Rock*, and with Helen Strauss's aid, looked for a new American publisher. His English publishers, Michael Joseph, stayed with him and by September he had moved to Harper Brothers, after a lunch meeting with the publisher, Cass Canfield Jr. He certainly hoped that *Fandango Rock* would sell as a film. Indeed, selling the film rights was probably a strong reason for holding on to the book so tenaciously. An offer of $200,000 did come in from a Texan film-maker, but in the end never came to fruition.

1959 started with a magazine tour. Helen Strauss had set up four commissioned articles for *Life* and *Holiday*: on the sherry country of Andalusia; the prehistoric caves of Lascaux in south-west France; the work of the US Save the Children Federation, from its Paris office; and the Greenjackets Regiment in England. Masters had laid on a welcome surprise present for Barbara at Madrid airport. Waiting there was Mike Rose. Barbara could not believe it and it took her a minute or two to realise Masters had so thoughtfully organised this.

Mike Rose remembers this trip vividly: 'We walked across from Jerez to Fuengirola, via Ronda, taking local buses. Jack was always pointing things out to me about the Romans or the Moorish occupation, or the wild life we saw. I still have a photograph of us at the beach in Fuengirola standing in front of a little old house with mountains behind and an old crone picking up sticks on the beach, no apartments in sight.' Mike was impressed by Masters's 'curiosity about everything around him. You'd walk down a street with him and he noticed things and knew an awful lot. He brought the street alive.'

Fandango Rock came out in early 1959, dedicated 'by the Author and the Typist to their collaborators in exacting arts of writing and friendship, Keith and Emily Jennison.' Critics inevitably noted its resemblance to Hemingway, with the descriptions of bullfights and Spanish life and the refrain running through the book, 'but this was Spain'. *The Times Literary Supplement* called it a 'rattling good yarn' and liked the suspense and tension between the Spanish town and the US air force base. The reviewer went on, 'the American characters are drawn with a delicate under-emphasis which can only be the product of the most intimate observation', a comment which would have pleased the developing author. The book's sales were good, as he had a devoted readership; it had sold 27,000 copies in the first four months in the UK alone, but the critical acclaim was moderate. Many felt it was not up to the standard of his Indian books and that it was too contrived. Chastened perhaps, Masters returned to Indian themes for his next novel. *Venus of Konpara* was about archaeology and adventure in India in the 1890s.

AT HOME
AND ABROAD
1960–1969

*V*enus of Konpara was written and published. Masters then turned to his second volume of autobiography covering his war years, provisionally entitled *Mercenary Calling*. This title was later changed to *Road Past Mandalay*. The novelty of the book was that it related the experience of war from the perspective of a member of the middle ranks. 'We have had much from disgruntled privates and self-satisfied Generals, but little from the Major and Lieutenant-Colonel level.'

As 1959 came to an end, changes were taking place at home and Masters was feeling a little frayed. 'The hectic Christmas season of goodwill is drawing to a close, thank God, and we can go back to hating everyone's guts. By this time next year I shall have become a Buddhist, and will announce that I am not going to give any cards or presents as it is against my religion; though very rich people can send me largeish checks for the benefit of my religious studies (viz my own navel and any twats available for studying).' He was now forty-five, a turning point, and his children were growing up: 'Susan, nearly sixteen, is turning into a beauty; rather short, but she's over five feet and that's all that matters. Martin gets longer and thinner every day, and talks about nothing but Triumph TR3s, and sometimes, his skis.' Masters had less control over his adolescent children. 'The kids return to school tomorrow; not that it will make much difference. They watch TV half the night and sleep till noon every day.'

Another turning point was Liz's wedding on 23 April in London. Her husband-to-be was a naval officer, Freddie Jefferson. Ever since Liz had come over for Christmas in 1956, Masters had taken a fatherly interest in her. Now he took it upon himself to give her some advice for her forthcoming marriage. He sent her a long eight-page letter just before her wedding.

I am writing because I am forty-five and very happily married, and,

because wherever we go, we see the wreck of marriages, and because
we have kind faces, we often hear the real truth as opposed to the
publicly given-out truth. Nine times out of ten, the failure of a
marriage is due to sex. This is not surprising if you grasp firmly the
idea that marriage is sex [a viewpoint he had already advanced in his
novels]. I do not mean that one spends one's entire time in lascivious
enjoyments . . . but the things that go wrong are very seldom published
in the way they ought to be. Sex is carried out, and has its seat, in
parts of our body which we hide away; which, if we do not keep them
clean, are apt to smell; we pee out of the same organs and worse is
not an inch or two away . . . if we do not accept these facts, we are in
trouble right away. Whatever attitude you have to adopt in public, in
private you must not be ashamed of sex or its organs or its extremely
earthy manifestations. You must therefore firmly grasp the principle
that sex is a damned good thing, and not in the least shameful. The
British upper class attitude, that it is much healthier and better to go
off shooting foxes, strangling salmon, or belting golf balls, and rather
caddish to enjoy sex, is the cause of much trouble. The most pitiful
and telling letter I have had in my life was from Tom Longstaff, now
over eighty and probably the greatest mountaineer who ever lived. I
sent him the ms of *Far, Far* to correct for mountaineering technique;
as you know there was a fair amount of sex in it, too. Tom, who had
lived his life in the tight lip, gentlemanly way, corrected my mistakes,
and then wrote, out of nowhere, 'sex is the most important thing in
life.' What had happened was that he lived about twenty-five years
with a wife, a lady, and presumably acted like a gentleman instead of
a man. They were divorced – or perhaps she died, I'm not sure; he
married again at about fifty, and this time found what was wrong the
first time. In the same vein we have Gen Frank Messervy, who
married like a gent, spent his time hunting and poloing and probably
despising sex – and ended up twice in the *News of the World* for
assaulting girls of fifteen, at the age of sixty plus. Nearer to home I
could point out three or four women who are unhappy because their
husbands treat them like ladies instead of like females on heat; the
trouble is only compounded, not caused, by the fact that these men
sometimes unleash on whores the passion their wives would love to
have – if they hadn't been taught it was unladylike, and learned by
experience that their husbands did not think it appropriate or proper
in the woman they had chosen to be the mother of their children,
chatelaine of Hinton St Admiral-Parva, etc.

Now men and women are different. The gravest mistake we make,
particularly men, is to imagine that this difference is confined to

physique. It is not, it runs right through the deepest recesses of our being. The two vital points, as regards sex are (1) that man likes the act, woman likes the man (2) for man, the act is of short duration, for woman, of long – 9 months.

And so on, for six more pages in similar vein. Liz, emerging from a relatively sheltered, though traumatic, upbringing, found the letter both shocking and impressive at the same time. She felt she was being treated as a grown-up, coming out into the adult world. She liked her new-found stepfather and admired him; any resentment she had felt towards him as the man who took her mother away had subsided long ago.

The letter stands as an autobiographical text as well. It states a defiant and idiosyncratic view of marriage, the separation of sex and love, and insists that a working arrangement can be built on this. 'The way to a good marriage is to recognize, on the outside, those controls which society enforces, while on the inside let your own wishes and tastes decide.' In his own marriage, an uneasy but working compromise had been achieved on this basis. For instance, Barbara could tolerate his infidelities if she also liked the other woman involved. Masters seems to be saying that provided you take a realistic attitude towards sex, then the marriage will survive.

At the heart of his relationships with women was the need to dominate and to control the relationship. In his novels the shadowy side comes out: women are sometimes treated harshly, often cruelly; sometimes they are seen as sexual vehicles, or are feared as likely to entice. Robin in *The Lotus and the Wind*, for instance, spurns his wife for fear of 'engulfment', despite her declared love for him. Although there is great emphasis on sex in his books, many of Masters's women are rather one dimensional, as if he feared them having a life of their own. The portrait of Victoria Jones is arguably more convincing when depicted by Rodney Savage than when she tells her story herself.

Liz's wedding took place in April at St James's, Piccadilly, and brought Masters and Liz's father, Hugh Rose, under the same roof. There was still ill-feeling from the divorce. Money was at the root of it. Masters put his side of things in his letter to Liz: 'I hope you do not think we are being miserly about your trousseau – neither of us are [sic] really stingy by nature; but your pa can certainly make me feel that way. He is apt to do something and then invite us to pay for it, a custom which arouses my worst instincts, since it is an old and generally sound policy to consult and obtain the agreement of those who you want to pay or help pay for something.'

In this letter Masters reiterated his side of the contentious issues in that divorce case.

> In order to obtain his assent to the adoption of Susan, who had, technically, to be his child, we had to sign papers agreeing never to seek custody of you two. As a matter of law I doubt whether those agreements would have stood up in law, since they were not relevant to the future of Susan; but we abided by them, thinking that your pa intended to remarry or at least bring you up himself. When he went out east and left you with Bunny and Pat [Pratt], it seemed to us that this was not quite fair; bringing you up himself was one thing but farming you out quite another. That was when we suggested we look after you, pa to retain all possible rights of seeing, consultation, decision, etc. He refused – only, suddenly, some years later when I had made some dough, to suggest that we should pay for your education. This we refused to do, since we had not been consulted at all; my private intention was to maintain some fluidity in finance so that I would be able to step in if things went seriously wrong.

It is difficult to disentangle all the threads. Hugh Rose did intend to look after the children himself, but when he was transferred with his regiment to Malaya, he had first asked his sister to help him out. This was the point when Barbara and Masters had initially hoped they might be allowed to look after the children, in 1947 when they came back to England. The divorce had been acrimonious and Hugh Rose would not budge, so the children went to foster parents instead. All this had been revived by the mention of money, when Rose expected Masters to pay for the trousseau. Masters had a horror of being used financially. His success had been hard-earned, achieved by his own hand in spite of the Establishment. The last thing he wanted was for others to feel they could cash in on that. It reawakened all his old resentment of the British upper classes and their high-handed manner.

In England for Liz's wedding, Masters went down to Wiltshire to see his childhood friend Eddie Waight. Eddie told him news of Lois. She was now married, and living with her army husband in Germany. Things were very difficult: she had been in and out of psychiatric hospital classified as a depressive, with occasional bouts of schizophrenia. Masters recalled his time with her, when she sometimes verged on instability and her frequent nightmares. He felt genuinely upset at this, as he told Eddie, because Lois had meant a lot to him during his Sandhurst years. She committed suicide five years later. His other childhood friend, Stanley Odlum, had since died of alcoholism.

Mike Rose was invited across to the USA that summer to join a family trip out West prior to going up to Oxford in the autumn. Martin recalls their journey. 'We all piled into the Station Wagon, a huge, nine-seater 1957 De Soto that we called the Observation Car as one of us would sit on the backwards facing seat in the tailgate with a pair of binoculars watching out for police.' They drove south through Arkansas, West Virginia, Kentucky and Oklahoma, camping and spending every fourth night in a hotel, as usual. 'It was a very instructive and exciting time, with a strong feeling of togetherness as a family.' Masters did most of the driving. Their journey continued through Texas, New Mexico, and Colorado, where the children went to the Diamond-G ranch in Dubois, Wyoming, while Masters and Barbara headed further east to California to see film contacts in Los Angeles. They had driven across the whole continent. Two weeks later the family was reunited and had a final camp together in the Tetons. Masters liked providing a wilderness experience for the young, teaching them to live in primitive surroundings, fishing for their own food, and, since it was bear country, sitting up all night round a camp fire waiting for a bear to appear. The huge plateaux, with their extensive views, made ideal riding country; a day's ride of 30 to 40 miles was not uncommon.

He worked on his autobiography while they were away. He describes the setting in the published postscript to the book: 'While I write at 9,000 feet above sea-level in the Absaroka Range of Wyoming, I can see the Wind River peaks to the south east and, when I climb the hill behind the cabin, the jagged tower of the Grand Teton to the west. Moose and elk and bear roam the forests and sometimes, between chapters, I walk up to the lakes below the cliff wall and catch a trout.' Harpers seemed pleased with the first draft.

Mike returned to England that September and wrote back saying he had the best time of his life during that summer. In October Masters wrote Alex, 'Things are pretty hectic round here what with the World Series being played and the football season in full swing and me preparing to get off on this long Asiatic trip. Now I have a mild fever and aching arms from three inoculations I got yesterday; and the kitten shat in the corner of the study . . .' The Asiatic trip was another magazine journey. Half a dozen articles on Pakistan and India had been commissioned by the *Saturday Evening Post*, *Holiday* and *Reader's Digest*. Masters left in November, and stayed first in Rawalpindi with an old Sandhurst colleague, Major-General Shahid Hamid, now a Minister in the Government and Director-General of Small Industries. Masters's first article was 'Kipling's Frontier, Then and Now'. He spent five days travelling round his old haunts – Bannu, Dera Ismail Khan, Wana, and Tank – and found the North-West Frontier as captivating as ever and physically little changed. 'Men still strode the roads and hills with rifles on their shoulders, and tribesmen descended from Afghanistan.' His companion was Commander Izzat Awan, 'a frontier Political Agent in the best tradition, tough and big in mazri pyjamas and shirt, smoking a pipe.'

Under the surface many changes had taken place, however. With the advent of Pakistan and an Islamic Government, the Mahsuds and Wazirs had dropped their warlike stance and agreed to be educated – something the British had never been able to get them to do. Masters saw this at first hand. 'At Wana, I was treated as a visiting VIP of the first magnitude, and hundreds of boys from six to seventeen were out on parade (the elders with rifles, the others with sticks) and put on gymnastic exhibitions. I had to look at their visitors' books, they learn and speak English poetry at the age of thirteen. They are exceedingly intelligent people and have seen that there is a better life than sticking a knife into your neighbour.'

His busy schedule meant he was on the move all the time and he went across to India to write other articles. In Delhi he met old friends such as the Sawhnys and stayed with a 4th Gurkha colleague, Moti Sagar, in his house there. For his main article, 'The Indian Army Today', he visited Jhansi and the Central India Horse, which his great-uncle had once commanded, and Subathu, the Gurkha training centre. These were festive occasions; he found himself welcomed back as an old India hand. In Subathu he was presented with a silver kukri; typically enough he introduced his Indian hosts to the art of making cocktails and then 'we hauled a couple of dozen wine bottles out of the cellars and tested whether they were still drinkable. They weren't, but it took us a long time to find out.'

He moved on to Dehra Dun for the Passing-out Parade of his old regiment, accompanied by Moti Sagar; he was impressed by the present-day Indian Army, the parade 'as good as any at the R.M.C. in my day.' In his article he wrote, 'the continuity of the Indian Army and its sense of the past was very moving. It seemed to me that the sepoy and NCO has improved since the days of the Raj. He is better educated, more alert and more independent, while retaining the basic qualities that make him what he was. The senior officers are of a quality that would be remarkable in any army. The hospitality, and the goodwill towards ex-British Service Officers is simply miraculous.' At Dehra Dun he looked at the inscription written there by Lord Chetwode, which epitomised for him the notion of service: 'The safety, honour and welfare of your country come first, always and every time. The honour, welfare and comfort of the men you command come next. Your own ease, comfort and safety come last, always and every time.'

Next he visited the temples at Khajurāho, the subject of another article, but overall it was a punishing schedule. As he wrote to Alex, after two months, 'the trip in Pakistan and India was very wearing; I had to fight like mad to get any work done at all, I mean, to find time to see the people I wanted to see, rather than go on an endless round of visits, tamashas, guest nights, special bara khanas and the like. I didn't seem able to get a happy medium – either I was guest of honour at successive parties, dinners, lunches and breakfasts, or I was sitting alone in a hotel room, knowing no one and writing. The frontier was fun though – looks just the same but tremendously changed in spirit.'

He had stop-overs arranged in Singapore and Bangkok and at Angkor Wat, which he compared to Khajurāho: 'both late flowering of Hindu art, Khajurāho more vital and erotic, Angkor more formal'. Then he went to Tokyo, and home, via San Francisco, by train – the California Zephyr to Chicago and the Twentieth-Century Limited 'at 80 mph all the way through a blizzard' to New York – arriving on 29 January 1961. Trains were still his favourite form of travel, and he was keen to use them 'before the car and plane strangled them.' He settled down to polish up his travel articles; writing them was a financially rewarding exercise, as he could get up to $1,250 for each article.

India stayed fresh in his mind. Once *Road Past Mandalay* was completed, his next book project was *To The Coral Strand*, another part of the Savage sequence, with a contemporary Indian setting, continuing where *Bhowani Junction* left off. It was his version of the 'staying on' theme that Paul Scott later wrote about. The central character, Rodney Savage, is no longer in the army, but working for a British firm and trying to come to terms with post-Independence India. When his firm, which builds dams, comes under Indian management, Rodney resigns, and sets himself up as a big game hunter for visiting rich English and Americans. At last Masters was able to work his Himalayan Holidays scheme into a novel. Rodney finds it hard to adjust to the changes about him. He feels nostalgia for the old India and resentment for the new.

Rodney becomes brigadier-cum-diplomat in a small Princely State whose independence is threatened. He has an affair with the Rani of a neighbouring state, who later betrays him. He must leave and just escapes arrest, retreating to a beach hut outside Bombay; Masters drew on his own experience and his stay at Juhu with Barbara in 1943 for the details. In the final part of the book, ensconced in his lair, Rodney reflects on British Indian history, disillusioned by the awareness that all that power and sacrifice has ended in defeat. A young English widow, who, like most of the women in the story, loses her heart to him – the book has its expected quota of sexual episodes, told with characteristic frankness – and looks after him; the book ends with a question mark over their future. Masters identified in some ways with Rodney and his nostalgia for the old India, but once again Masters is using his novel to test out ideas, such as the merits of staying in India. He seems to be implying that there is little place in present-day India for the likes of Rodney or for himself. History has moved on. The book conveys this by its authentic picture of that troubled period in Indian history.

Masters kept to his writing pattern. September to May were writing months, the summer for travel. In the winter Masters devoted time to planning the following summer's schedule. If the family was going to Spain he would write to Julio Nogues six months in advance, giving him precise instructions of which hotels to book on which days. Julio did as bidden and wrote back confirming the arrangements, his letter commencing 'Mi general'. For the summer of 1961 Masters devised a logistically complicated London-to-Spain bicycle trip for the younger generation on South Mountain Road. Martin was going with the two Anderson sons and two Simon sons, with Mike Rose in charge. Masters planned the whole thing down to the last detail in best staff-officer tradition. 'The admin instructions are a good deal more complex than anything I tackled in the army', he wrote at the time. The three families flew over to London at the beginning of June and bicycles and equipment were bought locally. The younger ones set off from Victoria Station for the first leg of the journey across the English Channel. Masters had mapped out an itinerary for them and their eventual destination was Santander in northern Spain, 750 miles away, where they would all meet up again. The boys had two weeks to get there, staying at youth hostels en route and averaging 50 miles per day. After seeing them off, Masters took the parental group for a drink at a bar opposite Victoria Station. Sydney Simon remembers his detailed but very precise instructions to the English barmaid to make Dry Martinis for them. She did her best, much to the impatience of other waiting customers, whom she berated petulantly with, 'Can't you see I'm working as a bloody chemist?'

Mike Rose, the future army officer in the making, kept firm control over the bicycling group. 'It went well, although there was a slight mutiny on the first hill outside Calais, which I quelled. After that they realised they were up against someone very hardline, and were not going to get any quarter.' They got to Santander on time, struggling a bit over the Pyrenees, as the bikes had no gears. They even managed to save some of the money given them for the trip and dutifully handed it back to their parents. Their bikes were sold in Spain for a profit. It concluded what had been a very satisfying venture for all concerned and one that lingered long in the memory of all the participants.

They all met up at Santander and went across to Huesca for the annual fiesta of San Lorenzo with its late-night dancing in the streets, jotas, processions and bullfights. A cannon went off at 7.00 a.m. each day to launch the festivities, and a bugler went round the streets waking people up. Eva Nogues remembers looking out of her window one morning and seeing Masters below with a loud-hailer alongside the bugler, urging people to bestir themselves. On these occasions Masters immersed himself fully in Spanish life, picoteando in various bars, eating very late lunches and sitting out in cafés until 3 a.m. or later.

By October he and Barbara were back in London for the publication of *Road Past Mandalay*. London was where many of those associated with the book lived, including most of his old wartime colleagues, several of whom came to the launch party. The book covered the period from where *Bugles and a Tiger* left off in 1939 and continued the narration through to the end of the Second World War. It had come out in America earlier that summer and met with favourable reviews. *Time* magazine praised it for the way the writing conveyed 'the peculiar, intense, masculine love a professional soldier has for the men he leads into battle'. Charlton Ogburn, the author of *Merrill's Marauders*, lauded it in *The New York Times* similarly, saying it made 'real and understandable the pride and appeal of soldierhood.' Even *The New Yorker* gave it their characteristic accolade, 'fashionably graphic' and 'helplessly impressionistic.'

Masters felt pleased with these reviews, but the English ones were eagerly awaited. Most reviewers felt he had captured the intensity of the Burma campaign with rare and impressive feeling, but others were more critical. There were suggestions that he had overplayed his hand and was claiming more than his share of credit for Chindit successes. It was a risk all writers of war memoirs run, and the Chindit campaign was a particularly fraught area, having been such a controversial subject. Masters had to some extent anticipated this by stating in his foreword that his purpose in writing the book was 'to tell the story of how a professional officer of the old Indian Army reached some sort of maturity both as a soldier and as a man'; in other words, he stressed that this was a personal view of things. He went on, 'Some parts of the story are very unpleasant – so was the war it records; others are almost painfully personal – but this is not a battle diary: this is the story of one man's life.' He was giving his perspective on events, not a comprehensive historical account.

His achievement was all the more remarkable in that he had no diary to guide him, but had to rely on his exceptional memory. 'I remember the whole thing with great clarity,' he wrote to his ex-Chindit colleague Alec Harper, 'and could probably walk the brigade's route again from end to end without more than one or two wrong turns; I have a photographic memory for places.' Part of his difficulty had been in recreating the intensity of Blackpool: 'I think all humans forget pain . . . it is, I believe, a psychological fact that the mind cannot reconstruct or really recreate pain, as for instance it can recreate loved sounds, sights, smells etc.' Yet he did manage, in this book, to do both. Shelford Bidwell, the military historian who later wrote *The Chindit War*, found only a few minor mistakes in dates. Masters's explanation was that they were 'very explosive events, and they have a great effect on you. If you have any sort of memory at all – and I have a pretty good one – you don't forget them.' His account of Burma is graphic and evocative, and the personal side is adroitly handled. It records his meeting with Barbara and their subsequent marriage.

His old adversary Bernard Fergusson was asked to review the book for *The Daily Telegraph*. Inevitably some of Fergusson's animosity crept in as he reminded the reader of their first frosty meeting in the jungle in India in 1943, 'I thought him conceited and coarse.' He refers again to Masters's early novels as exposing 'his streak of coarseness with no more reticence than a leper beggar', and in this book he takes him to task for introducing details of his personal life. Fergusson finds it 'embarrassing' to be told 'at length, how he bred his first child out of wedlock and how she attended his wedding to her mother a year later.' Gentlemanly conduct was at issue again. Bernard Fergusson wrote this review from what he called his 'lair' in Tuscany, comfortably ensconced in a distant land. Yet he does praise the book where praise is due: 'He writes wonderfully well despite the coarseness: not because of it', and this in spite of 'words that I was taught not to use in decent company let alone to print'. He calls the book overall 'magnificent stuff' and 'a major work', and concedes, 'I doubt if the business of fighting at the middle level has ever been portrayed as well. The weariness, the agonies and doubts of decision, the importance of putting a brave face on bad moments, the grief of sustaining casualties, the nomination of men to command forlorn hopes and their almost inevitable deaths, are retailed so vividly that the most chair-borne of readers will feel this might have happened to him.' The fact that Masters 'hides nothing, neither his moments of pride, nor those of abasement' brings out a grudging admiration. 'He writes superbly. He is not a hypocrite.' Yet Fergusson has to have the final word: 'I wish he would add to these

virtues a modicum of good manners, but I don't think he ever will.'
The running feud continued.

John Raymond of *The Sunday Times*, an earlier praiser of his novels,
had reservations about this book. He liked the 'crisp narrative, crisply
narrated', but was put off by what he termed Masters's 'cockiness' and
feared he must have been tainted by his American success ('Mr
Masters's temperament has suffered a powerful dislocation'). He ends
his review astringently with 'Go back East, Mr Masters', a hint of anti-
Americanism, the unforgiving side of envy.

Simon Raven, a shrewd observer of gentlemanly conduct, gave *Road
Past Mandalay* a sympathetic hearing in his *Spectator* review:

> *Road Past Mandalay* is at once an outspoken and an entirely equitable
> book. Indignation there is plenty, but never at the expense of truth;
> nor is truth itself permitted to reject compassion or to outrage privacy.
> I am easily bored by long battle sequences, muddled and repetitious as
> the best of them become; but in this case I was driven to read every
> word for the good reason that every word is made to tell. Lucidity
> unravels confusion, nice distinctions excuse the repeated pattern . . .
> the man speaks just as often as the professional soldier; and the man
> says that love and loyalty are better used to private ends, to the
> getting of happiness and children, and he illustrates the theme by
> telling his own love story with taste and dignity.

Masters warmed to these comments and to those of many of his ex-
colleagues from Burma, who nearly all expressed strong approval of
the book. His greatest pleasure came from an inscription Field Marshal
Sir William Slim wrote in a copy of his own book, *Unofficial Victory*,
which he sent to Masters in response to his signed copy of *Road Past
Mandalay*. Slim's inscription read: 'To John Masters, by age and more
than a bit of luck, I was your superior in times of war. Now in the field
of letters you have most decisively reversed our roles. Ayo Gurkhali,
Bill Slim.'

In the following winter of 1961 an offer came through from ABC
Television for Masters to make a documentary about Pakistan focusing
on the legacy of the British Empire. Masters would be the presenter
and would select and interview people on camera. Barbara went with
him and they left at the end of January 1962 to establish a base in
Lahore. 'It was hard but fascinating work. We took the cameras into
the High Court when it was in session and talked to lawyers in their
gowns and white bars – to show the continuity of the English legal
system. We visited cantonments and found the massed bands of the

Pakistan army practising for the Horse Show. I got them to parade in
full dress; organised a guest night at the 1st Punjab Regiment's mess;
had the guard of the old PAVO Cavalry (now just 11 Cavalry) turned
out – all this to show the continuity in the army. We spoke to students
at the University, and to the editor of the *Civil and Military*, at work in
Kipling's chair.'

Patrick Burke, head of the local Catholic school, was among those
interviewed. He went to meet Masters at Faletti's hotel beforehand.

> The door of suite no 5 was open and a cheerful fire burning in the
> grate. Masters rose from the desk and came towards me with
> outstretched hand. He radiated friendliness and an easy relaxed charm.
> He was casually dressed in a turtle-necked sweater and grey slacks. A
> tall man, his many years as an army officer had left an unmistakable
> mark on his bearing. He gave me a whisky. 'I won't go anywhere with-
> out my Johnnie Walker' he told me. Barbara came in from the bed-
> room, not exactly pretty but she had a face of gentle tenderness and a
> personality at once lovable and loving and, above all, dependable.

They discussed the film and Burke was told to report to the
Montgomery Club two days later. 'The filming began. I can still
picture Masters as he stood in front of the magnificent fireplace and
said "Here I am in the famous Montgomery Club of Lahore, Pakistan,
the guest of my English, Irish and Pakistani friends."' Each of them –
Philip Luckeys, the head of Lloyds Bank; Zal Manekji, an importer of
American cars; Zulfikar Ali Shah, head physician at the Mayo Hospital;
Anwar Moinuddin, a lawyer; and Tariq Ali, editor of the pro-com-
munist *Pakistan Times* – gave their views on the current state of
Pakistan, and the consensus was that British influence was still
prevalent in the administration and official business of the country,
and, of course, in the army.

Back home on 1 March, he was putting the finishing touches to *To
The Coral Strand* when a letter arrived out of the blue from colleagues,
or rather ex-colleagues, at Michael Joseph. The publishing house had
recently changed hands and been bought by the Thomson organisation, owned by Roy (later Lord) Thomson, the Canadian newspaper
tycoon. The joint Managing Directors, Peter Hebdon and Charles
Pick, together with another director, Roland Gant, felt they did not
want to stay on and transferred to Heinemann, though Hebdon later
returned to Michael Joseph. Charles Pick wrote to Masters suggesting
he join them. Masters sent the letter straight back, scrawling the words
'Fuck Off' boldly three times across its front page. It was a classic
Masters response – loyalty was not going to be traduced this way;

if anyone was to change agent or publisher, it would be his decision. *To The Coral Strand* brought him to the end of his current series of Savage novels. He had written eight in all, and this completed the historical span from the earliest days (*Coromandel*) to modern times. He still had his original list of thirty-five possible titles, but felt it was time to move on and try his hand elsewhere. He felt that he had, for the moment, said all he wanted to say about India. It repeated the situation with *Fandango Rock* a few years back, only now no theme came immediately to mind. As he wrote to Alex, he found himself 'staring at bits of paper and trying to get worked up to start on another novel.' Each preparatory stage before a novel was written was, as Barbara remembers, like a gestative period. He would sit before embarking on the writing and brood on his own for two weeks or more, eyebrows furrowed, thinking hard, getting the shape and outline of the book gradually into perspective. He remained incommunicado during this phase. It was like drawing up an appreciation again, seeking to summarise the essence and the objective of the book. Then he would go quickly to work in his study. He drew up charts of the outline and the characters, noting when they first appeared in the book, when they were first described physically and so on. He put these up on the wall too. A first draft would be typed out straightaway and quickly. He told Mollie Kaye he wrote the first draft of *Bhowani Junction* in thirteen days. The revisions, 'polishing' the book, might take six months. Mollie Kaye told him she could not work that fast. She had to write slowly. He told her, 'To hell with it, get it all down and then polish.'

An early heatwave hit South Mountain Road that May. 'It's over 90 here now, about 3.30 in the afternoon. Also pretty muggy but no one's got their swimming pools filled, the selfish rats.' He decided his next novel was to be set in Cape Cod and they planned a summer vacation there. They had been there before in 1959 and enjoyed it. This time, as he told Alex, they were going 'for the sake of the children, so that they can meet friends, sail, dance and generally live a "normal" summer life as it is lived here.' Susan was eighteen, and in her last term at St Mary's in the Mountains in New Hampshire, stricter and more regimented than North Country, where Masters had sent her to advance her academic progress. She had applied and been accepted for Stanford University in California, starting at the end of September. 'We are all pleased as it is the No 1 place where girls want to go – about 8,000 men and 500 women, and a very high scholastic and general reputation.' Martin was now 5 ft 10 in and 'built like a bean pole, and spends his whole time reading sports car books and playing the radio, pop music of the most ghastly type.' Martin was a talented piano player and visibly keener on music than soldiering. There had been a bad moment in his youth when Martin announced that he liked Liberace, much to Masters's horror. When Keith Jennison was told of this, he said, 'Let him be, he's only a kid, he'll get over it', but Masters found it hard to take. Martin had gone to North Country for a while, but was now finishing his sophomore year at Deerfield and would be sixteen on 21 July. 'On that day we are certain to become owners of another car, as he has been saving up for years and thinks of nothing else. My insurance rates on cars will go way up. Where he is going to park it I don't know.'

The Masters family left for the Cape on 11 June. They had rented 'a nice four-bedroom house' right on Pleasant Bay in North Chatham, close to the sailing club and the country club, 'which I may have to join, though I hate them. I am getting a 16 ft Bristol with 40 hp engine, which I will sell again at the end of the season, or rather at the beginning of next when there are some buyers. In 1959 I hardly dropped anything doing that with a smaller boat.' It turned out to be an enjoyable family summer. The sailing, swimming and the children's social life were much as expected. Masters had sketched out a plan for his new book, and set it against a backcloth of Cape Cod. He was busy acquiring local details. The book was soon to be entitled *Trial at Monomoy*, and was closer in structure to a thriller; it described how an American town on the Atlantic coast was threatened with annihilation by a blizzard. Its cast of characters includes a ruthless property-owning fascist who is a suppressed homosexual, a puzzled yet virile liberal, an over-sexed and shallow woman, and an under-sexed liberal woman whose sexuality blooms from the attentions of the puzzled male liberal and so on. For all its entertainment value, it was not one of his best efforts and lacks credibility. Years later when Allen Kaufman was visiting the Cape he stayed in a local motel near Chatham and mentioned the book to its proprietor. 'Oh that guy, oh sure, I remember him,' the proprietor told him. 'We nearly ran him out of town.' They felt that, in Somerset Maugham fashion, Masters had misrepresented them and betrayed their secrets.

Once the children were back in school and college, he and Barbara left for England, combining their annual walking holiday in Spain with the launch of *To The Coral Strand*. They headed for the Spanish Pyrenees and based themselves at Bielsa, a typical Aragonese village at the head of a valley, with great jagged mountains all round, gorges, cataracts and overhanging precipices. On their second day there, at the end of

September, they had set out to walk as usual, but almost immediately a severe pain started in Masters's left leg as he and Barbara were going up the village street. It did not leave him for three days, but he was determined to continue. On the next day Masters wrote in his log: 'I set off 10.00 a.m. on the mule road to Ala de Beret, finally made it by 1.10 p.m. – 3 hrs 10 min for 2,100 ft and about 4½ kms! I stopped every fifty paces. Felt awful but bloody well got there. Down in 1 hr 15 min (pain less downhill) legs still pretty bad, but reasonable especially on the steeper downhills!'

Masters had suffered a blockage in the circulation in his left leg; it was ironic for him to be incapacitated in this way since walking was what kept him fit and healthy. Walking now became painful. Barbara remembers: 'It was terrible. He'd walk for 100 yards and then turn pale green, he'd give me the stuff to carry and then walk another hundred yards. It was a bad summer, but he was determined to complete our schedule.' From Aragon, they went further south to Orihuela in Castile. On 23 October they listened to Kennedy's broadcast about the Cuban crisis and blockade: 'neither of us could sleep, general restlessness and a bad night.' The Masterses always took their powerful short-wave radio with them to listen to news programmes on the BBC World Service and to the Voice of America for World Series baseball when it was on. Otherwise, in the evenings, they mostly played Scrabble together; Barbara, with her four-leaf clover eyes, was the better player.

On their way back to New York, they went through London for the publication of *To The Coral Strand*. He gave an interview for BBC TV. 'I have now written the eighth and last book of the series dealing with the period in which the British were in India. The thing I was trying to do in the series as a whole was to create a truth of time and place. Somebody once called my books geographical novels, and I took that as a compliment because the air, the soil, the water, the smell of woodsmoke and cowdung and the particular kind of dusk of an Indian evening, the feel of mud in the rains, the kind of feel of the Himalayas at ten, twelve or fourteen thousand feet, are circumstances that give an event a particularly Indian reality rather than a general reality.' He was reiterating the Indian-ness of his books.

Part of his overall aim had been to paint a four-dimensional picture of the two hundred and fifty years of British rule there – 'a broad canvas of this period', as he called it. He felt that, Kipling aside, India and especially Indians hitherto had been under-represented in fiction, and this had contributed to the misunderstanding between races. The author Leonard Woolf tells the story of how when he was a government

official in Ceylon he could never make up his mind whether Kipling
had moulded his characters accurately in the image of British Indian
society or whether 'we were moulding our characters accurately in the
image of a Kipling story.' It was a telling observation. This 'mistreat-
ment' of Indians in fiction was something Masters sought to rectify.
Even Kipling had at times treated the Indian as 'half-devil, half-child'
and had written, 'The Indian is as incapable as a child of understanding
what authority means, or where is the danger of disobeying it.' He was
echoing the notion of the 'civilising mission' at the root of the imperial
idea. Masters only partly went along with this and wanted to convey
the Indian side of things as fully as the British. His proudest boast was
the compliment paid to him in 1957 by the contemporary author and
critic Khushwant Singh who wrote, 'Both Kipling and Masters understand India, but only Masters understands Indians.'

His heroes were unlike those of Maud Diver, 'all sunburn and stern
renunciation.' Masters looked beneath the sunburn. Skin had a special
and emotive significance to him and his books explore its symbolism, testing to see whether, beneath that skin, the two races could
meet or understand each other. This theme is carried through to his
last novel, *To The Coral Strand*, where Rodney Savage says: 'After
days and years and centuries, would there stand an opaque wall between true understanding, however clear the paintings each of us
put on the surface of the wall, in an attempt to communicate?' This
question had underpinned *The Deceivers* and *Bhowani Junction*.
Kipling, Masters felt, had stopped short with his 'you'll never plumb
the Oriental mind.'

Surface, the brilliant light and sheen of India, were important and
frequently evoked in his novels, especially the early Indian ones, but his
heroes are often more complex than they seem at first sight. They
suffer inner doubts and heart searchings. Their quest is often as much
for identity as for the enemy or the spy. William Savage never forgets
the spiritual dangers he runs in tracking down the Thugs. His struggle
is both with the worshippers of Kali and with himself. Rodney in
Nightrunners of Bengal, in the midst of overcoming hardships as he
escapes from the Mutiny, faces the bitterness of mind and heart that
these experiences have engendered in him. In *Far, Far the Mountain
Peak*, Peter Savage struggles with the urge to prove himself as a
mountaineer and is aware of the risks, as other people might be
involved. The peculiar affinity which develops between Robin Savage
and his adversaries makes *The Lotus and The Wind* more than just a
story of the pursuit of spies; it is about finding one's self and an act
of redemption.

Masters's reputation is, rightly, primarily that of a superb storyteller and was gained through the narrative power of his novels. They resemble adventures in the old-fashioned sense and make compelling reading. The organisation of material and plot is handled with great expertise. In the mainstream of British writers on India he is closer to Kipling than Forster. He admired Forster, though he had reservations about *A Passage to India*. Its picture of the country, he felt, was deceptive; the 'shading of greys to blacks, and uniting muddled chains of small hillocks into a sharp single mountain range' was overdone. India, in his eyes, was not like that, it was much more complex and opaque. With Kipling he shared an admiration for the Indian Army, which as an institution probably got closer to the 'real' India than any other segment of the British Raj. He also shares some of Kipling's belief in duty and action, and his gift for local colour.

In Masters's autobiographies, such as *Bugles and a Tiger*, his nostalgia for bygone India is often stronger. In the novels, by using the device of the Savage family as 'measuring rods' for the events going on around them, he can be more critical and can evaluate the merits of each historical situation and its corresponding imperial idea in a much more pragmatic manner. Both sympathy – and objectivity – can be expressed in this way. For instance, the Rani in *Nightrunners of Bengal* is depicted as intelligent, capable and patriotic. She is shown as being defeated not because her cause is unworthy, a standard British line about the Mutiny, or because she is lacking in courage, but because circumstances are against her, the forces of history are moving India away from the feudal order. Masters's objectivity is just as noticeable in the way he depicts the cruelty of his compatriots when they come to suppress the Mutiny and in the way he emphasises the humanity of many Indians who risked protecting the British at considerable danger to their own lives. His aim overall was to render what he saw as the essence of England's relationship to India: 'activist, decisive, a great love with also domination, and pragmatic rather than theoretical.'

He never saw himself as a propagandist, more as recording what he knew from personal experience. If there was a message, it was that the lack of personal contact with Indians ultimately doomed the imperial idea. It was the upstairs room mentality: 'the British did not allow themselves to feel India. They were like men in an upstairs room, secure, cut off'. Much of Masters's incentive to write was to recreate his 'lost' India. By naming it and putting it down on paper, and recreating it through imagination, he was forcibly coming to terms with its loss. Now, in 1962, he felt that process was through.

*

At the end of November the Masterses travelled back to the USA on the *Queen Mary*. Masters immediately saw his doctor, Dr Mack Lipkin, who diagnosed arterio-scelerosis with partial occlusion of the artery. Dr Lipkin told him he had to give up smoking – Masters smoked a pack and a half of Camels per day. True to form, he left the surgery, went out to his car, lit up his last cigarette, smoked it and never smoked again. Barbara, in loyal support, stopped too. A week later he went to Cornell Medical Centre for a plathysmogram which showed the occlusion had occurred at the junction of the aorta and left ilium. This onset of ill-health was a cruel blow; he had done his level best to keep fit, and now he was struck down with an indeterminate illness.

Further tests followed that winter. He wrote to Laurence Pollinger at the end of December, 'the long-term prognosis is for a gradual worsening of the condition, not steadily but by incalculable stages – I might drop dead tomorrow with a blockage of the brain, or might have nothing for 20 years, and then only a mild pain of the little finger. I am supposed to keep warm, take exercise so that the blood finds new ways to the leg round this blockage. I don't mind not smoking as much as I thought I would, but I do find it hellishly hard to concentrate, and will do so until I get used to not having a cigarette around.' Why this sudden attack should hit him is not clear. It had happened at a time when his life was in a state of flux, both as an author and emotionally: the letter about his Anglo-Indian ancestry had come through that summer. It was possible that the delayed after-effects of war – Burma and the Chindits especially, when he was half-starved and exhausted – might have contributed to it.

He was now forty-eight years old and these first intimations of mortality were making themselves felt. Changes were now taking place in nearly every sphere. His payments from MGM spread over nine years were ending, prompting him to consider living in a tax haven in the Caribbean. 'I have been foreseeing this condition for some time, but have not acted, partly because there was no need to and nothing much to be done, and partly because a couple of good breaks would have put my income up.' His writing career was heading off in a different direction, his children were beginning to leave home and now physical debility was hitting him. It was a time for stock-taking. In another letter to Pollinger that year he wrote, 'this seems to be the Year of the Woodlice for me,' and it was true, much that was hidden was coming out of the woodwork.

It was a difficult winter for the Masterses in 1962. Giving up smoking was tribulation enough, but now Masters's writing was not going all that well either; *Trial at Monomoy* was proving difficult to get into shape. Then he heard news that his father was in hospital in Exeter. It had been a very cold winter in England and Masters senior had slipped on the ice on his doorstep at Uplyme, trying to clear it away. The fall caused a rupture in his aorta (curiously both father and son now had complaints in the same area). Masters, with the circulation problems in his leg and the bad winter, was not keen to travel. Then his father suffered an aneurism when the rupture burst, and died quite suddenly on 14 January 1963, aged seventy-nine, in Exeter hospital. Had Masters known the seriousness of his father's condition, he would have flown over straightaway. Deep down, he was very fond of his father, and had felt protective towards him for the last few years. Masters was glad he had at least managed to spend time with him the previous autumn, when he had gone down to Uplyme and his father had met him off the train in Axminster in his old Rover and taken him for drinks with his golf club cronies. He would miss him. For all his impatience with him, there was a closer bond than might have appeared on the surface. He wanted his father to feel proud of him, and had enjoyed his parents' visits over to the USA that showed how well he was doing. Masters and his father shared other memories too, of India and the old days. Masters flew over for the funeral and stayed a week to get his mother settled.

A further trip to the Indian sub-continent was now in the offing. After the success of his 1962 film for ABC on Pakistan, their rival company, NBC, wanted Masters to present a programme on India's ability – and will – to resist Chinese communist aggression, now threatening their northern border. China had occupied Tibet in the 1950s and was poised for what looked like another invasion.

Masters welcomed the chance to return to India and the prospect of more television work. He liked being regarded as a TV presenter and an expert on Indian sub-continent affairs. Although primarily an author, he was always on the look-out for extensions of his writing and expertise. Films and scriptwriting had been one route, magazine article writing another, and now television seemed to be offering a third. Once again, Barbara went with him; she was an essential companion and helpmate on these trips. They left New York City on 24 September, taking a train – still their favourite way of travel – across to San Francisco to visit Susan, now a sophomore at Stanford University. Being plunged into a milieu where there were ten thousand students instead of a hundred as she had previously known was quite a shock to her. 'Nobody cared whether you went to meals or class,' she recalled. She had had a fairly protected upbringing, with no dating at high school, other than dances with nearby boys' boarding schools, and this was quite a contrast. She seemed to be settling in though, and her parents did their best to reassure her.

From California they flew to Tokyo on 1 October. 'We left the same evening for a remote fishing village in Yamaguchi Prefecture opposite to Korea on the Sea of Japan, where we spent a week in a Japanese inn finishing *Trial at Monomoy*. We worked every morning, and walked every afternoon and then after being ceremoniously wrapped into a kimono by the maid, who was charmingly ugly and sixty-five years of age, we bathed, ate, drank sake and fell back on the pillows to sleep.'

Now suitably refreshed, they flew on to Delhi, to be given an official welcome at the airport by Commander Nar Singh from the Indian Government Armed Forces Information Office and by Lt-Col Pyare Lall, their liaison officer. The Indian Government had given their blessing to the film and were secretly pleased it was being made, but the inevitable delays as official permissions were drawn up for their visit to the border area in Sikkhim left the Masterses with time on their hands. While waiting, Masters went down to the Rajputana Rifles Regimental Centre in Rajasthan to film the process of induction into the modern Indian Army, showing how a peasant or ploughboy was turned into a present-day Indian soldier. He was back on familiar ground, since his father had served with the 10th Rajputs, and felt at ease there.

Permission for Barbara to accompany him to Sikkhim was proving difficult to obtain. Nobody, other than the military, was allowed in the border zone: no newspaper correspondents, no Indian Army wives, no women, but Barbara was keen to go and Masters wanted her to. They went to see the Army Chief of Staff, General Moochoo Chaudary, whom Barbara knew from her Quetta days; he had been at Staff College with her first husband Hugh Rose. 'He looked at me and said, "Do you want to go as well?" I said, "Of course." "All right, we'll put you down as the specialist"', and he gave her a permit. They were billeted in a dak bungalow at 11,000 feet, and were well looked after, with a Jeep and driver at their disposal and cold weather clothes provided.

Masters set off for the border area every morning at first light with his film crew, and filmed until 2.30 p.m. Then they drove back down the precipitous road, part of which fell while they were there. In early November it was freezing cold at that altitude. To Masters's surprise and delight, his former battalion of 4th Gurkhas, under Lt-Col (now General) Kale, was there, and the film shows his reunion with them, dancing and drinking rum, dressed in a bright red mountaineering shirt covered in badges and Alpine clothes and boots. A fellow Gurkha officer saw the completed film and later wrote, 'he was showing all his grace and skill as a nautcher and his moving departure as he slowly walked to his Jeep with the Pipes playing *Auld Lang Syne* at 14,000 ft was a memorable sight.' Other troops he met there (exact numbers were not mentioned on the film for security reasons) included colleagues from earlier campaigns, the sergeant-major of the Dogras and a naik in the 2nd Battalion 11th Sikhs who had been in Waziristan with him in 1937, and five subadars, all veterans of the 1944 Chindit campaign and his own Subadar-Major Rudrabahadur Punanother, who had been with him as adjutant in 1940 at Loralai.

Despite the altitude of 14,000 feet, morale was high, which comes across in this film, and in the next sequence, down on the plains, preparedness was just as evident. Masters chose to illustrate this dramatically by arranging a special Parachute Brigade drop on the flat land in front of the Taj Mahal, as he put it, to 'symbolise in a single dramatic and colourful sequence the subject of our documentary'; namely how, with all its old traditions and monuments, modern India was nevertheless ready for such contingencies as a possible Chinese invasion.

Not since 1946 had Masters spent so much time with the Indian Army, and he found much that pleased him, the sense of continuity, and its great tradition of 'hospitality, grace and good manners.' The film, entitled *Jaiwan*, bears this out. It was shown both in America and England and was well received; Masters's confident manner as presenter was favourably commented on. Indeed, the Indian Government felt it may have contributed towards aid being granted to them by the US Government.

In the USA the Masters family was about to move house to somewhere smaller and easier to run. A newer, more modern house was available further up South Mountain Road. They went to look at it, liked it and bought it. It had full-length plate-glass windows, an ultra-modern kitchen, a long narrow room Masters could use as his study, a pool and wooded surroundings. It was set well back from the road, perched up at the end of a steep drive. They also traded in their bulky de Soto station wagon and bought a smaller Dodge. It had a special engine in it, 'a racing car for the street' as Martin called it. 'No one could pass it, and it reached about sixty miles an hour in two seconds.' Masters liked his cars to be different.

The new house was surrounded by plenty of animal life, which pleased Barbara. Racoons, and later skunks, appeared once the porch light was turned on.

People couldn't believe it. Once we had a party and someone said, 'Look at that.' A racoon was standing with his nose pressed against the glass. The racoons knew that if we had a party, someone was going to feed them and they'd rip round to the kitchen door as soon as they saw me moving in that direction. They were always funny to watch – particularly when you fed them spaghetti, as it got all tangled up in their dainty little fingers. We put out scraps, everything except orange peel, every night. They became so tame that if they were hungry they soon came and begged in broad daylight. Racoons all look the same as their markings are identical but the skunks were more individual, there was one we called Queen Victoria as she had a perfect white cap, with little ribbons off it.

Barbara's liking for these animals became legendary. Once Alan Anderson was driving down South Mountain Road at night and he saw a racoon walking along in the opposite direction to the Masterses' house. Alan stuck his head out of the window and shouted, 'The Masterses are that way.'

Masters was now working on a history of the First World War, commissioned originally as a series of articles for the *News of the World* in London to commemorate the outbreak of war fifty years earlier. Michael Joseph thought it would make a book, and it became *Fourteen Eighteen*, published a year later, in October 1965.

Once the manuscript of *Fourteen Eighteen* was completed, the Masterses went across to London that summer. They stayed at the Charing Cross Hotel. Masters preferred these large, comfortable Edwardian hotels attached to major railway stations. Another favourite was the Grosvenor near Victoria. London meant eating at good restaurants; his favourite was Wheelers in Old Compton Street, Soho, where he knew the manager, Peter Jones, and the staff well, and was always greeted as a long lost friend. He would invite agents or publishers there or to The Ivy or Boulestin or Quaglino's, where he and Laurence Pollinger usually met. Food mattered greatly to Masters. In London he enjoyed nothing more than traditional British fare: grilled Dover sole, half a dozen oysters and poached turbot were favourites at Wheelers. In his logs nearly all of his meals, and Barbara's if she was with him, were comprehensively recorded, including what was ordered and consumed, which dishes were successful, which overcooked or whatever. He was a fast eater, who attacked his food with gusto and enjoyed it. He was not averse to using his hands as a food purveyor, in the accepted Indian tradition. He would often try bits and pieces off other people's plates.

For their London visits the Masterses kept up a busy schedule, and spent money readily. He liked inviting friends or family to a meal in one of his preferred restaurants and insisted on paying the bill, not ostentatiously but out of genuine generosity. His day was fully occupied, meeting publishers or agents, doing research at the Imperial War Museum or the Royal United Services Institution, and shopping, but he always found time for at least an hour's walk each day, usually in a London park. Barbara and he would separate to visit their respective families: Barbara to see her mother in Claygate, Masters to see his mother or Alex in Farnham. His mother was now about to move to a flat close to Farnham and Masters went down to help her. He kept up with old army colleagues, such as Tim Brennan, and on this visit he met 'the Auk' for lunch at Quaglino's to discuss the history of the Indian Army the latter was still trying to get Masters to write.

After ten days in London, the Masterses moved to France, where they now kept a Peugeot Estate Car which they had bought early in the 60s for their European travels and kept on blocks for the winter at a friend's garage on the outskirts of Paris. They seldom spent long in Paris – a couple of days at the most – meeting friends, or going to the cinema, where 'blue' films were more readily available. This time they saw a 'so-called' sex movie, *Les Sexy Girls*, which proved to be 'about as sexy as an old bra thrown on a sofa.' Spain was always their destination and the pleasure of arrival there was undimmed. 'It is good to be in Spain – cheerful waitresses, plain food, animation in faces and gestures – French people don't smile when spoken to or smiled at – Spanish do.'

Masters became almost Spanish once he had crossed the frontier, as he now spoke the language fluently. He liked the quality of Spanish life, in a country that was tough, enduring, proud, defiant, its people gregarious and voluble. Spain had style, which he felt was rapidly disappearing in the twentieth century. The arrogant grace and insolence of its people reminded him of India, and he felt at home with their independence of manner, their head-high and straight-eyed look, their generosity, their old-fashioned sense of honour and respect for others. Spain has never been a country of half measures: its landscape which was austere and desolate at one moment, as in the plains of Castile, was rich and fruitful elsewhere, as in Aragon. It was a country where ordinary things became heightened. It brought out 'something bravely perpendicular about a man, something that makes him feel a finer, or at least an intenser, species than he is elsewhere'. Masters liked nothing more than going into a rural bar and emerging half an hour later, amid much back-slapping and protestations of 'hombre!', an intimate friend of its owner. He wrote a *Sunday Times* article about Spain that year in which he conveys many of these sentiments, writing of 'Spain's magnificent, starving, proud, generous, polite, unbendable individuals.'

Walking was the Masterses' main activity in Spain, but it was more than a form of relaxation. It was exhilarating being up in the hills, in the mountains, with the clear air and dramatic scenery and changing clouds, but it also fitted in with Masters's wish to give a sense of purpose to each day, the sense of getting somewhere, staking out a plan, mapping out a schedule, and then sticking to that schedule, and, on the walk, keeping up to the mark ('going well' is a frequent phrase in his logs). At the end of the day they felt a sense of fulfilment, of repletion, at having achieved their objective, at having covered the required ground and climbed so many feet. Masters's logs record to the minutest detail the exact tally of each day's walk. The precision of such recording mattered to him. Once that was done, they could go out and have a good evening with friends or at a restaurant. After every 100 miles walked, they celebrated with champagne at their evening meal.

Walking was not for dawdlers. Masters set the pace, stayed in the lead most of the way and stopped only briefly for refreshment or rest – a 'pit-stop' as it came to be known – not for admiring the view or chitchat. There were echoes here of the marches across the plains below Bakloh. Guests had to go along with this. Walking had an energy, a purpose to it, but it also offered an experience of landscape that tied in with Masters's philosophy. Landscape was there, a given; it was the surface of things that mattered to him. He was less concerned with what lay beneath or beyond – in common with many of his generation he distrusted such speculation. The world of Freud was kept firmly outside the door, though, interestingly, he shifted his views about this as he grew older, and his last novel, *Man of War*, has a sympathetically-drawn central character who is a psychiatrist. In place of the direct expression of feelings, however strongly felt, humour and bonhomie were much-used substitutes.

The mid-1960s were an unsettled time for Masters. He was in an in-between phase in his writing, having lost, or given up, the surer footing of his Indian novels, and had not yet found a suitable replacement. The house move had been a symptom of this and now he and Barbara thought of establishing a pied-à-terre in England as well. On their next visit, in May 1966, they rented a flat in Royal Avenue, Chelsea, for a month. By now he was working on his new novel, *Breaking Strain*, a new genre for him; it was to be a thriller about salmon fishing in the John Buchan mould. He worked at home while Barbara looked for a suitable flat to buy. She soon found one in Water Gardens, just off

Edgware Road. It was newly-built and had two bedrooms – one of which he could use as his study. Barbara, a keen ornithologist, later discovered to her great delight that the eleventh floor flat was on the flight line of Canadian geese between Kew Gardens and Regent's Park. They passed close to the windows at eye level.

Masters's mother was more and more a preoccupation on his London visits. He went to see her in Farnham. 'Difficult to know what she wants or thinks, she's now eighty, and there is still emotionalism, dislike of various people, pique, etc. but it is clear she doesn't want to go to a home unless it fulfils impossible conditions – it has to be in the middle of a town, large, cheap.' She was becoming a bit cranky: 'She hates Aunt Nancy, butlers, posh people, subordinates, etc.'

When they went to Spain for the summer, they invited Alice Mathews to be their guest. Alice remembers this trip with great affection.

> Spain's larger than life qualities appealed to Jack. His appetites were robust. He could enjoy a Rioja, a paella or broiled merluza without concerning himself with vintages and sauces. Women recognised his strong masculinity even in a casual encounter. Once we were astonished to find a meadow covered with small blue nylon tents in an otherwise primitive countryside and Jack asked a woman walking towards us what was going on. She explained that the wheat fields were farmed communally by a village further down and that it had always been the custom to move up and stay until the harvest was complete. Of course, there were sometimes interesting and unexpected results nine months later, but the tents made the harvest more comfortable. And, with a laugh and a leer, why didn't the señor join them for some fun?

It was an example of how quickly Masters merged into Spanish life. Alice pursues this point: 'Where Jack had been before, he was remembered. As we entered a remote cantina, the owner recognised Jack with an "hombre!" and immediately poured some of the heady local cider into a large glass, which Jack downed in the approved fashion – head back, glass at arm's length, to welcoming applause.' In a crowded Santander restaurant, the Rhin, the owner greeted them and found a table when none seemed available. On their walks 'Jack always led, followed by Barbara, then me, along a narrow trail. Jack's appearance was picturesque – tall, rangy, beak-nosed, topped by a wide-brimmed floppy felt hat, slung about with binoculars, camera and backpack, clothed in a long-sleeved shirt, trousers tucked into stout walking boots and wielding a very large black umbrella – used sometimes as protection from the weather, more often as a walking stick, occasionally as a weapon to fend off over-friendly cows or suspicious dogs.'

His attention to detail was very much in evidence. 'Every walk was planned meticulously, we walked a steady pace and rested, standing, for five minutes each hour. We had lunch (a merienda) and then a short nap or siesta which lasted so long and no longer. Our drives from one walking neighbourhood to another were similarly organised. Sight-seeing was minimal and Barbara and I had a standing joke that if we had a few minutes to spare for an interesting looking church, it was sure to be closed.'

As an example of his thoroughness, Alice recalls a walk that was more gruelling than anticipated because the local map was inaccurate. After it was over she lay down and wailed, 'But it was supposed to be an easy walk!' She remembers how Masters was concerned but quite firm. This was a foolish attitude: one could never tell what might be coming, what might be about to happen; one must always be prepared and maintain that bit of extra reserve which will see one through. Alice felt that Masters was driven by 'a real need to test, to push himself that was nervous as well as physical energy, a residue of the war.'

She remembers how short-tempered he became with waiters who did not follow his instructions and was often impatient with lengthy Spanish menus. He usually chose local specialities and had a liking for offal dishes, such as callos (tripe). In Spain, he was nearly always on the look-out for trains, mostly narrow gauge ones and the vanishing steam locomotives. Once they drove through a town that was a major railroad junction. Masters parked the car in the railway yards, leaving Barbara and Alice in it for some time and then came back with the photographs he wanted.

Breaking Strain was completed and then the winter was spent on magazine articles and correcting proofs. Through Laurence Pollinger Masters had met John Anstey who was in charge of the *Daily Telegraph* Weekend magazine. They got on well and Anstey was keen to commission Masters to do travel articles for him. He was just starting a series of pieces on 'Journeys of Discovery' to remote places. Masters wrote an article for him on Patagonia and Tierra del Fuego, where he had been in 1954. It was to prove a lucrative source of income in years to come. It also enabled Masters and Barbara to visit parts of the world they had never been to before. In February 1967 Masters took Barbara with him to write about the gold and opal miners of southern Australia. It soon became almost possible for them to name a part of the world they wanted to visit and then have Anstey agree to an article on it, all expenses paid.

On the way back from Australia, they stopped off in California to see Susan at Stanford. She had become embroiled in the 60s counter-culture of rebellion and hippie life. She had met and fallen in love with a fellow college student, Cyril Sia, a brilliant radical at Berkeley. They were married in 1965 while her parents were in Spain, and now lived outside San Francisco with their young daughter, Danielle. Cyril was Chinese by birth, but his family had left China after the Communist Revolution. A consequence of her marriage was that Susan had dropped out of college without completing her degree.

Masters and Barbara stayed at the Hotel President in Palo Alto. 'We went out at once to see Sue to find they had laid on a large dinner party – fourteen people including us. Some of the young men are weirdos, some not. Cyril has his hair to his shoulders and really looks strange – Sue fine, a little thin, but not bad.' They enjoyed meeting Danielle, 'a very good-tempered, strong child, nice-looking with huge eyes and very attractive personality.' The following day they took Sue and Cyril to dinner on Fisherman's Wharf in San Francisco, after which they all went back to the house in Palo Alto, where 'some sort of Wednesday night regular seance was going on in Cyril's study – loud rock and roll music, possibly the people smoking pot but no particular smell. As we had nothing to say and didn't want to join the session, we beat it. Bed, thankfully, midnight.'

Masters comments further on the evening in his logs:

> They are a strange lot, these Californian/Stanford/College types; no sense of responsibility or of future, but they lie around in the present, ignore laws and ordinary decencies of human behaviour outside their own set and don't clean up, or feel they have to for others, they live in squalor, generally cadging on society in one form or another – parents, scholarships, State funds, the capital that has been saved to build houses, universities, roads, businesses; no sense of what events or actions are for, what must be suffered or done to achieve, only the immediate reaction; altogether people with whom it is hard for any mature adult to communicate, particularly me. I think they all take drugs in one form or another, but not drink, they can't afford whisky and are anti-it too.

The hippie culture was clearly not Masters's scene, despite the liberality of some of his attitudes in other areas, such as his stand against racial prejudice in America and his membership of the American Civil Liberties Union. He disliked this sort of laxness and layabout mentality. He saw life as working hard, playing hard and then justifiably being entitled to the rewards. These laid-back Californian attitudes left him feeling perplexed, impatient and irritated, especially since his daughter was involved.

1967 saw a different summer companion on their walks in Spain, Chris Charnock. Masters had met her two years previously at Alex's house and noted in his logs at the time 'very luscious'. She was married and lived in London with her husband, and the foursome became close friends, meeting up whenever Masters and Barbara were in London. Chris Charnock had been able to help them with the decoration of their flat in Water Gardens and had taken responsibility for it while they were abroad. Masters found himself attracted to her and invited her to Spain to join Barbara and him for their summer walking. Her husband stayed in England.

There was something about travelling as a threesome that appealed to Masters. It was as if he needed two sorts of women with him, wife and mistress, mother and ayah, like the feted child in India. Photographs of the three of them in Spain show an apparently contented trio, Masters almost lion-like with his pride, but it must have been a strain for Barbara and she was often unwell on these occasions.

It was hardly surprising that Masters's next book was on Casanova and was dedicated to Tony and Chris Charnock. The idea had originated with the London publisher George Rainbird, who had wanted to publish a life of Casanova ever since he had read the original and complete version of Casanova's memoirs that had been reissued in 1960 by Librairie Plon in Paris and FA Brockhaus in Wiesbaden. Rainbird wanted to give his biography the usual 'Rainbird' illustrated treatment, and got in touch with Masters through Peter Hebdon at Michael Joseph. Masters remembered this:

> Rainbird approached me and said he was fascinated with the character of Casanova and would I do a book for him? He told me roughly what the guaranteed payment to me would be and how long I could take. I said: 'I don't know anything about the eighteenth century, George, why me? Why not pick on some scholar?' He said, 'You have a very strong narrative gift, and this Casanova is a man who jumped in and out of beds and battles, and there's a strong narrative. That is what is important. You can learn; you can just look up the books and read his autobiography to find out what happened. You can make it live. This is what you can do and the scholars can't.' So I was flattered and I thought, hell, this would be rather fun. I took it on.

John Hadfield, who was to be editor of the book, remembers Rainbird coming into his office afterwards and telling him that Masters wanted to do it, because Casanova was an 'adventurer after his own heart.' Hadfield adds, 'George Rainbird had a secret admiration for Casanova, as he himself was temperamentally a bit of a buccaneer and had an eye for women.'

Casanova was both a fascination and a challenge to Masters. Here was an adventurer and womaniser he could identify with to an extent. A Casanova sets out to conquer as many women as possible, partly for the pleasures of conquest, but partly to shift the centre of 'psychic gravity' to himself. Women in this respect need to be dominated, to be controlled so that he does not become beholden to them. The real aim is to avoid becoming dependent. It is an egocentric quest. In psychological terms, it indicates a hidden mother complex, or over-attachment, which the individual is seeking to free himself from.

Masters, not a womaniser on the same scale by any means, played at this at times, in his role as an 'educator' of women or husband-substitute. Such an outside figure, enshrined in the Casanova image, is often immensely attractive to women, as it enables them to move from the sexually passive role of 'child-bride' to a more active and expressive one. Masters had this in mind too; it was part of his lifelong crusade to enable people to discover their own strengths, including sexual ones.

From another angle, Casanova appealed to him as his 'free and explicit sexuality' was what Masters had often sought to convey in his novels. It explains his vexation in his early days with Helen Taylor when she criticised him for the sex in *Bhowani Junction*. He felt that his explicitness was accurate, that beneath the veneer of respectability, this was what really went on. His own experience told him it was. In Spain the woman on the hill mentioned by Alice Mathews had sensed his overt sexuality. Masters was like the 'picaro' figure in Spain who exerts a strong appeal as he has no ties and gives women the safety of anonymity.

The terms for the book were favourable: 65,000 words for an advance of £7,000. The contract was signed on 14 June 1967. He wrote a first draft quickly and then left with Barbara to carry out detailed research. They went to Czechoslovakia where Casanova had lived for much of his life, eventually dying there in 1797. Their destination was Prague. They picked up their Peugeot in Paris and drove east across roads slushy with snow. At the frontier, soldiers and police were everywhere, and they noticed how 'incredibly drab' the towns were before reaching Prague. It was early evening and unable to speak the language or to find the Park Hotel, Masters stopped a taxi and jumped in, while Barbara followed behind in the Peugeot. There was a curious assembly of guests staying in the hotel; the dining room was full of

Arabs and Chinese, with one empty table with a mysterious American flag on it. Masters spoke to the local Casanova expert, Professor Polisensky, who advised him to go to Duchov in the north where the original Casanova manuscripts were. Casanova had lived and worked as a librarian in his penniless old age in the castle belonging to the Count Waldstein and had died there, his 'chair' still extant when the Masterses visited the castle a week later.

From Prague they drove to Venice past snow-laden fir forests. 'Something I have wanted to see all my life, certainly since I read *Greenmantle* in 1930', Masters wrote. It was now wintery and bitterly cold, with ice forming on the lagoon and in the canals. They visited the dungeons where Casanova was allegedly put, and rooms normally closed off in the Doge's palace. They lunched at the fashionable Harry's Bar, 'obviously the place here: food was good, not unreasonably astronomic and the place full of caricatures: expatriate society queen, old aristocrat and two or three fairies with which Venice is so well supplied.' George Rainbird arrived to meet them and they took him to eat at the restaurant they favoured, the Citta di Milano: 'George likes his wine, drank large quantities and was not altogether coherent at the end, when he invited us for coffee and grappa at Florians in St Mark's Square.'

The writing of *Casanova* presented few problems. Masters gave it a fast-moving narrative, its style bordering on the colloquial; *The New York Times* reviewer called it 'gamey' after it was published in October 1969. It received mixed acclaim, which disappointed Masters. He had set out to portray Casanova as 'generous, mean, vindictive, proud, fawning, honest, lying, brilliant, stupid, unstable', but though the story runs at a cracking pace, somehow the book does not live up to its promise. The Rainbird treatment was effective and it was embellished by fine colour plates and contemporary prints, but for all that the sales were much lower than expected.

This muddled Masters's perspective even more as far as writing was concerned. His preceding book, *Breaking Strain*, had not been a success, the reviews were unenthusiastic and the sales relatively low. That seemed to put paid to the idea of writing John Buchan-type thrillers. *Casanova* was non-fiction, and he decided to take up another non-fiction idea for his next book. He had already got this in hand before finishing work on *Casanova*. The idea had originally been mooted at a Quaglino's lunch with Laurence Pollinger, namely to write a history of Gibraltar. The idea appealed to him, not least because it would involve Spain, both thematically and as a base for them to live while writing and researching the book. The Masterses had been advised by their accountant, Allen Kaufman, to live outside the USA for the next eighteen months to receive tax advantages. This meant that for the second half of 1968 and most of 1969 they were based at their flat in London at Water Gardens.

The Gibraltar book, later entitled *The Rock*, caused all sorts of difficulties. Its negotiations were started early in 1968, but the root of the trouble was Masters's lack of a regular American publisher since Viking. He had been through a succession of different American publishers in the 1960s: Harpers, the British Book Centre for *Fourteen Eighteen*, then Delacorte for *Breaking Strain*, while *Casanova* lacked an American publisher. Masters had been partly responsible for this, telling his American agents always to try to get him the best deal possible on each book.

When the Gibraltar idea was put up, Masters sent it around New York publishers via his agents. It was snapped up by a newly-formed New York publishing firm, Bernard Geis Associates, determined, somewhat aggressively, to break into mainstream American publishing. Geis came up with a strong offer of $35,000 for the Gibraltar book, keen to get Masters on their list as much for this book as for future ones. Their offer was made in February 1968 and, since it was much more than could be expected elsewhere as an advance, Masters jumped at it. A condition of Geis's offer was that they held world rights, which, somewhat precipitately, Masters agreed to.

It is an episode that he does not come out of too well. Admittedly his writing career was very unsettled at the time, but this did not justify his acting in a very high-handed manner towards his English agent and his English publishers. In a letter to Peter Hebdon at Michael Joseph, he put his side of the case.

> Recently I was approached by Bernard Geis Associates with a good offer for all rights in a book on Gibraltar, plus the usual options. The terms against which this offer is made are not normal, but then neither are Bernard Geis Associates' publishing techniques, nor their results. Since the offer precisely meets my needs, both as regards to subject and finance, and since I was unable to get what I was looking for before, I have decided to accept the BGA offer, and sign a contract with them on behalf of Bengal-Rockland Inc. This contract, since it deals with all rights, will of necessity end the publishing relationship between Michael Joseph Ltd and myself and Bengal-Rockland. When I say that I hope the break will be permanent you will understand that I mean only that I hope for success and continuity in this new approach.

He was leaving them very little room for manoeuvre, and it was a move that was both surprising and hurtful to Michael Joseph, who had loyally published his books through the years. Moreover they also understood they had an option on his next book. Masters ignored this and went on, 'Details of any matters outstanding between us can be settled, I hope, by Laurence Pollinger. This is not the moment to discuss our long and fruitful and happy relationship; but I am grateful for it, and hope that you personally, the firm, and everyone I was associated with there, got as much out of it as I did.'

Pollinger was treated in the same hasty and peremptory manner. 'The contract with Bernard Geis Associates is exactly what I want, in that the subject is right, the price is good, and I have only to deal with one entity.' By this he meant he wanted to have one worldwide agent, namely his American one, who could deal with world rights. Laurence Pollinger's services were being dispensed with, though 'I hope you will in any case still be associated in my other writing endeavours.' He was presenting Pollinger with a fait accompli. 'Bernard Geis is a controversial figure; but I think he has some exciting ideas, and am looking forward to working with them.'

Pollinger was justifiably upset and wrote back trying to deter him from going with Geis: 'They're publishing the near-porn *Candy and Edgar Henry* which contains the longest description of brutal intercourse I have read'. He also told Masters he had just had lunch with Geis's London representative 'who is likely to have his hands full during the next few months.' But Masters would not be put off. He told Peter Hebdon he had 'written single-mindedly for MJ for seventeen years, in spite of many and more lucrative offers elsewhere, through two major upheavals and several changes and desertions within the firm itself, and having advised some other writers to stay with you.' It was selective memory and he remained unrepentant. 'I could not understand the pain of your answer to my letter, which seemed inappropriate for the acknowledgement of perhaps unwelcome information about an undoubted right.' Michael Joseph released him from his next book with them, perhaps sensing that the Geis phenomenon was likely to be short-lived.

While all this was going on, Masters had found time to continue writing *Daily Telegraph* Weekend magazine articles for John Anstey. His new one was on the Pueblo Indians of New Mexico. Barbara and Masters left South Mountain Road on 17 April 1968, taking the Jeep to New York, where Martin, now at Columbia University, met them and drove them to La Guardia for a plane to Chicago. There they boarded the Super Chief train. It was an overnight journey through Missouri, Kansas and on to New Mexico, to Lamy Junction the nearest railhead to Santa Fe, which, despite its famous railroad name, had no terminal of its own. An Avis rent-a-car was waiting for them and they proceeded to Santa Fe.

The next day they went up to Taos to meet Frank Waters, an authority on Pueblo Indians and author of the classic text on their religion, *Masked Gods*. He lived in an attractive adobe house. Adobe is the mixture of mud, straw and water used to make the characteristic houses of New Mexico, which are rectangular-shaped, flat-roofed, brown or burnt sienna in colour with corners rounded and verticals sloping inwards towards the roofs. On the way to Waters's house they had already renewed their admiration for the vast, dry landscape and the glorious high, dry air, which they had known from previous, briefer trips. The West had always meant something special to Masters with its big sky and wide, open spaces and clear desert air. He was not alone in admiring these surroundings. D. H. Lawrence had lived close to Taos in the 1920s and had been enraptured: 'The moment I saw the brilliant proud morning sun shine high up over the deserts of Santa Fe, something stood still in my soul and I started to attend.'

Waters gave Masters advice on where to go and whom to see among the Pueblo Indians. Pueblo, the Spanish word for small town or village, was the name given to local Indians by the Spanish conquistadors in the sixteenth century when they first arrived from Mexico. They found the Indians living in villages rather than being nomadic as they expected. New Mexico now has nineteen pueblos in all, each a close-knit communal society, speaking six different languages among them, and mostly situated between Taos and Albuquerque along the Rio Grande. The Spanish conquistadors had originally seen the Indian cliff-top settlements glinting in the sun and imagined there must be gold there. Having subjugated the indigenous population in their usual brutal fashion, they attempted to convert them to Christianity. The Spanish were succeeded by the Mexicans. In 1848 New Mexico became part of the United States and the Indian pueblos were allowed to retain their autonomy as a 'nation within a nation', which they are to this day. However, they only got the vote in 1948. Nowadays, New Mexico, the fifth largest state in the USA, with a population of no more than a million and a half, boasts three distinct cultures existing side by side – Indian, Hispanic and Anglo (the name used for Americans).

The first pueblo Masters went to see was San Ildefonso, just north of Santa Fe, where he met its governor, Abel Sanchez. He found the atmosphere of San Ildefonso 'most interesting to see, very calm, and peaceful', and met some of its artists and potters. Communal life is more important to the Pueblo Indians than personal achievement, hence no work of art or pottery is ever signed. Ironically, while talking to Sanchez, Masters heard a megaton blast 700 miles away in Nevada. Modern and old were inseparable in New Mexico: only 20 miles away from where they stood was Los Alamos, where the atomic bomb had been invented.

Masters moved to another pueblo, Santo Domingo, where he had dinner with Preston Keevama, a 'broad, big man, with a round face, shortish, strong, gentle, a highly intelligent and good man.' The more he saw of these people, the more he liked them for their dignity and self-possession, but it was the landscape that appealed to him most strongly. Things looked right to him; it was like walking into a room and immediately feeling at home. The quality of light put him and Barbara in mind of Baluchistan, also 6,000 feet above sea level, with the same crisp air and desert scenery. Quetta and Santa Fe shared similarities, but each had a definable character of its own. Desert in this context meant not just sand but earth of every hue – pale gold to rose red – punctuated with sage and dark green juniper bushes. Within days the Masterses were seriously considering Santa Fe as a place to live.

For some time they had been contemplating leaving South Mountain Road. An era was coming to an end with the departure of their children and friends. They were ready for a change; they had been there twenty years and recent events were putting a strain on some of their friendships. Masters's intransigence over the Vietnam issue had alienated some of their more liberal friends and neighbours. He stuck to his militaristic view that the army had a job to do and should be supported at all costs – a 'my country right or wrong' viewpoint. The year before, Masters had been invited to a party at Sydney Simon's wife's house and some photographs were on display taken by one of the Andersons' sons of an anti-Vietnam demonstration with policemen hitting college students. Masters was furious that these were being shown round and stormed out of the house telling Mrs Simon she was no longer on his 'friends list'. Vietnam aroused all sorts of other spectres for him, not least that not only was Martin refusing the military, but he was also contemplating becoming a draft dissenter.

Santa Fe, by contrast, seemed like another world. A week after their arrival they went to see a real estate agent and enquired about the cost of property. Masters wrote in his log that night, 'we think we may move out to this area permanently.'

For his article he needed to witness Indian ceremonial dances. The

Masterses went to the Spring Corn Dance at the small pueblo of San Felipe on the first of May. The age-old plaza had sunk five feet below the level of the houses, 'for the earth has been pounded away by five hundred years of dances such as this'. Pueblo Indians allowed no photographers on these occasions since they believed that if a stranger took your likeness, they could then exercise control over you to your detriment. Non-Indian visitors had to remain silent and respectful in the presence of this 'infinitely un-Western' sacred ritual that made no concessions to tourism. Masters's observant eye took in the intricacies of the dance and apparel: 'At the corner of the plaza, where there is a gap between the houses, a thick phalanx of young men appears, their feet hidden by ankle trappings of black and white skunk fur. They have bare legs, arm bands of shells, bells below the knee, spruce sprigs tied to their arms and a spruce bough in each hand. They wear a white homespun kirtle to the knee, sashed on the right, and a full fox skin hangs from the small of the back, tail down. From above the knee to above the waist their brown skin has been whitened by ash and corn meal. There is a slight sheen of sweat on the fine torso, bare under the eleven o'clock sun.' It was his reporting at its best: it had a clear, visual, almost cinematic quality.

These ceremonies were evoking a sense of appreciative wonder: 'I close my eyes for a moment. Now that my attention is concentrated on the dancers rather than the spectators, I am stricken with doubt about the reality of what I am seeing. Can this elemental spectacle really be taking place, in the year 1968, in the United States of America?' Elsewhere civil unrest was rife, Martin Luther King's assassination had taken place and urban riots were threatening to tear the nation apart. Here he was witnessing another world, dancers whose self-expression and self-determination proclaimed 'the I AM of the last American Indians.' It immediately put him in mind of other 'primitive' peoples he had admired so much, the hill people of India and Spain, and at a deeper level other spurned and ill-treated people – such as his own family – 'evicted from one culture and excluded from another.' 'Where today', he asks in his article, 'are the Chippewas, Winnebagos, Mohicans? Where are the Five Civilised Tribes – Choctaw, Chicksaw, Cherokee, Seminole, Creek? Where are the Sioux and the Apache? . . . all gone or going, that-away over the hill. Betrayed by the weapons they trusted – the sharp tomahawk, the towering eagle feathers; dispossessed by force and lies of an enormous heritage; turned by time and treachery from proud nomad of the forest and prairie into an unsure, unhappy prisoner of a polluted soil.' The American Indian, he concludes, now 'shuffles into oblivion, his history recorded only in textbook evasions and Hollywood misrepresentations.'

His feeling for them and empathy with their plight comes through in his description of them. The dancing and rituals were a 'mystical celebration of the unity of all nature.' Religion was at the core of the Pueblo Indians' existence, they lived in harmony with nature and saw it as their duty each day to pray to the sun (their father) to help him cross the sky. If they stopped praying, the world would collapse.

He was back for a moment in the high Himalayas, where he had felt the same sort of oneness with his surroundings. The Pueblo Indians' reverence for landscape struck a chord in him. Watching this dance he could see these Indians were 'as much a part of this particular earth as the cottonwood trees, the roadrunners and the red cliffs', and he watched an old man carrying a pole 15 feet long, decorated with eagle feathers, shaking it over the dancers to release power to revitalise them, and invoking the spirits of nature to bring rain and impregnate the earth. Willa Cather had lived among this landscape and come to appreciate it. 'Here there was always activity overhead, clouds forming and moving all day long. Whether they were dark and full of violence, or soft and white with luxurious idleness, they powerfully affected the world beneath . . . the whole country seemed fluid to the eye under this constant change of accent, this ever-varying distribution of light.' She noted, too, that it was the Indian manner 'to vanish into the landscape, not stand out against it.' Masters realised he could easily live among such surroundings.

The agent took the Masterses to see sites being developed to the north of the town, but they were not quite ready to commit themselves. The only drawback to the area so far was the poor quality of restaurant food, both the local New Mexican dishes and more orthodox fare. After a meal at Frank's Steak House Masters notes 'this is not an inspiring gourmet centre!'

They drove further west in their hire car to Phoenix, Arizona, where they caught a plane to California. En route they had visited Chaco Canyon, giving a ride in their car to a Navajo who went with them as far as Zuni, where Masters bought a big silver and turquoise pendant for himself: 'I love the jewellery so much I wish I could buy masses of it for Barbara and me.' He wore this jewellery more and more, taking special pleasure in wearing it in London or New York where its incongruity at the offices of more restrained publishers stood out.

In California they saw Sue and told her of their plans for a possible move to Santa Fe. San Francisco seemed tawdry in contrast, as Masters noted in his logs, 'rude waitresses and shop attendants, dirty streets, dirty people.' He went with Cyril to Haight Street in the centre of Haight Ashbury to buy some 'soul food'. It was 'extremely depressing

– beards, filth, bare feet, shit, papers, smells, dark glasses for no reason, crowds of kids sitting on the sidewalk professing a new mendicant philosophy, and probably infected with all the mediaeval crabs and gonorrhea we worked so hard to overcome.' Even some friends of Sue's were not up to standard. 'The people were nice enough but two or more couples seemed to be living in the utmost squalor – all trash receptacles full to overflowing, dirt everywhere, the walls covered with psychedelic posters, many anti-US. They have the money for some things, but seem to choose deliberately to be dirty and degraded.'

It repeated his earlier exposure to hippie culture and the comparison with Santa Fe was more than he could take. He was glad to move on to Vancouver for their return trip home, this time on board the Super Continental train. The immigration officer at Vancouver airport recognised him, had read all his books and been at Cheltenham Junior School with him, which was a welcome relief. The train journey lived up to expectations, the scenery through the Rockies was spectacular, Mount Robson at 12,900 feet most impressive, and their bedroom comfortable, service and everything good. From Edmonton they flew home.

Just under a month later they were off to Europe; it was 5 June. Masters turned on his early morning clock radio to hear of Robert Kennedy's assassination in California. It 'threw a pall over the day'. His mood was already fractured by a visit from Martin the night before. 'Last night Martin came out and I told him I could not tolerate his evasion of the draft if he intended to do so, as he said he would. A painful time, because of course I love Martin.' It was doubly difficult as Martin had just graduated from Columbia and they had celebrated the event with a dinner two days previously at the Four Seasons in New York. Martin presumably felt he had to tell them his views before they set out for Europe.

For Masters events like the assassination only strengthened his view of 'the absolute necessity of obeying the law, however much you dislike its results.' Years before in *Bugles and a Tiger* he had rehearsed his present view: 'Whatever the country is doing, the regiment is clearly right in obeying the orders of lawful authority. This enables a man, by only a small exercise in schizophrenia, to be a disapproving citizen and an enthusiastic soldier at one and the same time.' His view was that once his country had entered Vietnam, it was the duty of every citizen to support it, however much he might privately doubt the wisdom of this move. It was the military view par excellence, and he expected Martin to follow suit. Now that Martin was standing up for himself, it was to lead to periods of partial estrangement.

In London the Masterses went to their flat at Water Gardens as temporary tax exile from the USA. Not that he was hard-up. Ever since *Nightrunners of Bengal* he had been comfortably off financially. Money mattered to him, an echo from his father's failure to hold on to his money. As his accountant, Allen Kaufman, remembers, he was very organised and methodical about money, always keeping detailed records of his expenditure on trips abroad, where he listed daily accounts of hotel and restaurant charges, gasoline costs and so on, which he then converted back into US dollars for Kaufman's accounts. He budgeted for so much to spend; any left over could be spent on good living, such as eating at a top restaurant in Spain.

Unusually perhaps for an author, he paid close attention to his investments, and liked to keep any spare money at work. Initially he used Merrill Lynch as his brokers, and gave them a certain amount of discretion, but he still supervised what was going on. Later he moved to Oppenheimer and Co who remained his brokers to the end. They told him he could speculate a bit, which he did. Some came out well for him, though he lost money on options trading and on the Chicago commodity futures market at one point. Otherwise, as Kaufman recalled, he usually selected stocks favouring utilities where he lived. In New City he picked out Orange and Rockland Utilities and made money on them, and he was an early investor in IBM. Overall not more than ten per cent of his income came from investments, the rest came from his writing and from the steady royalties from his books, more so than from high advances, which on average were about £3,000 per book with Michael Joseph. His royalties were paid into Bengal-Rockland, which then paid him a largeish monthly salary.

After a month in London, the Masterses left for France, now in a state of upheaval after the student riots of May 1968. They needed to go to Paris to pick up their Peugeot. The day before they left, Masters visited his mother, 'looking and acting more healthy than last time', and came back to London only to be caught in a horrendous traffic jam at Hyde Park Corner caused by 'communists marching down Park Lane in solidarity with French students and workers.' He felt little sympathy for them and, in best Marie Antoinette fashion, took himself and Barbara off to dinner at Antoine's in Charlotte Street. The headline in the evening paper on the next table read, 'France about to blow up again', and they were due to fly to Le Bourget next day, so 'all we can do is play it by ear and hope for the best with all antennae out.'

In the event, they passed through Paris without difficulty – 'not much sign of French trouble except one school we passed with chalked on the windows "lycée occupé"' – and drove for the night to the Loire Valley. Next day they crossed to Spain, feeling good – it was 'like being out of prison' – and set off for Huesca.

Spain was to feature more and more in their lives over the next year and a half. They spent two months there in the winter of 1968 and lived for the first three months of 1969 in a rented apartment in Cadiz while he was writing *The Rock*. It was not an easy book to write. As he stated in the foreword: 'After many experiments I wrote the book in two streams, one factual, one fictional; or if you wish I decided to cover the ground in two vehicles – one fast, one slow.' The main vehicle was the actual history of Gibraltar, but there came moments when he felt 'that we should stop the car, get out, step down and go on foot among the people, seeing, smelling, touching, hearing.'

Cadiz was close enough for periodic visits to Gibraltar and was typically Spanish, quiet, unspoilt, with good walks by the sea or inland to fortified towns like Medina Sidonia and Vejer, where they had lunches en route at small old-style Andalucian restaurants, such as the Venta de Argas, with its multi-patterned tiles and table tops with pictures of the feria of Seville and its good cheer – 'I always like a place where the customers say 'Buen Provecho' as they pass.' They would drive down to Gibraltar and stop off at the Reina Cristina Hotel in Algeciras before catching the ferry – 'terrible Brits at Reina Cristina, loud, superior, ignorant.' In Gibraltar he talked to officials and historians, met the Governor and the military attaché and members of old Gibraltar families, such as the Stagnettos and Gaggeros, and its leading politician, Sir Joshua Hassan. Gibraltar was full of paradoxes, 'British we are and British we stay' was marked everywhere on walls, yet it looked more like a mixture of Levantine bazaar and English country town. As a notable visiting author he was invited to judge a Miss Gibraltar competition, but his real purpose was to do research in the Garrison Library (founded by Pitt) and, through his military contacts, to visit the inside of the Rock and its hidden arsenals, galleries and caves.

In April the Masterses came back to London 'for a spell of frenzied work' to get the manuscript of *The Rock* ready by mid-June. He had re-written it three times in nine months. But, horror of horrors, Geis then turned it down; they did not think the end product was commercial enough. Masters was stuck and had to go cap in hand to Michael Joseph, who agreed to take him back. While in London Barbara flew out to Santa Fe to negotiate the purchase of a house there. They had put their South Mountain Road house up for sale during 1968 and heard that a buyer had been found for it for just under $70,000. That clinched their decision to move to Santa Fe.

SANTA FE
1970–1973

By early December Barbara and Masters were back in the USA. Eighteen months had elapsed since they were last there. Alan and Nancy Anderson met them in New York and drove them out to South Mountain Road for a final week of preparing for their move to Santa Fe and 'tying up a lot of loose ends which had been left dangling since we left the USA in June 1968.' *The Rock*, meanwhile, had been taken on by Putnam's as his new publishers in New York. This was good news, as they were a major publishing house. After the week was up the Masterses drove out to Santa Fe in their Jeep Wagoneer.

They set off on 8 December and arrived in New Mexico five days later. 'The views were tremendous, the air clear and dry; we saw snow on the peaks behind here from about 100 miles away.' They started moving in, their luggage and belongings coming in three main parts. One lot was in the Jeep with them, one was coming by moving van and another was coming from England by sea freight – including a table from Denmark. They ordered another car, a Chrysler New Yorker Sedan, as a replacement to their Lincoln, to be able to 'drive about really comfortably over the huge distances here in the west.'

The 'real chaos' began on Wednesday, 18 December, when the van came. 'We had all the furniture unloaded, including about fifty cartons of books; the telephone men coming to put in our phones, on bare walls, people coming to look at something the tenants had done wrong with the septic tank, others trying to sell us wood for the fireplace. The chaos continued all day, and in lessening fashion ever since. The afternoons have been madhouses of unpacking, washing, drying, stowing – the books are still in their cartons and will probably remain so for a long time, as there is not a single bookshelf in the house. There is a great view to the south as well as the view to the mountains to the east.'

Their home was a newish house on Circle Drive to the north of the town, but a month later they found it to be too new and too much of a false adobe house for their liking. They could not settle in it and soon started looking elsewhere. A more suitable house was available in Santa Barbara Drive 3 miles away to the east of the town. It was bigger, older, and more authentic, and its views of the distant San Pedro mountains out of the main window were stunning. They bought it from a divorcing couple and moved in at the beginning of April.

It was a typical, large, low-lying, single-storey New Mexican house, built more than a hundred years ago, and therefore old in American terms. The Masterses made various changes, such as installing a new kitchen with a central hob, so that both of them could cook, and changing the lighting in the house from its former 'Turkish brothel' effect to something more amenable. Masters's smallish writing room faced east; his desk stood against a blank wall, so as to minimise distraction, with a huge piece of furniture behind it for his papers and two large bookcases for reference books, travel documents and timetables. He put photographs of Spain on the walls. He enforced a strict no-disturbance rule while he was working, but an intercom to the kitchen was put in for dire emergencies. Another new and important installation was the sauna, roomy enough to accommodate up to six people. Outside, was a pool and tennis court and scenic views of mountains, uninterrupted by high-rise buildings, which were forbidden in Santa Fe. These views were a constant source of delight and the factor which had drawn them to the area originally.

Most of 1970 was spent settling in and getting to know their surroundings. Santa Fe's population was then twenty-five thousand inhabitants, a manageable sized town for them, but the real attraction was the huge 167,000-acre Pecos Wilderness beyond, and the Sangre de Cristo Mountains, the final part of the North American Rockies chain. He and Barbara started walking to explore these areas, buying all the available local topographical maps. Their routine was to get up at 5 a.m., just before dawn, and be on the road to their destination 'somewhere within 50 miles and somewhere between 7 and 9,000 feet up', and start walking by 7 a.m. Most days, they kept to below the tree line – New Mexico is far enough south for the tree line to be at about 11,500 feet – and walked amid forest full of deer and elk and, occasionally, bighorn sheep. Sometimes they went higher; by early summer Masters wrote, 'We have climbed the two highest peaks in the State, both over 13,000 feet, seen the tracks of a mountain lion, photographed innumerable wild flowers and have really come to know most of the country in and around the Pecos Wilderness in which no wheeled traffic is allowed.' After this initial period of exploration, he settled down to work again.

He was completing the first draft of *Pilgrim Son*, the third and final volume of autobiography, which took his story from leaving India in 1946 to his arrival in the USA and then up to the mid-1950s in South

Mountain Road, 'from British fighting man to American writing man'.
Such writing could be done on the spot and they did not go to Europe
that summer, though they went to California to visit Sue and Martin,
who had graduated from Columbia and was living in San Francisco
with his girlfriend Cheryl. Martin was carving out a career as a rock
and roll musician and selling second-hand cars. Their friend from
London, Peg de Fonbrune, had come to stay with them and they drove
her across with them. It was another typical lengthy car journey: six or
seven hours' steady driving per day, stopping at motels at night. Both
Masterses liked these epic journeys, trundling along the broad interstate
highways for three or four days on end.

Sue's marriage with Cyril had run into difficulties. After six years,
they were splitting up, and Susan was having to fend for herself, taking
a job in a bank. Cyril had proved to be too volatile a character for her.
When Masters saw Martin again, he 'hardly recognised him with hair
to shoulders and beard.' Much as he loved his children, Masters felt
uncomfortable in these surroundings. Long hair and hippies made him
irritable. On the third evening they all went to dinner, using Cheryl's
car. The parking attendant tried to get a 75 cent parking fee from
Cheryl, at which point Masters 'blew my stack' – an indication of the
mounting pressure within him, a trivial over-demand suddenly breaking
his tolerance. In the altercation he dropped his wallet; the next day he
noticed it missing and assumed the parking attendant took it, in
revenge. He was $140 the poorer and keen to leave California.

In Santa Fe he joined a monthly dining club, the Quien Sabe, frequented
by professional people, writers, artists and so on. Dick Stern, author of
The Towering Inferno, whom he had known in Rockland County and
was now living in Santa Fe, took him along initially. It was a convivial
group that went in for serious discussion. There he met, among others,
Tom Jameson, a retired engineer, and they struck up an immediate
friendship. Jameson was also a keen walker, and Masters invited him
to join Barbara and himself on their walks. He was looking for walking
companions and even invited a secretary, Charlotte, he met at the bank
where he had opened his account. At the same bank a week later, he
met Tom Hamill. Masters liked the look of him immediately and told
him. 'Meet me next Wednesday at 7 a.m. at my house.' Hamill was a
younger man by some twenty years and an artist resident in Santa Fe.
Masters took him to Hermits Peak, a difficult climb at the best of
times, but more so for a beginner or first-timer. 'Looking back I realise
he did this for every beginner to test them out. He didn't say a word,
and there I was swearing away under my breath at every step with

him behind me', Tom recalled. It was a hike of more than 13 miles. Masters wrote up his own account of that day:

> Sunday September 13th: first day out walking with Tom Hamill. We set off at 6.30 a.m. with Tom, Charlotte and Barbara. Lots of mist hanging about below, high cloud above when we started off from Jack's Creek, having seen scores of deer. The walk was good, though always in mist, with one or two drops of rain. We were walking as though in an amorphous inverted bowl. A wrangler and dude on horses passed going down, the former with a gun or rifle. We left the girls at a camp just below the lake. Tom and I went on up to the summit. I meant to stop there, but it was still in cloud and mist, blowing rain, and bitter cold, so we turned right round (12.38) and went down fast.

It had been a tough and arduous climb, no quarter given. 'Tom has a big, booming voice and is a nice chap, probably shy and woman-shy particularly owing to having had no father and a strong mother. Charlotte took him off when we got home and as he had told her he was impotent, temporarily at least for various reasons, we thought the girl was going to try to uphold the honour of womanhood. This a.m. I called her at the bank and asked her whether she had been able to raise the flag on Mt Hamill and she said she had done her duty for God and Country but it was impossible.'

This testing of newcomers was to become more frequent, as if Masters wanted to see whether they came up to the mark, to his level of competence. He treated them brusquely and aggressively, putting them through their paces. It was partly the military man in him, pushing his Gurkha troops to the limit, getting them to stretch themselves, to make one last effort – he had been through the mill himself, so others should do likewise.

Tom and he got on well together. Indeed Masters was to become a sort of father figure to him. Tom admired him as a 'great teacher with almost total recall, and a storehouse of historical facts.' Masters used to talk to him about many matters, perhaps finding it easier to talk openly to someone younger than himself and practising in a different artistic field, which meant less rivalry on both counts. Kipling, for instance, had found it easier to talk about his work to the explorer Feilden. Tom noticed how Masters would 'open up and talk' on their walks. 'We were both engaged in a process, in the struggle to create, and he didn't like to talk shop with other writers.' There may have been other similarities as well; Masters was very much a visual writer, concerned to render the surface of things in the way a painter does and to trust what he saw.

Tom did not always like it when the talk turned to his 'women prowess': 'I thought it was cynical. He would say a few things to me, amusing things. He started off talking about his father in India, how he would go all around the Indian countryside screwing women, so long as they were Indian, and of how his father was known in the regiment as "smell-of-a-cork John" because of his liking for drink.' Once Masters had got that preamble out of the way, Tom asked him if he had inherited any of his father's prowess in this direction 'and he smiled about that and told me a few of his escapades.'

As their friendship developed and they went on more walks together, Tom saw other sides of him. Once they came upon a man stuck in the sand in Tejon. 'My first reaction was to help the guy out. I said, "Let's give him a push with our hands." Masters said, "I wouldn't do that, Tom. He's made a mistake, he shouldn't have been there in the first place."' Tom insisted that people did make mistakes and that they should help him out. Masters eventually backed down 'as I had put him in an accurate light. He was then rather like a helpless child, "How are we going to help him out?" so I had to take the lead, so we did.' Masters did not like weakness or bad planning.

As their social circle increased, the sauna became an important facet of their life. Early on Masters made a point of inviting guests to share it with them. That first summer, 'on 25 June the Jamesons came for sauna at 6 and enjoyed it, rather to their or at least her surprise.' Wives and husbands had to be naked in front of apparent strangers. Men were more used to this with their collegiate locker room or sports ground experience, but for many wives it was quite a shock, and a trap. They felt they had to follow their husband's example and not be thought timid. It would be 'bad form' to refuse in the presence of the famous author. Masters was again putting people through a trial by ordeal, a testing of nerve and openness. However much he saw saunas as something convivial, and nakedness as nothing to be ashamed of, there was a double-edged component here, a hidden aggression, pushing people hard or pushing them further sometimes than they felt comfortable.

The sauna was very much his show and he enjoyed being master of ceremonies. The routine was to spend five minutes in, five minutes out. Guests, once they got used to it, mostly enjoyed the experience; it was novel, uninhibited, and heralded a new set of social relationships that the newly-arrived Masterses were bringing with them. He saw it as breaking new ground, shifting the boundary between host and guest. Not all wives agreed to it, nor did some husbands. Yet a common response was that it seemed alarming initially to have to take all your clothes off and walk across the room in front of all those people, but afterwards they would say, 'Well, what's all the fuss about?'

After a sauna they would each gulp down two shots of aquavit and then have cold beer as a chaser, and, if there was snow on the ground, roll in that too. Tom Hamill 'loved it very much. It was Bacchanalian, but the saunas were pure, pristine.' Masters had put up flagrantly revealing *Playboy* pin-ups on the walls, with legs spreadeagled, but the intention was a sort of joke within a joke, a frontal attack on inhibition and prudishness rather than trying to generate sexual arousal. The saunas were not in this sense sexual overtures, though innuendo had its field day. They were clearly an outlet for his exhibitionism and a far cry from English respectability, his old enemy.

Pilgrim Son was ready by the end of October and he sent it off to his editors, Walter Minton at Putnam's and Raleigh Trevelyan at Michael Joseph. A reader's report came back from Michael Joseph commenting on the rather loose construction of the book and its slangy writing. Masters was furious. He wrote back that the reader 'is a prig and an ass, and I'm surprised at Michael Joseph's setting such a nitpicking grammarian to read my Ms'. But in all fairness, it was not one of his better pieces of writing, and not up to the standard of his two previous volumes of autobiography.

Times were changing at Michael Joseph. Edmund Fisher was now managing director, following the sudden death of Peter Hebdon at Copenhagen Airport early in 1970. Hebdon, a decisive and blunt Yorkshireman, had taken Masters back into the fold after his debacle with Geis Associates; he and Masters had always got on well personally. Edmund Fisher was a friend too: Masters had first met him when he was working for George Rainbird at the time of the *Casanova* book. Fisher, who was twenty-nine years old, was young to be a managing director. Masters was pleased by the appointment and invited him out to Santa Fe for Christmas 1970.

Masters met him at the airport in Albuquerque and, after a drink, took him to his car. He said to Fisher, 'Do you want to drive my car?' Fisher agreed and was soon behind the wheel heading back to Santa Fe, whereupon Masters kept pressuring him to 'drive faster, go on faster. There's a faster driver behind you – what are you going to do about it?' Fisher recalls, 'It was said as a sort of joke but it wasn't really a joke. Next he would suddenly say, "Go on slam on the brakes," and then he mopped his brow. It was said to test my nerve, and perhaps he needed to feel a military man again, to feel that there were men in his platoon that could be relied on not to crack.'

Two days later there was another endurance test, as Fisher had rashly told him he liked walking. They set out the next day, as Masters recorded in his logs:

> Saturday, 2 January, 1971. Edmund Fisher said he wanted a good walk while he was here and had come specially equipped with a strong pair of shoes, so I worked out something which I thought would be suitable – from the St Peter's Dome fork down the Cochiti Canyon, up to the look-out corner, then back to the car, about 5 hours. We got going at 9.15 in sunny weather, and all went well till we were a couple of miles down the Canyon. Then the path all but vanished and we were in snow, scrambling over logs, up the side of the hill, in the stream bed on the ice, etc. Edmund's shoes were plain leather soles, and he was slipping very badly, but the real problem was that he had no balance or confidence and was getting into a panic in perfectly easy places, nor could he be helped. He was soon sweating heavily though it was cold, and turning a nasty shade of green. Finally, when the trail was supposed to turn up to the Dome road there was no trace of it, and after half an hour's scrambling around on a steep hillside I decided we must go back the same way we had come. It was a little easier somehow, except that Edmund was by now very tired and we had to keep the pace down, add lots of short halts, etc. Then with about an hour to go on the short cut we were taking (a logging road) it began to snow, and snowed harder and harder all the time until we reached the car at 2.30, having made pretty good time, all things considered. Then there was much relaxation, whisky and beer drinking, and soon all was forgotten – we had a sauna that night and then drove to Lamy in the snowstorm for dinner; quite a day.

These laconic entries reveal little of the drama involved; Masters used his logs primarily as fact sheets. However, there is little doubt that Masters was pushing Fisher, deliberately picking a challenging itinerary. As with Hamill, it was part aggressive friendship, part a sort of male bonding through trial by ordeal. Masters was living up to his self-designated, expatriate role as a tough man of action, who had been through 'the cannon's mouth'. He was allowing no shilly-shallying, no half measures. Englishmen from a public school background were special targets and were put through this gruelling baptismal fire. There were hints in this of a subtle form of revenge at all the slights he had suffered in the past at school or at Sandhurst or with his first year in a British regiment in India (having brandy butter rubbed in his hair all those years ago). Now firmly on his own terrain, he could call the tune as he liked. Edmund Fisher, an old Etonian, clearly passed muster and remained a close friend.

Fisher was intrigued at seeing Masters in America. The country manifestly suited him. He had greeted him with, 'Hi, pal', at the airport. Fisher could see that, for a person of Masters's type, America offered opportunities that he would not find in England and few of the restrictions he might have felt had he stayed in England and become part of the Establishment. Edmund never heard him run England down nor complain; the sense of the grass being greener on the other side was alien to him, and what nostalgia he had was reserved for India. He was temperamentally averse to whingers 'or patsies', or people who complained of times not being what they were. In all his logs there is seldom any complaint when things go wrong; they may be described as bad, but rarely as disappointing.

In Santa Fe he was quick to avoid being typecast as the Englishman abroad. Whenever English people showed up in Santa Fe, Masters showed little interest in meeting them. His American friends could not understand this, but it had a long history. In the South Mountain Road days, he tended to deflate any excessive Anglophilia in his American friends. When the Jennisons once enthused about English cathedrals, he called them 'just heaps of dark junk'. At other times, his Englishness was very much in evidence. The Jennisons remember driving with him through the verdant countryside of Vermont, not dissimilar to England, when he burst forth singing the lines from Blake's *Jerusalem* about 'England's green and pleasant land'. His Englishness was often highly valued by Americans, who saw more of it in him than he did himself, not least his accent and his military bearing. He was the sort of person you noted immediately he entered a crowded room. They liked his use of language and his ability to play with words, either in a debunking sense or teasing out their origin. A favourite example was the word 'sincere', deriving from the Latin for 'without wax'; in other words, without falsehood.

He had no 'side' as Fisher noted and he was a very good host in Santa Fe. Fisher recalls, 'I was taken around everywhere, met his friends. He usually laid on something each day or, if not, I was given the keys of the car. We all went out together to Lamy Junction, a favourite restaurant of his in a converted dining car in an old steam train. Masters ordered "surf and turf" [steak and lobster] for us all. He'd down two or three boilermakers [beer and a shot of whisky] beforehand and then have wine at dinner, but he drove home without any trouble.'

Masters had asked Fisher to come out so as to discuss new developments in his writing career. An offer had come in from Doubleday in New York to write a book for them. The executive editor there,

Stewart 'Sandy' Richardson, had contacted Don Gold at William
Morris and suggested Masters write a book on the effect of the First
World War on Indian soldiers who had been brought suddenly to the
front line in France at the very outset of the war, and the conflicts this
aroused with their belief in the 'superiority' of European civilisation.
Masters was heartened by this offer. It would be a return to Indian
themes again, which he knew after his less than satisfactory writing
excursions of the 1960s was where his best writing had come from. He
told Gold to negotiate a contract for him. Doubleday then suggested a
package of two novels, the subject of the second being 'the pressures on
a British commander in the Persian Gulf area who profoundly
disbelieves in the East of Suez withdrawal policy and in fact rebels
against it.'

The terms were good, a guarantee of $40,000 for each novel against
the normal US and Canadian rights, the first to be delivered by
February 1972 and the second by September 1973. It put him back in
harness again and on familiar terrain after nearly ten years. The subject
of the first novel had special significance for him. His uncle Alexander
had been killed at Festubert in the first months of the war fighting
alongside Indians in the 34th Sikh Pioneers. Even before he started
research, he knew enough about this unfortunate episode in the war
when Indian troops had been rushed to the front more or less as
cannon fodder and had been split up from each other needlessly. The
shock to them was immense, as was the racial hostility they
encountered. Masters knew Frank Richards's excellent *Soldier Sahib*,
which conveys the feel of this.

Masters met Sandy Richardson for the first time in New York early
in May on his way through to Europe. They had lunch at the Four
Seasons, and he described the meeting afterwards. 'Sandy has a funny
lop-sided look about the eyes, grey hair, humpy but turned out to be
very nice and relaxed.' He handed in his work in progress on the novel
and on his way back through New York later that summer called in to
Doubleday again. 'They are all very enthusiastic about the new book
and talking in large sums of money. I may need to re-negotiate my
original contract upwards . . . altogether most encouraging.' They were
heading for their usual summer's walking, but he had had a check-up
first with his local doctor, Dr Streeper, who diagnosed angina pectoris
in its early stages. He had noticed a shortness of breath recently. The
doctor advised him to exercise steadily and take nitroglycerine pills
whenever pain threatened.

Their first stop in Europe was Switzerland, where the clear mountain
air would help his angina. They were in St Moritz on 12 May when he

got a telephone call from Joan, Alex's wife, saying that his mother was seriously ill and going visibly downhill 'and the nurse doubted whether she would last a week.' He and Barbara flew back immediately and Alex met them at the airport. His mother had fallen down in her room and had broken her right femur. She was now in St Peter's Hospital, Chertsey. Masters found her 'in some distress'. Worse still, her operation had to be put off for two days as her breathing played up and they had to perform a tracheotomy, 'so now she will not be able to speak for some time.'

His mother's illness had a strong impact on him. In an unusual bout of introspection, his logs note its psychosomatic effects on him. On his first two nights back in England, he could not sleep properly and on the Saturday morning he had to take a nitroglycerine pill. He was 'not good, getting worse all day until after I had seen Ma', and he notes, 'so perhaps it was a psychosomatic thing, inner tension, etc: it is still not good p.m., but it is better than it was.'

Monday, 17 May was the publication day of *Pilgrim Son*: 'I walked to Michael Joseph, signed and sent off a number of copies of the book, did interviews, lunch at Empress, p.m. to BBC for more book interviews.' But his mind was more on his mother's illness and the middling reviews of the book did not help. *The Times Literary Supplement* found it 'often opinionated, often truculent, sometimes slapdash, and poorly proof-read, but it contains passages of excellent descriptive writing and throughout reflects the intense energy and diversity of interests of a man with the will and ability to set goals for himself and reach them, and as such commands one's own interest, and admiration.' At least its main thrust had come through – the 'metamorphosis from British fighting man to writing man and American citizen' – but it had been written in a bit of a hurry and this shows at times.

The next day he visited his mother and found her in better physical shape than before, 'with a valved tube in her throat, but correspondingly more distressed psychically, begging us not to leave her, praying to God to help her.' Then, four days later, he went by train to see her. She was 'going downhill', lying on her side barely able to speak, 'very grey and her arms seeming to go raw and puffy. The staff nurse told me she had been talking in the morning about how I was going to get her into a private ward but to me she only said "turn over" and "it hurts" [about her leg]. A miserable time.' On the following Monday his psychosomatic attacks returned. 'Bad morning for me, couldn't walk any distance, then to hospital, a couple of heart blinks on the way in the hospital but perfectly OK from the time I actually saw Ma on; she is sinking and looking worse each time. This time she wanted her teeth taken out and looked about 120.' The next day they went down to Boxford in Berkshire to stay with fellow writer George Shipway,who was helping with the research for his First World War book, *Ravi Lancers*. It was a rainy, overcast, dull day. After lunch, he went out for a walk on the Lambourn railway tracks with George and then on by himself. 'Barbara came out to tell me that Alex had called and Ma was dead. She died about 2.30. Sad, but the way I saw her last, welcome.' It was a deep blow to him as he had always felt very attached to her. He had not liked these last drawn-out stages, feeling powerless to do anything about it, which was never a situation he felt comfortable in. They went out that evening for dinner to the Swan in Streatley with the Shipways. 'Big argument at night over America, anti-America, etc. Went to bed late, full of whisky, but at least it took my mind off Ma.' He still felt chest pains over the next two days and had a bad coughing fit the day before the funeral at Aldershot Crematorium. 'The service was short but moving, as always.'

He and Barbara left the next day for the second part of their summer in Europe, choosing the cooler climes in Denmark and Norway. Walking in the crisper air suited him and his angina improved. On 5 June he wrote, 'We finally got back to hotel at 6.30 after 2.25 hours hard going, quite fast, the best day I've had in 2 months, very encouraging.'

Ravi Lancers (its original title had been *Lotus in Picardy*) was completed early in 1972, on schedule. Feeling pleased with it and the way his writing career had picked up (the second novel, *Thunder at Sunset*, was also now on the stocks), he gave Barbara and himself a treat, something they had been planning for a long time, a two-week rail holiday in Switzerland. They left in mid-January and, starting in Geneva, went over every mountain pass that a railway crosses in the Swiss Alps, a figure-of-eight trip between Geneva and Vienna that lasted two weeks. They would spend the morning on the train, going over a scenic pass, and then get out at a major town, such as Interlaken, book into a decent hotel, spend the afternoon on a three- to four-hour walk, have dinner, go to bed and proceed the next day as before, i.e. moving on from Interlaken to Zurich and so on. It was a wonderful holiday for both of them. Swiss railways, punctual to the second, were another form of rail travel, less nostalgic than steam, but offering a pleasing exactitude.

With another novel completed, he turned to the possibility of a film tie-in, and wrote to David Lean in March 1972 suggesting a film of *Ravi Lancers*. He knew David personally from his Korda days and they had met again in Spain more recently when Lean was filming *Dr Zhivago* near Soria. The USA pre-publication schedule for *Ravi Lanc-*

ers was looking promising, and Masters felt he was back to the good old days, with its selection as an alternate by the Book of the Month Club, and a high first print run of between 20,000 and 25,000.

The pattern of his year was well set now: steady writing through the winter and summer travel in Europe. He felt confident again now that he was writing about the East, and life at Santa Fe had developed along the lines he hoped, with plenty of outdoor walking and an increasing circle of friends, but with more space and an easier pace than at South Mountain Road. He wanted to take some of these new friends to Spain with him that summer, notably Tom and Ann Jameson and Tom Hamill. He got pleasure out of showing friends 'his' Spain and the delights of Spanish hill walking. It enabled him to relive his own discovery of the country in the process. He was generous too, and they came as his guests. He always drew up an exact address list in advance, giving dates and hotels they were due to stay in, with the proviso: 'Do NOT send any important messages by letter; even airmail takes 14 days or more and sometimes does not arrive at all; and will almost certainly never catch up with us. Send postcards for fun; important stuff by cable or telephone.'

He and Barbara went ahead of his guests because he wanted to call in to see Sandy Richardson in New York. He arrived for their lunch at Gloucester House wearing a thin bolo bootlace tie and Southwestern buckskin coat instead of the expected and more formal town jacket and tie. He very nearly was not allowed into the restaurant, but this was a habit and a way of dressing he was to adopt in major urban cities, such as New York and London – a clear and pointed statement about his difference and defiance of orthodox conventionality. Publishers, especially the more traditional-minded, were rather taken aback by this, but he refused to make any concessions. It was his distinctive mark and he usually added some Navajo jewellery, such as his favourite silver pendant with turquoise fillings. Perhaps it was a hidden dandyism, 'the pleasure of causing surprise in others and the proud satisfaction of never showing any oneself', as Baudelaire wrote. 'Dandyism is a setting sun; like the declining star, it is magnificent, without heat and full of melancholy. But alas! the rising tide of democracy, which spreads everywhere and reduces everything to the same level, is daily carrying away these last champions of human pride' – sentiments which Masters might well have echoed.

In London he went to see Laurence Pollinger and to a regimental reunion at the English Speaking Union, this time, more discreetly, wearing his Gurkha Brigade tie and avoiding what one of his colleagues there called the Rhett Butler look. They also saw Mike Rose, who arranged for them to attend a Changing of the Guard in the forecourt of Buckingham Palace. Mike was making great strides in the army, now with the Coldstream Guards and later with the SAS (reputedly leading the storming of the Iranian Embassy in London in 1981). He was the army son, or step-son, that Masters had always longed to have.

The Jamesons arrived in London and he took them with him for a typical English weekend at George Rainbird's country house at Whichford in Warwickshire, which was unusual since Masters normally avoided that sort of traditional English country life. He gives a vignette of the occasion in his logs:

> Sunday, 11 June: pissing with rain. We walked 3½ miles towards Barton. To lunch came Edmund Fisher, Mac and Anthea Hastings – all sorts of good food, ending with rhubarb tart and Chateau Yquem. Everyone stayed on, talking and snoring in a dimmer, greener atmosphere until I announced I was going to bed. Marvellous British drawing room comedy-type conversation at the meal and afterwards, Mac H name dropping. Lena, Jamesons and I walked 2½ miles in the rain to prepare ourselves for dinner, rivulets running down the roads, green distant views and back to hot bath and Sunday supper, which, at my suggestion, was sausage, eggs and bacon – excellent, lacking only beer. We later watched lousy British TV, which finally bored us to bed.

Tom Hamill joined them in London and they left for six weeks' walking and climbing in Spain. Each day commenced with a shot of anis at breakfast and concluded with thirst-quenching beers at the end of the walk. 'I didn't ever recall seeing a more respectful face than that of the little chica as she watched us demolish eight large bottles of ice cold lager in about five minutes'. Drink mattered to Masters. Since his army days, he had always liked his drink, and drank fully but never got drunk. He came from a generation that drank quite strongly as part of everyday life; a drink at lunchtime and in the early evening were regular features. In Spain the day was started this way. Alcohol was a boost, and perhaps in psychological terms for him, as for many writers, was what Malcolm Lowry saw as a form of mental anaesthetic, a means of 'stopping or at least slowing down this beautiful but ruinous construction of labyrinths'. Masters, his sensitive side so often under wraps, may have used drink as a cover from showing how much he cared, or rather of not wanting others to see that side of him.

For Tom Hamill the trip in Spain was memorable. 'A portion of brain is still in the Pyrenees, I'm still there up here.' Masters had given him the trip for free, in return for two paintings of his. They came back to London in time for the launch of *Ravi Lancers*. He did his usual round of radio interviews, meals with family and friends at either Prunier's, the Ivy or Rules, before eventually heading home via New York to Santa Fe on the Southern Railways' 'Southern Crescent' through Virginia and Georgia. 'Lots of blacks came on board, general good feeling and camaraderie.' He felt strongly about racial prejudice in America, and had been a subscriber to the NAACP (National Association for the Advancement of Colored People) ever since he first went to North Carolina in 1948 and was shocked to see the separate entrances and amenities for whites and coloureds. The Masterses always made sure their children went to schools that included blacks. The train trip was the longest they had ever done – 2,557 miles – and ended at El Paso where a welcoming committee of Jamesons and Hamill waited to drive them home.

CHILI AND MARCHING SOCIETY
1974–1975

The relationship with Doubleday was thriving. Sandy Richardson wrote to Masters early in January 1973: 'the *Ravi Lancers* continues to sell well and we're on our way towards the twenty-second thousand: may it flourish.' In the same letter, Richardson put forward an idea for a next book on a British general in the twilight of his career who decides to write his memoirs, having been offered a large sum to do so by his publishers. His memoirs were to be written with the help of his aide who learns too much, or the 'truth', about him, and the book would focus on the dilemma this poses. Richardson's letter ended with, 'It seems to me that with your marvellous gifts such a book could be dramatic, full of humanitarianism and detail, bitchery, jealousy, honesty and dissembling. Yet the result should be upbeat. What do you think?' Masters was taken by the idea and began to develop it. It became his next book project after *Thunder at Sunset*, and was eventually *The Field Marshal's Memoirs*.

For most of his writing career the initial impetus for his books came from the American end. He discussed book projects with his agent and editors there first, even though their subject matter was predominantly English or 'Indian'. His books sold as well in America as in England; his readership there was fascinated by the new world he was presenting to them when he was writing about India, or they liked the strong adventure-like narrative, and action, of his other books. The strongest editorial relationship he had was his first one with Helen Taylor and Keith Jennison at Viking, but relationships with Michael Joseph were always strong. Robert Lusty, his first contact at the time of *Nightrunners of Bengal*, became a close friend and they stayed in each other's houses on visits to their respective countries. Lusty's wife remembers particularly how much their children looked forward to Masters's stay. He was a larger-than-life character to them, with his bolo tie and Western boots, and they liked his sense of fun.

By now his working day in Santa Fe was clearly established.

I get to work every morning at the same time. I'm in my study about 8.00 and I've found over the years I can't really work much beyond noon. So I do about four hours, and I'm a very fast writer. I'll get a chapter of twenty-five to thirty pages written in that time. I do it over again two or three times, but each draft takes roughly the same amount of time. During the first three or four years of my writing career I used to work in the afternoons and sometimes the evening as well, but I found that I just couldn't take it. I'd start getting faint, so I learned to take naps [in South Mountain Road he had prefaced his afternoon disappearance for a nap with the old army euphemism, 'I think I'll go and study for the Staff College']. And recently having had heart trouble, I take a nap and a walk every afternoon. Then I deal with what I call administration; I write to children and insurance companies and banks, arrange travel plans, anything other than the original creative work.

He kept by his desk a Notebook of Notebooks in which he wrote down and numbered queries as they arose about his writing. For each character he kept a card index system going, linked to the wall-chart on which he placed their arrivals and disappearances.

The afternoon walks had become more and more popular with the Masterses' friends whenever they were invited. By the end of 1972, Masters decided to organise his walking. Existing arrangements were often too haphazard, as this entry in his logs shows: 'one by one everyone ratted on this walk for various reasons until in the end it was only Tom and me.' By forming a nucleus of regular walkers, the whole thing could be put on a more organised basis. He instituted the Santa Fe Chili and Marching Society early in 1973. The name was derived from the chilli stew served at the end of the walk from the tailgates of vehicles and the New England Chowder and Marching Societies that had fought in the Revolution against the Redcoats. He had run a sort of prototype walking group briefly in Rockland County, but nothing of this size. He could put his logistical and organising skills to work, reviving the John Masters who could spend hours looking through Bradshaw's railway guide or fixing the fine details of the bicycle trip to Spain, the highly competent staff officer.

The basic principles were that once a member joined the society he had to stick to the rules, mainly to be available to walk every Wednesday morning, come rain, snow or sunshine. The rules were made up by Masters. It was very much his show; the running joke was that it was a democratic society where only one person had a vote. All planning and adminstrative tasks were done by him, a godsend for someone who liked and needed, almost obsessively, to have things organised and ordered and scheduled. There were positive sides to this as well; it meant the day was well-spent, time was fully used up and his detailed planning allowed people to get the most out of the situation he was putting them in, and, as they soon remarked, it stretched them further than they had anticipated. A member later commented: 'the walks were an opening for me into a new way of life; being on foot all day in the mountains, my body learning how surprisingly far it could walk, the beauty of the forest and its inhabitants, the stresses of heat and cold and fatigue, all taught me something new.'

Mostly it was Masters's abundant energy that animated these occasions, and the surplus of energy that accounted for his frequent impatience with those slower of mind and limb than himself. He had the added attraction of being the outsider, a powerful figure in this context, showing locals more of their own surroundings, getting them to appreciate it fully for the first time. What he brought to it, above all, was a rich vein of humour, very much his own particular brand, part self-parody, part imitation of army orders of the day, part prep-school humour, part Wodehousean in its mocking of English customs. He was clearly in a more relaxed mood these days, able, at long last, to shed the taboos that had haunted him.

Humour was vested in the bulletins he issued regularly with the latest news of the society and its members. Reading these gives a distinct flavour of the organisation. The first bulletin, in typical style, describes the Table of Organization of the Society:

Big Chief Tamales	2
Leading Tacos	2
Ordinary Tacos	4
Burritos	as requisite

Tamales, Tacos and Burritos are Mexican food terms; a taco, for instance, is a type of pancake. It was his spoof on army establishments. The first list of officer appointments was as follows:

Big Chief Tamales [BCT]	Masters BP
	Hamill TF
Leading Tacos [LT]	Masters J
Ordinary Tacos [OT]	Jameson A
	Wilburn P
	Robertson P
Burritos [BTO]	Jameson TH
	Casady P

Surgeon General to the Society – Shultz PT.

These early members became the nucleus of the society, though other friends such as the Sterns and the Noyeses came on the first walks, and were gradually enlisted.

Rituals were all important. First, the early start before dawn; Susan remembers being up for one of the early walks and the excitement of feeling you are the only person wide awake in the whole world. Then on to a rendezvous point at the start of the walk 10 to 20 miles away, a quick gulp of tequila, or a concoction of dark rum, consommé and Worcester sauce, served hot, which Masters termed Nelson's Blood, from the legend of Nelson's body being kept in a cask of rum on its way back to England from Trafalgar.

Not long after this Masters wrote a *Daily Telegraph* magazine article 'Leaving the World Below', which catches the mood of these occasions.

> The clock-radio alarm pulls me out of sleep, in the dark, every Wednesday: 4.15 a.m., an hour later the others arrive, sharing rides to the house for transfer to our Jeep Wagoneer (eight cylinder, automatic shift, four-wheel-drive, high- and low-ratio gearbox). Today it's Borrego Mesa. Some of us are in our sixties, none under forty. It is still dark outside, a cool wind blowing from the south, as we travel up the Interstate, the lights of Los Alamos glittering like a flung necklace 35 miles away across the valley of the Rio Grande. What final nuclear escape is being prepared for us over there?
>
> I am watching anxiously for the light to show the cloud pattern. It's a fifty minute drive to Elk Mountain, full daylight, the sky ominously streaked toward the Staked Plains down there, 60, 100 miles away in the early haze. We are at 11,360 feet where the rocky road ends. All out, packs on. Barbara's going to drive the Wagoneer round to the Iron Gate, our destination. Maps out, explain the route, a formal slug of tequila all round, fire in the empty stomach. Some have breakfast but I never do; it pushes angina that much further away when the stomach isn't demanding blood for digestion.

The walk starts, a 20-mile hike or more, planned in detail by Masters, with him in the lead. Then,

> angina comes on, I get forewarnings. Stop, count ten slowly, on, counting. A hundred and forty paces, here it comes again. Better make it 100 paces at a time. They stand around . . . and wait standing. I start again, slowly, counting. Above 12,000, climbing it can get bad, especially if the wind is cold. Then there is danger of arrhythmia, the heart specialist says.

I just want out, every Wednesday, from comfort, food, ease, and
the world of the mind and the imagination. I come out for positive
reasons – to find and enjoy wilderness, big skies, loud water and
mountainflowers, but there is no doubt I am also escaping. I'm not
worrying about my writing at this moment, only about the route,
about my comrades and myself.

Halt for food; I eat raisins – eight. 'Fifteen minutes.' Lie back, close
my eyes, feel the water of the storm we have just passed through
dripping from my hat on to my shirt. What a blessing we have
received that we are able to come, at intervals, into this place! Since
we left the blacktop (paved road) we have not seen another human –
several eagles and jays, some of the cattle that graze the heights all
summer, untended, the wild turkey and the blue grouse. A great
horned owl swoops silently through the pines close over our heads.
We grin at each other, shaking heads in admiration and buckle into
the gradient.

They cover 23 miles in all. 'We are alone in all the vastness of the Pecos
Wilderness. But it is very different from being alone in the padded cell
of the writer, alone with the work of creation. No one can help me
there. Here we help each other just by being. Tomorrow, back to the
cell; today, escape to comradeship, the shared tasks, the shared sweat
and cold and weariness. Every Wednesday somewhere out into the
Jemez or the Sandias or the Ortiz or the Sangre de Cristo, somewhere
between 5,000 and 14,000 feet, on grass or rock or snow, among fir or
ponderosa or Gambel's oak.'

A final seasonal ritual was the St Vita's day lunch, derived from the
notion that if St Vitus dances, then St Vita walks, at the Rancho de
Chimayo outside Santa Fe, when speeches would be made and Honours
and Awards donated. For the first season these Honours all seemed to
go to their leader.

The group was rapidly forming itself into a prized and competed-for
society, which its members felt privileged to be a part of. For many
who had come to Santa Fe to lead a leisurely or retired existence, it
soon became the highlight of their week, despite the arduous nature of
the walks.

Thunder at Sunset was completed during 1973. The Masterses' European tour took in a trip to Greece to stay at George Rainbird's house
at Lindos, Rhodes, but Greece compared unfavourably with Spain.
For Masters, Greece represented 'all we dislike about the Levant,
unprincipled, grasping merchants, dirt, inefficiency, now allied to

SANTA FE CHILI & MARCHING SOCIETY

Honors and Awards, 1972-1973 Season.

The Awards Committee is pleased to announce the following grants of honors and awards:-

Council's Belt of Honor to the Hottest All Round Jalapeño	LT MASTERS J
Moshe Dayah Prize for Humility & Meekness	LT MASTERS J
Richard M Nixon Award for Honesty	LT MASTERS J
Zsa Zsa Gabor Silver Girdle for Chastity	LT MASTERS J
WC Fields Memorial Plaque for Abstinence	LT MASTERS J
General Gurbax Singh's 4th Gorkha Rifles Silver Buckle to Champion Pathfinder	LT MASTERS J
General Bewoor's 11th Gorkha Rifles Silver Buckle to Second Champion Pathfinder	LT MASTERS J **
Betty Friedan Prize for Machsimo	LT MASTERS J
Leo Durooher Award for Modesty	LT MASTERS J
Prize Stud (selected by the Woman's Club)	LT MASTERS J
Governor's Prize for Intelligence, Charm, Courage, Wit, and Good Looks	LT MASTERS J

[signature]   Pres. Awards Committee

Juan Maestros   Member

जुन मास्तर   Member

** The dirty shit eating cunt sucking bastards said I couldn't have both and gave this one to that sniveling pimp Hamill but its mine mine mine mi

contempt for all who come to be squeezed.' Spain was still his spiritual home.

The following winter, the Masterses took another trip to India. Anstey had commissioned an article for the *Daily Telegraph* weekend magazine but Masters needed to arrange expenses with him beforehand. A secondary, or combined, reason for going was to donate his medals to his old regiment.

> Expenses on the sort of job I am doing are never going to be cheap. There is usually only one decent hotel in the place and it is expensive. I do a lot of entertaining of locals and informants. We always have to hire a car, a big one to hold the camera equipment and often 4-wheel drive because of the local conditions, and we drive it the hell of a long way. I do not think it unreasonable to ask for a 1st class air fare to and from the site as this then enables me, at not much extra cost to me, to take Barbara, who is invaluable as a secretary and accountant, and to go into harems, the woman's world of the place, etc. When submitting income tax returns to the US Govt it is always accepted that if a man is travelling on business, but with his wife, two thirds of the full hotel bill is a reasonable approximation of what the man would have spent by himself; and I use this formula with you. I pay for Barbara's meals separately. If we rent a car then she comes free as we would have to rent one anyway. I could go on, but this will suffice to indicate that in my opinion the expenses cannot be reduced.

It was obviously a sensitive area for Masters. He was not extravagant nor did he seek to abuse his position, but he liked, and needed, to travel in style.

Barbara and he left for India on 19 September. It was his fifth journey back since leaving in 1946, but the first for ten years. The Jamesons came with them. Masters's old friend from his Sikkhim visit in 1963, the retired General Jangu Sataravala, now head of the Taj Ashoka Hotel chain, sent his assistant to usher them through customs with VIP treatment. They were staying at the Taj in Delhi. The customs went very quickly but then, typically of India, they had to wait forty-five minutes for their luggage, Masters sweating heavily in his 4th Gurkha hat and commenting wryly 'no Master Race to get their own way'.

His *Telegraph* article was to be about the India of today and the army in particular, and whether mechanisation and industrialisation had hindered or improved India's recent progress. He used the device of a discussion group set in the house of a prominent merchant in Delhi, similar to that of his friend Reggie Sawhny, the guests each contributing their own viewpoint on the country: the merchant criticising the frequency of strikes, how 'everyone is getting too greedy in an increasingly consumer society'; the general complaining that people are getting lazy and undisciplined; the young Indian radical advocating a cut in population growth and offering Maoist views; the politician claiming an advancement in India's standard of living. Masters's view concurred with the latter. Compared to the India he knew thirty-seven years before, with its 'creaking hand-operated fans, no plumbing, no telephones, water heated in old oil cans for your bath and tough chicken curry at every rest house and railway restaurant', living conditions were now immeasurably better, with 'air conditioning, running hot and cold water, good and varied food, the old and the new adjusting side by side, fewer people as beasts of burden. India is not only making its own goods but a lot of them are high quality. People are becoming less distinctly Hindu or Muslim, high caste or low caste and more Indian. It's the birth of a nation.'

He sums it up by saying, 'I think Indians have got to accept a strange idea, that India's a young country. Ideas of fundamental importance, such as socialism versus capitalism, freedom versus direction, excellence versus universality, the genius of the individual against the responsibility of the state, all these are being fought out here, and the battlefield is going to be untidy for some time to come. Untidy, but stimulating.'

It was an optimistic enough view. Broadly speaking, Masters adhered to J. K. Galbraith's view that India was an 'anarchy that works'. Its contradictions and paradoxes were intrinsic; chaos was never far below the surface, but the country continued to function nevertheless, absorbing change and intervention as it had done throughout its history.

Masters made the most of his travels round India, his curiosity aroused, comparing now with before, talking to as many people as he could find, his Hindi still serviceable. The tone of his log for this trip is observant, interested and critical where necessary. He spoke to a railway man, who told him: 'our standards are changing . . . I mean that we Indians used to give value to many things – saintliness, asceticism, family, caste, intelligence, scholarship . . . now we give value only to money. Whether they realised it or not, people used to accept part of their wages in esteem, the esteem in which their work or their training was held – public respect, if you wish. Now only money matters. That's why we're in the dark.'

The railways were still the guardians of old traditions and the ghost of British India still stalked their corridors. Masters and the others travelled by train whenever possible. 'I wouldn't have missed it for anything. An Indian railway station is still the place to see and meet India, seething, chanting mantras, sleeping on the platform, rushing hither and thither under huge bundles and cans and parcels, washing at the taps . . . when I wrote *Bhowani Junction* I had, after all, got it right.'

Being a guest of the army was always an advantage. 'As long as you stay with the army it's great. The rest of India is a mess, not an offensive mess, but if you put yourself in the hands of the army, things work.' His regiment was in Lucknow and they went there for the October festival of Dussehra. Entertainments were laid on for their first evening by the Gurkha troops. 'At midnight a trio of 4th Gorkah soldiers came on stage, two of them dressed in an approximation of the clothes my wife and I had worn when arriving in Lucknow that morning. They began a funny skit about us – my rusty Gorkhali, the way I had asked a rifleman about his caste and home, the mannerisms of my walk and stance. I leaned over to the General and said, "My god Gurbax, when have they had time to write and rehearse all this?" "I don't know," he said "but they did it somehow." "They haven't changed," I said "except that they're called Gorkahs and not Gurkhas."' Masters's evident pleasure, pride even, at how little had changed is apparent.

His article reiterates this. He found the army 'in excellent shape. It's much bigger and more conspicuous than it was in our time, but it's certainly no less good. The discipline's there, of course, but I think the army also sets an example of integrity and efficiency to the rest of the country, and it still has the old dashing, debonair quality.' The imperial baton that he had earlier hoped to see passed on as the legacy of the Raj still seemed to be in place.

The next day they attended the major Dussehra ceremonies, the sacrifice of live buffalo. Every year an animal was beheaded on the parade ground with a two-handed sacrificial kukri by a Gurkha soldier. It was a tense and critical moment – if the head was not taken off cleanly in a single blow then bad luck was expected to befall to the battalion for the next year. This time all went well and the executioner came over to have the ceremonial white turban wound round his head. The General, Gurbax Singh, turned to Masters and told him to tie it. Masters protested that the battalion commander, Colonel Bammi, should do it as usual. 'No,' said the General, 'you're back with your family. This is your regiment, and you joined it before anyone else here.' It was more than thirty years since he had last tied such a puggaree, nevertheless it came back to him, as hundreds of eyes watched.

After Lucknow they went up to the hills, to the Kulu Valley: 'the hill people filled the road from side to side. Our driver increased his speed in response to the challenge, his horn bleating without cease. Somehow, as miraculous as the parting of the Red Sea, the river of humanity parted to let us through.' It was the country he knew and loved from former days. 'The maize lay golden on the rooftops, drying, and the strings of chillies hung on the walls. The air was crisp in that mid-morning, the sky cloudless, snow glittering along the northern horizon and high on both sides of the valley. This was the fringe of the country in which I had placed *Far, Far The Mountain Peak* and, though it was my first visit, I felt that I was coming home.' Indeed Bakloh was only three valleys away, no more than 50 miles as the crow, or eagle, flies.

From Kulu they went to Kashmir and stayed on a house boat on Dal Lake, 'a wooden marvel in Neo-Edwardian Gothic over 150 feet long, equipped with three double bedrooms, a dining room and a heavily carved drawing room full of bric-a-brac, dubious water colours and red upholstered furniture'. Srinagar had changed since he was last there in 1937, 'but less than I have. It bustled and throbbed as of old, with the addition of motor traffic and Western hippies.' Could he ever get away from them? 'Many of these wore white robes as the proper garb to seek enlightenment, but ate and drank well in all the best western-style restaurants – a phenomenon also conspicuous in Delhi.' They trekked up to the Yamhar pass at 13,700 feet, with six pack ponies and six men. It was cold at night so they built huge fires in the snow, lost in the vastness of the Himalayan night.

In Delhi at the Taj, they were due to leave, but a clerk from the travel agency came up to him: 'You are John Masters, isn't it?' He shook Masters delightedly by the hand and cried, 'Oh Sir, please to write more books. You write so *superfluously*! It has been *lovable* meeting you', and he moved off waving and bowing simultaneously, a fitting epitaph, Masters thought, to his visit to India. They were back in London in time for his fifty-ninth birthday and a celebratory dinner at Wheelers with members of his family, and home in Santa Fe by 1 November.

Returning home was always a pleasure now, not least because it meant he was reunited with the Chili and Marching Society for their walks and for the exercise of the idiosyncratic humour of the bulletins he issued.

A favourite winter outing for the society was to Platoro in Colorado, a disused silver mine, near which they would stay in a small hotel and hike each day for four to five days. An established ritual of this visit was for Masters to disappear at one point during a hike and be 'discovered' by the group sitting naked, guru-like, beneath a large tree, adopting the lotus position and reciting over and over again the mantra 'Om'. Barbara would go ahead too and would be hidden away with his clothes.

SANTA FE CHILI & MARCHING SOCIETY

Bulletin # 20

1. REWARDS & PUNISHMENTS

(a) Gallantry: On May 29, 1974, at the Nambe R., Surg. Gen. SHULTZ P was attacked by a man-eating trout approximately 3 inches long. With great skill and courage he defended himself and the whole party to such effect that he succeeded, though severely wounded in several parts of his self esteem, in killing the brute. As a reward for his feat Surg. Gen. SHULTZ P will feed the Society smoked trout (or carp) before Sep 30, 1975.

(b) Murder: On May 21, 1974, at Caballo Mtn, OD NOYES N, on seeing a rare and beautiful flower, did pluck it, asking "What's this?" The proper questiong should have been "What was this?" Sentence: to be stripped of rank and clothing; smeared ALL OVER (including all nooks and crannies) with honey; tied out on an anthill; and left to the mercy of the ants.

2. DISCIPLINE

On recent walks some members have been observed enjoying themselves in public. This will cease immediately.

3. THE IGNOBLE ORDER OF THE IRREMOVABLE FINGER

The IOIF carries no insignia except an invisible halo of shame, which is to be worn for 3 months from the date of the act for which the Order is awarded. Since records have been kept the following awards have been made:-

Apr 28 71	BCT HAMILL T	Believing his alarm clock ran on electricity
Oct 21 71	BCT HAMILL T	Losing himself on a motorable road in broad daylight
May 8 74	BTO CASADY P	Believing his Jeep would run without ga
May 8 74	LT MASTERS J	Failing to consult an oculist
May 21 74	Rec. BOGERT M	Losing Society property, viz. a walking day
May 27 74	BTO CASADY P	Driving a Jeep while asleep
Jul 10 74	BTO CASADY P	Littering (on the same day he earned Palm & Elbow to this award)

4. ENLISTMENTS

MONKS J, Gent. of this County has been enlisted in they rank of Burrito, totake precedence immediately bbfore BTO CASADY P; and is appointed Town Crier.

WILBURN P, Artist, has been enlisted in the rnak of Burrito, to take precedence immediately before BTO CASADY P; and is appointed Bouncer.

2

5. WALK DISCIPLINE

Walkers may normally go at their own pace on steep trails; but to avoid IOIF awards all are reminded of the standing orders relating to independent walking:

A. Before going ahead or dropping back check with the leader of the day where you should in any case stop, so that control can be re-established.

B. Be sure you know what and where the final destination is, also intermediate destinations, snak halt sites, etc., if any.

C. Unless specifically instructed otherwise NEVER pass a trail fork, whether signposted or not. STOP and wait till all have been clocked in and the route established, before going on. Keep a very sharp eye open for all such forks.

D. If the trail peters out, eg in meadowland, STOP and wait till control has been -re-established. When all are walking through forest free form, or across country, make sure you can see and be seen by others.

6. SEASON 1974-1975

The first walk is scheduled for Wed Nov 20 1974. Weather permitting, we will go down the whole length of the Peralta Canypn, starting from the Valle Grande.

Off Season walks, 1974, are being organized on a Committee basis by various members, who will keep the Society informed.

7. AWARDS

Members will be pleased to learn that the Foundation for Democtratic Institutions, Washington DC, has awarded our Society its Gold Medal. The citation is too long to give in full here but some relevant extracts are: ...*share and share alike ... ample opportunity for discussion ... all decisions made by secret ballot ... purely voluntary co-operation ... no action taken unless vote for it was unanimous ... public participation in the decision making process ... rights of protest and dissent strictly upheld ... smiling early morning faces ... friendly and harmonious crepitation ...*

8. EXECUTIVE CLEMENCY

Ref. para 1 (b) of this Bulletin: In consideration of good work done beagling a lost trail on May 1, 1974, the sentence on OD NOYES N is modified as follows: -Delete the words "rank and"; "tied out on an anthill"; for "the ants" substitute "the Leading Tacos".

9. REPORT ON SEASON 1973-1974: During 57 walking days a quorum of the Society has covered 820.5 miles and climbed 128,000 ft in New Mexico, Colorado, Nevada, England & Kashmir. The average per walk day has been 14.4 miles and 2246 ft. The Members have unanimously voted to present the Head Ghillie with a Brass Trumpet as reward for his unparalleled skill in not losing even one of the cretinous nincompoops he was responsible for.

J Masters LT

J Masters, Head Ghillie 7/17/74

1974 saw a change of agent in London. Masters had been thinking of this for some time. Much as he liked Laurence Pollinger, he realised now that Pollinger was getting on and he wanted someone younger and more vigorous. He wrote to him from Spain in the summer of 1974:

> for a great many years now it has been clear to me that it would be better for me to have all my literary affairs managed by one agency. As I live in the USA and will visit Europe less often, the agency should clearly be American. Many factors including your increasing retirement from the day to day conduct of your business have decided me that the change must be made now. Accordingly L P Ltd will cease to represent me or Bengal-Rockland after any contracts arising out of *The Field Marshal's Memoirs*. My agent, world-wide, will thereafter be the William Morris Agency. We have had a long and profitable relationship and I hope you will agree that the time has come to part amicably and with good will. You have about nineteen works of mine to deal with. In any case, part we must – so with thanks and good wishes – I am – Yours, John Masters

Pollinger was 'shocked' by this, but went along with it. Masters was not being wholly honest with him, as he saw another agent, Ed Victor, over lunch at Wheelers that autumn in London. Ed Victor, an American but very much the up-and-coming agent of the moment in London, had a high opinion of Masters's novels, rating *Nightrunners of Bengal* one of the finest pieces of twentieth-century historical fiction; he became Masters's new London agent.

1975 was a 'normal year, which meant that I worked hard on a book, then walked hard before starting on another book.' His walking that year took him to Scotland in May.

> It was pretty cold in Skye and very cold in the Cairngorms, but we only got rained on once in ten days and ate a lot of haggis. While there I attended the annual dinner of the Highland Counties branch of the Burma Star Association at which I was guest of honour. Tim Brennan, former CO of the Cameronians was also a principal guest. Several of us had drinks with the Provost before the dinner and were then escorted down the main street by the Royal British Legion band. There was a large attendance and all in all it was a moving occasion.

The Field Marshal's Memoirs was published in London on 27 May 1975. Masters found himself very busy with interviews, 'rushing around like a chicken with its head cut off', to the BBC, then Wheelers for a publishers' lunch and more radio interviews the next day, plus an

Bulletin # 21

1. A DIVINE MESSAGE FROM OUR PATRON, FOUNDER, AND HEAD GORGONZOLA,
COMMODORE MUJHE K. WALLBANGER:

Valued subjects‡! --- It has been brought to Our notice that various goodfellows and goodladies enjoy Our Society's walking regime and would welcome the opportunity to accompany you good peasants who actually do the walking. As Our repute and word of our sybaritic way of life spreads the number of such excellent people will doubtless increase. Where will it all end? (Knows God, and the undersigned.) We therefore deem it expedient to publish Our policy on this matter, viz:

The maximum number of walkers on any walk shall be12. All designated Members shall be asked first for each walk, three to four days in advance. If a Member opts out for a walk, he may NOT change his mind later. (Do not ask the Head Ghillie where a walk is going. Except in summer he doesn't know until I appear to him in a dream the night before the walk, and tell the clot.) The vacant places to complete to 12 will immediately be offered to those on the MK List, which shall consist of people who wish to join us, and who are well recommended by a few Members and accepted by Me. The offers will be made in rptation, ie if for say Nov 20 Nos. 1 and 2 on the MK List are asked, then on Nov 27 No. 3 will be asked first, and so on back to No. 1.

There will be óne exception to the Rule of 12, ie that all designated Members of the Society shall be accepted for any walk even if the number goes above 12.

Obviously Members may not bring friends, visitors, or relatives along without working out something well in advance with the Head Ghillie. We do not want to be harsh or dogmatical, and perish forbid elitist, but twelve is enough on any trail at any one time, and it is also two car loads. Enough is enough.

We would welcome suggestions on this matter. It might be possible, for instance, to set up a second walk day, on weekends perhaps, where there might be dogs, dancing girls, hookah smoking, three-dimensional chess without boards, and long stops for purposes of nature and mutual admiration. This second walk will NOT be organized by the Head Ghillie.

The designated Members of the Society as of this date are: Jameson 2, Masters 2, Hamill 1, Robertson 1, Noyes 1, Shults 1, Wilburn 2, Catron 1, Bogert 1, Monks 1, Casady 1 -- Total 14. Recommendations are invited fot the MK LIst.

God bless Us .... Mujhe kaas!

November 19, 1974   BY COMMAND. Mujhe K. Wallbanger

****   ****   ****   ****   ****   ****   ****

2. WALK DATES : Weds Nov 27, Dec 4, Dec 11, Dec 18. Thurs Dec 26,
Jan 2 1975
3. ERRATA: In line 33 of our Head Gorgonzola's Divine Message,
after "nature" add "study"; for "admiration" substitute *DELETED*

LT

Nov 19, 1974   Head Ghillie & Chief Bottlewasher

interview with *Punch*. Ed Victor met him and tried to interest him in a project on Indian railways. Nowadays, instead of a station hotel, he and Barbara stayed with Peg de Fonbrune, now married to Michael Man, at Bolton's Court. He was back in the England he liked: 'supper here tonight – sausages, broad beans, tomatoes – great!'

On 13 June he went down to Stoke Poges for his 4th Gurkha Regimental Remembrance Day, meeting many old colleagues, a 'very moving' occasion, with the regimental band playing on the lawn in full dress. This was followed by their annual dinner in London at the East India and Sports Club – 'same crowd, plus a few.' An account of this appeared in the 4th Gurkhas Newsletter: 'On Remembrance Day Masters was in his usual good form and still sporting the Rhett Butler *Gone with the Wind* neckwear which he wore when he was with us three years ago. After all, Rhett was Quite A Chap, but I see in the regimental album that he was wearing a Gurkha Brigade tie on some occasions during his visit to the 1st Battalion in India 1973, which fits him better!' Masters usually contributed exotic accounts of his own progress to these newsletters each year.

Back in Santa Fe he used the Chili and Marching Society Bulletin 27 to outline his reasons for walking: 'I walk for spiritual and mental satisfaction, and for physical self-discipline, and subject to increasing infirmity and general dottiness my walks are as long and hard as I can take. I am delighted to have the comradeship and support of anyone who shares these general values, aims, and abilities, subject to a reasonable limitation on numbers. I am willing and I believe able to organize walks, but only for those who want to do my kind of walk. For those of you who don't, or can't stand my face – God bless you one and all, and do not bother to read further; there are plenty more where I came from.' And he could still be a martinet in insisting on orders being carried out. Only half-jokingly he awards one member a 'solid Gold Brick for the most imaginative series of excuses and explanations to avoid uphill work that these ears have heard since attending Defaulters' parade of the 1st Bn Duke of Cornwall's Light Infantry in 1934.' To give an indication of the sorts of walks they undertook, in the 1975–1976 season they walked on forty-six days, covered a distance of 739 miles in all and climbed a total of 104,600 feet, which gave a daily average of 16.08 miles and 2273.91 feet. It was vigorous going and an example of both their stamina and dedication.

We can be sure Masters was in his element here, and the tone of these bulletins and the testimony of his colleagues in the walking group confirm it. He was at his happiest among them on these walks. Just as the Kaghan Valley with Barbara in 1942 had represented a high point for him in his late twenties, so these years when he was in his early sixties represented another high water mark. He was fully himself, relaxed, generous, ribald, gregarious, but still in charge. He was in the fortunate position of doing what he liked, where he liked: a global citizen who had at last found his spot on the globe, which was not always so easy. In the novel that he published in 1976, *The Himalaya Concerto*, he had this to say about modern frontiers: 'The tragedy was that most of the extraordinary places in the world, once difficult of access for purely physical reasons had now disappeared behind far more impenetrable barriers of national suspicion, security and xenophobia.'

LOSS OF EDEN
1976–1982

1976 marked the launch of a major writing project, a trilogy of books on the First World War, and a turning point in Masters's writing career. It was a subject that had strong personal associations for him. He had been born in the year the war started and much of his early childhood had been lived in its shadow. Like many other writers, Masters was returning to his childhood towards the end of his life, exploring themes that had lain dormant for years, partly to put the record straight, partly to recapture some of the lost feeling from that era. In a letter at this time to his friend Air Marshal Sir Peter Wykeham, he wrote,

> I feel very much the same way as you do about the sense of twilight that falls over 1914–1918. I still feel it was a warmer time – people helped you, rather than let you die in a gutter. It is almost indescribable, this feeling, but for me one very strong image of it is a deserted railway station platform somewhere in the remote country, gas lamps burning hazily through the November dusk; and being alone on it, waiting for a train, to catch or to meet – the sense that the train would come; that no one would step out of the shadows and mug you; that if you went into the waiting room there might be someone there who would say nothing, but be warm, a presence.

These images from childhood, the perennial railway station, representing hope and purpose and recalling his journeys north to stay with relations, and the images of warmth and security, the enveloping maternal presence of the waiting room and the certainty that the train would come, that mother, or father, would return, all speak of a secure pre-Oedipal world, safe from harm.

Images as powerful as these sprang from a pervasive nostalgia in him. The word nostalgia comes from a combination of two Greek words, nostos 'return home' and algos 'pain' and hence conveys the sense of yearning mixed with sadness that Masters felt both about India and his childhood. The Edwardian world before the war paralleled India in many respects; as his contemporary, the writer Paul Scott, puts it: 'The product of the Raj was, of course, rule; rule in the form of benevolent despotism or, as it was called, paternalism, which meant that it was supposed to be stern but just. It was a Victorian concept. In India it endured into the 1940s. In England belief in it did not survive the Great War but it lasted until the war began which is why for me the Raj does not convey a musty Victorian interior but a perpetual Edwardian sunlight.' That Edwardian sunlight, idealised perhaps in memory, was to suffuse the writing of the trilogy.

The turning point in his writing had been facilitated by his new literary agent, Carl Brandt, in New York. Masters had first met Brandt some years before at a dinner party with Sandy Richardson. They had got on well, not least because Brandt was also a keen walker. Tall, good looking, an Ivy League type, Brandt was the sort of forward-looking agent Masters needed. After his break with Pollinger, he had continued with William Morris Agency, but he had not been altogether happy with them, especially when they wanted to increase their rate to 15 per cent in 1975. Masters mentioned all this to Dick Stern, whose agent was Carl Brandt. Brandt was scheduled to visit New Mexico anyhow and the two of them went on a hike together in the Pecos Mountains, which was the determining factor in Masters's decision to switch agents; his London business was handled by Brandt's correspondent there, A. M. Heath.

Shortly after Brandt left New Mexico, Masters wrote to him outlining his writing plans:

> It was good seeing you, even better getting to grips, by your help, with the future of my writing career. After we had been beating about the bush for some time you asked me flatly what I *wanted* to do, as opposed to what might be expedient or profitable on a short-term, one-shot basis. I told you . . . and would now like to tell you again, in, I hope, a better organized way. I want to compose and write a great work in novel form, that is not about the Great War of 1914–1918, but IS that war. As I said in another place [his preface to *Fourteen Eighteen*] 'The French Revolution destroyed a social system that had flourished in Europe for almost a thousand years; the Great War destroyed Europe itself. The French Revolution destroyed faith in Church and Sovereign; the Great War destroyed faith in God and Man and was the most far-reaching and all embracing event of the past two centuries, perhaps of all recorded history.'

He was setting out to write a magnum opus. He told Brandt of the surge of inspiration it had created in him. 'As I continued my mental exploration, themes and sub-themes, plots, characters and events poured down on me in so strong and increasingly powerful a torrent that I felt I had opened the flood gates of a giant dam, and that the pent and towering waters would sweep me away unless I managed, struggling, to close the gates. But I could not close them and I have instead been swept to a conviction that there is a book to be written here as powerful as those waters; and that I can write it.' During much of his organised and at times over-planned life, these intense emotions were kept at bay – even in his novels, which relied on narrative rather than introspection for their impact.

He was now in full Tolstoyan flow.

> The tensions and events that will make the book do not have to be created by me: they are there in the time, and have only to be embodied: – the struggle between old and new ideas in society, warfare, politics, economics, industry, women's place and rights, labor and medicine, sexual mores, behaviour patterns; colonialism, capitalism, the conquest of the air, radio. The roll goes on and on, far too long for me to attempt to recount here even if I had the full tally, which I can not have until I have made a much more detailed study. It is enough to say now that it was a time of drastic and continuous change, of unparalleled courage and inventiveness, unparalleled stupidity and selfishness; and that the passion of some was matched only by the disillusion of others.

Marshalling these disparate events into a co-ordinated pattern, and readying himself for a test of his writing and organisational skills had all the makings of a full-scale military campaign. He had always prided himself on being a professional writer, and now he set himself a real challenge. He told Brandt his personal motive for writing his biography:

> The enormity of the subject might have intimidated or even bored me (and my readers) if I had not long been impelled by personal interest and involvement. I had three uncles killed in action on the Western Front and three others served there; my father was wounded and decorated in the Eastern theatre; as a cadet and officer I was taught by and served under men who had fought throughout. The British Army which I entered as a 2nd lieutenant in 1934 was not preparing to fight that war again, but its conduct and ways of thought – good and bad – were rooted in Flanders. And, more important, not only the Army's; the England I grew up in and went to school in was a mixture, not yet an amalgam, of pre-war feudalism and post-war unrest, of a splendidly decaying past and a vital but often ugly present, of combined love and hatred towards all tradition; and the Great War was the link between every one of these states.

There was a sense of reprise in taking up the family history again, only sketchily used in the early Indian novels.

America, Masters's host nation, would need to be included. It was where the bulk of his reading public lived. 'The role of the United States in the novel would have to be much as it was in reality; beginning almost off stage, gradually and willingly being dragged in, to play finally a decisive part and to reach its own maturity as a world power. My overall plan is to have US representation in the books more or less equivalent to US representation in the war, as seen from the British position.' This would present problems, as the American troops did not train in England but went straight to France, nor did they fight alongside the British; yet Masters wanted the hero of the book to be an American, Johnny Merritt.

Masters planned to have twenty major characters covering three generations and four main social levels, and the structure of the work would divide into three phases, corresponding to the three stages of the Great War itself. First, the 'Palladian calm and Olympian confidence of 1914' that led into the 'debonair moves and quixotic emotions of the first open moves of the war', and ended with the fighting grinding to a halt in 1915 and the stalemate in trench warfare. Secondly, the grim years of 1916 and 1917, 'when the universal mood changes from high hope to despairing determination', the slaughter becomes 'monstruous' and new inventions and new modes 'begin to undermine all previous norms'; this phase ending with the arrival of American troops in France and the collapse of Russia into revolution. Thirdly, the violent swings of 1918, 'the heights and depths of the German offensive and Allied counter offensive, the fall of Germany, final victory, final exhaustion; and then 1919 – exploration of the battlefield to catalogue the wounded, bury the dead, identify the missing, and applaud, sometimes wryly, those who are building the new world out of the rubble of the old.'

It was clearly going to be a massive undertaking and Masters estimated he would need three volumes, each of about 160,000 words – 500,000 words in all – with four years to complete them at the rate of one volume every sixteen months.

The summer of 1976 was spent in Europe: 'We had the usual year – went to England, saw relatives and friends, and then to the Dolomites and Spain for walking. The Dolomites are scenically superb, and there are many good hotels, the trails are well marked . . . and only man is vile, in the form of thousands upon thousands of German and Austrian tourists, on the roads, the trails, the hotels, the peaks everywhere. Several times, crossing some enormous Alpine meadow, we were faced by what looked like the Prussian guard advancing at Mons towards us, in mass.' His imagination appeared already to have begun its offensive against 'the Hun' on the tourist trails of Europe.

Masters always had mixed feelings about handing over the leadership of the Chili and Marching Society while he was away. Like many a charismatic leader, part of him was loath to delegate. He entrusted the arrangements for the walks to a trio of established members: Polly Robertson; Bill Chudd, formerly in charge of New York's juvenile bureau; and Carl Overhage, an ex-MIT physicist. Masters left explicit instructions behind: 'These leaders will be better mannered and more considerate than the Head Ghillie, but must be assured the same surly obedience. Please do not propose substantial changes in the Society's normal walk routines and customs; it will only Cause Trouble Later.' Bulletin 33, published on his return, remarks that the detachment of the Society that had remained in Santa Fe had 'in an ill-advised attempt to make their Leader look like a piker walked 216 miles in 17 days at an average of 12.71'. He immediately awarded the Ignoble Order of the Index Finger to them all and warned that 'details of these awards are being kept in pectore; this is just to let you know that Big Brother was watching.' He was keeping tabs on them, even at a distance.

Carl Brandt conducted the negotiations with US publishers for the proposed war trilogy and fixed up a deal in September 1976 with Reader's Digest Press, a contract worth more than $100,000 for the three books. The first volume would be called *Now God Be Thanked* after the Rupert Brooke poem which speaks of England being 'wakened from sleeping' as people throng to the recruiting stations, imbued with patriotism and a fervent sense of justice: two facets of the essential code of pre-war society that Masters wanted to bring out in this first volume. Bruce Lee was to be his editor at Digest. He flew out to New Mexico with Carl Brandt to meet Masters. 'I liked Jack immediately. He had the same ruthless approach to life as did my father, who was a highly decorated infantryman in World War One. So when Jack said he wanted to write a trilogy that explained the pain and suffering of the Great War – at home as well as on the battlefield – I could relate to what he wanted to do.' Masters wrote to him on 4 November with a progress report: 'I have been working on the trilogy for nearly a month now and have amassed a hundred or so pages of notes, and a card index with an imposing list of characters and characteristics. I have followed each character in turn through the whole period of the three books, noting what he did, what happened to him, how and where he impinged on other characters. I then had a series of so to speak vertical lists, one for each character. By dividing these into three horizontally, I had a list of what each character did in each book. By collecting all the horizontal strips I saw what was to be included in each book.' He was using his familiar pre-writing planning, mapping the book out in advance.

Masters told Bruce Lee that 'detailed research must wait till I have shaped the book sufficiently for us to know what area has to be researched. If we try to research every angle of the Great War before writing we won't get Book 1 done till Easter 2040.' He did enlist the help of two researchers in England, Major Martin Fuller, formerly of the 4th Gurkhas, and Marjorie Caton-Jones, who worked for John Anstey at the *Telegraph*. He told them what sort of research he was after:

> One is where I need facts of some kind or other. The other is where I really need a visual presentation. Suppose I have a scene in a country town magistrate's court (I probably will have) – an explanation of legal procedures can be got for me by my cousin, an ex-lawyer in England. But what did the court look like? How were the spectators dressed? Laborious explanations might be found; a picture in a magazine would do it all. This is only one example of a fact which will come up again and again and the solution of which is vital to the books, for I must have colour and a sense of reality as well as narrative and characterisation.

The more he shaped up his forthcoming campaign, the more exhilarated Masters was at the prospect ahead. 'It's a great feeling to have a big job cut out, a long term commitment made', he wrote to Alex, still the recipient for his confidences and hopes for the future. 'I have been working hard for a month, and it will go on all the time, though not too frantically I hope; that will depend really on how "right" the first draft of the first novel comes out. If the editors like it, we will have found a form on which to build the other two as well.' Michael Joseph had come in on the deal and were offering £27,000 for the proposed three books.

Masters's sixty-second birthday was on 26 October. He wrote, 'I don't feel any older from the inside, but looking at myself in the mirror realize what the chicks are seeing, from the outside, so adopt an Ancient Mariner pose.' The Marching Society had celebrated their annual Head Ghillie's Tiffin on the same day with a get-together for all the Society's walkers at the Masterses' house at 12.00 p.m., for a barbecue meal of chicken, saffron rice and beer. Guests were warned not to bring birthday presents – anyone bringing them would be 'sent into lunar orbit'. The Tiffin was accompanied by an afternoon slide show, when Masters showed slides of his summer walking and the Society's seasonal walks. Occasionally he would slip in a nude slide, often the wrong way up, by 'accident', and then go through a lengthy rigmarole of inserting it the right way up, and then the wrong way again, to the groans of spectators and the dismay of some of the non-walking wives present and the more conservative guests.

Barbara's birthday was a fortnight later and they decided to celebrate together, going down to the new fish store in Santa Fe, the Fish Net, and buying two dozen Blue Point oysters and two chicken lobsters, which they ate while listening to the Presidential Election returns on 3 November. Jimmy Carter was voted into office. He was not Masters's choice, as his allegiances had shifted to the right and were now firmly with the Republican party.

The high-spirited tone of the Chili and Marching Society bulletins continued throughout 1977. On 5 May a dire warning emanated from the Head Ghillie in Bulletin 38 that 'shepherds who lose their sheep, sheep who bleat out of turn, will be awarded a hot fudge enema to be administered on the spot by the Surgeon General', and an equally stern reminder that no backsliders would be tolerated. 'The walk on April 20 consisted of 1 sick, 1 convalescent, 5 short walkers, 4 walkers. Early on we also encountered three mousefinks posing as members of the Society, but they quickly scuttled back into their holes when challenged.' Yet they managed to keep up a high average of 14.81 miles on the 37 walking days they had in the winter of the 1976–1977 season.

For most of 1977 Masters was writing at full stretch, prodding his English researchers to investigate details of social and military customs and sending out a continuous stream of letters to experts in England. Marjorie Caton-Jones recalls that he was absolutely meticulous about detail and often asked several people the same question. No research stone was left unturned. Masters told Martin Fuller to check the exact times of trains from Brighton to London in 1914 and said that if he did not there would always be someone who wrote in complaining that there wasn't a 9.34 in 1914. Accuracy of research was all-important to him and he used any contacts he had, from Lady Falkender for information about 10 Downing Street to the Italian owner of a restaurant in New York he frequented for the correct Italian translation of colloquial terms.

By April Masters had finished the first draft of 170,000 words, a phenomenal output for just over four months. It was time for a short break and a quick visit to California to see Martin and Susan. Martin was playing piano in a rock and roll band at a club called Hobo Joe's in west Los Angeles – 'good band, noisy of course.' Sue came from San Francisco to see her parents in Los Angeles. She had remarried, to another Chinese American. It was unusual, to say the least, to find her marrying two Chinese husbands, a leaning towards the Orient that was finding expression in her generation too. Was she, in the Jungian phrase, living the unlived life of parents and living out their hidden secret?

More research was needed for the trilogy, so Masters thought he would combine on-the-spot research with a trip to Europe, notably to the battlefields of the Somme, and then go to Spain for his 'annual attack on the waistline'. Spain was always full of surprises. His logs recorded unusual incidents during this trip. He mentions the 'strange German couple we encountered near Cervera who walked 200 ft or more apart, he shouting at her over his shoulder in conversation'. Elsewhere he recorded the encounter with an old roadmender, a caminero, he knew from previous years, full of 'joyous greetings, back slapping, embraces and much animated talk', and the unexpected sight of mountain shepherds hurling their dogs into a lake in a competition to see who could throw theirs the furthest. Later, up in the Pyrenees near Portalet, a huge white Pyrenean sheepdog attached himself to them and walked with them to the telesilla (chair lift), trotting below all the way up to the Pic du Midi, staying with them all day, chasing a few cows unsuccessfully, standing in water to cool off, and then descending again with them. The observant eye of the author was on the lookout for such details; the military man, meanwhile, kept track of distances covered, miles walked, feet climbed, weather conditions and, more and more, the state of his health.

He had to be careful about his angina, which might flare up suddenly. One night outside Huesca he was 'awakened soon after four in the morning by fibrillations, very wild and intermittent, I slept till 5 when reawakened and stayed up till 6.15. Barbara awoke then too deciding what to do next. We decided to go to Huesca to see a heart man and get a proper prescription.' The doctor told him to take it easy and to stick to fizzy drinks and lower his alcohol intake, which was not easy for him as his morning anis, evening whisky and dinner wine were very much part of his routine, as were the boilermakers (beer with a whisky chaser) after a walk.

Masters and Barbara stopped in New York to see Bruce Lee and Carl Brandt on their return journey. The book was now being published by McGraw-Hill, where Bruce Lee had moved after the Reader's Digest Press was disbanded. Nowadays Masters did not like to stay too long in New York. Bruce Lee remembers, 'You could tell that every hour in smoggy New York was agony for him. His face would get redder the longer he stayed. One always knew his heart was yearning for the clear air of the high mountains.' He and Bruce usually had dinner at the Seafare of the Aegean on 56th Street, where Masters prefaced his meal of striped bass posilipo, a spicy fish stew, with a shot of Quervos Gold tequila, followed by a Coors Light Beer.

By the end of November Masters had finished the third draft of *Now God Be Thanked* and sent out chapters to elicit the corrections and comments of the experts who had helped him. Barbara typed out five copies, one each for Brandt, Bruce Lee, Michael Joseph, Mark Hamilton of A. M. Heath and Masters.

One area of the book that was worrying Masters was the homosexual theme. One of his main characters, Tom Rowland, serving as a commander in the Royal Navy, 'discovers' his homosexual inclinations. He is attracted to a rating on the same ship and wants to have an affair with him. Masters needed to know whether this was feasible or whether social attitudes and naval practice at the time would have forbidden it. He asked Peg Man to show the relevant passages to any naval officers she knew. She did so and reported back that 'both the naval officers who read your chapters said that never in a thousand years would someone of the rank of Commander, no matter what his private inclinations might be, indulge in even the briefest homosexual practice with one of his ratings'; and she added, 'Actually they were both deeply shocked at the explicitness of the descriptions and of course naval officers of the old school, in spite of their reputation for booziness and gaiety, are, in fact, surprisingly conventional.'

Masters was clearly determined to include the passages he had written and wrote back to her asking her to pass them on to another friend of hers, Admiral Sir Caspar John, the son of Augustus John, because 'having been brought up in an artistic environment he will not be so shocked at the possibility of Tom being a queer'. He wrote in the accompanying letter:

> I am sending you these chapters in the hope that you will be able and willing to read and correct them. I cannot believe that with a total naval experience of six hours [visiting HMS *Emerald* and going on board HMS *Yarra*, both in Basra in 1941] I have not made mistakes – that all the orders are correct ones, correctly worded – that the ranks and jobs I have guessed at and given people are correct – in a word that a naval officer reading the chapters would nod and say 'the author has been in the service.' So I ask could you please read the

chapters, and correct in pencil on the ms wherever I have used wrong words, phrases or situations?

What he really wanted was advice on

the second problem which is dramatic rather than technical. As I have said, Tom Rowland is a homosexual, so far suppressed. In the navy of 1914 this makes him a figure of tragedy; his story through three books is going to be his recognition of himself, his unavailing struggle to reconcile his life in the Navy, which he loves, and his training, with this condition; and finally his new start in the world of the civilian homosexual – a new start and a way of life which have been made possible by the changes in society brought about by the war. The naval readers have been unanimous that never never would a Commander R N have homosexual relations with a rating. I imagine it must be rare – but can one really say 'Never'? If so, under what authority? I personally know four army officers of good regiments and family, who were cashiered and in one case committed suicide for this. Heaven knows how many more there have been throughout the past two centuries. It seems to me that the readers might as well swear that Commanders R N never, never catch measles from ratings; the diseases strike where they will. I could easily have Tom Rowland keep a hold on his propensities while at sea; but then I have to split his personality sooner than I want to, and sooner than is good for a strong portrayal of his agony. It is much more powerful if he hates and despises homosexuals, yet is compelled to recognize that he is one, in the most disgraceful circumstances, and the most contrary to all his training – i.e. with a rating in his own ship. In Book Two he is gradually torn apart into the two personalities . . . and finds that they cannot live together. In Book Three he makes peace within himself by abandoning the old Tom, and surrendering to the new. Does this seem to you to be an impossible course for a naval officer's life, in the massively changing world of 1914–1919?

In itself it was the sort of technical, or dramatic, problem he was facing with many characters in this trilogy: how to combine ideas, such as the changes in social attitudes wrought by the war, with credible characters. This example is of interest because it shows his persistence, and interesting, too, in that he was so determined to include a homosexual figure and portray him in a sympathetic light. For Masters, perhaps this was curiosity about, or acknowledgement of, his own other than heterosexual side.

This may seem surprising in someone so apparently masculine, macho even, but writing was partly a vehicle for self-exploration as well. Tom Rowland here offers him an opportunity to get in touch with a sexuality hitherto missing from his novels. His own sexual orientation had been under scrutiny over the years, not least because of his fascination with the subject. He gave a hint of this with a remark he made during a South Mountain Road party when he told a group of friends that he would not mind at all being a woman for a year and 'having that sword thrust into me.' The sexualisation of experience was a theme close to his heart, and the reversal of sexual norms, as suggested in his remark, would fit in with this.

At any event, he was determined that Tom Rowland should hold on to his homosexuality, despite the doubts of the naval experts. Tom mattered, too, because he was 'breaking every tenet his class holds dear, and which, of course, he does too – in spite of himself.' The paradox this posed, the perennial evaluation of the dictates of class, was another theme Masters was setting out to explore in this book. Much of the book describes a deferential society that reached its apotheosis in the Edwardian era. It is curious that Masters here seems almost to be enshrining the class-ridden society in an aura of beneficence, when he had spent so much of his life going against it. His argument would have been that he needed to show it first in its full extent, via his three Kentish families, before showing how it broke down after the war, but one cannot help feeling that his sympathies were with its existence. The nostalgia for a Golden Age is encapsulated in the title of the trilogy, *Loss of Eden*.

Responses to the completed draft were mostly positive, but comments were made once again on the excessive sexual description. His English editor, Alan Brooke, wrote,

> it is not the quantity of the sex that bothers me, but the brutality and perversity of some of it. Scenes that I would particularly like toned down, or deleted, are: (a) Tom's homosexual affair with the sailor (b) Stella's lesbian encounter with Naomi (c) the incest reference (d) Stella's loss of virginity. This last scene is necessary of course but I still feel that her conversion from virgin to sexual raver is a rather too sudden one for the period! I don't think these suggestions are puritanical; it's more a question of trying to highlight the divergences from a sexually repressed society; the impact, I feel, is weakened if too many of the characters are behaving against the social grain.

Masters did not agree. He felt his readers looked to him to give them sexually explicit scenes, to 'write in another rape' as he had put it to Mollie Kaye.

Now God Be Thanked was nearing completion. 'We are now down to the nitty gritty of Draft IV now, me working ahead making final corrections, Barbara typing about three chapters behind, and then me correcting her typed stuff; when you are dealing with six copies of each draft, the rooms rapidly silt up with little cartons containing MS; and my nightmare is a fire before it is all done, so soon I start carrying one whole set to the far end of the house, so that everything doesn't go at once.'

Bruce Lee rang up to say that he and everyone at McGraw Hill was delighted with the book. He felt Masters's novel was 'a work from his heart, a cry from his soul. There are a number of instances in which one can see Jack, the soldier, in the characters. One, I recall, is the sniper shooting the German in the knees – a Christmas present of his life. Or in the field hospital, or in the antipathy of the line officer for the neat, well-dressed, well-fed Staff.' Bruce promised extensive promotion; they were going to spend $100,000 on publicity and advertising, and planned a first printing of 75,000. This was welcome news, less appealing was having to do all the publicity work at publication time. He told Bruce he would not do it for anything like that length of time (three weeks). 'I like TV and radio and lecture and personal appearances, and am good at them, the professionals say. But I have learned in the past three or four years that it is exactly that sort of activity which ends up in acute fibrillations in the middle of the night, visits from doctors at 3 a.m., or worse. The heart won't take that sort of non-physical pressure any more; so if there is to be anything of the sort, it must be cut to a week at the most.'

Masters really did look to be on a winner, as even better news came through by the beginning of November: Ballantine (Bantam) had offered to pay $500,000 for the paperback rights. Masters was still battling on with the Royal Navy chapters, but then he had a 'great stroke of luck'.

I had a letter a fortnight ago from one David Scott saying he was going to visit Los Alamos, and was the brother of Minden Scott, 5GR, killed close to me in March 37 in Waziristan; and son of H St G Scott, who commanded 2/4 GR in the 20s, and could he visit me. I said yes, and it turned out he was Rear Admiral Sir David Scott, Britain's Chief Polaris Executive; he was a midshipman in *Revenge* about 1937 on and said he had driven all the pinnaces, steamboats etc and was fairly proficient still at the words of command stuff. So I begged him to read the MS – he had time to do Chapter 13 [At Sea, Sept 14 1914] very thoroughly, and asked me to send him Chapter 32 [North Atlantic Dec 1915] to his office, where he would be happy to deal with it as soon as he could. The great thing was that I was able to

ask him questions face to face. He seemed to enjoy remembering back
to those dim dead days; and we did give him a 2″ steak, garlic bread
and salad! I'm going to stick with his advice, whatever it is, and go
down with my colours nailed to his mast.

After a brief pause, he started work on the second volume in August
1978; the final draft was due to be submitted by January 1980, in
seventeen months' time. He launched into his familiar tight schedule
and no disturbances were allowed. Barbara's daughter Liz was due to
come and stay with them that summer with her second husband, Tony
Stubbs. A date had been fixed, but since they were passing close by
beforehand on their way to Los Alamos they decided to call in.
Masters answered the door and would not let them in. He reminded
them their visit was scheduled was for such and such a date, and that
was it, they were expected then. Barbara was in the house and she
managed to get him to agree that they could at least stop for a drink,
but then they had to leave.

Scheduling was all-important. For the Masterses' daily life a rota
was drawn up and pinned up in the kitchen: shopping at 10.30 a.m.,
pre-lunch drinks at 11.45, lunch at 12.15 precisely, evening drinks at
5.30, etc. If either he or Barbara was late with one of these tasks, the
other would look at his or her watch and remind the tardy one. Soon
after they arrived, house guests were given a blank timetable to fill in
with visits they expected to make; Masters would then fill in all the
arrangements he had made on their behalf. He wanted them to account
in advance for all their movements during their stay. Ad hoc arrangements were not good enough. This controlling side was relentless, as if
he needed to keep people near him under control for fear that they
might otherwise impinge unduly on his life. Everything had to be
planned. Yet it never produced the dead hand of conformity. Social
occasions with the Masterses were always convivial and enjoyable.

Masters's punctuality was legendary and woe betide people who
were late. Back in the South Mountain Road days Keith Jennison had
tested him. The Jennisons had invited the Masterses for dinner at
7 p.m. and Keith went to his front door at that precise moment to see if
they were coming. Just as he opened it on the dot of 7 p.m., Masters's
hand was reaching up for the knocker.

London publication of *Now God Be Thanked* was scheduled for
11 June 1979. Alan Brooke was keen for Masters to do publicity in
London. Masters restricted this to what was absolutely necessary. 'For
London, let's say two interviews and one lunch or dinner. You have a
whole-time author here, but only a part-time performing seal. I will not

see anyone from *Punch* by the way; the two little squirts who interviewed me for them a couple of years ago were too busy trying to make me out an alcoholic Colonel Blimp that they invented words and attitudes for me to fit.'

His physical condition, as he told Alan Brooke, was getting no better. He now had the arthritis in his neck, and it 'hurts like hell some of the time, and a little all the time.' The pain in his left shoulder and arm stemming from angina came on in the morning, making it hard for him to write, but he was having traction and doing neck exercises. 'It has improved; also my temper a bit.' By evening it had usually disappeared, enabling him to sleep well. To Vald Heiberg, an old West Point friend, he wrote about this time: 'We are breaking up slowly as we advance into decrepitude. Barbara has just developed phlebitis in the left thigh; but the doctor seems to hope he can cure that soon. These of course on top of my angina and Barbara's sciatica. Still I manage to take my hikers out every Wednesday, 15 miles +. So it isn't too bad.' Considering the degree of his discomfort these were mild complaints indeed.

The second novel pleased Bruce Lee. In mid-March he reported, 'I have been reading *How Long O Lord* with great pleasure. You write so well and the pace of the book is wonderful. One really has the feeling that people are being swept along by a great tornado of events.' Masters was still writing at speed, up to 6,000 words a day, his pace not slackening despite his physical shortcomings. He was, as Bruce Lee later commented, 'always the consummate professional. His angina might be giving him terrible pain, but he would never let it interfere with the subject of work. God knows how much pain that cost him.' The book had in fact expanded to about 1,100 manuscript pages and was on a bigger scale than anything attempted before.

That May the Masterses went to California to see Martin, whose first record, of tunes 'nearly all of his own composing', had just been released. He had sent his parents a copy. 'I think it is very good,' Masters wrote in a letter to his brother, 'he plays a very boogie-woogie sort of piano, which I have always liked, and also sings in it. We are all trying to help him promote it and get it played by disc jockeys everywhere.' Their relationship had improved of late and Masters was giving Martin his full support.

At the end of the month Masters left with Barbara on his publicity tour for *Now God Be Thanked*. In Chicago he was inundated with a full schedule of interviews for radio and newspapers, which left him feeling 'like the good soldier Schweik, doing my job, obeying orders.' Then he moved on to New York in time for the 4 June publication day. He spent the morning at the offices of McGraw Hill, conducting interviews for *Newsday* and *Daily News*, then had lunch at Park Perigord with McGraw's President, Victor Keyserling. Later he joined Barbara and Bruce Lee, Carl Brandt and his wife Clare at the New York Yacht Club for drinks and a peek at the America's Cup before dinner at Seafare of the Aegean.

Two days later Masters met Bruce again at the Grand Central Oyster Bar to talk over the second volume. 'Most of the points he made were sensible, though they really have their minds made up beforehand about sex' – a familiar bone of contention. Alice Mathews had come down to New York as their guest for the weekend. She gives her picture of Masters on this occasion: 'On Sunday Barbara wasn't feeling well and stayed at the hotel while Jack and I went for a walk around Central Park. The weather threatened rain so Jack carried his familiar black umbrella and we joined the joggers on the wide footpath. Joggers of all shapes, sexes, costumes, Jack and I looking very conservative. The rains came and the joggers vanished – Jack opened the umbrella and we finished the walk at the regular brisk pace in an empty park.' It was a triumph of constancy over fickleness, a generational defiance and supremacy; Masters, the man for all seasons, marched on when all joggers had scattered.

From New York he crossed to Dublin, then to London for a busy publication day. Rising before 6 a.m., he got in his early morning walk along the Embankment for an hour before starting on newspaper interviews, then lunch with Peter Grosvenor, literary editor of the *Daily Express*, and more interviews in the afternoon, including Kaleidoscope for BBC Radio 4. On his way back to his hotel at Charing Cross, he passed Foyle's bookshop window and saw its display gratifyingly full of his book; less welcome in another window was the sight of Mollie Kaye's paperback edition of *The Far Pavilions*. They had temporarily fallen out over its publication in the USA, professional jealousy coming into it. Mollie had invited him to her New York launch party expecting him to come and share in her success, just as she and Goff had in his over the years, but he had simply sent a note through his agent saying he was unable to do so.

Michael Joseph laid on a celebration that evening at Restaurant Lafayette in King Street, St James's, in a downstairs private room. 'Excellent salmon trout, good party, but too much of much – Bob and Babs Lusty, Anthea Joseph, Victor Morrison, Alan Brooke, and a lot of twatlets. Home in hired car.' The book took off well initially and was fourth on the bestseller list, despite a 'catty' review in *The Daily Telegraph*, but 'very good ones' in the *Daily Mail* and *Daily Express*.

He appeared on BBC TV's Word for Word book discussion programme that same week, with Robert Robinson and Germaine Greer. Asked about the current wave of nostalgia for India, he said it was probably for a code of honour and probity in public affairs that now seemed to be missing from British public life. It had been upheld typically by the Indian Civil Service in lonely outposts, people of the highest integrity with 'a strong moral sense of duty which is being submerged by chicanery and graft in the Western world.' Germaine Greer said that she preferred his books to those of Paul Scott. Scott 'made a tremendous effort to understand the Indian mentality which doesn't exist any more than the European one does, whereas Masters doesn't try at all and is content to let the Indians be Indians'. It was a perceptive and important comparison, and one which, as Masters pointed out, echoed Khushwant Singh's earlier one about him in relation to Kipling.

It brings into focus the question of what was Masters's India. It was not the Raj so much as a preference for an India untainted by the British, often primitive and in distant or outlying areas. Towards the end of *Bhowani Junction* Masters has Rodney Savage say: 'This was my India . . . because these people had no desire to become like me, nor I like them. There had been a place for me round such fires as this for three hundred years. The Ranjits and Surabhais, who were trying to change themselves, didn't light bonfires and dance round them. They read Paine and Burke and spoke in English because the ideas they were trying to express did not exist in their own language.'

This hankering for an 'old' India, one where generations had trod, linked up with his own family's five-generational stay in India, its roots deeper than that of the Raj. He returns to this theme in *To The Coral Strand* when Rodney retreats to a primitive hovel on the beach near Bombay as far as he can get from the 'new' India. This refrain stayed with Masters. Barbara relates that after his last visit to India in 1973 he was not keen to go back again – the country had changed too much for his liking. He found an outlet for his longing for the old India and its physicality when he wrote the introduction to an exhibition catalogue entitled *The Glory That Was India*, in 1982. There he reiterates his feeling for India with 'its space, closeness, giant mountains, large visions . . . above all the people and their kindness and inherent gentleness, both allied to an unrivalled capacity to endure, a stubborn will to live in the way their forefathers lived, in harmony with the land beneath their feet, the waters that flow past their doors, the circumambulant Indian air – now hot, close-embracing, now distant, sharp and bitter cold.' This yearning for an unmarked and physically powerful landscape motivated him in his choice of other primitive and remote surroundings, whether in the Pyrenees, the Picos de Europa or in New Mexico outside Santa Fe. In his novel *The Breaking Strain* he had anticipated this and described New Mexico as having these qualities: 'this was what life ought to be like . . . primitive, clean, companionable.'

That summer Joan Buresch and John Talley were the Masterses' guests in Spain, both were Santa Fe Chili and Marching Society members and Jungian analysts. Joan was struck by how different Masters was in Spain. This was man's country and he almost ignored her throughout their stay, a sharp contrast to Santa Fe where his 'sense of the joy of planning and his warmth and leadership and the evident enjoyment he got out of stretching everybody', and the way he had 'of being beside you when you were in trouble on a walk without passing around sympathy', was much in evidence.

On this Spanish trip, however, it seemed different. Admittedly he was not well and not on his best form. Being with him in Spain felt like being on a mission. At dinner, talk was of practicalities, what had happened that day, plans for the next day, with none of the speculative talk they had enjoyed with him in Santa Fe. In Spain conversations of this nature, such as a discussion of a historical question, were curtailed. He talked more to John, man-to-man stuff; 'You couldn't transgress on him, or joke him out of it,' and it was a shock to her.

On this trip Joan Buresch sensed what the loss of India meant to Masters. She felt he had left his heart there. It created a paradox, 'here's a real person, who can't be a real person', as if the real person was something of an artefact, built on this sense of loss. This came through in his role as leader of the walking group, especially with the bulletins with their double entendre, half serious ('these are my orders'), half joke ('it's all make believe'). It was play-acting to some extent but it was also an outlet for his real charm, which he was able to express fully these days.

There were inevitable echoes of his beloved Gurkhas in forming a group like the Chili and Marching Society. Groups generate a sense of belonging and all Chili and Marching Society rituals retained this element, whether at a sauna (Masters argued that it was good for group cohesion for members to take their clothes off in front of each other), or at their get-togethers, or as expressed in the bulletins with their orders of rank.

The group clearly mattered to Masters and he was hurt when people did not value it as highly as himself. Once when a member showed a preference for skiing in place of walking on some Wednesday mornings, Masters asked him to give up his membership as there were others waiting to join, but he was hurt by this episode. As he told a colleague, 'I guess he doesn't really like me.'

To the group as a whole he was a sort of ideal father figure, heroic too, leading his tribe into the wilderness. Outsiders could not understand why so many comfortably-off citizens of Santa Fe should submit themselves to this weekly gruelling ordeal. Most had originally gone to Santa Fe to retire and lead a life of comfort and ease, or at any rate a self-directed one. Yet here they were being dragooned at the crack of dawn each Wednesday morning, bidden, no questions asked, to do tasks that would stretch them physically and mentally. It seemed to answer an unmet psychological need in them. Americans are less easily regimented than the British. However, the aura Masters brought with him was not just the cachet of being the stranger in town, but, more powerfully, the mystique of the ex-Indian Army colonel and Gurkha officer, steeped in military tradition, allied to the forceful image of the Englishman who was a bit of a martinet, a bit fierce and crusty, and definitely not someone to get on the wrong side of. All this generated a frisson, and a keen following. Competition was kept to a minimum. Masters managed to make them all feel equally valued.

Masters's confidence and sense of knowing exactly what he was doing on the mountain gave them a protected feeling. He could take them through good times and bad, as an ideal father should, and bring more out of them than they thought they were capable of. There was excitement, too, in being taken into unknown territory, into unexpected adventures. Dramatic escapades lingered in the memory, like the 'Retreat from Moscow', when they were caught in a snowstorm at Borrego Mesa, and the famous 'Snow-blind walk', when the glare of the sun suddenly caught them unawares.

Masters revived in many of them the forgotten ability to play, the child in the adult. Play presupposes a certain distance from oneself, the capacity to stand back and not to take oneself too seriously. Masters was in touch with this side of himself at this stage in his life, as was evident in the bulletins. Reviving this capacity to play was something they all grew to appreciate. For Masters it was a release. He had spent much of his adult life proving to himself, and to others, his competence and competitive edge. Now he could let his guard down and enjoy himself. Photographs show him at this stage as relaxed, clowning almost. One shows him after a sauna, wearing his kimono bought for him as a present from Japan, a saturnine and relaxed look on his face, the old warrior at rest. It epitomises his current mood, and hints too at the underlying sense of absurdity that went with it, the Englishman who was not an Englishman any longer, yet remained very English.

It was a felicitous period for him. Now at last he was able to throw off the taboos of the Raj. The Indian novelist Manohar Malgonkar made a perceptive comment in this respect:

> The British officers of the Indian army were rather like an isolated tribe, who looked down upon those who did not quite belong. Masters's early days in the regiment must have been full of daily slights, and the regimental wives must have delighted in rubbing salt in all pinpricks. Alas, for his part, Masters must have made an ideal foil striving to prove himself by hard work and study and, at the same time, hankering for full acceptance – witness his exultation at some fellow (pure-British) subaltern rubbing rum butter into his scalp at a Christmas shindy in the mess. His quite outstanding war record shows what an excellent officer he was – but also how hard he tried. I feel that it was not till he had made a success of himself and become an American citizen that he was able to shed away the taboos of the Raj. Did he, I wonder, ever learn to laugh at the orthodoxies of the pukka-sahib?

He did, as the bulletins show.

Masters was comfortable with the men in his group. There was little rivalry for leadership. Even though some were older, they were content to be younger siblings, fitting in to the role assigned to them, similar to that of his beloved Gurkha troops, the same unquestioning obedience and robust sense of humour as they struggled across difficult terrain.

Tim Heald, a young English writer whose parents lived in Santa Fe, went on one walk in 1979.

> Masters seemed a bit wary of me, I thought. Very courteous but not a hundred per cent keen on the idea of a younger British writer. It was very much Masters's show. He led the main group at what seemed to me an extremely professional sort of shuffle and we only stopped when he said so. He had an old tobacco tin with nuts and raisins but you were only allowed to stop for something like thirty seconds every half hour. Any longer and you'd stiffen up, or something. I felt there was a lot of Gurkha and Southwest folklore banging around. I remember his US cavalry cap with the crossed kukris and how leathery his face was, almost like a Navajo. I was mildly disappointed not to get to know him better especially in a place like Santa Fe that was so outgoing but I suppose he went to Santa Fe to get away from people like me.

Now God Be Thanked was not selling as well as had been expected. This was depressing news after all the build-up and publicity. After their

1979 summer in Spain the Masterses passed through New York on the way home, and he talked it over with Bruce Lee.

At home on 25 August, Masters now found it difficult getting back to work, as he wrote in a letter to Peter Wykeham ten days later: 'We are home again, and after a week of doing nothing except sort out the mail, and answer letters unhurriedly. I am supposedly ready to get back to work on Volume Two, but I feel a strange lethargy and think I'll go out and have a beer or two instead. It takes me days to get back into work after a long break like this . . . I walk around the work like a dog trying to settle, getting ever closer but not actually doing anything creative, just making preparations, dusting off things, arranging card indexes, anything rather than touch the paper.' He was dispirited about the poor sales of the first volume of the trilogy, but his professionalism soon returned and he was back into his work schedule before long. The second volume was completed by the end of the year. He sent it to Bruce Lee, who wrote back praising the improvements but sounding a note of caution about the pace of the book, 'it may be too slow. There are times when it moves like the wind. In other places it seems ponderous . . . but, Jack, you are such a master at creating characters that I hesitate to suggest cutting.'

However, on 15 February 1980, Bruce Lee wrote to him telling him he wanted to bring the second volume in at the same length as the first. This meant cutting some 250 pages. Masters was furious, reminding him that when he had sent in the final draft of *O Lord, How Long?* on 8 December, it was then 1,239 pages and that he had

> heard no more from anyone until February 14th when I was told that it had to be cut by nearly twenty per cent. This was the first intimation that I had had from anyone that there was a limit on the length of the book I could write, or what the limit was. Since *The Far Pavilions* is considerably longer and since I presumed that McGraw Hill and Michael Joseph can count past 999 I thought I could write what was necessary for the book. You will recall that the original prospectus for the trilogy envisioned books of 150,000 words each but no protest was made when the first one came to 250,000. So instead of being able to work to a figure which I could at least understand, even if I disagreed with it, and cut say four lines from each page, the work has been submitted to butchering in large chunks.

Masters was particularly irate because he felt that what had been 'hacked out' was everything that 'gives colour, feeling and background to the story – the spirit of the RFC, the feel of rural England, what people are fighting for, the interaction of minor characters, the reminders placed at intervals so that the reader won't forget them.' Nor was he happy about the last minute deletion of additions he had made,

> a systematic attempt seems to have been made to cut out anything to do with Johnny Merritt, though I was asked in August to enlarge the US presence in the book. The book visibly bleeds from these gashes; sentences and phrases end abruptly, chains of thought are broken, loose ends left trailing, beginnings lead nowhere, chapters vary wildly in length. To sum up I think I have been given a lousy deal by my editors. We could have had a good book of the length you now apparently require; we do not; we have a collection of bones, with little flesh and less spirit.

He was feeling understandably aggrieved at having his book pruned so drastically. The emotional investment in the book had always been strong, because of the personal and family associations. Masters had conceived this trilogy as his magnum opus, and this made it doubly difficult for him to climb down. But climb down he did, like the professional writer he always was. Most of his writing life had been punctuated by 'tiffs' with editors, such as Helen Taylor in the past, and after an initial flurry he usually succumbed to his editor's better judgement. Now he agreed to make the required cuts. By 28 March Bruce Lee was writing to him: 'Thank you for returning the ms of Volume Two so promptly. It looks good and reads even better.'

The book came out on 14 October 1980, with the title *Heart of War*, but it failed to do well either in its reviews or its sales. It suffered, as the first volume had, from being top-heavy with research, with too much use of contemporary newspaper accounts inserted in the text. It was as if Masters was trying too hard to give it solidity and had lost much of the narrative flow, which was usually his strength, in the process.

He did not feel happy with his publisher's efforts. 'McGraw Hill's presentation of *Heart of War* was miserable,' he complained to Bruce Lee. 'Once they did not get a Book Club or big paperback sale, after the poor sales of *Now God Be Thanked*, they decided to cut their losses. There has been no publicity that I know of, I certainly was not asked to do any radio, print or TV appearances; in Santa Fe no one knew the book were coming out unless I told them.' Masters's hurt and disappointment were understandable. He had put immense effort into these books by his own reckoning, and now he stood rather like a weary battle commander seeing his troops scatter in disarray, the clamour of battle fading away and facing the ashes of defeat.

The third volume, *By the Green of the Spring*, suffered similar truncating. Inevitably dispirited, Masters was left wondering whether McGraw Hill would indeed go ahead and publish it or 'do it on the cheap, and as secretively as possible, as they have done with *Heart of War?*' By the end of the year he was asking Carl Brandt: 'Where do I go from here? What next?' To a Chili and Marching Society member, he admitted he was 'nearly writ out'. Ideas for his next book included one about the USA. 'I have lived in this country long enough to be able to tackle a suitable US subject. The thing I know most about is the Civil War and railroading, but not those two together, that's an area that has been overworked', he wrote to Brandt. He also considered writing a book on the US Air Commando in Burma, which would have a small British interest. 'I worked with Air Commando in 1944, know some of them, and am to be their guest of honour at the annual reunion this March.' At least with Brandt he felt confident to try out several possibilities and was confident of his guiding hand.

In the end two possibilities emerged. One took up an idea that had originated in discussions with Bruce Lee. This was for a novel about a man 'coming of age and preparing himself' between the wars in the first half of the twentieth century: 'someone like Bill Slim – a man of comparatively humble origins, whose profession was not going to be that of war; but who is dragged into World War I as a young man, stays on for various reasons, and through personal and professional vicissitudes comes of age in time to become the sort of military commander England needed in 1939.' The attraction of this book would be that it could draw upon some of his own experiences between the wars.

The second alternative was for a book that harked back to *Bhowani Junction*. Bruce Lee felt there was still a market for such a book. Masters sent Brandt an outline for *Valentine*, about an adventuress in India who has liaisons with five different men from a Maharajah to a European businessman. She is meant to be a 'hell of a woman, intelligent, unscrupulous and of course beautiful,' but the idea was too contrived and pseudo-exotic, and nothing came of it.

Just as he was about to start work on the first idea, Bruce Lee was fired from McGraw Hill in an organisational shake-out. McGraw Hill then vetoed the book Lee and Masters were shaping up together, provisionally entitled *The Commander*. Their sales and publicity division were against it. Masters was suddenly left high and dry, back in the very unwelcome position of being without an American publisher. Michael Joseph had agreed to do the book but Masters was not happy, nor did he feel it would be 'economically wise' to proceed with an English publisher alone. His writing life came to a standstill. Then Bruce Lee signed up with William Morrow as senior editor and

Masters joined him there. By November Morrow had agreed to pay $60,000 for *The Commander*, and Michael Joseph were putting up £12,500 for it.

Curiously, no sooner had they done this than George Rainbird came up with an idea for a 70,000-word personal essay on India, 'on the India you have loved and remembered and how it has changed, contrasting the urban and rural, rich and poor, beautiful and ugly.' £25,000 was on offer for it. Masters thought about it at length before turning it down. As he wrote to Carl Brandt:

> I have been looking carefully into the project as it interests me. I find problems: (1) it would be hard for me to write 70,000 words on India with any coherence. I found it difficult to do much the same to the tune of 5,000 words for an introduction to a picture book earlier this year [this was for *The Glory That Was India*], (2) the text would have no coherence or narrative line and could be no more than random reminiscences or thoughts on India, (3) it would take a lot of research re changes and India is not a restful place for a researcher as I have various forms of heart trouble which should keep me moving peacefully or not at all. So I feel I have to turn it down.

The Commander idea breathed new life into his writing. Slim, on whom it was loosely modelled, was one of his heroes. He was back to writing about India on the North-West Frontier and Spain during the Civil War, and creating fast moving battle scenes that could bring out the full pace of his narrative after the slower-moving trilogy of the First World War. Masters felt he could get inside his main character, something he had not really been able to do in the trilogy. His own 'years of preparation' in India and Burma, when he first tasted real command, were coming into play.

For his new book he needed to know about the Spanish Civil War. His protagonist, Bill Ryder, volunteers to fight on the nationalist side, as a means of getting first-hand experience of modern warfare. Masters had always been fascinated by the Spanish Civil War and frequently discussed it with Spanish friends. He wrote to Hugh Thomas, whose book on the subject he admired, asking for more detailed information. Thomas's book, he wrote, had been much appreciated by Spanish friends, not least because 'it could only have been written by someone young enough not to have lived through the Spanish Civil War, and someone not Spanish, anyone else would still, even at that date, have foundered in angry rhetoric and partisanship.'

Len Deighton was invoked as another source of information, on tank warfare in 1940 as featured in his book *Blitzkrieg*. Deighton wrote back enthusiastically, 'We're all John Masters fans in this house', and helped him as best he could. In thanking him, Masters invited him to stop off in Santa Fe the next time he was visiting the USA.

Bruce Lee was immensely pleased by the first draft of *The Commander*, 'a real, page-turning read. You have done an incredible job. The book has a reality and immediacy to it that will win a large audience.' He was near to being back on his best form. His London agent, Mark Hamilton, called it 'vintage Masters', and it was true – the fighting and battle scenes are as vivid as anything he wrote and the progression of his central character is convincingly done. Autobiographical details inevitably creep in. The senior officer, Morgan Lloyd, who encourages Ryder's abilities and ambition bears a distinct resemblance to Murray-Lyon, who played a similar role for Masters.

Health worries intruded more and more as 1982 went on. His angina and arrhythmia led to repeated shortness of breath. The Wednesday walks became literally an uphill struggle. He could manage 50 yards or so, but then needed to halt and rest. He would wave the others on, unable to stay in the lead as of old. Bill Chudd recalls how he would look up at a hill in front of them and normally he would assess it as 400 or 550 feet, but now he said, 'It's a two nitroglycerine hill.'

Nevertheless Masters kept up his walking schedule with the Chili and Marching Society and was much cared for by them. For the past several years an oxygen tank was carried for him, just in case. Aware of his increasing disability he had offered to resign as its leader, but they would not hear of it. They cosseted him like an old stag nearing his end. In October they had their annual Head Ghillie's Tiffin. 'It went off very well. The chef d'oeuvre was a singing telegram from Fritz and Romona Scholder, in New York, which consisted of a belly dancer and a stooge with a radio; she did about 15 minutes of hoochie-koochie to great applause. We cooked kedgeree for 30 people and everyone drank a lot of beer.' Romona, a young and attractive member of the walking group, had always been wary of joining a sauna session. Masters had never asked her, but she had made up her mind to refuse his invitation. The only trouble was Masters never did ask her! She realised that it was all part of his clever psychology, for the moment he did eventually ask her some two years later, she instantly agreed.

Christmas came and Martin, Sue, recently divorced from her second husband, and her three children came to stay. It was typical Santa Fe weather. 'We have a white Christmas all right, snowing off and on and the temperature rising from 18° in the middle of the night to 30° in the middle of the afternoon.' It was good to have all the family together.

FINAL MONTHS
1983

After Christmas, Masters's mood darkened. He became convinced they had run out of money. He wrote to his brother on 15 January 1983: 'We have suddenly found that we are in a very parlous financial condition; how it turns out depends largely on how much for and how soon we can sell this house, which we are putting on the market. Down the road a couple of years or so things look very black, with no remedy in sight. In the circumstances there is no chance of our being able to visit Europe, or anywhere else; and therefore I have decided to sell the Peugeot. Will you sell it for what you can get?'

It was a bleak statement that had little foundation in fact. Masters's money worries were largely a figment of his imagination, and there was no justification for selling the house. His income from recent books had been lower, especially after the not very successful *By the Green of the Spring*, but he still had a steady flow of royalties from his early Indian novels, now extensively available in paperback. His private income was steady, he was paid $3,000 per month from Bengal-Rockland and his stock market investments totalled well over $200,000. So why the panic? The most likely explanation was a physical one. The effect of angina was causing oxygen starvation in the brain and was producing a form of siege mentality. His controlling, obsessive side had come to the fore. It was working overtime. In his letter to Alex there is a sense of foreboding and he ends it with, 'Let me know if there are any problems with the car. We are in a very worried state, but trying to keep a stiff upper lip.'

Many writers have fallen into this sort of despondency towards the end of their lives. Hemingway, for example, tormented by money worries, drove down to his local bank at night and, seeing the lights on, became convinced they were counting his money in order to take it away. Perhaps the isolation of the writer, working on his own and creating his own world, has something to do with it. The continual effort of moving dead weight across paper, of providing the impetus, can lead to premature exhaustion. In Masters's case the strain had been there all along. He was an intensely driven man who resorted to continuous activity as a means of regulating his energy. His relentless scheduling had been a way of overcoming the fear of standing still, of feeling the burden of his heart's ache, but now his heart was under too much pressure. He had channelled this inner tension outwards and now the pressure was beginning to turn inwards and, like many angina sufferers, he was becoming unusually pessimistic.

He pressed on with the idea of selling the house for some weeks, even suggesting to two close friends of theirs, Bob and Priscilla Bunker, that they should move in with them. Otherwise, he and Barbara would buy a small apartment in Santa Fe and move in there. Barbara did her best to support and not alienate him; she realised he was in an unbalanced state when he started selling some of his most prized possessions, such as his Gurkha trophies and inscribed silver marriage gifts. But, fortunately for her, Santa Fe was a small enough place for these to be located easily and bought back on the quiet. Whenever Masters asked Barbara to sell things for him, she would hide them away instead.

Whatever else, he stuck to his writing, and *The Commander*, later entitled *Man of War*, was still on his desk and needed more work done on it, principally the minor revisions suggested by his English and American editors.

He kept up his Wednesday walking group as much as he could, but it was clear he would have to do something about his health. He hated being unwell. Among the walking group was David Kyger, a young doctor, and Masters consulted him and his own doctor, Dr Streeper, and they both recommended by-pass surgery, feeling he was a good candidate for it. He took them at their word and agreed to have the operation. He wrote to Alex at the end of February: 'This is primarily to let you know that I am going down to hospital in Albuquerque next week on March 1 to have a cardiac catheterization, from which they will decide what sort of obstruction I have in my coronary artery, and what to do about it, probably by-pass surgery. We will keep you informed, though it will take time unless something final happens in the next few days. Both ops are considered pretty safe – 1 in a 100 and 1 in a 1,000, but accidents will happen.' He asked about the Peugeot and whether they had managed to sell it and pay the money in to his Coutts account. 'And let me know of any expenses you personally have incurred on my behalf; and thanks for everything. No more now, as I have lots on my mind'.

Barbara drove Masters to the Presbyterian Hospital in Albuquerque; Susan went with them. He was well enough to walk and check himself into the hospital. The heart operation took place two days later and he seemed to come out of it satisfactorily. He was up out of bed and walking around with a stick, talking and doing his exercises two days afterwards. Susan had stayed on to await the outcome, but seeing him well and seemingly on the road to recovery left for California again.

A few days later the surgical wound started to redden and became infected. This infection took hold and suddenly they were in difficulties. Susan returned and recalls how 'terrible it was for my mother who was staying locally with friends in Albuquerque to go in every day and the medical authorities would tell her some line or other.' They were very guarded in their prognosis. Susan stayed with her mother at a friend's house close to hospital. 'So we just slept there and spent all time at hospital. It was terrible as he was non-responsive. He had about six extra ops. We kept asking the doctors and they said "We'll try this, we'll try that."' Later on his kidneys failed and he went on dialysis, then his gall bladder went gangrenous and had to be taken out, followed by liver biopsies. In the end he was in a deep coma, on dialysis and a lung respirator part of the time. Martin flew out from Los Angeles. 'We decided he wasn't going to come back and was slowly wasting away, so we agreed to turn the kidney machine off, and it took a couple of days. We didn't stay down in Albuquerque as it was too hard.' He died in the early morning of Saturday, 7 May, two months after he had gone into hospital. Susan remembers how the hospital 'called us when he died, I slept with mother that night as we had expected it.'

Martin found the whole episode an appalling and harrowing experience.

> That lingering was terrible, a nightmare. My last memories of him were seeing him on an awful motorised table that he was put on to stop him from getting bedsores. It brought me to my knees. I thought I was prepared for it, could cope with it, but I couldn't. It was not a good way to die, it was terrible. I feel there was negligence of some kind, his heart was in good enough shape as otherwise he wouldn't have lived for so long afterwards, but I didn't want to bring it up at the time as it would have distressed my mother who was upset enough as it was. I felt so empty afterwards and angry. I wanted to say something at the wake but I couldn't as I felt angry, confused, mad and upset.

For Barbara especially it had been an exhausting and emotionally-draining ordeal, not just the terrible and unexpected loss of her husband, but the uncertainty and powerlessness, and the difficulty of getting a clear picture from the doctors of what was going on. Those two months had been a prolonged agony. Friends came and helped, the walking group especially. They took it in turns to come down to Albuquerque and visit Masters's bedside and be with Barbara and the children.

He was cremated without a religious service. Friends gathered at his house to remember him afterwards. His ashes were then scattered, appropriately enough, over the Pecos Wilderness, outside Santa Fe. They were taken up in a plane belonging to their friend, Bill Mauldin, the political cartoonist. Barbara, Sue, Martin and Mike Rose, who had flown over for the funeral, went up in the plane, as did Phil Shultz, representing the walking group. Bill Mauldin joked to Barbara, 'I told you I'd get Jack up in this crate some day.' Masters had previously refused all invitations to fly with him. Phil Shultz recalls looking down out of the plane window at the moment the ashes were scattered and seeing a herd of elk below looking up, a symbolic presence.

Sue stayed on to help her mother. The estate needed sorting out as Masters had always handled most of their financial matters, and Barbara was faced with a mountain of paper work. Sue stayed on longer, and eventually decided to leave California altogether. She and her children lived at first with Barbara while she took a job in real estate. Then she started seeing David Kyger, whom she later married. Barbara decided she did not want to go on living in the big house and put it up for sale but retained a portion of the land to the west of the main house with a favourite view on it, and there she built a smaller house for herself in the traditional adobe style, and a guest house alongside it. Sue and David contemplated buying the big house, but when it was appraised for the estate it was at a level they could not afford. Eventually it was sold for more than $400,000. Masters left his family comfortably off, and the royalties from his books continued to provide a steady income for Barbara.

The news of Masters's death took many of his friends and colleagues by surprise. He was only sixty-eight and few had known of the full extent of his last illness. Many distant friends heard the news on the BBC World Service or from obituaries in English or American newspapers. John Brook wrote a typical obituary in *The Guardian*:

He was quite simply determined to tell the truth about men and war, and, if the critics sneered that his characters were cardboard, they had no idea of the men he had lived, fought and got drunk with. To some, his mountaineering and tiger-hunting image were over the top. Who would believe that Gurkhas' eyes glow red before they kill, that they can run full pelt down a vertical slope, rifles correctly positioned? Or that 10,000 travellers were murdered each year and buried beneath

camp fires on India's roads? But, as he said, he wasn't in the business
of handing out spectacles to blind men.

Letters poured in from friends and literary associates. Carl Brandt
wrote: 'We have all lost a friend, a wonderful friend who gave us a
look at worlds which we never knew were there and of his own
generosity took us into them. In a certain sense he serves as model for
me – for he was a man who did what had to and should be done, but
then grasped life and shook it vigorously for his own delight and
amusement. We will miss him. We will miss the idea of him.' Bruce Lee
wrote: 'Rarely have I experienced working with someone so professional. You always knew the next draft would be better', a reflection
echoed by Alan Brooke from Michael Joseph: 'We have lost an author
of great and lasting distinction but also a man whom I have always
admired and respected enormously – a man of unshakeable loyalty and
integrity, both in his writing and in his relations with people.' Old
friends on South Mountain Road, such as the Andersons and the
Glenns, wrote to Barbara, as did Keith Jennison: 'I have written, or
started to write, about twenty times. The words came out muddy and
trite. But what the hell can I say? For weeks I pretended I hadn't heard
the news. That doesn't work. We were too close for too long. I suppose
what I have settled for is just remembering ALL the great times. I have
an acute enough sense of loss to get a hint of how you feel . . . Take
care of yourself. I don't worry about you. I saw the lioness in you just
as Jack did.' The strength of their relationship was commented on by
many, including Peg Man: 'You were the most wonderful wife to Jack
– no wife could possibly ever have been better. Not only did you help
him in his work, and show great selflessness in falling in with his wishes
over many things, both great and small, but, though he was a strong
character (and often rather demanding!) you gave him the most marvellous loyalty, and the calmness and strength of your own quiet and
resolute character, and I know how much he actually depended upon
you.' For others it was his 'fuzzy hug and kiss, bawdy chuckle, and pat
on the behind' that lingered in the memory.

The walking group were devastated by his loss. As their founding
father, guiding spirit, animator and administrator, he was literally
irreplaceable. 'He taught us to stretch ourselves, to hike longer, climb
higher, go faster than was comfortable or easy. This last year he always
pushed himself harder and quietly withstood greater discomfort than
he ever expected any of us to do, and I am honestly sorry he didn't
have the quick end to his life on the trail, going up a mountain, that he
so very much had earned and deserved. His dying, like a soldier badly

injured in battle, his body unable to heal, gave us all time to reconcile ourselves to the fact of his dying and to try to prepare for his being gone. So even in dying he prepared and supported us', one member wrote.

The Chili and Marching Society did go on, and still does, its leadership alternating. I went on a walk while researching this book in Santa Fe, and caught the flavour of earlier walks, experiencing the exhilarating thrill of being up in the hills above Santa Fe in such a purposeful way. I met many of its members who all testified to Masters's unique presence. Barbara still lives in Santa Fe and her daughter Liz now lives next door in the guest house. Susan is in Oklahoma with David Kyger and their children, Martin is in Los Angeles, and Mike Rose is scaling the heights of the British Army.

The publication of *Man of War* took place posthumously, and was well-received by critics and admirers. It was a fitting climax to Masters's writing career. His appeal to readers was still there as a writer who, initially, in a drab post-war era, had produced books that were exciting, knowledgeable and appealingly risqué. Readers immediately sensed he knew his stuff, describing a far-off world that few of them were ever likely to get to. As his books appeared, they trusted him not to get it wrong, and trusted him, too, to produce strong narratives, laced with the right amount of drama, violence and sex to keep the blood racing. His books had their own unmistakable signature. A reader would silently nod to himself and say, 'Yes, that was how it was.' Once *Nightrunners of Bengal* had appeared, he developed a steady readership on both sides of the Atlantic.

In writing, he aligned himself with Conrad's aim 'to make you hear, to make you feel, to make you see.' He was foremost a chronicler of British India, recording how it felt to both sides, Indians as well as British. In time his contribution may be valued more highly now that the first wave of nostalgia for the days of Empire and the Raj has passed. His books may well stand the test of time for their authenticity and the rounded depiction of British India. *Bugles and a Tiger* and *Bhowani Junction* in particular may well occupy their own corner as unique documents. Indians rate his books highly, more so at times than those of Forster or Paul Scott, for these reasons.

It was an outstanding achievement to write twenty-five books in just over thirty years, keeping up a pace that never slackened. Just as his books were a quest, so it was with his life, with its high water mark being the Independence of India. Each half of his life brought success. In the army he advanced rapidly up the scale and as a writer he quickly gained, and sustained, early fame. Being uprooted from India marked him indelibly but he was determined to do something about it. In the end he refound his roots, and discovered a more than satisfactory replacement for India in the hills of Spain, in Rockland County and in Santa Fe and, above all, in his writing. The sense of belonging that had eluded him in his youth was eventually found.

He treated the world globally, picking landscapes that really meant something to him and finding congenial people to share them with. He was impelled, and relieved, to escape the strictures of post-war Britain. He thrived on that escape. He needed to go to America to make sense of the paradoxes of his life and eventually to shed the taboos of his youth. He was an Englishman who could only feel himself English in the way he wanted to be English by not living in England. In Santa Fe he was the Head Ghillie, in London he wore his Southwestern bolo tie and Navajo jewellery. He had become his own man, and it was America that made him. 'It was America that enabled me to write . . . I lost my self-consciousness there.'

APPENDIX

Sales of Works by John Masters
published by Michael Joseph
(courtesy of Laurence Pollinger Ltd)

1   *Nightrunners of Bengal*   Published 4th June 1951   Advance £332
    Home   20,686
    Export   15,876
                    _____
                    36,562

2   *The Deceivers*   Published 25th August 1952   Advance £200
    Home   17,761
    Export   12,627
                    _____
                    30,388

3   *The Lotus and the Wind*   Published 11th May 1953   Advance £250
    Home   15,499
    Export   10,599
                    _____
                    26,098

4   *Bhowani Junction*   Published 10th May 1954   Advance £3,000
    Home   37,460
    Export   37,743
    Bookclub   235,000
                    _____
                    310,203

5   *Coromandel*   Published 18th April 1955
    Home   19,133
    Export   14,404
                    _____
                    33,537

6   *Bugles and a Tiger*   Published 23rd January 1956
    Sales from 1968   *Estimate from 1956–68*
    Home   1,811   Home   5,500
    Export   528   Export   4,500
                 _____   _____
                 2,339   10,000

7 *Far, Far the Mountain Peak* Published 20th May 1957
   Sales from 1964   *Estimate from 1957–63*
   Home   5,154   Home   13,500
   Export   741   Export   12,500

                     5,895   26,000

8 *Fandango Rock* Published 15th June 1959
   Sales from 1969   *Estimate from 1959–68*
   Home   2,856   Home   7,500
   Export   345   Export   6,500

                     3,201   14,000

9 *The Venus of Konpara* Published 26th September 1960
   Home   19,037
   Export   14,709

                    33,746

10 *Road Past Mandalay* Published 4th September 1961
   Home   29,281
   Export   19,799

                    49,080

11 *To The Coral Strand* Published 12th November 1962
   Home   20,908
   Export   12,332

                    33,240

12 *Trial at Monomoy* Published 2nd October 1964   Advance £2,000
   Home   13,790
   Export   8,038

                    21,828

13 *Fourteen Eighteen* Published 30th September 1965   Advance £2,000
   Home   4,306
   Export   3,513

                     7,819

14 *The Breaking Strain* Published 2nd October 1967   Advance £2,000
   Home   11,367
   Export   5,211

                    16,578

15 *The Rock* Published 18th May 1970   Advance £2,500
   Home   5,888
   Export   2,374

                     8,262

16   *Pilgrim Son*   Published 17th May 1971   Advance £2,500
     Home   4,010
     Export   1,260

                         5,270

17   *The Ravi Lancers*   Published 4th September 1972   Advance £2,500
     Home   12,516
     Export   2,871

                         15,387

18   *Thunder at Sunset*   Published 20th May 1974   Advance £2,500
     Home   9,020
     Export   4,619

                        13,639

19   *The Field Marshal's Memoirs*   Published 27th May 1975   Advance £3,500
     Home   7,471
     Export   2,563

                        10,034

NOTES

ABBREVIATIONS

JM – this covers papers relating to John Masters in the possession of Barbara Masters and Alex Masters, and includes nearly all the family letters between 1937 and 1983 that are quoted here. John Masters lived abroad from England during most of that time and was an assiduous letter writer, both to his parents and to his brother Alex, and, after the latter's marriage in 1947, to Alex and his wife Joan. He wrote as frequently to publishers, agents and friends, keeping them informed of his movements and progress as an author. Barbara Masters also let me see the 'History of the Masters Family' written by Alexander Masters in 1903, as well as John Masters's 'logs' of foreign trips, walking expeditions and so on (from Garhwal 1945 to the end of 1982). These logs, some thirty-five in all, cover nearly two thousand handwritten pages. I also looked through the two volumes of Chili and Marching Society Logs and Bulletins between 1970 and 1982, some of which have also been quoted in the text. When letters and interviews are referred to and are not followed by (JM), they were to and with me.

BU – John Masters's papers at the time of his death, mainly connected with his First World War trilogy, *Loss of Eden*, were given as a gift by Barbara Masters to the Department of Special Collections, Mugar Memorial Library, Boston University
LP – Correspondence between John Masters and Laurence Pollinger 1952–1982
MJ – Correspondence from the archives of Michael Joseph
NL – Newsletters issued annually by the 4th P. W. O. Gurkha Rifles Officers' Association
SB – Scrapbook kept by John Masters since 1934, containing personal documents relating to his army career and life as an author
VP – Correspondence between John Masters and his editors at Viking, Keith Jennison and Helen Taylor, 1949–1959, now lodged in the archives of Viking Penguin, New York

John Masters wrote three volumes of autobiography which are here abbreviated as follows (page references to these and his other books refer to the English edition unless otherwise stated):
BT – *Bugles and a Tiger* (1956)
RPM – *Road Past Mandalay* (1961)
PS – *Pilgrim Son* (1971)

1 *Family Origins*

1   To be Anglo-Indian: for the history of the Anglo-Indian community and their place in British India, my main sources of information have been: Frank Anthony, *Britain's Betrayal in India, The Story of the Anglo-Indian Community* (Bombay, Allied Publishers, 1969); V. R. Gaikwad, *The Anglo-Indians* (London, Asia Publishing House, 1967); Geoffrey Moorhouse, *India Britannica* (London, Harvill Press, 1983); Herbert Stark, *Hostages to India* (Calcutta, Star Printing Works, 1936).

2   The Masters family's connection with India: 'A History of the Masters Family' by Alexander Masters, 34th Sikh Pioneers, Ambala, Punjab, India, August 1903 (JM). Most of the information about the Masters family through the nineteenth century comes from this.

2   Eurasian (as Anglo-Indians were then called): the term Anglo-Indian came into official use in 1911 to accord with the census drawn up that year. Previous appellations had included Eurasian, East-Indian, Indo-Briton and the more colloquial but pejorative 'country-born'. From 1911 Anglo-Indian predominated, though Domiciled European is also used (for a fuller discussion of this see Anthony, Chapter 1, Who is Anglo-Indian?).

3   For the early years of the British in India and the influence of the East India Company, see Edward Thompson and G. T. Garratt, *Rise and Fulfilment of British Rule in India* (London, Macmillan, 1934).

4   'The education imparted': Austin D'Souza, *Anglo-Indian Education, a Study of its Origins and Growth in Bengal up to 1960* (Bombay, Oxford University Press, 1976), 89.

6   William Steuart had gone out: the following letters (pages 6–7) are taken from the Charles Steuart papers (MSS 5040–1) in the Department of Manuscripts, National Library of Scotland, Edinburgh.

8   The 'University Graduate': letter from Don Alney, Principal of La Martiniere School for Boys, Calcutta, 19 February 1988.

8   Memsahibs needed to maintain a sense of superiority: the best account of this I have found is Kenneth Ballhatchet, *Race, Sex and Class under the Raj*, Chapter 4, On the margins of social distance (London, Weidenfeld and Nicolson, 1980).

9   'Or have we some strange': Shakespeare, *Henry VIII*, Act V, Scene iv.

12 'I didn't comment': letter to Alex Masters, 17 August 1962 (JM).

12 'the genuine counterjumper': the 'University Graduate' who succeeded William Masters at La Martiniere.

13 'takorari': troublesome or contentious, see Rev. Thomas Craven, *Hindustani Dictionary* (Lucknow, Methodist Publishing House, 1911).

13 'Jim Corbett, or the Skinners': Jim Corbett (1875–1955) was a big game hunter and author of *Man-Eaters of Kumaon* (Bombay, Oxford University Press, 1946). His family had lived in India for generations. Corbett National Park in Uttar Pradesh is named after him. James Skinner (1788–1841) was the son of a Scottish soldier and a Rajputani woman. He was famous for founding Skinner's Horse in 1809 – often known as the Yellow Boys from the colour of their uniform – the senior regiment of Indian Cavalry at the time of Independence. Skinner, revered in his lifetime for his panache and bravery, was known as 'old Sikandar', a corruption of Alexander the Great. He built both a mosque and the church of St James in Delhi. For a more detailed account of his life and problematic relationship with the British, see Anthony, 24–29. Other prominent Anglo-Indians have included Sir Eyre Coote, Commander-in-Chief after Clive, who married the Eurasian daughter of Job Charnock, founder of Calcutta, General Sir John Hearsey, a key figure at the time of the Mutiny, Field Marshal Lord Roberts, hero of the 1879 campaign from Kabul to Kandahar, Lord Liverpool, Tory Prime Minister for fifteen years (1812–1827) and Elihu Yale, founder of Yale University, formerly Governor of Madras, who married a woman of mixed blood and had three children by her.

2 *India 1914–1919*

14 Fort William: see Jan Morris, with Simon Winchester, *Stones of Empire* (Oxford University Press, 1983).

14 His baptism is recorded in *Bengal Baptisms*, vol 402, folio 136 (1915) at the India Office Library. His father's regimental movements are from Indian Army List at same.

14 'I travelled about India': this comes from a summary of Masters's life that he wrote for his step-grandson, Edward Rose, in April 1982. Edward was writing a mini-biography of him as a school project.

15 For a description of the role of ayahs, see Charles Allen, *Plain Tales of the Raj* (London, André Deutsch, 1975), 23 (this and other page references are from the 1983 paperback Futura edition).

16 the dreaded chee chee: both a manner of speech and a pejorative term for Anglo-Indians. The invaluable *Hobson-Jobson*, written by Yule and Burnell in 1886, defines chee-chee as 'a disparaging term applied to half-castes or Eurasians and also to their manner of speech. The word is said to be taken from chi (Fie!) a common native (South Indian) interjection of remonstration or reproof, supposed to be much used by the class in question. The term is, however, perhaps also a kind of onomatopoeia, indicating the mincing pronunciation which often characterises them. It should be added, however, that there are many well-educated East-Indians who are quite free from this mincing accent.' Colonel Henry Yule and Arthur Coke Burnell, *Hobson-Jobson, being a Glossary of Anglo-Indian Colloquial Words and Phrases, and of Kindred Terms.* Geoffrey Moorhouse adds other terms such as kutcha butcha (i.e. half-baked bread – fully baked being pukka). Masters lists some other terms in *Bhowani Junction*, 13, when Patrick Taylor says, 'we didn't look like English people. We looked like what we were – Anglo-Indians, Eurasians, chee-chees, half-castes, eight-annas, blacky-whites.' Such derogatory nomenclature forced Anglo-Indians to be excessively concerned about their appearance, and led to the prolific use of skin-lightening creams.

16 'to roam at will': Michael Edwardes, *The Sahibs and the Lotus* (London, Constable, 1988).

16 'My Hindustani': PS, 376.

3 *England 1920–1927*

19 'It was hard to have someone foisted on you': interview with Major-General Cyril Edge, June 1987.

19 'All through the time': Allen, 36.

19 'Separation made us immensely': *ibid*, 35.

20 'prep school was long corridors': PS, 376.

20 'closed compartments': *Bhowani Junction*, 274.

20 The Waight family: interview with Edwin Waight, May 1987.

22 'Jackie and Alex, get away': interview with Alex Masters, May 1987.

4 *Wellington 1928–1932*

23 Wellington was, and still is: for the history of Wellington, I have consulted Dr David Newsome, *History of Wellington College* (London, John Murray, 1959),

and for Masters's stay there, Colonel David Fladgate, Secretary of Old Wellingtonian Society, and Dr Heather Tomlinson, College Archivist.

23 A contemporary of Masters remembers: I am most grateful to the following contemporaries for their reminiscences of both Masters and Wellington: Major-General R. Burges, Lieutenant-Colonel E. Edlmann, Lieutenant-Colonel F. Edmeades, Theo Hetherington, Dr William McKean, Major Ainslie Miller, Dr Michael O'Flynn, Richard Peel, J. R. Strachan, Lieutenant-Colonel Patrick Turner, Lieutenant-Colonel Desmond Wakely.

24 Wellington was 'in every possible way': T. C. Worsley, *A Flannelled Fool* (London, Alan Ross, 1967).

24 'I arrived on a winter evening': PS, 377.

25 'The boy who came a term': Giles and Esmond Romilly, *Out of Bounds* (London, Hamish Hamilton, 1935). Esmond, later killed in the Spanish Civil War, inserted a pacifist leaflet in hymn books at Wellington on Remembrance Day 1933.

25 'Jack and I paired off': letter from Dr William McKean, June 1987.

26 'There were some very good English masters': Edward Rose, school project.

27 The head of the English department: R. StC. Talboys, *A Victorian School, being the Story of Wellington College* (Oxford, Basil Blackwell, 1943).

27 'diminished and disparaged element': Worsley.

29 'in the costume which they all seemed to affect': Talboys, 41.

30 Michaelmas Report (SB).

30 'It was always autumn at Wellington': PS, 377.

32 'Baa Baa Black Sheep' in Rudyard Kipling, *Wee Willie Winkie* (London, Macmillan, 1890).

5 *Sandhurst 1933–1934*

33 'After we had taken my bags': BT, 36.

34 'smell-of-a-cork Masters': PS, 376.

35 'It's no laughing matter, Mr Masters': BT, 46. For a general history of Sandhurst I have used Hugh Thomas, *The Story of Sandhurst* (London, Hutchinson, 1961) (in his introduction he refers to Masters as the 'Balzac of India'), and Alan Shepperd, *Sandhurst* (London, Country Life Books, 1980); for details of Masters's stay there I am indebted to A. M. Orgill, Senior Librarian, RMA Sandhurst (letter, 9 May 1988).

35 'In 1933 I disliked': BT, 40.

36 David Niven, *The Moon's a Balloon* (London, Hamish Hamilton, 1971).

36 'I gritted my teeth': BT, 51.

36 'I had already survived': BT, 51.

37 'had been kind enough': BT, 57.

38 In later years a libel action was threatened by Sergeant-Major Giddings after Masters retold this tale in Lilliput in the early 1950s, i.e. before Masters wrote *Bugles and a Tiger*.

39 'Officers wobbled': BT, 68.

6 *India 1934–1938*

44 'No one ever found out': BT, 209.

45 'as craggy as the country': Philip Mason, 'Foreword' in Charles Chevenix-Trench, *The Frontier Scouts* (London, Jonathan Cape, 1985), viii.

45 'No man who has read a page': Lord Curzon in a speech on receiving the Freedom of the City of London, 20 July 1906.

45 'I unlearned my Sandhurst drill': BT, 26.

46 'There was always excitement': interview with Colonel David Davidson, July 1987.

47 'an ambitious person': interview with Brigadier H. C. Pulley, June 1987.

47 'Oh ecstasy! – hard fingers': BT, 23.

48 'floundering about, like a blind puppy': BT, 20.

48 'My code has never been quite the same': BT, 30.

50 'erratic brilliance': BT, 76.

50 'bit of a know-all': interview with Major Robin Hodson, May 1988.

52 'In the one year, I grew up ten': PS, 378.

52 'One day my name will be on one of these': this and the following quotations about his life at Bakloh come, unless otherwise stated, from *Bugles and a Tiger*, Chapter 3 onwards.

53 Gurkhas occupied a special position: details about the Gurkhas and their history have come from Colonel J. M. Macaulay DSO, *History of the 4th Prince of Wales's Own Gurkha Rifles*, Vol III, 1938–1948 (London, William Blackwood, 1952), and Vols I and II by Ranald Macdonell and Marcus Macaulay; David Bolt, *Gurkhas* (London, Weidenfeld and Nicolson, 1967); Lieutenant-General Sir Francis Tuker, *Gorkha* (London, Constable, 1957); Sandro Tucci, *Gurkhas* (London, Hamish Hamilton, 1985); H. D. James and D. Sheil-Small, *The Gurkhas* (London, Macdonald, 1965); plus interviews conducted in India in April 1988 with Brigadier Raj Bir Chopra, Major-General G. S. Nagra, Lieutenant-General Moti Sagar, all past members of the 4th Gurkhas, and visits to Bakloh and Subathu 4th Gurkha Museum.

58 'the appalling sweep': Rudyard Kipling, *Kim*, quoted in BT, 144.

59 Masters cites: BT, 150.

60 'drowsy repletion': BT, 248.

61 'looked neither to left nor right': BT, 177.

61 'I didn't have to live': BT, 178.

62 'If you got captured': Frank Baines, *Officer Boy* (London, Eyre and Spottiswoode, 1971), 145. Baines was the son of Sir Frank Baines KCVO, but opted for a bohemian life. Having fought on the North-West Frontier and with the Chindits, he then became a monk in a Hindu monastery for three years before running a tea-chest repairing business in Calcutta and writing a daily newspaper column entitled 'Mirror, Mirror'. His autobiography, *Look Towards the Sea*, was written in 1958, while he was working as a navvy digging holes on number 1 platform in Victoria Station.

64 The Pathans adhered: for information on the Pathans, see Philip Mason, 'Foreword' in Chevenix-Trench, *The Frontier Scouts*; Sir Olaf Caroe, *The Pathans 550 BC – AD 1957* (London, Macmillan, 1958); James W. Spain, *The Pathan Borderland* (The Hague, Mouton & Co, 1963); and Peter Mayne, *The Narrow Smile* (London, John Murray, 1955).

64 'these fierce men': BT, 212.

65 send the British political agent: for background material on the North-West Frontier, see Chevenix-Trench, *The Frontier Scouts*; Philip Mason, *A Matter of Honour, An Account of the Indian Army, its Officers and Men* (London, Jonathan Cape, 1974); Michael Barthorp, *The North-West Frontier* (Dorset, Blandford Press, 1982); Lieutenant-Colonel C. E. Bruce, *Waziristan 1936–1937* (Aldershot,

Gale and Polden, 1937); Sir William Barton, *India's North-West Frontier* (London, John Murray, 1939); Major-General J. G. Elliott, *The Frontier 1839–1947* (London, Cassell, 1968); Charles Miller, *Khyber* (London, Macdonald and Jane's, 1977); Victoria Schofield, *Every Rock, Every Hill, The Plain Tale of the North-West Frontier and Afghanistan* (Buchan and Enright, 1984).

65 'Scouts on the move': BT, 204.
66 'the station of a dream': *Collected Letters of T. E. Lawrence*, ed David Garnett (London, Jonathan Cape, 1928), 614–615.
66 'All this happened': BT, 25, echoing Kipling's lines, 'Two thousand pounds of education/Drops to a ten-rupee jezail'.
68 'fast and furiously': interview with Colonel John Strickland, July 1988, who also gave me much information about Bakloh and 4th Gurkha life.
68 'I was in Tocol's': letter to Alex Masters, 6 June 1937 (JM).
68 'We were sniped at': *ibid.*
69 Masters mentions this: BT, 262.
69 'attain a physical release': *Far, Far the Mountain Peak*, 92.
70 'Inside me my spirit sang': BT, 266.
71 The tiger skin used to hang in the mess at Bakloh but now has pride of place in the dining room at Subathu Gurkha Training Centre.
73 an Indian officer . . . might never: interview with Major-General M. K. Palit, April 1988.
73 'To read any political account': Mason, *A Matter of Honour*, 444.
74 'they seemed set': BT, 287.

USA 1938–1939

75 'most attractive': interview with Norah Collins, October 1988.
75 'nothing was missing': BT, 287.
76 'simultaneously as wild': BT, 291.
76 'Honolulu is a hell of a place': letter to Alex Masters, 18 December 1938 (JM).
76 'For four days': *ibid.*
77 'Jack's arrival': letter from Alice Mathews (then Westfeldt), June 1987.
78 'I loved New Orleans': letter to Alex Masters, 13 January 1939 (JM).
79 'I had suddenly fallen in love': BT, 298.

India and Quetta 1940–1942

82 Loralai week: interview with Lieutenant-Colonel Paddy Massey, March 1991.
83 'tremendous zest for living': letter from Val Roberts (now Lebern), 19 February 1988.
84 'Nothing ever had to be said twice': BT, 330.
84 'Weallens kept persecuting me': letter to Alex Masters, 16 September 1951 (JM).
85 'and it was all a game': RPM, 24.
85 'like firemen trying': RPM, 25.
85 their marching orders – to Iraq: see Charles Chevenix-Trench, *The Indian Army* (London, Thames and Hudson, 1988), 158.
86 'There, standing in an open field': RPM, 57.

87   'I shall be sorry to lose you': R PM, 69.
87   'She nodded pleasantly': R PM, 77.
89   'Goff had to work hard': interview with Mollie Kaye, February 1987.
90   'it was electric': R PM, 84.
91   'From all over India': *ibid.*
91   'One of the women in the party': R PM, 100.
91   other contenders: interview with Barbara Masters, April 1987.
93   'his wife must have vision': *Far, Far the Mountain Peak*, 91.
94   'Soldiering was all': R PM, 104.
94   'under heavy shadows': R PM, 107.
95   Quetta Report (S B).
96   'I had been too long away': R PM, 111.
96   'My father grew': letter from Val Roberts.
97   'Don't you understand': R PM, 112.
98   'The Kaghan valley': Dervla Murphy, *Full Tilt* (London, John Murray, 1965)
      201.
98   Masters waxes lyrical: R PM, 118–125.
99   'The tent, the cooking fire': V. S. Naipaul, *Among the Believers* (London, Andr
      Deutsch, 1970), 173.
99   'My life, my love': R PM, 124.

9   *Chindits and Burma 1943–1945*

103   The Chindit idea: sources I have consulted include: Louis Allen, *Burma, The Longes
      War 1941–45* (London, J. M. Dent, 1984); Shelford Bidwell, *The Chindit Wa*
      (London, Hodder and Stoughton, 1979); Raymond Callahan, *Burma 1942–194*
      (London, Davis-Poynter, 1978); Michael Calvert, *Prisoners of Hope* (London
      Jonathan Cape, 1971) and *Chindits – Long Range Penetration* (London, Pan
      Ballantine, 1973); Richard Rhodes-James, *Chindit* (London, John Murray, 1980)
      Sir William Slim, *Defeat into Victory* (London, Cassell, 1956); Christopher Sykes
      Orde Wingate (London, Collins, 1959); plus interviews with Tim Brennan
      Shelford Bidwell, Michael Calvert, Alec Harper, Desmond Whyte and others
      and letters from A. Bass, D. Foxall, C. Hard, F. G. Holliday, Brigadier P. Mead
      J. Wilkinson and others.
107   'I saw a young nubile girl's': R PM, 143.
107   'You're going to die': R PM, 146.
108   'Jack welcomed me': interview with Michael Calvert, March 1989.
108   'My reception was inevitably chilly': Bernard Fergusson, 'Magnificently at War
      Daily Telegraph, September 1961, book review of R PM.
109   'They got absolutely tight': interview with Mollie Kaye.
109   'He was one of the most extraordinary': interview with Richard Rhodes-James
      March 1988.
113   'That's Brigade HQ': R PM, 196.
114   Wingate's death remains a mystery. Allen, 344, cites as the likely cause 'a frea
      storm, as it looks as though the plane suddenly decided to turn back to Imphal'.
115   'limey-hater': *The Stilwell Papers*, ed. Theodore White (London, Macdonalc
      1949), 267, 'what a mess the limeys can produce in short order', and 29(
      'Glamour Boy'. Masters's own view of Stilwell was given on R PM, 155: 'a
      unmitigated disaster for inter-allied relations.'

15 The Chindit cause wilted: Slim's reaction to Wingate's death was characteristic: 'Without his presence to animate it, Special Force would no longer be the same to others or to itself. He had created, inspired, defended it, and given it confidence; it was the offspring of his vivid imagination and ruthless energy. It had no other parent. Now it was orphaned.' Ronald Lewin, *Slim* (London, Leo Cooper, 1976), 183.

16 'a highly trained staff officer': interview with Tim Brennan, January 1987.

17 'When we received orders': Dr Desmond Whyte, 'A Trying Chindit', *British Medical Journal*, 18 December 1982.

18 'I shall not forget': RPM, 235.

19 'My men were being worked': RPM, 243.

19 'complete confidence': RPM, 243.

20 'a rather gaunt looking': letter from F. G. Holliday, June 1989.

20 The pilot, Jack Gallagher: letter from Bob Moist, 1st Air Commando Association, Broderick, California, November 1988.

21 'Having failed to eject': Rhodes-James, *Chindit*, 142.

21 'the first man': RPM, 258.

22 'At about noon': RPM, 260.

23 Meeting with Upjohn: in a letter Masters wrote to Shelford Bidwell on 16 December 1977, he stated: 'the first I really knew of 6 NR's whereabouts was a signal to them repeated to us, after we had left Blackpool, ordering them to move towards us and gather the remnants. I sent a rude signal to Joe [Lentaigne] saying we were not remnants but in a cohesive unit, under my command; and that I did not intend to hand over to anyone unless relieved. I knew Gordon Upjohn at the RMC and he was very helpful when we met near the pass between Blackpool and Mokso; I asked him to act as rearguard and hold the pass for sure, which we did.' (BU).

24 'He was given an impossible task': Rhodes-James interview.

24 Bidwell, 229–230.

25 Allen, 358.

25 'sitting stripped': Bidwell, 230.

26 'blur of cloud': RPM, 269.

26 'we were falling against': RPM, 276.

26 Mogaung: for the American angle, see Charlton Ogburn, *Merrill's Marauders* (London, Hodder and Stoughton, 1960). Calvert's 77 Brigade actually captured Mogaung but Stilwell's public relations staff put it out that the Chinese had done so. When Calvert heard this, he signalled back: 'The Chinese having taken Mogaung, 77 Brigade is proceeding to take Umbrage.' Legend has it that Stilwell's staff started earnestly looking for this new map reference.

26 'All the men sleepwalking': *ibid*.

28 Post-war evidence: see Allen.

33 'Those six hours were the summit': RPM, 304.

34 'from the smell of death': RPM, 309.

34 'I drive cars that way': interview with Barbara Masters.

35 'The fact that': Slim, 468.

35 'I stood back': RPM, 311.

37 Divorce documents (SB). Attitudes towards officers resigning their commission may have been modified by Auchinleck's own marriage breaking up that same year when his wife went off with Air Chief Marshal Sir Richard Peirse.

38 'This mattered': RPM, 322.

138   Churchill 1937, from letter to Lord Linlithgow, Viceroy of India, 3 November 1937 (see Martin Gilbert, *Winston Churchill V* (London, 1976), 886). Masters felt that Churchill neither understood nor liked India.

139   'This was the life': RPM, 324.

139   'in scenery and climate': Frank Smythe, *Kamet Conquered* (London, Victor Gollancz, 1932).

140   'Willy Weallens walking': RPM, 328.

141   Pete Rees wrote: letter from Rees 5 August 1945 (SB).

141   Log, Garhwal 45.

10   *Delhi 1945–1946*

142   'too enthusiastic': letter to Alex Masters, 29 September 1945 (JM).

142   'bald, burly': PS, 22.

143   under Auchinleck: for an inside view of this period, see Major-General Shahid Hamid, *Disastrous Twilight* (London, Leo Cooper, 1986). Hamid was Private Secretary to Auchinleck 1946–1947.

143   'Having my papers': PS, 22.

143   As Independence loomed: for events leading up to Independence, see Michael Edwardes, *The Last Years in British India* (London, Cassell, 1963); Leonard Mosley, *The Last Days of the British Raj* (London, Weidenfeld and Nicolson, 1961); B. N. Pandey, *The Break-Up of British India* (London, Macmillan, 1969); Trevor Royle, *The Last Days of the Raj* (London, Michael Joseph, 1989); Wilfrid Russell, *Indian Summer* (Bombay, Thacker and Co, 1951); C. H. Philips and Mary Doreen Wainwright, *The Partition of India* (London, George Allen and Unwin, 1970).

144   Masters's own view: PS, 34.

144   Annual Report for 1946 by McLeod (SB).

146   'We were simply pressing': PS, 30.

146   'I was backed off': letter to Alex Masters, 25 April 1946 (JM).

146   'Sunday lunches': PS, 30.

147   Philip Mason: interview, February 1988.

149   'I got the message': PS, 40.

11   *England 1947–1948*

150   'strangers in a foreign land': PS, 52. In a later interview (18 May 1979) with F. A. de Caro and Rosan Jordan at Santa Fe, Masters had this to say: 'I went back to England in 1946 to do teaching at Staff College. I didn't know it was going to be my last job. No plans had been made for India yet. But I did look forward to being back in the England I'd known as a boy, grown up in and loved, but as a man I found it quite stifling, quite mentally enclosing. I was feeling a closing-in of ideas. A sense I wasn't free to think whatever thoughts I wanted to think. This is partly the fact of being who I am. As long as I stayed in England I was entrapped. I was in a certain pattern. I needed to break away. Coming to America made me see England through different eyes. Eyes that saw it rather than lived it.'

150   'After the geographical space and freedom of India': PS, 53.

151 Chindit Reunion menu (SB).
153 'I was cut adrift from my past': PS, 59.
154 'how could Aldershot': PS, 54.
154 bond between them was very close: in the de Caro/Jordan interview, Masters adds: 'That is the tradition of the Indian Army to get very involved. You get drunk with the men and they carry you back to bed. British Army officers to some extent and certainly American officers are always amazed at the contrast between the iron discipline of the Indian Army and the extreme freedom in other ways. But the reason, as Philip Mason points out, is that there was such an enormous, inherent gap between a British officer and a raw recruit, an Indian recruit – the one could never become the other in the early days – that you could let your hair down far more because there was no possible chance of the guy taking advantage of you, and certainly they never did. You're not expected to marry before you are about thirty because you have to devote those ten years to playing football with the men, going out shooting and taking them with you hunting, snipe shooting, checking the Himalayas, whatever. At night when we'd finish – not every night, but twice a week – I'd go up to the lines and have a rum in the canteen with the soldiers, or Gurkha officers would take us to their mess and we'd sit around and drink rum and eat little pakoras, curried meat patty things, and quite frequently I'd finish up getting pretty soused, but we had to be on parade the next morning. We might have been falling down dead drunk the night before and singing indecent Gurkha songs with the Gurkha officers but my subadar would greet me with no trace of a smile on his face and salute and report the parade state, the whole thing cut off.'
154 'It sounds as if': letter to Alec Harper, 1 March 1952 (JM).
155 'If they don't want the 4th': PS, 56.
156 'warm-hearted vulgarity': *The Notebooks of Raymond Chandler* (New York, Ecco Press, 1976), 19.
156 'because each of them has a blues': interview with Lieutenant-Colonel R. N. D. Williams, June 1991.
157 'To live as a family unit': PS, 62.
157 'the idea of launching my family': PS, 60.
157 'If I stay': interview with Alex Masters, May 1987.
158 'most intelligent officer': report by Lambert (SB).

12   *USA 1948–1952*

161 'Life alternates': letter to his parents, 29 February 1948 (JM).
162 'walking along the edge': PS, 97.
162 Lardner suggested: letter from Rex Lardner, son of Ring Lardner, 18 May 1990.
162 'Lardner was a good host': 'In Spite of Gollancz', *Books and Bookmen*, March 1964, 12.
163 'We enter an India': 'Through the Films Darkly', *Atlantic Monthly*, September 1948.
163 '*The New Yorker*'s loss': letter from Jacques Chambrun to John Masters, April 1948 (SB).
165 'As long as I remained': PS, 104.
165 'I had dealt': *Books and Bookmen*, 13.
166 'At that point I sat down': *Sunday Times* interview with Gavin Lyall, 14 January 1962.

167 'there is no introspection': Angus Wilson, *The Strange Ride of Rudyard Kipling* (London, Secker and Warburg, 1977).

167 Masters hadn't particularly liked the book: 'I have a very low tolerance for yoga and yogis and transubstantiation and meditation and anything like that, especially when people associate a higher spirituality with it, if only because it's not American or English. They chant, the Indians, holy as hell, but we're not. And there are all kinds of secrets that they know that our people don't know in a spiritual sense.' (de Caro/Jordan interview.)

171 'the goddamnest interview I ever had': interview with Keith and Emily Jennison, August 1988.

171 'I would have preferred': *Books and Bookmen*, 15.

172 'the physical and psychological hinge': PS, 142.

172 'My approach to writing': *Contemporary Authors*, Vol 110, 336.

172 'like men in an upstairs room': Foreword to US edition of *Nightrunners of Bengal* (New York, Viking, 1951), viii.

173 'an English girl had no business': *Nightrunners of Bengal* (London, Michael Joseph, 1951), 16.

173 'If you want': *ibid.*, 30.

173 'I killed my husband': *ibid.*, 263.

173 'the rebellion will go on': *ibid.*, 371.

173 'The Company is not going to lose India': *ibid.*, 323.

174 'inherent melancholy of power': Foreword, viii.

174 'The chains could have': *ibid.*, vii.

174 'for most of us': *Nightrunners of Bengal*, 31.

175 'of dyspeptic mien': *Books and Bookmen*, 16.

176 'Life continues to be hazardous': letter to Alex and Joan Masters, 25 November 1948 (JM).

176 'essential guts': PS, 148.

176 'at night I could hear': PS, 148.

177 'crisp crack and crash': PS, 133.

177 'When Jack went cold on you': interview with Keith Jennison.

177 'You know when we first met': PS, 154.

179 Dr John B. Watson, *Psychological Care of Infant and Child*, 1928.

179 'the solitary confrontation': PS, 166. Two hundred thousand TV sets were sold every month in the United States between 1948 and 1950. In 1950 seven million sets were sold as a result of the Korean War and the McCarthy hearings.

180 For a biography of Major-General Sir William Sleeman, 1788–1856, see Sir Francis Tuker, *The Yellow Scarf* (London, J. M. Dent, 1961), or read Sleeman's own *Rambles and Recollections of an Indian Officer* (London, Hatchard, 1844), or for his account of Thug vocabulary and rituals, *Ramaseeana* (Calcutta, Military Orphan Press, 1836).

180 Masters planned for him to disguise himself: a precedent was that of the Anglo-Indian Bombay Police Commissioner, Charles Forjett, who sat disguised for many nights at the time of the Mutiny in 1857 with conspiring Sepoys of the Bombay Native Infantry Regiments and thereby forestalled an uprising in Bombay. Masters himself had used disguise as a Burmese to recce the site of Blackpool.

181 Captain Philip Meadows Taylor, *Confessions of a Thug* (London, Richard Bentley, 1839). Taylor himself had been involved with the suppression of the Thugs in India, and the Introduction to his book gives a valuable account of the history of the Thugs.

181   'It was the only time she broke down': PS, 175.
182   'a complete series of readings': PS, 176.
182   'Finished your manuscript': letter, 19 October 1949 (SB).
182   adopted Fabian tactics: interview with Keith Jennison.
184   'Before you blow': Helen Taylor to John Masters, 6 February 1950 (VP). The following exchanges of letters from February 1950 onwards between Masters and Helen Taylor and Keith Jennison at Viking are all taken from the archives of Viking Penguin, New York.
186   'Jack seems to be able': Barbara Masters to Masters's parents, 25 June 1950 (JM).
186   'We explored the White Mountains': PS, 203.
186   'The transformation which we knew': PS, 199.
188   'the mystique cutting across': PS, 202.
188   'as a present': see Robert Lusty, *Bound to be Read* (London, Jonathan Cape, 1985), 142, and *At the Sign of the Mermaid* (London, Michael Joseph, 1986), 59.
189   'Nanny was mad as a hatter': letter to Alex Masters, 15 November 1950 (JM).
189   'More and more I feel': letter to his parents, 3 December 1950 (JM).
190   Orville Prescott, *New York Times* Book Section, 19 January 1951.
190   The sales figures: *Nightrunners* sold over 300,000 in its first eighteen months. For overall UK sales figures and advances on Masters's books by Michael Joseph see Appendix.
191   'H'm, no date': letter to Alex Masters, 8 February 1951 (JM).
193   'A good, a very good place': PS, 216.
193   'What haunts a foreigner': Alastair Reid, *Whereabouts, Notes on being a Foreigner* (Edinburgh, Canongate, 1987), 18.
193   'We spend a good part': *ibid.*, 30.
195   'Subject: – Writing Plans': letter to Keith Jennison, 10 July 1951 (JM).
197   Christopher Sykes, *Orde Wingate*.
197   The Great Game: for an up-to-date book, see Peter Hopkirk, *The Great Game* (London, John Murray, 1990).
198   'for what I don't know': PS, 227.
198   'I had set up a target': PS, 227.
199   'I want something': *The Lotus and the Wind*, 218.
199   'that every human quality': *ibid*, 219.
199   'The exhaust beat': PS, 230.
199   'the writing business prospers': letter to Alex Masters, 16 September 1951 (JM).
200   'What worried me': *ibid*.
200   'Jack was the great man': interview with Alex Masters, May 1987.
201   'We settled back': PS, 231.
201   'We had not come': PS, 232.
202   'Our experiment in Connecticut': PS, 234.
202   'We find the couldn't-care-less attitude': PS, 242.
203   'very reasonable, not dear at all': PS, 245.
203   'in his old-fashioned suit': PS, 246.
203   'nasty ship': PS, 246.
204   'England, their England': PS, 250.
204   For their arrival and much information about their time in Spain I am indebted to Julio Nogues and Antonio Lacoma, interviewed in August 1987.
205   'Everything felt vaguely familiar': PS, 256.
205   'the two countries': PS, 261.
206   'females in tight-bottom skirts': Log, Spain 1952 (JM).

206 'The central figure': C. P. Snow in *The Sunday Times*.
207 'the marriage between his hero': Marghanita Laski, *Observer*, August 1952.
207 'I seem to be in danger': letter to Alex Masters, 9 November 1952 (JM).
208 skipping off across the Atlantic: other writers' reputations suffered similarly for living abroad, Auden and Isherwood, for example, and later even Graham Greene.
208 'She came down': interview with Liz Rose, April 1987.
209 'She swims at ninety-one': *Sunday Graphic*, 9 July 1950.
209 'an old gorgon': PS, 274.
209 Alexander Korda had married Merle Oberon, an Anglo-Indian by birth, who always maintained she was born in Tasmania rather than Calcutta.

13   Bhowani Junction *1953–1954*

211 'I am more than half way through': letter to Alex Masters, 9 November 1952 (JM).
211 'I could tackle it now': PS, 248.
212 Interview with Wilfrid and Sheila Russell, March 1989. *Indian Summer* was published by Thacker and Co, Bombay, 1951.
212 'pale coffee skin': these jottings and personal descriptions are taken from record cards among the John Masters papers in the Mugar Memorial Library at Boston University (BU).
213 'I've been four years': *Bhowani Junction*, 24.
213 'I don't despise anyone now': *ibid.*, 26.
213 ' "Home? Where is your home?" ': *ibid.*, 25.
214 'She couldn't desert her people': *ibid.*, 345.
214 'not entirely happy with the book': Helen Taylor to John Masters, 15 June 1953. This next exchange of letters about *Bhowani Junction* took place between June and August 1953 (VP).
214 Harrison Smith, 5 June 1953.
216 'Rodney is meant to be': letter to Wilfrid Russell, 24 February 1953 (JM).
218 'Alex paled': PS, 299.
219 'the immediate future is an opaque fog': letter to Alex Masters, 4 October 1953 (JM).
219 'the Golden Fleece was inside you': *Coromandel*, 317.
219 'I know now that the magic mountain': *ibid.*, 319.
219 'wise, beautiful, understanding earth': *Coromandel*, 288.
219 Meru is the holy Mount Sumeru, or Mount Kailas, sacred to Hindus and Buddhists as the home of Shiva and the Centre of the World.
219 Reviews of *Bhowani Junction*: John Barkham, 28 March 1954; Orville Prescott, 26 March; *Time* magazine, 29 March.
220 'The photo of me': letter to Alex Masters, 9 May 1954 (JM).
220 For sales of *Bhowani Junction* in the UK, see Appendix.
220 'the most spectacular flight': from log, 'Diary of a Visit to Chile', March 14 – April 11 1952 (JM).
220 'whole scene' and 'Sitting in my hotel': *ibid.*
221 'Their lunatic fisher husbands': *ibid.*
221 Masters got the highest sum Hollywood had ever paid to an author, his $155,000 exceeding the $80,000 paid previously to James Jones for *From Here To Eternity*.

222 'if she wants to give it': letter to his parents, 25 April 1954.
223 Review of *Bhowani Junction* by Angus Wilson, *Observer*, 23 May 1954.
223 'We are beginning to knock hell': letter to Wilfrid Russell, 27 April 1954 (JM).
224 'My publishers': *ibid.*
225 'I shall become an American citizen': letter to Laurence Pollinger (LP).
225 Glenn recalls: interview, August 1988.
225 'We have had Pa and Ma': letter to Alex Masters, 20 October 1954 (JM).
226 Masters describes this party: PS, 375.
226 The idea was to spread the money: interview with Allen Kaufman, August 1988.
226 'We are putting the old 'uns': letter to Alex and Joan Masters, 9 November 1954 (JM).
227 'As I had gone up': PS, 381.

14   *USA 1955–1957*

228 'incisiveness of decision': PS, 385.
228 'I saw . . . the long views': PS, 387.
229 The Indian Government opposed making a film version of *Bhowani Junction* 'as the book was a caricature of Indian politics and life, a far from complimentary presentation of the communal life of Anglo-Indians and a libel on the British Army. It revelled in vulgarity and sex and the clumsy device of slandering Indian leaders and the Indian character through the mouths of Anglo-Indian railwaymen and British colonels was too thin to deceive anyone'. This was reported in the *Hindustani Times*, 11 October 1954. Masters, in a letter to Alex at this time, claimed Nehru was in favour of the film but did not want to offend members of his Government. The Delhi correspondent of *The Daily Telegraph* reported on 20 October that the film had been definitely turned down on the grounds that it 'will create bitterness, especially among Anglo-Indians'. MGM took it instead to Lahore, and used the main railway station there (see illustration on the back jacket).
230 'It gave me quite an eerie feeling': letter to his parents, 5 March 1955 (JM).
230 'What really sold us': interview with Barbara Masters.
230 'I was miserable': interview with Martin Masters, April 1987.
231 'My first boarding school': interview with Susan Kyger, April 1987.
232 'I had a wonderful time': letter to Alex and Joan Masters, 9 July 1955 (JM).
233 Harrison Smith, *Saturday Review*, 10 February 1956; Compton Mackenzie, *The Spectator*, 10 February 1956; Bernard Fergusson, *Sunday Times*, 5 February 1956.
233 'I must have had a score of letters': letter to Alex Masters, 4 March 1956 (JM).
234 letter from Cuba: NL (1956), 51.
234 'Ma and Pa are here': letter to Alex Masters, 15 March 1956 (JM).
235 'We will not stress culture': Log, Spain 1956 (JM).
236 'when he met me': interview with Liz Rose.

15   Fandango Rock *1958–1959*

238 'I am almost totally bewildered': letter from Helen Taylor, 16 May 1957 (VP).
239 'perhaps the roughness': Helen Taylor, 27 May 1957 (VP).

239 Mollie Kaye tells: interview, February 1987.
240 'don Cesar may certainly': letter to Helen Taylor, 29 May 1957 (VP).
241 'You will know': letter to Helen Taylor, 15 January 1958 (VP).
242 'We walked': interview with Mike Rose, June 1987. Rose subsequently made his name in the Falklands: 'the brilliant and single-minded officer commanding 22 SAS threw out ideas like some strategic word-processing machine. He was forty-two, an Oxford PPE graduate, stepson of the novelist John Masters, with the sort of hawkish good looks Hollywood might impose upon a Commanding Officer of the SAS. A Coldstream Guardsman who had served with the SAS all over the world . . .'. Max Hastings and Simon Jenkins, *Battle of the Falklands* (London, Michael Joseph, 1983), 186.
242 'rattling good yarn': TLS review, 19 June 1959.

16 *At Home and Abroad 1960–1969*

243 'We have had much': NL (1955), 48
243 'The hectic Christmas season': letter to Alex and Joan Masters, 5 January 1960 (JM).
243 'I am writing because I am forty-five': letter to Liz Rose, 28 December 1959 (JM).
247 'While I write': RPM, 337.
247 'Kipling's Frontier, Then and Now', published as 'The Uneasy Battlefield', *Sunday Times*, 2 December 1961.
248 'The Indian Army Today', *Saturday Evening Post*, 1 April 1961.
249 'the trip in Pakistan': letter to Alex Masters, 9 January 1961 (JM).
249 'both late flowering of Hindu art': NL (1962), 20.
250 'Mi general': interview with Julio Nogues, August 1987.
250 Letter from Sydney Simon, 17 October 1988.
250 'It went well': interview with Michael Rose, June 1987.
251 *Time* magazine, 25 August 1961; Ogburn, *New York Times Book Review*, 20 August 1961; *The New Yorker*, 16 September 1961.
252 'I remember the whole thing': letter to Alec Harper, 30 August 1963 (JM).
253 '*Road Past Mandalay* is at once': Simon Raven, *The Spectator*, 8 September 1961.
253 'It was hard but fascinating work': NL 15 (1963), 51.
254 The publishing house: interview with Alan Brooke and Lusty, *Sign of the Mermaid*, 117.
255 'Each preparatory stage': interview with Barbara Masters.
255 'It's over 90 here now': letter to Alex and Joan Masters, 19 May 1962 (JM).
257 'I set off': Log, Spain 1962 (JM).
258 'we were moulding our characters': Leonard Woolf, *Growing: An Autobiography of the Years 1904–11* (London, Hogarth Press, 1961), 46. This reference comes from Allen J. Greenberger, *The British Image of India, A Study in the Literature of Imperialism 1880–1960* (Oxford University Press, 1969). Other sources on this topic are Shamsul Islam, *Chronicles of the Raj, A Study of Literary Reaction to the Imperial Idea towards the End of the Raj* (London, Macmillan, 1979), and Bhupal Singh, *A Survey of Anglo-Indian Fiction* (Oxford University Press, 1934).
258 'half-devil, half-child': Kipling, *The White Man's Burden*, 1899.
258 'The Indian is as incapable': *The Writings in Prose and Verse of Rudyard Kipling*, Outward Bound Edition, 36 vols (New York 1897–1937) 1,88.

NOTES TO PAGES 258-281

258 'Both Kipling and Masters': Khushwant Singh, *The Statesman* (Delhi), October 1957.
258 'all sunburn and stern renunciation': J. K. Stanford, *Ladies in the Sun: The Memsahibs' India 1790–1860* (London, Galley Press, 1962), 37.
258 'After days and years': *To The Coral Strand*, 133.
258 'you'll never plumb the Oriental mind': 'One Viceroy Resigns' in *The Definitive Edition of Kipling's Verse* (London, Hodder and Stoughton, 1943), 69.
259 'shadings of greys to blacks': PS, 146.
259 'the British did not allow': Foreword to US edition of *Nightrunners of Bengal*.
260 'the long-term prognosis': letter to Laurence Pollinger, 29 December 1962 (LP).
261 'Nobody cared': interview with Susan Kyger.
262 'We left the same evening': NL 16 (1964), 26.
262 'He looked at me': interview with Barbara Masters.
263 'he was showing all his grace': NL 17 (1965), 53.
263 'Jaiwan' means literally 'young man' but has come to be used as 'rank and file of a service unit', the 'boys'.
264 'People couldn't believe': interview with Barbara Masters.
265 'about as sexy': Log, Spain 1964 (JM).
265 'something bravely perpendicular': Jan Morris, *Spain* (London, Penguin, 1982). Masters's *Sunday Times* article was published on 22 March 1964.
266 For walks in Spain I am grateful to the reminiscences of many friends invited to walk with the Masterses, namely the Andersons, Brandts, Cassadys, Sterns, Tom Hamill and others.
267 'Difficult to know what she wants': Log, Spain 1964 (JM).
267 'Spain's larger than life': letter from Alice Mathews.
269 'We went out at once': Logs, USA 1965 (JM).
270 'Rainbird approached me': *Contemporary Authors*, vol 110, 335.
271 Letter from John Hadfield, 7 February 1988.
272 'Something I have wanted to see': Log, *Casanova* 1968 (JM).
272 *New York Times* review of *Casanova*, 7 December 1969.
272 'generous, mean, vindictive': *Casanova*, 10.
273 Most of the information and correspondence about the dispute over *The Rock* came from the files in Laurence Pollinger Ltd.
275 Frank Waters, *Masked Gods: Navaho and Pueblo Ceremonialism* (University of New Mexico, 1950). Other texts are Bertha Dutton, *The Pueblos* (New York, Prentice Hall, 1976) and Willa Cather, *Death Comes for the Archbishop* (New York, Alfred A. Knopf, 1929) and Lawrence Clark Powell, *Southwestern Book Trails, A Reader's Guide to the Heartland of New Mexico and Arizona* (Albuquerque, Horn and Wallace, 1964).
275 'The moment I saw': D. H. Lawrence, September 1922, in Harry Moore, *The Priest of Love, A Life of D. H. Lawrence* (London, Heinemann, 1974).
276 Vietnam: some of the origin of Masters's views on the split between military and political imperatives can be traced to his time on the North-West Frontier, where the role of the political agent and the military often diverged.
277 For his article 'The Tribe that didn't go That-Away': *Daily Telegraph Magazine*, 27 September 1968.
277 For a comparison of Gurkhas (Gurung tribe) and North American Indians, see Peter Mattheissen, *The Snow Leopard* (London, Picador, 1980), 58.
278 'I love the jewellery': Log, BJ 35.
281 Account of stay in Cadiz and Gibraltar from Log, *The Rock*, 68/9 (JM).

17   *Santa Fe 1970–1973*

282   'The views were tremendous': round robin letter January 1970 (JM).
283   'We have climbed': NL (1971), 58.
284   'Looking back': interview with Tom Hamill, April 1987.
285   'Sunday September 13th': Log, vol 1, Chili and Marching Society (JM).
286   sauna on 25 June: *ibid.*
287   Fisher recalls: interview with Edmund Fisher, June 1987.
290   'Sandy has a funny lop-sided look': Log, Albajaca 71 (JM).
291   'and the nurse doubted': *ibid.*
293   Baudelaire, *Le Peintre de la vie Moderne*, IX 1864 (see *Selected Writing on Art and Artists* (London, Penguin, 1972), 421).
294   'Sunday, 11 June': Log, Franciberia 1972 (JM).
294   Douglas Day, *Malcolm Lowry* (Oxford University Press, 1974).

18   *Chili and Marching Society 1974–1975*

297   'I get to work every morning': *Contemporary Authors.*
297   once a member joined the Society: I am grateful to all those members of the Chili and Marching Society who spoke to me about their association with it.
299   Nelson's Blood: Masters's recommended ingredients were: 'dark rum, consommé or bouillon, Worcestershire sauce or tabasco. To prepare: Stand to attention, place right hand over left breast, and sing *Hearts of Oak*. Work out how many fl. oz. of the mixture are required. In a saucepan make a consommé or bouillon (from Bovril, beef extract cubes, consommé, beef broth or other means) to ⅔ of the total quantity required. If using concentrated canned consommé make it a stronger meat taste. (Nelson was in that cask a good many days.) Add a few dashes of tabasco and/or a teaspoonful of Worcestershire sauce. Heat the mixture. Meanwhile heat the interior of the Thermos flask or flasks with very hot or boiling water. As soon as the bouillon begins to bubble, pour in the rum to complete quantity required, i.e. ⅔. When the Nelson's Blood now begins to boil, quickly pour into the Thermos flask or flasks. BE SURE TO EMPTY OUT THE HOT WATER FIRST. Cap and wrap the flasks in newspapers or an insulated bag. Sing *Admiral Benbow*, stand at ease.' SOP 478, 21 January 1974 (JM).
299   'Leaving the World Below', *Daily Telegraph Magazine*, 30 July 1976.
300   'all we dislike': Log, Bajapo 73 (JM).
302   'Expenses on the sort of job': letter to Laurence Pollinger, 4 January 1974 (LP).
303   'I think Indians': 'Times Past Times Future in Bharat', *Daily Telegraph Magazine*, 18 March 1976.
303   'our standards': Log, Bharat 73 (JM).
304   'As long as you stay': *ibid.*
304   'the hill people': *ibid.*
305   clerk in Delhi: *ibid.*
308   'for a great many years': letter to Laurence Pollinger, 21 September 1974 (LP).
308   'It was pretty cold in Skye': Log, Atholl Brose, 1975 (JM).
310   'On Remembrance Day': NL 28 (1976), 44.
311   'The tragedy was': *The Himalaya Concerto*, 48.

19   Loss of Eden 1976–*1982*

312   Wykeham, a World War Two fighter pilot, was called by Hemingway one of his personal heroes and among the bravest men he knew (see Carlos Baker, *Ernest Hemingway: A Life Story* (London, Collins, 1969), 523–4 and 550).

312   'The product of the Raj': Paul Scott in *John Kenneth Galbraith Introduces India*, eds. Frank Moraes and Edward Howe (London, André Deutsch, 1976), 74.

313   'It was good seeing you': letter to Carl Brandt, April 1976 (BU).

315   'The role of the United States': letter to Bruce Lee, 4 November 1976 (BU).

315   'We had the usual year': NL (1977), 101.

316   'Now God be Thanked': from Rupert Brooke's poem 'Peace' (1914).

316   'I liked Jack immediately': letter from Bruce Lee, 4 February 1991.

317   'detailed research must wait': letter to Bruce Lee, 4 November 1976 (BU).

317   'One is where': letter to Marjorie Caton-Jones, January 1977 (JM).

317   'I don't feel any older': letter to Alex Masters, 6 November 1976 (JM).

319   illness in Huesca: Log, Passing Bells 1 (JM).

320   'both the naval officers': letter from Peg Man, 5 December 1977 (JM).

320   'having been brought up': letter to Admiral Sir Caspar John, 11 December 1977 (JM).

322   'breaking every tenet': letter to Shelford Bidwell, 16 February 1978 (BU).

322   'We are now down': *ibid*, 16 May 1978 (BU).

323   'I had a letter': *ibid*.

324   'For London': letter to Alan Brooke, 5 January 1979 (MJ).

325   'We are breaking up slowly': letter to Vald Heiberg, 25 March 1979 (BU).

325   'I have been reading': letter from Bruce Lee, 7 March 1979 (BU).

326   'Excellent salmon trout': Log, Passing Bells 111 (JM).

327   'This was my India': *Bhowani Junction*, 328.

327   *The Glory That Was India* (London, Collins, 1982).

328   *The Breaking Strain*, 77.

328   interview with Joan Buresch and John Talley, April 1987.

330   letter from Manohar Malgonkar, 25 December 1987.

330   'Masters seemed a bit wary of me': letter from Tim Heald, 1 November 1987. de Caro/Jordan interview: 'I came to Santa Fe because it's got interesting people. It's got wonderful country for my hobby, walking, so we came here and we haven't been sorry. We've met very nice people. I really don't want to meet any more people. I know enough people already'.

331   'heard no more': letter to Bruce Lee, 15 February 1980 (BU).

332   'McGraw Hill's presentation': letter to Bruce Lee, 15 February 1980 (BU).

332   'By the green of the spring' is from the Siegfried Sassoon poem 'Aftermath': 'Have you forgotten yet? Look up, and swear by the green of the spring that you'll never forget.' Masters had wanted to call his trilogy *Passing Bells* (from the Wilfrid Owen poem, 'What passing bells for those who die as cattle?'), but another author, the American Philip Rock, had already taken the title shortly before him, much to his annoyance. He had already used *Passing Bells* as the title for several Logs.

335   'It went off very well': letter to Alex Masters, 29 October 1982 (JM).

20   *Final Months 1983*

338   Susan returned: interview with Susan Kyger.

338 Martin found: interview with Martin Masters.
339 'He was quite simply determined': *The Guardian*, 9 May 1983. Other obituaries appeared in *The Daily Telegraph*, 7 May, *New York Times*, 8 May, and *Times*, 9 May.
342 'It was America': from 'Notes from the Editors' in *Now God Be Thanked* (Pennsylvania, Franklin Library, 1979).

BIBLIOGRAPHY

JOHN MASTERS'S BOOKS:

Nightrunners of Bengal [1951] Viking Press and Michael Joseph
The Deceivers [1952] Viking Press and Michael Joseph
The Lotus and the Wind [1953] Viking Press and Michael Joseph
Bhowani Junction [1954] Viking Press and Michael Joseph
Coromandel [1955] Viking Press and Michael Joseph
Bugles and a Tiger [1956] Viking Press and Michael Joseph
Far, Far the Mountain Peak [1957] Viking Press and Michael Joseph
Fandango Rock [1959] Harper and Michael Joseph
Venus of Konpara [1960] Harper and Michael Joseph
Road Past Mandalay [1961] Harper and Michael Joseph
To The Coral Strand [1962] Harper and Michael Joseph
Trial at Monomoy [1964] Harper and Michael Joseph
Fourteen Eighteen [1965] Michael Joseph and British Book Centre, NY
The Breaking Strain [1967] Michael Joseph and Delacorte
Casanova [1969] Michael Joseph and Geis Associates, NY
The Rock [1970] Michael Joseph and Putnam's
Pilgrim Son [1971] Putnam's and Michael Joseph
The Ravi Lancers [1972] Doubleday and Michael Joseph
Thunder at Sunset [1974] Doubleday and Michael Joseph
The Field Marshal's Memoirs [1975] Doubleday and Michael Joseph
The Himalaya Concerto [1976] Doubleday and Michael Joseph
Now God Be Thanked [1979] McGraw-Hill and Michael Joseph
Heart of War [1980] McGraw-Hill and Michael Joseph
By the Green of the Spring [1981] McGraw-Hill and Michael Joseph
Man of War [1983] McGraw-Hill and Michael Joseph.

Other bibliographical material is referred to under the relevant chapter in the Notes.

INDEX

Allcard, Ethel, 148, 150
Allen, Louis, 125
Allison, Commander, 111
Anderson, Alan and Nancy, 175, 264,
    276, 282, 340
Anderson, Maxwell, 168
Anglo-Indians (*see also* Eurasians), 1–2,
    211, 229, 346, 347, 359
    Master's attitude toward, 12–13
Anstey, John, 268, 274, 301, 317
Atlantic Monthly, 163
Auberjonois, Fernand and Laura, 175,
    179, 201, 210
Auchinleck, Field-Marshal Sir Claude,
    88, 142, 147, 236, 265

'Baa, Baa Black Sheep', 32
Bailey Gate, Uplyme, 39, 61
Baines, Frank, 62, 350
Bakloh, 49, 52, 55, 58, 266, 305
Balaban, A. J. and Carrie, 175
Baluchistan, 44, 81
Bannu, 65, 66
Bareilly, 42
Bayona, 235
Bedford, 10
Bengal Famine 1943, 107
Bengal Lancer, 167, 232, 356
Bengal-Rockland Inc, 225, 280, 308
Bidwell, Shelford, 124, 252
Blackpool, 173, 252
    as 'block', 117–123
    lay-out, 118
    assessment of, 124
Bogert, Mickey, 306, 309
Bottlesford, Wiltshire, 20, 38, 176
Brandt, Carl, 319, 326, 333–4
    first meets Masters, 313–14
    agent for *Loss of Eden*, 316
    appreciation of Masters, 340
Brennan, Lt-Col Tim, 116, 119, 139, 140,
    151, 265, 308
Brook, John, 339

Brooke, Alan, 322, 324, 326, 340
Buchan, John, 166, 266
Bunker, Bob and Priscilla, 337
Buresch, Joan, 328

Cadiz, 281
Calcutta, 1, 14, 159
    killings in 1946, 147
Calvert, Brig Michael
    as Chindit, 106, 108, 111, 114, 117,
        123–4
    post war, 151, 207
    and capture of Mogaung, 353
Camberley Staff College, 147, 151
Cameronians (1st Battalion), 106, 112,
    119, 122, 126
Cane, Peter, 36, 142
Cardew, Cornelius, 2
Casady, Phil, 298, 306, 309
Cather, Willa, 278
Caton-Jones, Marjorie, 317
Chambrun, Jacques, 163, 166
Chandler, Raymond, 156
Charnock, Tony and Chris, 270
Cheltenham Junior School, 18–19
Chevenic-Trench, Charles, 349–51
Chili and Marching Society, 73, 316, 328,
    340–1
    founded, 297
    Bulletins, 300–1, 306–7, 346
    Head Ghillie's Tiffin, 317, 335
Chindits 1952, 207
    111 Brigade, 101, 106, 111, 114, 123–8
        Masters appointed commander, 115
    formation of, 103
    concept of strongholds, 106
    training, 107
    fly-in to Burma, 112
    assessment of, 128
    disbanded, 130
    reunions post-war, 152, 207
    books on, 352
Chudd, Bill, 316, 335

Churchill, Winston, 105
 views on British Empire, 138
Close Border Policy, 44
Cochran, Col Phil, 107
Collins, Norah, 75, 80, 83
The Compleat Indian Angler, 81
Congress Party, 72, 83, 174
Conrad, Joseph, 198, 341
Corbett, Jim, 13, 347
Crow, Cecilia and Caroline, 5, 7
Curzon, Lord (Viceroy of India 1899–
 1905), 45

DCLI (Duke of Cornwall's Light
 Infantry), 39, 42, 43, 52
Daily Telegraph, 252, 268, 274, 299, 301,
 302, 317
Darling, Maj-Gen Douglas, 39
Davidson, Col David, 46
de Caro, F., 354, 355
Deighton, Len, 334
Diver, Maud, 258
Dodds, Col Bill, 157, 177
Donner, Vyvyan, 161
Doubleday, 175, 289–90
Dunn, Barbara, 76
Durand Line, 44
Dussehra, 54, 60, 304

East India Company, 2, 3, 5
Eastbourne, 18
Edge, Cyril and Mary, 19
Empress of Japan, 75, 148
Eurasians, 2, 4, 8, 346–8
 language of, 'chee-chee', 16, 348

Fairweather, James, 49, 52, 56, 66
Fakir of Ipi, 64, 65
Fergusson, Bernard, 108, 207, 233, 252
Fisher, Edmund, 287–9, 294
Forester, C. S., 166
Forster, E. M., 259, 341
Fort William, Calcutta, 2, 11, 14, 348
Forward Policy, 44
Fuller, Maj Martin, 317

Gallagher, Jack, 120
Gardner, Ava, 221, 229
Garhwal, 139–40, 161, 346
Geis Associates, Bernard, 273–4, 281
Geschwind, Herman, 76, 79

Ghatera, 101, 103, 107
Gibraltar, 281
Giddings family, 18, 20, 23, 38
Glenn, Armon and Lucie, 225, 340
Gray, Diana, 35, 37
Great Game, 45, 197
Guinzburg, Harold, 182
Gulmarg, 128
Gurkhas, 53–4, 86, 106, 127, 130, 147,
 310
 Masters' first visits, 49
 history of, 53–4, 350
 history of Masters's regiment, 55
 training year, 56–8
 split-up after Independence, 153–4
 centenary reunion 1957, 241

Hadfield, John, 270
Haggard, Rider, 198
Hall, Desmond, 170, 175, 232
Hamid, Maj-Gen Shahid, 247
Hamill, Tom, 284–5, 293–4, 298, 306,
 309
Hamilton, Maj-Gen Goff, 88, 109, 229
Hamilton, Mark, 335
Harper, Lt-Col Alec, 120, 127, 154
Harper Brothers, 242, 252
Heald, Tim, 330
Heath, A. M., 313
Hebdon, Peter, 254, 270, 273, 274, 287
Hedley, John, 110
Hemingway, Ernest, 336
Hobson-Jobson, 348
Hodson, Maj Robin, 42, 49, 50
Holliday, Fred, 120
Hope, Eleanor, 168
Howell, Miriam, 175, 188, 220

India, British, 62, 262
 attitudes to race, 3, 8
 memsahibs, 8
 1857 Mutiny, 9, 54, 171
 childhood in, 15–19
 separation from, 19
 social life, 58
 club life, 59
 ordinary soldier's life, 59
 sexual mores between the wars, 59
 Independence, 144, 147, 153, 354
Indian Army, 248, 304, 355
 composition of, 43

and leave, 60
and politics, 72
post-war reduction, 143
Iraq, 85

Jameson, Tom and Anne, 284, 286, 289,
    293, 298, 302, 309
Jennison Keith, 175, 177, 194, 202, 238,
    256, 296, 324
    first meets Masters, 170
    as editor, 182, 187ff, 214ff, 233
    and Masters's move from Viking,
    241–2
    appreciation of John and Barbara
    Masters, 340
Jennison, Emily, 170, 177
Jennison, Nicky, 235
Jervis, Lois, 29, 32, 39, 61, 79, 246
John, Admiral Sir Caspar, 320
Jordan, Rosan, 354, 355

Kaghan Valley, 97–8, 129, 139, 311
Karachi, 17
Kashmir, 59, 305
Kaufman, Allen, 225, 255, 273, 280
Kaye, Mollie (Hamilton), 88–9, 109, 228,
    239, 255, 326
Kilpatrick, Ann, 78
Kim, 5, 58, 197, 200
Kipling, Rudyard, 5, 19, 32, 58, 107, 176,
    197, 285
    influence on Masters, 86, 167
    Masters visits his home, 199
    comparison with Masters, 258
Korda, Alexander, 209, 214, 218
Kyger, David, 337, 339

La Martiniere, 5, 7, 9
Lacoma, Antonio, 205
Lahore, 50, 253
Lardner, Rex, 162
Larpent, Douglas, 129, 140
Laskier, Frank, 170
Lawrence, D. H., 275
Lawrence, T. E., 66
Leach, Lt-Col 'Bulgy', 89
Lee, Bruce
    first meets Masters, 316
    as editor, 317, 319, 323, 325–6, 331–3,
    335
    appreciation of Masters, 340

Lentaigne, Maj-Gen W. D. A., 119, 123,
    126, 140
    first meets Masters, 68
    and Chindits, 102–13
    appointed Wingate's successor, 114
    appoints Masters to command 111
    Brigade, 115
    problems with Stilwell, 120
Linlithgow, Marquess of (Viceroy of
    India 1936–1943), 83, 160
Loralai, 81, 82
Lusty, Sir Robert, 188, 296, 326

McCarthy, Senator Joe, 210, 225
MacGillicuddy, Mike, 113, 126
Mackay, Col Hamish, 133, 202
McKean, William, 25
McLeod, Roddy, 142, 144
Maine, 50, 185–6
Malgonkar, Manohar, 329
Malim, F. B., 24, 29, 31, 165
Man, Peg (de Fonbrune), 284, 310, 320,
    340
Mandalay, 132–3
Mason, Philip, 72–3, 147, 349
Massey, Lt-Col Paddy, 82, 88, 90
Masters, Ada (née Coulthard) (1882–
    1971), 148, 204
    early life and marriage, 12
    as mother to Masters, 15, 19
    post-war England, 157–8
    visits to USA, 203, 225, 234
    old age and illness, 267, 280, 291
    death of, 292
Masters, Alex (1917–   ), 66, 151, 191–2,
    232, 265, 291
    birth, 17
    school, 20–1
    relationship with Masters, 21, 67, 191–
    2, 200
    prisoner of war, 95, 142
Masters, Alexander (1886–1914), 14,
    290
Masters, Annie (1859–1954), 10–11, 21,
    209, 222
Masters, Barbara (née Allcard)
    (1910–   ), 208, 281, 339, 341
    early upbringing, 91
    first meets Masters, 91
    attraction to Masters, 92
    relationship with Liz and Mike, 93,

134, 155, 159, 208, 236–7, 242, 246, 341
agrees to marry Masters, 100
divorce from first husband, 101, 134, 137
gives birth to Susan, 112
marries Masters, 134
gives birth to Martin, 148
strength of relationship with Masters, 181, 228, 240, 340
and Masters's death, 338
Masters, John (1844–1901), 10–11
Masters, John (1883–1963), 34, 39, 81, 85, 148, 203
birth and childhood, 10–12
joins Indian Army, 12
marries Ada Coulthard, 12
during World War I, 15
retires from India, 28
works as swineherd, 28
relationship with Masters, 33, 61, 151, 157, 179, 203, 226, 230, 267
visits to USA, 203, 225, 234
death of, 261
Masters, John (1914–1983)
birth, 12
childhood in India, 14–17
first visit to England, 18
schooling
at Cheltenham Junior, 19–20
at Wellington, 23–32
and trains, 20, 39, 42, 176, 199, 223, 292, 303
relationship with Lois Jervis, 29, 32, 39, 61, 79, 246
Sandhurst, 33–41
and USA, 38, 76, 155, 162, 199, 224
appointed to Indian Army, 39
return to India, 42
year with DCLI, 44–52
on North-West Frontier, 44–5, 62–9
at Bakloh, 50, 52–59, 69–72
joins 4th Gurkhas, 53
and mountains, 58, 70, 98, 139, 232, 266, 310
bachelor life in India, 59–60, 75, 81, 83–4
leave to England, 61, 72
kills tiger 1938, 70–1
first visit to USA, 77–80
at Loralai, 82

goes to Staff College, Quetta, 88–94
meets Barbara Rose, 91
decision to marry, 100
complications with divorce, 101, 134, 137
joins Chindits, 103
at Blackpool, 118–23
effect of Chindit campaign, 128–9
joins 19th Indian Division, 130
relationship with Pete Rees, 132–3
at fall of Mandalay, 133
marries Barbara, 134
in Delhi, post-war, 142–8
returns to England 1946, 149
at Staff College, Camberley, 150–9
decides to emigrate, 156
and money, 157, 226, 280, 336
in USA 1948, 160ff
becomes author, 165ff
moves house, 168, 178, 194, 201, 263, 278
life on South Mountain Road, 168ff
changes agent, 175, 220, 234, 308, 313
immigration problems, 176, 179, 225
Nightrunners of Bengal accepted, 183
travels to Europe, 204–9, 232, 293
liking for Spain, 205–6, 235, 265, 267
writes *Bhowani Junction*, 211ff
return visits to India, 241, 248, 262, 303
changes publisher, 241–2, 273, 282, 289–90, 316, 333
illnesses, 257, 260, 292, 325, 335–6
angina, 290, 299, 319
moves to Santa Fe, New Mexico, 282
and saunas, 286, 335
and drink, 294
starts Chili and Marching Society, 297
writes *Loss of Eden* trilogy, 312ff
enters hospital, Albuquerque, 337
death, 338
tributes, 340–1
relationship with:
mother, 15, 19, 61, 158, 226, 234, 267, 280, 291
father, 15, 33, 61, 151, 157, 179, 203, 226, 230, 234, 261
brother, 21, 67, 191–2, 200
Barbara, 91–4, 156, 181, 228, 240, 340

children, 151, 179, 224, 229, 255,
  269
step-children, 294, 324
BOOKS
first stories, 19
plan of thirty-five Indian novels, 166,
  171
literary influences on, 166–7
working methods and technique, 169,
  172, 186, 228, 255, 297
designs colophon, 176
aims as writer, 238, 257, 341
Nightrunners of Bengal (1951), 172ff,
  181, 184ff, 187, 229, 308, 348
The Deceivers (1952), 107, 180ff, 204–
  5, 236
The Lotus and the Wind (1953), 45, 96,
  195, 197, 245
Bhowani Junction (1954), 211ff, 214–
  19, 221, 225, 229, 239, 303, 327, 333,
  341
Coromandel (1955), 218, 229
Bugles and a Tiger (1956), 14, 33, 43,
  231, 233, 271, 341
Far, Far the Mountain Peak (1957), 69,
  93, 234, 238, 305
Fandango Rock (1959), 238, 242
Venus of Konpara (1960), 242–3
Road Past Mandalay (1961), 86, 124,
  126, 135, 243, 251
To The Coral Strand (1962), 249, 254
Trial at Monomoy (1964), 255–6
Fourteen Eighteen (1965), 264, 313
The Breaking Strain (1967), 266, 268,
  272, 328
Casanova (1969), 270–1, 287
The Rock (1970), 272, 281–2
Pilgrim Son (1971), 181, 283, 287,
  291
The Ravi Lancers (1972), 292, 295–6
Thunder at Sunset (1974), 296, 300
The Field-Marshal's Memoirs (1975),
  296, 308
The Himalaya Concerto (1976), 311
Now God Be Thanked (1979), 322ff,
  332
Heart of War (1980), 332
By the Green of the Spring (1981), 332,
  336
Man of War (1983), 334–7, 341
Masters, Martha (1802–1883), 2, 9

Masters, Martin (1946–   ), 149, 151,
  168, 223, 243, 250, 256, 263, 335
birth of, 148
at school, 179, 230, 235–6
liking for music, 256, 325
and Vietnam, 279
in Los Angeles, 284, 318
at death of father, 338–9, 341
Masters, Susan (Kyger) (1944–   ), 129,
  134, 139, 149, 151, 168, 243, 278,
  299, 335
birth of, 112
at school, 179, 230, 236, 255
at Stanford, 261
marriages of, 269, 284, 319, 341
at death of father, 337–9
Masters, William (1773–1819), 2
Masters, William (1803–1868), 2, 4, 7, 9
Mathews, Alice (née Westfeldt), 77, 160,
  161, 168, 178, 210, 267, 271, 326
Mauldin, Bill, 339
Meadows, Taylor, 181
Merchant, Ismail, 236
Messervy, Gen Sir Frank, 135, 244
MGM, 221, 229
Michael Joseph, 280–1, 291, 326
  as Masters's publishers, 188, 242, 264,
    273–4, 287, 296, 317, 333–4
  changes at, 254
Miranshah, 66, 103
Mogaung, 117, 126
Morris, Jumbo, 112, 115
Mountbatten, Lord Louis (later Earl
  Mountbatten of Burma), 111, 113,
  115, 130, 153
Mugar Memorial Library, 346
Murphy, Dervla, 98
Murray, Iain, 37
Murray, 'Moke', 52, 58
Murray-Lyon, Col David, 55, 57, 66,
  69, 82, 335
Mystic, Connecticut, 186

Naipaul, V. S., 99
The New Yorker, 162, 251
Niven, David, 36, 157
Nogues, Julio, 205, 250
Noyes, Stan and Nancy, 299, 306, 309
North-West Frontier, 43, 146, 167, 247
  tribal wars on, 44
  and columns, 46

life at stations, 46
piquet duty, 46
Masters there in 1936, 62
political agent, 62
Frontier scouts, 65
books on, 350

Odlum, Stanley, 21, 162, 246
Ogburn, Charlton, 251
Olson, Charles, 224
Overhage, Carl, 316

Pathans, 44, 45, 62, 64, 350
Pethick-Lawrence Commission, 144
Platoro, Colorado, 305
Pollinger, Laurence, 222, 234, 264, 268,
    293, 343, 346
  becomes Masters's agent, 188
  and Korda, 209
  introduces John Anstey, 268
  and *The Rock*, 272–4
  and change of agent, 304
Pueblo Indians, 274ff, 361
Pulley, Brig Chris, 42, 47, 50
Putnam, 282

Quetta, 35, 44, 81, 84, 88, 276
  Staff College, 88
  social life, 90
  Club, 91
Quit India Movement, 97, 107

Rainbird, George, 270–1, 287, 294, 300,
    334
Rangoon, 135, 137, 146
Ranikhet, 139, 141, 147
Raven, Simon, 253
Raymond, John, 190, 253
Razmak, 43–4
Rees, Maj-Gen Pete, 130, 134, 135, 137,
    138, 140–1
  description of, 132
  at fall of Mandalay, 133
  importance to Masters, 133, 138
Rhodes-James, Richard, 121, 127, 159,
    207
  impressions of Masters, 109–10
  assessment of Blackpool, 124–5
Richardson, Stewart, 290, 293, 296, 313
Ricketts, J. W., 4
Roberts, Brig. Michael, 96, 100, 140

Roberts, Val (Lebern), 83, 96, 101
Robertson, Polly, 298, 309, 316
Romilly, Esmond, 24
Rose, Barbara (*see also* Masters,
    Barbara), 91
Rose, Edward, vii, 346
Rose, Hugh, 92–3, 101, 134, 155, 208,
    245
Rose, Elizabeth, 245, 324, 341
  childhood, 93, 129, 134, 208
  visits to USA, 236–7
  marriage, 243
Rose, Brig Michael, 242, 250, 293, 341,
    360
  childhood, 93, 129, 134, 208
  visits to USA, 236–7, 246–7
Royal Military College, Sandhurst, 23, 33
Russell, Wilfrid and Sheila, 212ff

Sagar, Lt-Gen Moti, 248
Sandhurst (*see also* Royal Military
    College), 23, 33, 37, 38
Santa Fe, 276, 281, 283–4, 293, 297, 342
Saugor, 130, 134
Sawhny, Reggie, 212, 248, 302
Scholder, Romona, 335
Scott, Rear-Admiral Sir David, 323
Scott, Paul, 249, 327, 341
Shultz, Phil, 298, 306, 309, 339
Sia, Cyril, 269, 278, 284
Sia, Danielle, 269
Simon, Sydney, 250, 276
Singh, Khushwant, 258
Skinner, James, 13, 347
Sleeman, William, 180
Slim, Field-Marshal Sir William, 86, 111,
    114, 135, 180, 253, 333, 334
Smith, Harrison, 214, 233
South Mountain Road, 168, 263, 276,
    281–2
Something of Myself, 19
Spain, 167, 235, 238, 257, 265, 281, 293,
    294, 300
  Masters's first glimpses from aeroplane,
    147
  first visit, 204–5
  similarity to India, 205
Spock, Dr Benjamin, 179
SS Canton, 75
Stern, Richard and Dot, 284, 299, 313
Steuart, Charles and William, 5–7

Stilwell, Gen 'Vinegar Joe', 114, 120, 126, 140
Strauss, Helen, 220, 229, 233, 236, 242
Strickland, Lt-Col John, 42, 52, 68–9

Talboys, R. St C., 27, 29
Talley, John, 328
Taylor, Helen, 271, 296, 332, 346
  as editor at Viking, 182ff, 214ff, 231, 238, 241
Thapa, Biniram, 101
Thapa, Daljit, 96–7, 101
Thomas, Hugh, 334
Trevelyan, Raleigh, 287
Trisul, 139, 158

Upjohn, Gordon, 123
Uplyme, 61

Victor, Ed, 308, 310
Viking, 182–4, 231, 241, 346

Waight, Eddie, 20, 246

Waters, Frank, 275
Wavell, Field-Marshal Sir Archibald, 88, 103, 153
Waziristan, 17, 43, 62
Weallens, Lt-Col Willie, 84, 87, 95, 140
Wellington, 23–9
Whyte, Dr 'Doc', 110, 122, 126, 129, 140
William Morris Agency, 290, 308, 313
Williams, Bill, 42, 50
Wingate, Maj-Gen Orde, 196
  founds the Chindits, 103
  early life and personality, 103
  appearance, 106
  death of, 114, 353
  character and reputation, 128
Woolf, Leonard, 258
Worsley, T. C., 24
Wykeham, Air Vice-Marshal Sir Peter, 312, 363

Yeats-Brown, Francis, 167

Zinnemann, Fred, 223, 225